# UNIVERSITY OF WALES SWANSEA
## PRIFYSGOL CYMRU ABERTAWE
### LIBRARY/LLYFRGELL

Classmark    DA675. L5

Location

D1381398

The Apprenticeship of a Mountaineer: Edward Whymper's
London Diary 1855–1859

edited by Ian Smith

LONDON RECORD SOCIETY
PUBLICATIONS

VOLUME XLIII

# THE APPRENTICESHIP
# OF A MOUNTAINEER:
# EDWARD WHYMPER'S
# LONDON DIARY
# 1855–1859

EDITED BY

IAN SMITH

LONDON RECORD SOCIETY
VOLUME XLIII

© Ian Smith 2008
ISBN 978–0-900952–43–2

Printed and bound by Q3 Print Project Management Ltd, Loughborough

# Acknowledgements

Because Whymper's niece Amy Woodgate chose to deposit all her uncle's diaries and journals with the Scott Polar Research Institute, I was given a delightful environment to work in and have particularly benefited from the enthusiasm, encyclopaedic knowledge and helpfulness of Robert Headland, the now-retired archivist. His interest in Edward Whymper, and his welcome have been continued by his successor, Naomi Boneham, and the library staff. Their unfailing helpfulness (along with the regular morning and afternoon teas served in the museum) made the Institute a pleasure to frequent. Publication of Edward Whymper's London diary is by permission of the Scott Polar Research Institute.

All those descendants of Whymper and his brothers, whom I have contacted, have been helpful and enthusiastically interested in their 'Uncle Ted.' I would particularly like to thank Bill Whymper for introducing me to his various relatives. In the possession of his mother Joan Whymper (whose husband John was the grandson of William Nathaniel Whymper, and great-nephew of Edward) is an album of family history, originally started by Josiah Whymper, which she most kindly allowed me to read. Another grandson of William Nathaniel Whymper, Timothy Woodgate, collected many notes, letters and pictures relating to his family's history. These are now in the possession of his widow, Eva Woodgate, who bravely excavated them from her attic and allowed me to bear them away to peruse.

Whymper's granddaughter Nigella Hall generously showed me the material she has relating to her mother's childhood. It has also been my pleasure to meet Susan Block, Jeremy Cogswell, Michael Petter, Steve Bennedik, Jill Hetherington and Richard Webb, who all share my interest in their family. Harry Smith and Greg Lewin have also most generously shared the results of their own research into the Whymper family history.

Whymper was a member of the Alpine Club for fifty years and his spirit still hovers over the club. Many of its members have shared and encouraged my interest in Whymper, among them Jerry Lovatt, Glyn Hughes, Bob Lawford and Peter Berg. Yvonne Sibbald, until recently the librarian, was especially kind in keeping me abreast of worldwide interest and enquiries in Whymper.

Simon Brett and John Lawrence, both active members of the Society of Wood Engravers, have been most generous in spending their time explaining to me the finer details of their noble craft. I would also like to thank Louise Hurrell and Steve Milton for sharing their interest in the world of nineteenth century wood engraving, and the artists associated with the Whympers studio, North, Walker and Pinwell. Louise kindly brought to my attention what is almost certainly the earliest known illustration of Whymper, kept in the Department of Prints and Drawings at the British Museum.

Even as a librarian myself, I have been continually struck (but, of course, should not be) by the unfailing courtesy and helpfulness of librarians and archivists from around the world. The British Library is always a delight in which to spend the day. Also deserving of mention for help which went towards this volume are the Haslemere Educational Museum, the National Library of Scotland, Virginia Murray at the John Murray Archive (prior to its relocation to Edinburgh), the Baptist Library at Regent's Park College, Oxford and the Minet Local History Library in Lambeth. The availability of the Family Record Centre in Islington was particularly welcome, until its recent removal to Kew. The website http://www.cricketarchive.co.uk/Archive/ proved useful in confirming that Whymper's accounts of cricket matches at the Oval were invariably accurate. In tracing the many individuals mentioned in the diary I have used the nineteenth century census records and the registers of births, deaths and marriages, now made available online by the National Archives.

Alan Lyall was most encouraging when I first set about delving into the life of Edward Whymper, and has always been happy to share his interest and extensive knowledge of the subject. As well as his own personal encouragement and suggestions, Robin Eagles has provided astute editorial guidance, and has spent much time attending to the details of the text and the production of this volume. Lastly I have to commend my wife, Eleanor, who, for several years now, has happily shared our small flat, fortuitously situated in the locale of this diary, with the author of that diary, Mr Edward Whymper.

# Table of contents

# Illustrations

# Abbreviations

AJ        Alpine Journal
SPRI      Scott Polar Research Institute, University of Cambridge
BL        British Library
MPMB      Maze Pond Minute Book
MPAB      Maze Pond Account Book 1844 – 1861
SPCK      The Society for Promoting Christian Knowledge
NWCS      New Water-Colour Society
RA        Royal Academy

# Introduction

## *Edward Whymper's family background*

I had ideas floating in my head that I should one day turn out some great person, be the person of my day, perhaps Prime Minister, or at least a millionaire. Who has not had them? They have not left me yet: time will show if they be true or false.[1]

The seventeen-year old Edward Whymper was a restlessly ambitious young man, but could have had no idea how, just eight years later, he would return to London from his triumphant, but tragic, ascent of the Matterhorn, to find himself the centre of attention.

The Whymper family had been established in Suffolk at least since the early seventeenth century, and owned the country seat of Glevering Hall, near Wickham Market, until the end of the eighteenth century.[2] Edward's grandfather Nathaniel Whymper (1787 – 1861) was a brewer and town councillor in Ipswich, who had eight surviving children by his first wife. Nathaniel's second son Josiah Wood (1813 – 1903) came to London with his older brother Ebenezer, when their mother died in 1829. They settled in Lambeth, in Old Paradise Street, and soon took up the rapidly developing trade of wood engraving. Josiah Whymper studied watercolour painting with Collingwood Smith and must have been making a reasonable living, as he soon married a woman one year older than himself, who died when she was only 23.[3] He married again two years later, this time to a penniless orphan. After the early deaths of her father, an impoverished clerk, and her mother, Elizabeth Claridge had been adopted by the philanthropically-minded Samuel Leigh, a prosperous cashier at the Bank of England (and presumably the employer of Elizabeth's father), who lived with his two sisters in a grand house in Peckham. Excluded from any inheritance, Elizabeth was educated to work for a living, but this necessity was avoided when 'the prettiest girl he had ever seen,' was noticed by the handsome young Josiah Whymper in the Baptist chapel attended by himself and the Leighs. When told that the object of his desire had no prospects, Josiah's

---

1. 15 December 1857.
2. The surname was variously spelt Whimper or Whymper. In about 1856, Edward's father Josiah regularised his family's surname to Whymper. The Ipswich side of the family were usually referred to as Whimper. Throughout the introduction and appendices the spelling Whymper has been used.
3. Mary Ann Whymper's death was recorded at the parish church of St. Mary's at Lambeth, next to where they lived, in October 1835. The marriage certificate of Josiah Whymper's second marriage in August 1837 describes him as a "widower." See also, Seymour J. Price, 'Maze Pond and the Matterhorn.' *Baptist Quarterly* 10, no. 4 (Oct 1940): 204.

confident reply, 'money no object,' secured his bride. Elizabeth Claridge was eighteen when they married, and was to bear Josiah's eleven children.[4] The tenor of Edward's diary entries, and his puzzled comment about Samuel Leigh's funeral ('I am obliged to attend.'), suggest that he only knew of him as another family friend from chapel.[5] The youngest Whymper boy was however given the forenames Samuel Leigh.

Josiah Whymper was by now settled at Canterbury Place, Lambeth Road, where Edward was to live for nearly fifty years.[6] Lambeth Road runs east from the site of the old horse ferry across the Thames, to St George's Circus. At one end was the Bethlem Royal Hospital for the insane, greatly expanded in 1835, and at the other, by the river, was the parish church of St Mary's at Lambeth, and the Archbishop of Canterbury's Lambeth Palace. The central block of the Bethlem Hospital is now the Imperial War Museum; the parish church of St Mary's closed in 1979, and became a museum of garden history, run by the Tradescant Trust. As the Whymper household grew, they moved into rented premises on the other side of the road at 4 Lambeth Terrace, keeping Canterbury Place as the work premises. When the family moved to Haslemere in the summer of 1859, leaving Edward to run the business in London, he moved back into Canterbury Place. (Neither building survived the Second World War.)

Josiah Whymper's first son, Frederick, was born at Canterbury Place in 1838. Edward, the second son, followed on 27 April 1840. The two boys were close as children and Edward always looked up to his older brother. Fred was an easy-going, sociable character, who, after an adventurous start in life, settled into a relaxed existence in London as a jobbing writer, journalist and theatre critic. Edward took nothing for granted, but grew up with the deeply inculcated consciousness of a second son, that everything had to be worked for. As they left school and made their way in the world of work, Edward had more in common with his next brother, the quiet and undemonstrative Alfred (born 1843). The Whymper family grew steadily: Henry Josiah (1845), Elizabeth, the first girl (1848), Joseph (1850), Frank (1851) and Charles (1853). During the period of the diary came William Nathaniel (1855) and the youngest boy, Samuel (1857). The last child Annette was born in November 1859, just a few weeks before her mother's death.

None of Josiah Whymper's children ever knew that he had been married before meeting their mother. Josiah Whymper, in fact, was strangely reticent about his family and background. After his mother had died in 1829, his father Nathaniel married twice, further adding to his large family. Josiah Whymper hated his stepmothers, never told his children about their grandfather's second wife, and refused to recognize his father's third wife.

---

4. The details of Elizabeth Claridge's early life are described in an undated note written by her youngest child, Annette, now in the possession of Eva Woodgate, and can only have come from Josiah.
5. 11 November 1856.
6. Renaming and renumbering of the streets and terraces by the Post Office in 1876, turned 20 Canterbury Place into 45 Lambeth Road.

He had a difficult relationship with the side of the family that remained resident in Ipswich, and according to Charles Whymper, those settled in London 'swore the Ipswich lot were rascals and had made muddles and so on, which all made JWW nearly mad, as he kept seemingly the whole lot.'[7] When an old man in the 1930s, Charles could still remember himself at thirteen, being sent out delivering money to various impecunious relatives, down in London to benefit from the good will of the hard-working, business-like Josiah Whymper.

Josiah Whymper had been brought up as a Baptist, and twice every Sunday the family would walk to the Baptist chapel at Maze Pond, near London Bridge, where they had their own pew. Josiah was involved in many of the chapel committees, was elected deacon in 1855, and much of their social life revolved around the chapel.[8] Edward's sisters, Elizabeth and Annette, were later active members of the Congregational church in Haslemere, but the Whymper boys, apart from Charles, did not keep any particular attachment to the Baptist creed. Alfred became a Church of England clergyman.

At the age of nine, Edward followed his brother Fred to the small private school, Clarendon House, run by Conrad Pinches, just around the corner from Canterbury Place.[9] This minor private academy operated in a single room in a large terraced house in Kennington Road. Edward clearly benefited from the influence of his driven, ambitious father, as his first report shows his position in a class of about thirty pupils to be third, fourth or fifth in all subjects. In the succeeding years he always came top in geography, natural philosophy, arithmetic and lectures. The school had a rule, (introduced, perhaps, to deal with the precocious young Whymper), that pupils could be awarded no more than three prizes each year. The box of school reports and certificates for good conduct which Whymper kept all his life, contains many commendations given in the absence of the prize that would be his due, but for the fact that he had already secured his quota of three that year. He learnt to write a reasonable, formal French, which stood him in good stead all his life. Clarendon House described itself as a 'Classical and scientific school' and did provide a thorough, modern and practical scientific education. Whymper's exercise books show he had a good grasp (for a twelve or thirteen year old), of such subjects as magnetism, heat, galvanism, mechanics, pneumatics, physiology, binary compounds and steam engines. His next brother Alfred followed him as a pupil at Clarendon House.

---

7. Notes made by Charles Whymper, in November 1935, for his niece Gladys, with a pencil note at the top 'you had best burn when read.' These notes are in the large bound volume of Whymper family history, started by Josiah Whymper, which passed to John Whymper, grandson of William Nathaniel, and are now in the possession of his widow, Mrs Joan Whymper. The notes left by Charles Whymper, probably in the 1930s, are the source of the information about his father and grandfather.
8. Price, 'Maze Pond and the Matterhorn', 202-208.
9. The building is now 164 Kennington Road. Whymper's school reports, commendations, certificates, notebooks, and letters written to his father in French, are at SPRI MS 822/39; BJ and MS 822/1/1-9; BJ.

Years later, Whymper said that the economic impact of the Crimean War had terminated his schooling earlier than intended.[10] Most box wood, the basic material used for wood engravings, came from the Black Sea area, so the price may have risen when the war started, early in 1854. However, the conflict with Russia certainly stimulated the demand for cheap illustrated news, although, two years later, Whymper thought, 'It is certain that the war has done us (the engravers) a great deal of harm.'[11] For whatever reason, by the age of fourteen Edward Whymper's formal education had finished, and he started his apprenticeship as a wood engraver in the family firm.

## Wood engraving

Josiah Whymper took up wood engraving at the right time. For at least fifty years, from the 1830s onwards, wood engraving was the means by which people would receive most of their visual representations of the outside world. A wood cut is a relief made with a knife or scooper, on a piece of plank, working with the grain. Metal engraving, which developed at the same time early in the fifteenth century, creates an intaglio design on a plate, the ink held in the depressions on the plate. Engraving on metal allows much finer, more detailed and more intense impressions, but it is more expensive and greater pressure is required to draw the ink from the incisions, so the metal wears out relatively quickly. Woodcuts, giving a much stronger image based on broad outlines, were widely used for cheaper, popular pictures, and mass-produced devotional images.

The first to combine the artistic richness of metal engraving with the relative cheapness of wood was Thomas Bewick (1753 - 1828). Born in Ovingham, on the Tyne, Bewick had been apprenticed to Ralph Beilby, a jeweler, metalworker, and engraver on copper of book illustrations. Seeking to achieve the same richness of detail and intensity, given by copper engravings, Bewick started using the end grain of planks of wood. This is harder than the side plank and allows the engraver to incise a greater range of fine lines and tinier details. A small burin, the engraving tool, is held in the palm of the hand, between forefinger and thumb, and eased gently across the surface of the block, leaving a shallow impression. Thus the required white space in the illustration is cut away, and the remaining relief surfaces are inked over, as in a traditional wood cut. However, the finer lines, greater detail and more minute engraving on the hard wood, give a denser, richer print. Box wood, being a relatively cheap hard wood, was preferred, but the trunk is of small diameter, and Bewick's illustrations are small vignettes, roughly two inches by four inches. Such engraving on wood had almost certainly been tried earlier in metalworking practices, but Bewick was the first British artist to make a living from book illustration, and is generally credited as the father of wood engraving. He specialized in small, intense scenes of natural history for the growing popular interest in

10. *The Times*, 24 May 1892, 10.
11. 1 January 1856.

the study of birds, animals and the natural world. Whymper had a deep attachment to the history and traditions of the art of wood engraving, and later owned two small wood blocks, on which he noted that they were engraved by 'the celebrated Bewick of Newcastle.'[12]

The unprecedented expansion of working class education, the growth of religious publishing, and the enormous distribution of cheap tracts and Bibles, had a massive impact on working class literacy and created a demand for printed materials. The SPCK, founded in 1698, started publishing books in a serious way in the nineteenth century. *SPCK*, along with the *Religious Tract Society*, which started in 1799, would provide much fruitful employment for the Whympers. The manually operated printing press had not changed much in 350 years, but from 1814, the steam powered printing press quadrupled production of such newspapers as *The Times* to over 1,100 copies an hour. The large printing firms, such as Clowes, were using steam presses from the 1820s, enabling cheap, mass produced publications to become a commercially attractive possibility.

Engraved relief wood blocks fitted into the letter-press (which metal plates did not) and could be printed simultaneously with the text, allowing pages to contain both text and pictures. The first publisher to grasp the importance of mass-produced imagery was Charles Knight, who, in 1832, started the weekly *Penny Magazine*, on which Josiah Whymper was able to find employment early in his career. *Punch* and the *Illustrated London News* started ten years later, and by 1850 the *Illustrated London News* had 100,000 readers. The Crimean War (1854–1856), together with the development of the telegraph in the 1850s, stimulated the demand for news, accompanied by appropriate illustrations. The immediacy created by the telegraph, the rapid distribution of printed materials by the railway, and the growing audience for cheap, accessible stories, stimulated a demand for pictures to accompany the text. There were photographers working in the Crimea, but communication technology still had a long way to go before their efforts could be published simultaneously with the reporting that they illustrated.

In 1817, there were fourteen wood engraving firms in London, by 1852, forty-seven and by 1872, 128 firms.[13] Newspaper stamp duty was removed in 1855, and paper duty in 1861. The expansion and near completion of the railway network in the 1850s and 1860s, made the distribution network quicker and cheaper. Wood engraving always lent itself to a form of domestic industry, and many of the most notable names in the business belong as much to families, as to gifted individuals. Apart from the Whympers, other important wood engravers in London were Joseph Swain, who engraved the Punch illustrations, and the Dalziels, who started about 1840. The Dalziel brothers worked on such prestigious projects as Edward Lane's *Arabian Nights* (along with Josiah Whymper), the illustrations by

12. See, Jenny Uglow, *Nature's engraver: a life of Thomas Bewick* (London: Faber and Faber, 2006). Whymper's Bewick wood blocks are in the Department of Prints and Drawings, British Museum.
13. Eric de Maré, *The Victorian woodblock illustrators* (London: Gordon Fraser, 1980), 7.

Ill. 1 Josiah Whymper and his older brother Ebenezer ("a screwish man", 22 March 1857) by Frederick Walker, photograph © National Portrait Gallery, London; collection unknown.

Sir John Tenniel to *Alice's Adventures in Wonderland*, and Moxon's edition of Tennyson's poems, with its pre-Raphaelite illustrations.

When Josiah Whymper and his brother Ebenezer started their studio they offered apprenticeships, but as they established a reputation for the quality of their work, aspiring artists approached them, or were passed on by other big firms, such as the Dalziels, and they were able to advertise, 'first-rate wood engravers may have employment.'[14] By the early 1840s, the Whympers' name would appear as a selling point in advertising for books on which they had worked.

Frederick Walker (1840 - 1875), Charles Green (1840 - 1898) and John William North (1842 - 1924) all received training in the Whympers' studio during the period of Edward's diary, and went on to become respected

14. *Times*, 1 March 1841.

artists, beyond the wood engraving industry. Edward formed a close friendship with North, joined him on sketching trips at home and in the Alps, and later used his work in *Scrambles amongst the Alps*. Walker became another friend who, although of a shy, nervous disposition, shared Edward Whymper's enthusiasm for rowing.[15]

Thomas Bewick had drawn his own designs on the wood block, or worked directly with the burin, but as wood engraving became an integral part of industrialized mass-production in the 1830s and 1840s, there arose a division of labour between artist and engraver. Typically, an original drawing would be passed to a second draughtsman to transfer to a wood block, then a third person would engrave the design. Commonly, the artist's name would be cut into the block, sometimes also the engraver's name. Less commonly did just the engraver sign the block, but the Whympers were of sufficient status to have their name appear regularly on the illustrations they engraved. Two strands of wood engraving practice developed during the middle decades of the century – the semi-industrial facsimile engraving for popular, cheap editions, magazines and newspapers, advertising, tobacco, tea, and biscuit wrappers and the like, and the more artistic reproduction of high-quality illustrations. Such artistic, pictorial engraving would be paid at a higher rate than jobbing work, and by the 1880s, when photographic technology began to replace facsimile engraving, the expert wood engraved illustration was highly regarded as a skilled art form.

Although there is a brief reference in Edward's diary to work on matchbox packaging, the Whympers principally worked on book illustrations for the upper end of the market, supplemented with regular work for such periodicals as *Leisure hour* and *Home friend*. Early in his career Josiah Whymper was engraving illustrations for French periodicals and books. His first significant book-illustrating commissions were Charles Knight's three-volume edition of Lane's *Arabian Nights*, and a profusely illustrated work on classical Greece.[16] He then engraved illustrations for an eight-volume pictorial edition of Shakespeare, also for Knight.[17] Later, when established as a prestigious engraver, Josiah Whymper worked on finely illustrated editions of Walter Scott's *Marmion, The lay of the last minstrel* and *Lord of the Isles*.[18]

15. 28 May 1859.
16. Edward Lane, *The thousand and one nights, commonly called, in England, The Arabian Nights' Entertainments* (London: Charles Knight, 1839). This was the first translation into English, from the original Arabic, of *The thousand and one nights*. Josiah Whymper is credited as the engraver of thirty-seven of the illustrations, which are by William Harvey, a pupil of Thomas Bewick. Christopher Wordsworth, *Greece: pictorial, descriptive and historical* (London: William S. Orr, 1839), for which Josiah Whymper engraved twenty-two illustrations.
17. Charles Knight, ed. *The pictorial edition of the works of Shakespeare* (London: Charles Knight, 1841-3).
18. Walter Scott, *Marmion: a tale of Flodden Field* (Edinburgh: A & C Black, 1855); *The lay of the last minstrel* (Edinburgh: A & C Black, 1854); *Lord of the Isles* (Edinburgh: A & C Black, 1857).

The nineteenth-century enthusiasm for natural history provided frequent work for the Whympers, engraving the illustrations for the increasing number of guides, catalogues and encyclopaedias produced by writers such as Josiah Whymper's friend, Philip Gosse. Travel narratives, guidebooks and descriptions of archaeological discoveries (Josiah Whymper engraved the illustrations to Austen Henry Layard's books about Mesopotamia and Nineveh) were also fruitful sources of employment. Since the 1830s Josiah Whymper had been regularly employed by the publisher John Murray and he was involved in Murray's most successful publication during the period of Edward's diary, David Livingstone's *Missionary travels and researches in South Africa*, published at the end of 1857. Having crossed the continent from west to east, and been the first European to see the Victoria Falls, Livingstone's narrative was an eagerly awaited volume, which demanded lively, action-filled illustrations. The Whympers were engaged to engrave them, and most of the work was done by Josiah, although one engraving is credited to Frederick. The artist who drew the illustrations on the wood blocks, and had a large part in choosing and designing the subjects, was Joseph Wolf, who worked from sketches made by Livingstone, or his ideas as described to Wolf. Wolf, however, did not have a high regard for the explorer's visual sense, 'he would propose subjects; but there was no handle to what he said. He had a thing in his mind that couldn't be illustrated.'[19] Wolf did not think much of the engravings either, and Josiah Whymper's African scenes are lacking in atmosphere or mystery. Wolf may not have liked the wood engraver's treatment of his drawings, but Livingstone's book was the start of a long and fruitful association between the natural history painter and the Whymper family.

While Wolf was unhappy with the engravings, Livingstone was not enthusiastic about Wolf's drawings. His illustration of 'The missionary's escape from the lion' drew particular dismay from Livingstone, who wrote to John Murray,

> The lion encounter is absolutely abominable. I entreat you by all that's good to suppress it. Everyone who knows what a lion is will die laughing at it. It's the greatest bungle Wolf ever made. … It really must hurt the book to make a lion look larger than a hippopotamus. I am quite distressed about it.[20]

David Livingstone was a demanding person who did not readily understand another's point of view, and the Whympers found him difficult to work with. When Livingstone received proofs of the illustrations from the printer, he covered them in notes and instructions to Josiah Whymper, demanding modifications and improvements (see illustration 2). The book, however, was immensely successful and made Livingstone a fortune in royalties. Other important books for which the Whympers engraved the

19. Wolf's words quoted in A.H. Palmer, *The life of Joseph Wolf: animal painter* (London: Longman, 1896), 124.
20. David Livingstone to John Murray, 22 May 1852, quoted in *David Livingstone and the Victorian encounter with Africa* (London: National Portrait Gallery, 1996), 180. The illustration appears on page 13 of Livingstone's book.

illustrations during the period of the diary included editions of *Aesop's Fables* (for which Wolf and Tenniel drew the illustrations), Byron's *Childe Harold's Pilgrimage*, published by John Murray and Bunyan's *Pilgrim's Progress*, published by James Nisbet.

Wood engraving was well-paid work, when available, and the 1850s and 1860s were the heyday of wood engraved illustration. When still only 26, despite having spent his last seven summer holidays in the Alps, Edward could plan an expedition to northern Greenland that was to cost him £900, an extraordinary amount of disposable income for a young man to have earned himself. The usual charge for one engraving was six guineas, and the Whympers charged nearly the same again, if they had organized the transfer of the drawing onto the wood block, paying some of that to the artist.[21] John Murray's ledgers detail all the payments made for each book they published, and indicate the value of a skilled wood engraver: £330 for the illustrations to Hooker's *Himalayan Journals* (1854), £242 for David Livingstone's *Missionary Travels* (1857, the artist Wolf received £75), £157 for *Aesop's Fables* (1858; Tenniel was paid £57 for his illustrations).

Josiah Whymper studied watercolour painting with William Collingwood Smith, and in 1854 became a member of the NWCS.[22] The Times said of him,

> Mr Whymper is one of the most facile and industrious workmen in the society, and his many drawings of Surrey Commons and high-banked lanes, crowned with park palings have an unmistakable look of outdoor truth, and a freshness that bespeaks many of them actual studies made on the spot.[23]

Edward, however, complains in his diary of his father's painting distracting him from the money-earning business of wood engraving. The diary does, though, give a picture of Josiah Whymper's social world of London-based landscape painters, (usually aspiring to membership of the NWCS), who would turn their hand to whatever illustrating work might earn them some money – Harrison Weir, Percival Skelton, David McKewan, Samuel Read.

21. Receipt from Josiah Wood Whymper to the *London Society*, for engravings, 1 July 1868, BL Add. MS 46666, f. 106; and 12 September 1870, BL Add. MS 46664, f. 3. On 1860s wood engraving, see particularly, Paul Goldman, *Victorian illustrated books 1850-1870: the heyday of wood-engraving: the Robin de Beaumont collection* (London: British Museum Press, 1994); Forrest Reid, *Illustrators of the sixties* (London: Faber and Gwyer, 1928); Joseph White, *English illustration – 'the sixties' 1855-70* (London: Constable, 1897).
   £900 in 1867 was roughly equivalent in spending power to £50,000 today. A skilled labourer would have been lucky to earn 10/- a week, and a professional clerk or civil servant might have earned £200 a year. Whymper's trips to the Alps each summer cost him about £50 (in 1865 he spent £100).
22. The *New Water-Colour Society* was started in 1832 in opposition to the more restricted and establishment *Society of Painters in Water-Colours* (usually known as the *Old Water-Colour Society*, founded in 1804). In 1863 the *New Water-Colour Society* became the *Institute of Painters in Water Colours*, and in 1884, the *Royal Institute of Painters in Water Colours*.
23. *The Times*, 19 April 1858.

What was the teenage Whymper doing during his years of apprentice-ship? The usual terms of engagement at Josiah Whymper's studio were that apprentices worked three days a week, with the remaining time theirs to earn their own money, hence Edward's frequent concern about using his time profitably.[24] Josiah Whymper encouraged his pupils to visit the public galleries, and acquaint themselves with the products of the established art world. At work Edward's principal task was transferring designs and draw-ings onto the whitened wood blocks, usually by tracing the original. Occasionally the Whympers would work from an original drawing, but just as often they would copy a sketch onto the wood block, or make a tracing of another engraving or photograph. Drawing onto a wood block for an engraving is quite a different skill to conventional sketching; the draughtsman has to know just what information the engraver needs, what lines and shading are required and what can be left to the engraver to supply. The drawing has to be precise, so that the engraver knows exactly what thickness of line to cut. The Dalziels complained of Dante Gabriel Rossetti's drawings, which 'made use of wash, pencil, coloured chalk, and pen and ink, producing a very nice effect' but were quite unsuited to being reduced to the black and white of printer's ink.[25] Rossetti, however, said of his work for Moxon's <u>Tennyson</u>, 'It is a thankless task. After a fortnight's work my block goes to the engraver, like Agag, delicately, and is hewn to pieces.'[26]

Edward's more routine tasks involved cutting up the trunks of box wood to provide blocks of the required size, whitening over these blocks for the draughtsmen, preparing overlays and underlays – shaped sections cut from a proof print to give an extra layer of thickness, or thinness, to alter the light and dark on subsequent printings – and arranging the finished wood blocks for the printer. Established wood engraving firms – particularly the Dalziels – would act as quasi-publishers themselves, designing a book around selected illustrations, and frequently a publisher would ask the engravers to select suitable subjects to enhance a particular book. As he became more experienced Edward was charged with reading various volumes, to 'pick places for cuts.'

Learning the art of drawing onto the wood block provided a thorough knowledge of the requirements of the engraver, but from the mid-1860s drawings were often photographed directly on to wood blocks. Although his diary contains few references to actual engraving, once his apprentice-ship had finished, this was what Edward Whymper was most concerned with. In the Whymper's family firm most blocks would be worked on by a variety of engravers, depending on their strengths – whether for figures, scenery, foreground, background, sky or architecture – and it was this work that Edward Whymper would supervise, usually touching up and finishing

---

24. John George Marks, *The life and letters of Frederick Walker A.R.A.* (London: Macmillan, 1896), 7, describes the apprenticeship terms at Whymper's workshop.
25. George Dalziel and Edward Dalziel, *The Brothers Dalziel: a record of fifty years' work in conjunction with many of the most distinguished artists of the period 1840 – 1890* (London: Methuen, 1901), 86.
26. W. Minto, ed., *Autobiographical notes of the life of William Bell Scott* (2 vols., London: James R Osgood, 1892), ii. 36.

the details himself.[27] Although his older brother Frederick had trained as the engraver, he never continued with this, but set about making a living as a painter. Apart from some watercolour sketches made on his first trip abroad, Edward left virtually no original pictures, but his best engravings on wood are among the finest reproductive work produced in that medium.

### The Whympers' social world in South London

When Josiah Whymper settled in Lambeth around 1830, it was a crowded, busy area rapidly taking over the fields and gardens on the south side of the river. The ease of access for goods and materials provided by the river made Lambeth into a growing hub of industry. The Clowes' printing works at Waterloo, employing 600 people, was the largest in the country, and next to them was Stephen's ink factory. In Westminster Bridge Road was the Maudslay iron works, and in South Lambeth Road, the Beaufoy's vinegar brewery. The river made Lambeth a thriving centre of pottery and among the many concerns, large and small, were the Whympers' friend Stephen Green's works by Waterloo, and the Doulton factory in Lambeth High Street. The extension of the railway from Nine Elms to Waterloo in 1848 only helped to increase the noise and dirt, which finally caused the Whympers to move their residence to Haslemere in 1859, unfortunately too late for Mrs Whymper's health.

The diary indicates that the Whympers' social acquaintances lived not in the immediate area, but in the more salubrious and rural suburbs of Streatham, Clapham, Peckham, Brixton and Camberwell. Their social life emanated from the Baptist chapel at Maze Pond, situated until the 1870s where Guy's Hospital now is, by London Bridge. Josiah Whymper had come from a Baptist family in Ipswich, and he and his wife became members of Maze Pond in 1845. Josiah immediately threw himself into the life of the chapel, sitting on committees, helping to audit the accounts, acting as messenger to new applicants, and in 1855 he was elected a deacon. For seventeen years the pastor had been John Aldis (despite surviving an accusation of gross immorality by his servant, Sarah Bishop)[28] who resigned after several years of declining congregations. His resignation letter bemoaned his failure to make any impression upon the poor working class area in which he worked, 'I cannot bear the sight of so many empty pews; I am yet more depressed by the very small spiritual results of my labour.'[29] The chapel membership of 329 at the end of 1855 had fallen to 235 five years later.[30] Samuel Booth, whom the Maze Pond members hoped would

---

27. SPRI MS 822/37/1-2; BJ, 'Proofs of wood engravings' contain many proof prints of the Whympers' engravings from the 1870s with the names of the individual engravers pencilled in around the side, indicating the parts of the print on which each had worked.
28. MPMB 1840-1860; Aldis was cleared by an inquiry in September 1847.
29. John Aldis to the members of Maze Pond Chapel, letter read 4 November 1855, MPMB 1840-1860.
30. Spurgeon's Metropolitan Tabernacle at the Elephant and Castle had 5,311 members in 1891; A.C. Underwood, *A history of the English Baptists* (London: Baptist Union, 1947), 218.

take the place of John Aldis, referred to 'the peculiar difficulties attendant upon a ministry in this place,' and went on, 'The position of your chapel, and the character of the surrounding neighbourhood, leave me little hope of increasing the congregation to any large degree.'[31] The Whympers' friends – all members of the chapel – were lawyers, merchants, factory managers, underwriters, bankers. Thomas Hepburn, whose daughter Emily became Josiah's third wife, had his leather-making works nearby in Bermondsey, but lived in a fine house on Clapham Common. Surrounded by the densely-packed and growing poverty of the slums and rookeries of Southwark and Bermondsey, the prosperous Maze Pond community set up committees to carry out good works among the poor, but certainly did not want the great unwashed within their chapel walls. When finally they persuaded James Millard to replace John Aldis as pastor, he resigned after five years. 'They have been, as you well know, years of trial and disappointment.' Millard's comments suggest that the minister's desire for closer engagement with the local population did not accord with the congregation's conservatively respectable middle class attitudes. He hoped that, 'God will be pleased to make the church a more abundant blessing to the teeming population of your neighbourhood.'[32] Edward's remarks on Charles Spurgeon hiring the Surrey Gardens music hall suggest that the Maze Pond establishment viewed Spurgeon's popularity with some disdain.[33]

Although from a commercial background, working with their hands for a living, and inhabiting a crowded, working-class area of London, the Whympers regarded themselves as educated people who operated in the world of art and literature. Acceptance in established social circles was a background theme that ran through Edward Whymper's life, and it is noticeable in the diary how he emphasises their association with the artist John Gilbert, and Gilbert's connections with the government and the royal family. Indeed, Edward's frequent references to his father's social activities seem to be a subconscious insistence on their right to a position in accepted society. Membership of organized societies, Maze Pond, then the NWCS, provided a position in established society. Josiah Whymper belonged to the Southwark Book Society (most of whose members seem also to have been associated with Maze Pond chapel), attended artistic *conversazione*, and became a full member of the NWCS.[34] Edward, never a naturally gregarious person, preferred the stability and established social procedures of clubs and societies. The diary shows his zeal for the organ-ized world of cricket clubs, although 'the Peckham Rye Albion Cricket Club of which I am a member … are a rather queer, beery lot and I must mind that I am not drawn into their bad habits.'[35] Surrey Cricket Club first

---

31. Samuel Booth to William Beddome, 2 January 1857, MPMB 1840-1860.
32. James Millard to the members of Maze Pond Chapel, 25 May 1863, MPMB 1861-1871.
33. See for example 20 October 1856.
34. For book societies, see Paul Kaufman, 'English book clubs and their role in social history', *Libri* 4 (1964-5): 1-31. Josiah Whymper's book club was probably an arrange-ment whereby subscriptions were charged and volumes were bought for the members to borrow.
35. 12 April 1859.

played at the Kennington Oval in 1845, and by the time that Whymper had become such a keen supporter they were probably the strongest county in England. From 1856 to 1859 they played twenty-nine games of which they won twenty-six. Whymper kept his interest in cricket all his life, and was able to fit his games in to his busy working life and his summer's mountaineering. He was a member of the Alpine Club for fifty years until his death, and regularly attended the meetings and dinners of the Royal Geographical Society, of which he had become a fellow in 1865.

However the diary does reveal the socially varied nature of the people with whom Edward came into contact every day. A friend who knew Whymper well at the end of his life described his 'knack of scraping and continuing acquaintance with neighbours and fellow residents entirely out of his own station.'[36] Although critical of the Greenlanders' dislike for work, Whymper did have an innate appreciation of the nature of their lives and an awareness of their ability to exist successfully in a difficult environment. Particularly among printers and engravers there was a culture of radicalism and liberalism – W.J. Linton and Henry Vizetelly for example – but this was not shared by the Whympers. Probably as a comment for a lecture, Whymper later remarked:

> I have always looked upon the theodolite as a revolutionary kind of instrument, as an instrument for levelling all things, and as a good conservative I have hitherto declined to travel in its company.[37]

The diary shows Edward's dislike, almost certainly following his father and his father's circle of friends, for the local radical and liberal politicians.[38] Whymper never came to accept the unbridled *laissez-faire* capitalism of mid-nineteenth-century Whigs and liberals, and remained all his life a believer in old-fashioned, established practices and social behaviour. However, Edward's grandfather, Nathaniel, was a Liberal town councillor in Ipswich and well-known in the town as a Chartist supporter, which probably had much to do with Josiah Whymper's antipathy toward his family in Ipswich.[39]

## Edward Whymper's later life

Either unmentioned during the period of his diary, or more likely, shortly after it closes, Whymper completed his apprenticeship as a wood engraver. He then set about following his brother as an illustrator of landscape, and went on a walking and sketching tour of Somerset with his fellow apprentice, John William North. While planning an artistic tour of the continent,

---

36. Coulson Kernahan, *In good company: some personal recollections of Swinburne, Lord Roberts, Watts-Dunton, Oscar Wilde, Edward Whymper, S.J. Stone, Steven Phillips* (2nd ed., London: Bodley Head, 1917), 158.
37. Edward Whymper, 'Diary for the year 1872', SPRI MS 822/4; BJ.
38. See, for example, 19, 21, 28 April 1859.
39. Nathaniel Whymper chaired a Chartist meeting in Ipswich calling for an extension of the franchise, just a few days after the great demonstration on Kennington Common, April 1848. See, *Ipswich Journal* 22 February 1840, 2 November 1844, 22 April 1848.

a commission from William Longman (a member of the Alpine Club and the publisher of its journal) to make sketches of Mont Pelvoux in the Dauphiné, meant that Whymper spent his summer in the Alps. Meeting Leslie Stephen and other Alpine Club luminaries in Zermatt, Whymper was introduced to the world of mountaineering, and he was captivated. He returned the following year, 1861, kitted out with ropes and ice axes, and began his mountaineering career by making what he thought at the time was the first ascent of Mont Pelvoux. The summer of 1862 was spent in a succession of attempts on the Matterhorn, reaching a point on the mountain higher than any previous attempts. His work the following year permitted only one serious attempt on the Matterhorn, but in 1864 Whymper joined forces first with Adolphus Moore, then the cartographer Adams Reilly, to make a ground-breaking series of first ascents in the Dauphiné and around Mont Blanc.

1865 was to be his own great campaign, finally disposing of the still unclimbed Matterhorn, before returning to serious sketching. In an astonishing four weeks, Whymper made the first ascents of four peaks, including the Grandes Jorasses and the Aiguille Verte, and three new passes, before finding himself in Breuil, under the Matterhorn. After a series of misunderstandings, coincidences, and some duplicity on the part of his expected guide, Jean-Antoine Carrel, Whymper fell in with the young Lord Francis Douglas, brother of the Marquess of Queensberry. Set on the Matterhorn, they crossed to Zermatt to arrange guides, and there met Charles Hudson, a senior member of the Alpine Club, with a young but inexperienced protégé, Douglas Hadow, also hoping to climb the Matterhorn. The two parties agreed to climb together. Hudson's guide Michel Croz (with whom Whymper had climbed the previous year) and the Taugwalders, father and son (employed by Douglas), made a party of seven. The first ascent of the Matterhorn was achieved easily enough by the previously untried Hörnli Ridge, but on the steepest part of the descent, just below the summit, the young Hadow lost his footing, dislodging Croz and pulling Hudson and Douglas after him. Next on the rope after Douglas, the elder Taugwalder braced himself, as did Whymper behind him, but the thin cord joining Douglas and Taugwalder was snapped in mid air by the weight of four falling bodies. Croz, Hadow, Hudson and Douglas, still roped together, fell 4,000 feet to the glacier at the foot of the mountain. Paralyzed with shock, Whymper and the Taugwalders returned to Zermatt the following morning, after a wretched night on the mountain. Just twenty-five years old, this tragedy effectively ended Whymper's serious mountaineering in the Alps.

Whymper had always been fascinated by the Arctic, and now planned an expedition to penetrate the then unknown interior of Greenland. In 1867, with a young Scottish naturalist, Robert Brown (who had studied at Edinburgh University and had met Whymper's brother Fred in Vancouver) he travelled from Copenhagen to Jakobshavn, in Disko Bay. A lack of arctic experience and a local influenza epidemic meant that Brown and Whymper failed to penetrate the Greenland ice cap, but they explored the coast of Disko Bay and made a valuable collection of Miocene fossil plants. Although Whymper had welcomed the young naturalist's participation, Brown was contemptuously dismissive of Whymper, whom he regarded as a 'mere artist,' (but was paying for the expedition), and these two young men had a difficult relationship. Five years later, Whymper returned to Greenland, this time alone, and circumnavigated Disko Island, as well as ascending a peak of nearly 7,000 feet. He hoped to make another expedition to the far north, using a small steamship, and spending the winter in Greenland, but his applications for funds to the Royal Society and the Royal Geographic Society, were pushed to one side by the Royal Navy's attempt on the North Pole in 1875–6, under George Nares.[40]

In between his two trips to Greenland, Whymper turned his Alpine experiences into a book, telling the story of his epic, but ultimately tragic, quest of the Matterhorn, in *Scrambles amongst the Alps*, published by John Murray in 1871. As well as being one of the finest mountaineering tales, the book is significant for the quality of the illustrations, designed and engraved by Whymper, and their integration with the narrative. Drawn on the wood by a variety of artists (rather than being transferred photographically), and hand-printed to Whymper's specifications, the dramatic, life-like quality of the illustrations was widely remarked. 'We do not know of any collection of engravings which so thoroughly brings back, not merely the form and relief of the mountains, but their very spirit.'[41]

The Whympers' wood engraving business, now run by Josiah and Edward together, prospered as a provider of high quality illustrations to travel, natural history and scientific narratives. They were employed by John Murray to organize all the illustrations for the English editions of Heinrich Schliemann's books about his excavations in Troy and Homeric Greece. A volume effectively published by the Whympers, under Macmillan's imprint, as a showcase for the work of Joseph Wolf - *The life and habits of wild animals, illustrated by designs by Joseph Wolf* - is as much a testament to the artistic quality of their wood engraving, as it is to Wolf's animal drawings.

Frustrated in his attempts to win financial support for further Arctic exploration, Whymper found an outlet for his growing interest in science, by travelling to Ecuador in 1879–80 to investigate the effects of altitude, about which virtually nothing was then known. With the two Carrel cousins, Jean-Antoine and Louis, employed as guides, Whymper made the first ascent of Chimborazo, then the highest separate mountain known to have been climbed. Seven other first ascents were made, along with the then highest camp, when Whymper and the Carrels pitched their tent at 19,500 feet on the crater rim of the live volcano, Cotopaxi. The resulting book, *Travels amongst the Great Andes of the Equator*, finally published

40. 'Mr Whymper would do well to delay his application to the RS for funds for his Greenland excursion until next year.' Edward Sabine to Robert Scott, January 1873, Alpine Club Archives, 1922/B35.
41. 'Hours of scrambling exercise – Tyndall and Whymper', *Saturday Review* 32 (8 July 1871), 59. See also, Leslie Stephen, 'Mr. Whymper's "Scrambles amongst the Alps"', *Macmillan's Magazine* 24 (May-Oct 1871), 305; 'Scrambles amongst the Alps', *The Hawthorn* 1, no. 1 (April 1872), 47-8.

by John Murray in 1892, is a delightfully written account of his adventures, as well as a monument to the then dying art of wood engraving.

Ever since his youthful involvement in the Architectural Photographic Association Whymper had maintained his interest in photography, and was only prevented from taking a camera to Greenland in 1867 by the cost. He did take a camera there in 1872, and returned from Ecuador with more than a hundred photographs. However, by the 1890s photographic technology had removed the need for the wood engraver in the reproduction of images, and Whymper found other means of earning a living, writing guidebooks to Zermatt and Chamonix, and giving lectures on mountaineering, illustrated with lantern slides of his own photographs taken in the Alps. Through his book, *Scrambles amongst the Alps* (which appeared in four further editions in his lifetime) and his dramatically illustrated lectures given all around the country, Whymper did more than anyone to popularize the growing sport of mountaineering.

Revising his guidebooks, he went every year to the Alps, then in 1901 he persuaded the Canadian Pacific Railway to finance some exploration of the Rockies around Banff and Lake Louise, to publicize the company's facilities. With four Alpine guides, many new trails were explored and some first ascents made, but Whymper's heart was no longer in challenging mountaineering. He revisited Canada four more times, one summer walking 500 miles along the line of the railway, but made no new ascents. When nearly sixty-six years old Whymper married Edith Lewin, the young niece of his landlady, and bought a house in Teddington. They had a daughter, Ethel Rosa (who herself would climb the Matterhorn), but after four years Whymper's wife left him for another man, and sued for divorce. On his annual visit to the Alps, Whymper fell ill in Chamonix and died on 16 September 1911. The whole village formed a procession behind his funeral cortege.

### *The diary and the editorial method*

Edward Whymper's first diary fills six carefully ruled exercise books, and was begun on 1 January 1855. Unfortunately the first two pages are missing. On the inside cover of the first book he wrote, '1855 – Book 1st. Commencing Jan 1st 1855 and ending Nov 30, 1855.' He numbered sequentially the 193 pages of the six volumes, which start at page three.[42] The pages of the first four volumes are divided into three columns, and in the first book entries go across the columns then down; from Book Two the entries read down the column, then across the page. In Books Five and Six the pages are divided into two columns. There is a running header pretty much throughout, with the month or months, usually in bold, centred. His final entry, recording a game of cricket on 15 October 1859, fills the sixth notebook, and almost certainly this was when Whymper ceased keeping the diary. Throughout the last volume, covering 1859, there are ever more

---

42. Book One goes up to page 28; Book Two is pages 29 to 60; Book Three, pages 61 to 83; Book Four, pages 84 to 113; Book Five, pages 114 to 157; Book Six, pages 158 to 193.

blank spaces when he was too busy to make an entry, and never had time to go back and do so. Nearing the end of his apprenticeship (which he may have completed during the period of his diary, but did not record), and with his father and the rest of the family relocating to Town House in Haslemere, Edward was increasingly busy managing the firm's affairs in Lambeth, and probably did not have the time to start another volume. During the month following the closure of his diary, his youngest sibling, Annette, was born, and John Murray, whose offices in Albermarle Street Whymper would visit on a regular basis, published Darwin's *Origin of species*. We are also deprived of his thoughts on the death of his mother in Haslemere, less than two months after the diary finished.

Whymper usually filled in his diary every night, keeping it locked in his bedroom, but (a habit he kept all his life), he would often write up periods some days later.[43] Another more frustrating habit he retained, was to leave a space in his journal for the description of particularly important or striking events until he had the leisure, or perhaps sufficient hindsight, to write up a full and more thought-out account, but then never does so. Probably he fully intended to explain how he came to be in 'rather a queer position' with Miss Wilson in March 1859, as he left space in his diary, and also meant to describe where he went in Norfolk in September 1858, but the loss of immediacy takes away his desire to record the events. Most distressingly his Alpine journal for 1865 finishes ten days before the ascent of the Matterhorn, though he had plenty of time to describe the days leading up to the fateful climb. Whymper always had a practical approach to the literary and artistic value of his writings, and, on this occasion particularly, was waiting to record a narrative of triumphant success or narrow failure. Sadly, events overtook his journal. In his otherwise complete two volumes of journal kept in Ecuador, the day of the first ascent of Chimborazo, 4 January 1880, is left blank.

Whymper was not a regular diarist and with one exception his first diary is the only one recording his time in London.[44] He kept detailed journals of his two expeditions to Greenland, and his great trip to Ecuador, then recorded his annual visits to the Alps from 1893 onwards. His first travel diary describes his introduction to the Alps in 1860, but he only began keeping this two weeks after leaving London. He kept no journals for 1861 or 1862, when he began his Alpine climbing and made his most determined attempts on the Matterhorn, but almost certainly followed his life-long practice of keeping notes on scraps of paper. This he did when he met Carrel in the Alps in 1869, made a melancholy second ascent of the Matterhorn in 1874, re-visited Zermatt in 1876, and on his return to the Alps after 16 years in 1892. He certainly made many other visits to the continent between 1870 and 1895, on walking tours, sketching, visiting acquaintances and lecturing, without keeping a record.

43. See his entry for 5 October 1857.
44. Whymper, 'Diary for the year 1872', covers the whole of the year, during which he was in Greenland from May to November.

   Almost certainly all the journals which Whymper kept have survived; he was methodical about keeping everything, stretching back to his school reports when nine years old. When he died he left everything to his executor, his brother William Nathaniel, who had the unenviable task of clearing out Edward's house in Teddington. William Nathaniel Whymper worked all his life for an insurance company in the city, and on his shoulders fell the responsibility for his brothers' variously muddled financial affairs. Edward's first diary, his Alpine notebooks, all his journals from Greenland and Ecuador, and the Alpine and Canadian journals kept meticulously over the last 20 years of his life, passed to William Nathaniel's daughter, Amy Woodgate, who kept them in her house in Surbiton, until shortly before her death. In 1968 she deposited her uncle's papers with the Scott Polar Research Institute in Cambridge, and they were later bequeathed to the Institute by her son Timothy Woodgate. Frank Smythe read through all Whymper's papers while they were in Amy Woodgate's possession, and in his biography of Whymper he published about a quarter of the first diary.

   The text reproduces Whymper's manuscript, keeping his spelling, abbreviations and, as far as possible, his punctuation. Sometimes what is likely to be the same name is given various spellings, but Whymper's usage has been kept. Occasional interpolations are made in square brackets where Whymper has accidentally missed a word. Places where he deliberately left space, but then never used it, are also indicated by square brackets.

# Edward Whymper's London diary 1855 – 1859

1855 – Book 1st. Commencing Jan 1st 1855 and ending Nov 30, 1855

*[NOTE: First two pages missing]*

27. Began 'Toast rack'. Cold day. In the evening went to Mr Swinfens at Kennington. No news whatever.

28. Sunday. Went in morning to Maze Pond, to hear Rev. J. Aldis, and in the evening staid at home on account of my cough. Cold and dry. No news.

29. Went on with 'Toast rack' and began 'Steel,' cut up some wood and went to Mr Darby at Carpenter Smith's Wharf. Cold day. No news. Mr Swinfens is engaged to work again. A good many away in the shop ill. We have a good deal of business, although it is said Dalziel the engraver discharged 7 hands the other day.

30. Finished 'Steel' cut up wood and drew 'Fag' over again and cut out overlays. Snowing and hailing almost all day. No news. Cough not much better if at all.

31. Finished 'Fag' and cut up wood and whited a large quantity of wood for Gosse the naturalist. Mamma and Papa gone to a party at Collingwood Smiths, the artists. A rare occurrence for them. Fred to Mr Eastty's, I staid at home on account of my cough and eyes, see 23rd of this month. Had very heavy falls of snow all the day. The wind very high.

1 **February**. Whited a quantity of wood. Drew 'Signature' and began 'Volute.' Very cold, but not snowing. No news. It is said that the French have now 1000000 men in the Crimea and that ours have dwindled away down to 12 or 14000.

2. Went on with 'Volute' and altered 'Steel' and 'Saltspoon.' Papa went to Peckham today, to Mr Leigh's to ask him to preach at Maze Pond some time in March, which he complied with. Mama went to the Ragged School to a treat given to the girls. Today the MINISTERS RESIGNED in consequence chiefly of a motion made by Mr Roebuck in the House of Commons to inquire into the conduct of the war, and the ministers, not wanting an inquiry, resigned. However, there will be one. The Queen sent for Lord Derby, but he refused to try and form a cabinet because Mr Gladstone and Lord Palmerston would not take office under him. The popular voice is for Lord Palmerston, but he has very little favour in the Queen's eyes. A cold day and snowing. Guns firing all day long. No reason known. (I suppose they must have been practising somewhere).

3. Went on with 'Volute.' A half holiday. Staid at home. It rained in the night and then froze, which made the roads in consequence like glass. Thawing in the afternoon, altogether a most awful mess. My cough almost gone.

4. Sunday. Went morning and evening to hear Mr Aldis at Maze Pond. Thawing, raining and a thick fog. A most filthy day for walking. Cough going away and Fred getting one. The Russians make frequent sorties from Sebastopol.

5. Finished 'Volute' and began 'Saltspoon.' A filthy day for walking. Castle our apprentice came back today after having been away nearly 3 months from rheumatism. Took the Societies books home in the afternoon. No news. The Queen after sending for everyone but the right person, at last sent for Lord Palmerston, and it is understood that he has undertaken to form a cabinet.

6. Finished 'Saltspoon' and altered a clock of Mr Gibson's drawing. A drizzly day. No news. Lord Palmerston has consented to form a cabinet. My mother's pea soup affair at the 'Ragged School' came off tonight, but I have not heard the result yet.[1]

7. Drew 'Saltspoon' over again, and went on with soup plate and traced some cuneiform characters belonging to the British Museum. No news. Cold and dry. No ministry formed yet. My father went to Mr Gilbert's.

8. Traced some more hieroglyphics. Snowed last night and all today. It lays very thick on the ground. A ministry formed with Lord Palmerston for Prime Minister, Lord Panmure Minister of War. With the exception of these, the ministers are the same. My mother is trying to get a blind boy into the school in St George's Fields and went her rounds today canvassing for votes for him. She was pretty successful and very sanguine.[2] Plenty of our business doing engraving, advertising for hands.

9. Went on with 'Soup plate' and went to Mr Gibson's. Cold day. No news. My mother going about for her blind boy. Our servants when they went down stairs early this morning mistook the snow sweeper (Hopkins) for a thief and came running upstairs tumbling over one another, frightened out of their wits.

10. Finished 'Soup plate.' Thawing and freezing. The thermometer 27° in rooms. No news. Thieves got into No 8 tonight and went in some gardens but were frightened away. The first number of the new illustrated paper (started in opposition to the Illustrated News) came out today. It was pretty good but not good enough to compete successfully with the other.

11. Went to Maze Pond twice, hearing Mr Aldis both times. Very cold, the snow however being beaten down, makes very good ground to walk on. My father has written to Lord Shaftesbury about the blind boy, but he has

---

1.  The Ragged School, on Newport Street, near Black Prince Road, was built by Henry Beaufoy and opened in 1851. Both Whymper's mother and father were on the committees (of which there was one for each sex). Originally with a classical portico and two wings, only the south wing still stands.
2.  The School for the Indigent Blind was founded in 1799, moved to St George's Circus in 1811 and was enlarged in 1838. Funded by subscription, an annual guinea gave each subscriber one vote for each vacancy, hence Whymper's canvassing. The school took boys and girls, who had to be at least 12 years old, and were instructed in handicrafts, reading and writing, and sometimes, music. Elections were held twice a year, in May and November.

not seen fit to return any answer. Mrs Moore, who kept the house of business for us, went yesterday with her husband, on route for Australia.

12. Drew 'Spear' and 'Steel' over again. Cold day. No news. Bentley the publisher has failed for a large amount it is said, but he will still continue his business. The book meeting is going to take place next Wednesday week and we are to have a juvenile party after it (the next day) if all is well. We returned to the old way of working, 9 hours a day and being paid on Saturday, the other way not being found to answer well

13. Began soup tureen and began a piece of bacon. Very cold and snowing slightly. No news. Lord Russell is going out as plenipotentiary at Vienna for something (I don't know what). Bentley owes his paper maker between 8 and 9000£. My mother gave away the pea soup at the Ragged School again tonight. It seemed to answer very well. It was distributed to upwards of 100 boys and girls.

14. Went to Mr Read's. He was not fortunate in getting into the Old Water Colour Society, but he says he will try again. Very cold. No news. Some professor of astronomy has prophesied either today or tomorrow there will be the heaviest fall of snow that there has been for 60 years. The Thames is partially frozen and a great quantity of ice floating in it. The price of coals reaching up very high. I drew today 'Rectangle,' a diagram, and cut up a great deal of wood and began 'Plough.'

15. Cut up a lot of wood, went on with 'Plough' and went to Christian Know. Soc. Very cold. No news. The river is frozen over at Richmond and thousands of people skating and sliding on it. It was predicted by different persons that there would either be a great thaw or a good fall of snow on this day, but there was neither of them, so they were disappointed. My father, mother and Fred went to the photographic exhibition this evening.

16. Finished 'Plough' and drew 'shallow' and cut up a rare lot of wood, which though it may be good exercise is not good practice. Today my mother went to Peckham to Miss Leigh's and my father to Blackheath to Mr Gilbert's. Mr Watson of the Deaf and Dumb School has turned out a great number of introductions in the vocabulary, which occasioned a disturbance with my father. Admiral Saunders Dunderhead[3] is appointed to the command of the Baltic fleet, Seymour $2^{nd}$ in command. No news, except our army in the Crimea (if it may be called so) is in a little better condition. Very cold, the wind blowing very hard. It changed today.

17. Began 'Type,' cut up a lot of wood and went to the bank. Never having been there before, I nearly lost myself there. No news except that they seem to be nearer a general assault than they were before in the Crimea. Freezing hard, the Thames quite chocked up with ice. Last night an enormous fire took place near Blackfriars Bridge, which burnt down a flour mill, a timber yard, a lime wharf, a bottle warehouse, Sir J Rennie's house with his valuable models, and another enormous factory (I don't know of what), besides a number of private houses. The fire continued burning all night and today. Mr Braidwood the superintendent of the brigade, had a

---

3.  Sir Richard Dundas (see Appendix 1).

son in law crushed in the ruins, a great pile of timber. It is said that several other lives were lost.

18. Went to Maze Pond twice. Mr Aldis preached in the morning, and a student in the evening. Very cold but not snowing.

19. Drew 'Spear' again and finished 'Type.' No news. The fire is estimated to have done 150000 £'s worth of damage. Very cold. The river is so much frozen over that some people skated on the ice below London Bridge.

20. Touched up 'Type', went to London road, the Blind School and the Blackfriars Road and cut up and whited a lot of wood. Very cold. Sky clear and no indications of snow or rain. Tomorrow the Book Society meet at our house, the second time since my father has joined it. It is rumoured the Emperor of the French intends visiting the camp in the Crimea.

21. Began 'Wreath' and went to Butterworth's, Clowes', Fariner's, the Plumber's etc. Tonight we entertained the Book Society. It was a pretty full meeting and we had a very pleasant party. Tomorrow our juvenile party comes off. No news. Very cold. The sky appears as if we should have a great deal of snow.

22. Went on with Wreath and went several errands. No news. A little snow. Thawing towards the evening. The ice on the river is doing immense damage to the shipping. Some of the ships have been torn from their moorings and are drifting backwards and forwards with the tide. To-night our juvenile party came off. We had a good many games, some music, chemical experiments, etc.

23. Finished Wreath. Gladstone the Chancellor of the Exchequer, Mr S. Herbert the Secretary of War, and Sir J. Graham 1st Lord of the Admiralty have resigned their places. Snowing a little all day and very cold. I have a bad headache, shivering sensations, etc. Yesterday some bread riots took place in Whitechapel and the mob did a considerable deal of damage to the workhouse.

24. Began 'Writing' and cut up wood etc. The cold weather broke up today. The sun at 12 o'clock was pretty warm and it continued thawing all the rest of the day, making the streets in a great mess. Mr J. Hume the financist died lately. No news. Tonight my nose bled considerably, a thing which it has not done for 6 or 7 years.

25. Sunday. Went to Maze Pond twice. Mr Aldis preached both times. The streets are in an awful mess as it has been raining in the night. No news. My headache going away slowly, it gives considerable trouble.

26. Finished 'Writing' and began a Vase. No news. Not so mild as yesterday. No successors appointed to the resigned ministers.

27. Went on with the 'Vase' and went out to different places. No news. All day dull, wet and the roads very dirty. A good deal of business being done at our shop. We had a ticket for a concert at the Blind School sent us today; they are said to be very good.

28. Went on with 'Vase', went to Mr Read's, and cut up some wood. Mild day and roads in an awful state. Nearly all the ice disappeared off the river and the ships consequently released. The price of coals is falling. There has been an attack of the Russians at Eupatoria, no certain intelligence has as

yet come of it. My mother distributed soup again at the Ragged tonight to 100 boys.

## MARCH

1. Went on with the Vase, traced something for my father and cut out some overlays. No news. Rainy and mild. In the evening we had Mr Aldis and Mr Spurgeon visited my uncle[4]. We keep on sending letters off for votes for our blind boy.

2. Finished the Vase. No news. A little rain and more mild. I went in the afternoon to Mr Bernal's collection in Eaton Square. I saw some fine armour, a great number of curious old watches and other things, old pictures and a very great quantity of curious and rare old china and glass. A great number of people there. Catalogues sold at 8d each. It is said Mr Bernal ruined himself by making this collection, which is valued at 70,000£s. The Government was solicited to buy it but refused and it is now going to be sold by auction.

3. Drew Shoestring and cut up some wood. In the afternoon I went to Mr Gilbert's at Blackheath. He was not at home having gone to a dinner at the Mansion House. Yesterday in all probability the most important event took place that has happened in my lifetime. I mean the death of the Emperor Nicholas I of Russia. Yesterday afternoon a telegraphic despatch was received of the dangerous illness of the Czar, almost immediately another, with an account of his having taken his last leave of his family and then another with the news of his death. In the House of Lords it was announced last night by Lord Palmerston. He is said to have died of an apoplectic fit. The evening editions of today's papers say that the younger and more tyrannical of the emperor's sons has assumed the crown, at the desire of the more numerous party in Russia. The whole thing is disbelieved by many persons on account of the numerous lies that have been received before, but this account certainly seems to wear an aspect of truth, and is believed by the majority of the people. Now is the time for the ministers to press the siege of Sebastopol, for being without orders the generals must necessarily be uncertain as to what they are to do, and of course there will be division of opinion among them. If they take it (of which at this time there is a great chance) and the milder prince ascends the throne, we shall be able to dictate much better terms to him, but if we do not and the fierce one ascends, the army in the Crimea will be in a worse condition than ever. The weather is mild and showery. No other particular news except that Lord Lucan is on his way home and Sir G. Brown is recovered.

4. Sunday. Went to Maze Pond both morning and evening, and heard Mr Aldis both times. Pretty mild all day and sunshiny. Mr Leigh is going to preach at Maze Pond next Sunday. Mr Aldis I believe is going to Dublin to preach for some benevolent society.

5. Began a part of the Elgin Marbles and cut up some wood. A beautiful day. No news. I made my first deposit today in the savings bank.

---

4.   Ebenezer Whymper (see Apendix 1).

6. Went on with Elgin marbles. Went to Clowes and Bradbury and Evans and cut up some wood. A fine day. It is reported that the Grand Duke Michael of Russia has been poisoned, but it is not believed, and there is news that the King of Denmark is dangerously ill.

7. Went on with 'Elgin marbles', cut up wood, went out some errands and began drawing some toys made by the Russian prisoners at Lewes.[5] A fine day but colder. It is expected that Parliament will be dissolved, because the Emperor of the French does not like the enquiry of Mr Roebuck's committee on the conduct of the war.

8. Went on with the 'toys', cut up some wood. Went to Mr Soper's the artist's. A fine day but cold. No news excepting that Menschikoff is recalled from Sebastopol and Gortschakoff put in his place. The china at Mr Bernal's sale is realising fabulous prices, two small vases alone fetching 1850£s and one other 1300£s.

9. Finished toys and went some errands. A very cold day. The inclement weather returned again, snow falling in the afternoon. It is said that there has been an earthquake at Bursa in Asia Minor, in which 2000 people were killed. My father bought some nice large maps at an auction today, rather cheap, as also some Saturday magazines.

10. Redrew a good part of Elgin marbles. Very cold, snowing pretty fast in the morning. No particular news. The railway is getting on in the Crimea pretty well; 1½ miles being finished. Tomorrow Mr Leigh preaches at Maze Pond. The manifesto of the new Emperor of Russia is very warlike. He declares his policy to be that of Catherine and Nicholas, consequently that of aggression.

11. Sunday. Went to Maze Pond twice, morning and evening. Heard Mr Leigh preach both times. Had Mr Beddome to tea. Cold day, snowing in the morning and evening. No news.

12. Drew 'Toast rack' over again, and did various jobs. A drizzly day with some good hard showers. No news. The pictures in Mr Bernal's sale are fetching good prices, the first day's sale realized as much or more than they thought the whole would realize. The death of the Emperor of Russia is said to have been caused by the violent excitement produced by the King of Sardinia joining the allies. It brought on a severe fit of passion which lasted several days. He was going to confiscate all the property of the Sardinians resident in Russia and numberless other mad things.

13. Finished Toast rack. Fine day, tolerably warm. No news. My mother went out canvassing Peckham and Camberwell way with rather bad success.

14. Began drawing 'Wash stand', cut up some wood and went out some errands. Fine day. No news from the Crimea. The expedition of the Emperor of the French appears to have been given up for some reason. The Vienna conference commences today.

15. Was out walking almost all day. In the morning went to Mr Prior's and Mr Reid's and in the afternoon to Mr Dare and canvassing for the blind

---

5.   Some 350 prisoners had been taken at Bomarsund on the Åland Islands in the Baltic, in August 1854. They were mostly Finns and local islanders.

boy, and had rather bad success. It is said that a large part of the town of Sebastopol is in flames and that they are making rapid progress for the bombardment. My father went to his conversazione tonight with Miss Hepburn.

16. Went on with 'wash stand' and cut out overlays. Rained a good deal in the night, but was fine all day. No news. The Baltic fleet is being rapidly assembled and there is talk also of the formation of a channel fleet.

17. Went on with 'Wash stand' and cut up a great deal of wood and whited it, and cut out some overlays. Rainy day. Our water pipes thawed today and burst in several places. No news excepting the French have had some combats with the Russians before Sebastopol, but nothing of importance is done.

18. Sunday. Went to Maze Pond twice, morning and evening. Heard Mr Aldis both times. A showery day. No news. It is reported that the Turks are beaten in a battle at Eupatoria. Next Wednesday is the day appointed for fasting. There will be a service at our chapel in the morning.

19. Monday. Went on with 'Wash stand' and cut up and whited a lot more wood. I have done very little drawing lately owing to walks and cutting up wood. Dull day. The Russians have sunk 3 more ships at the entrance of the harbour at Sebastopol, because our batteries now command the ships and set them on fire and they prefer sinking them to having them burnt.

20. Went to Mr Gibson's, cut up wood and began sampler. All the afternoon went out canvassing for the blind boy, but with very bad success and gained a fearful headache. Fine day. No news. A report of the French defeated in a battle before Sebastopol. Tomorrow is the day appointed for fasting and prayer, consequently our shop is shut up.

21. Being the day for fasting (which I did not) and prayer, our place was not open. Went to chapel in the morning. Fine day, but strong wind and very cold. No news. The Lord Chancellor had a narrow escape from being smashed yesterday, a large stone sheet they were hauling up for the houses where he was, smashing the roof in etc.

22. Went on with the 'Sampler' and cut up some wood. Drizzly day, rather cold. The 1$^{st}$ of the 4 points is formally ratified by all the powers at Vienna. No news from the Crimea. A bridge at Bristol has been carried away by a barge striking one of the piers, several lives lost.

23. Finished 'Sampler', went to Butterworth and Feath's [Heath] and the Society for Promoting C. Knowledge and cut up and whitened some wood. Dull, cold day. No news excepting large convoys of provisions and ammunition have entered Sebastopol without our army being able to prevent them. The canvassing for votes for our blind boy progresses pretty favourably I think.

24. Finished Wash stand and cut up some wood. Dull day. No news. Part of the new Baltic fleet has departed, but the remainder will not be ready in less than 2 months. Tomorrow is quarter day. We have now been 3 years in this house.

25. Sunday. Quarter day. Went to Maze Pond twice, morning and evening; heard Mr Aldis both times. Mr Leigh preached at Regent Street chapel.

Dull day. Dry and cold. Mr Green has got us a few votes more for our blind boy, so that now I think we may reckon we have ¾ the needed number.

26. Monday. Cut up some wood. Drew the formation of the wall of some place or other, and began a Grecian coin. Fine day. No news whatever.

27. Went on with coin. Went out the whole morning canvassing for blind boy. Dull day, raining in evening. The whole of the editions of the Paris papers have received orders from the Emperor to say nothing henceforward about the war, not even so much as the removal of one regiment from one part of France to another. A telegraphic despatch was received today announcing that the Russians attacked the whole line of the British, but were repulsed with great loss; they also have opened their batteries again.

28. Finished the Grecian coin. A very dull, drizzly day. No news of any kind. My mother got some more money today for the blind boy, and Fred is going out tomorrow canvassing for him.

29. Finished Vegetable dish and cut up some overlays. Fine day. My mother went to Peckham. It is said the Russians are assembling a great force near Eupatoria, being determined to take it from the Turks.

30. Drew 'wristband' and altered 'wash stand.' Fine day. Hailing occasionally. No news.

31. Began redrawing wash stand! In the afternoon went canvassing for the blind boy, pretty good success. Fine day. No news whatever. Tomorrow is my brother Alfred's birthday (the 1st of April).

**April**

1. Sunday. Went to Maze Pond twice, morning and evening. Heard Mr Aldis both times. Today is Alfred's birthday. He is 12 years old, and the 3rd in the family. A fine day. No news.

2. Drew 'Scraper' and went to Mr Smithers in the afternoon. Fine day. No news. My father dined and supped with Mr Green today. It is pretty generally understood that the Emperor of the French will visit this country about the middle of this month.

3. Altered 'Scraper' and began 'Screwdriver.' Showery day. No news. Father went to dinner today at Mr. Hepburn's. The paper that started in opposition to the Illustrated News has at length died after a short life of 10 weeks.

4. Finished 'Screwdriver' and went to the deaf and dumb asylum. Fine day. No news. Mr Read came to tea today. I have been subject to bad headaches lately, which are not at all agreeable, may they go quickly.

5. Went on with Wash stand and went to Butterworth's. Tomorrow being Good Friday (truly so to us) we have a holiday. Fine day. No news. Preparations are being made to receive the Emperor of the French. My uncle John comes up to London tomorrow, being one of his very few holidays.

6. Good Friday!! *bun day for ever!!! Went in the train to Wandsworth and walked on to Putney Common and back. Uncle John did not come. This is the finest day we have, very hot indeed. The particulars of the attack of the French on Sebastopol arrived today whence it appears that they suffered severely and we lost a good many officers

7. Went out canvassing for blind boy; bad success. The first proxy came to our house today; one of mine. Began a Grecian coin in afternoon. No news.

The Emperor of the French will stay upwards of a fortnight in London. Fine day, not so hot as yesterday. Committee of inquiry into the mismanagement of the war progresses but slowly; we hear now but little about it. The ministers are doing all they can to hush it up.

8. Sunday. Went to Maze Pond twice, morning and evening. Heard Mr Aldis both times. No news. Dry day, windy and very dusty. Uncle John came up today to see us, and returned this evening to Watford.

9. Easter Monday. Stamped the numbers on the vocabularies and cut up some wood. Went to Mr Ellis' and went on with 'coin.' No news. Fine day. Dry and dusty. We received 10 or 12 today. The proxies are now coming in thickly for our blind boy. The Baltic fleet left Spithead for the Downs last week, where it will wait for orders.

10. Went to Kensington, Mr Read's and went on with the coin. Very dusty day. No news. A rumour today that the allies had attacked Sebastopol. Up to today we have had 490 votes sent us for the blind boy.

11. Helped my father to finish his pictures in order to send them in to his gallery today. He sent 7 one of which he sold a few days before to Mr. Hepburn. I finished drawing the coin and drew 'Segment' Fine day. Raining in the evening. No news. The Emperor notified to the Corporation of London, that he would visit the city, which visit I understand will cost them about 9000£s. They can well afford it.

12. Began an electric light lamp and went in the afternoon to Mr Weir's at Peckham. A fine day. No news. The day that is fixed for the coming of the Emperor of the French is I believe Monday next. A number of English ships of war have gone to escort him over to England.

13. Finished the lamp and went out canvassing for the blind boy, the last time I hope. We have now 640 votes. Drizzly day. No news. The Russians it is said lost 2000 men in their last sortie and the French 600 by it.

14. Began the Winter Palace of the Emperor of Russia. Fine day. Next Monday is my mother's birthday. No news.

15. Sunday. Went twice to Maze Pond, morning and evening. Heard Mr Aldis both times. A beautiful day, very hot. No news. The Emperor and Empress of the French come up tomorrow by the South-eastern railway, I believe from Dover. Tomorrow is my mother's birthday. Blind boy progresses, we have now 746 votes.

16. Went on with 'winter palace' and went to Mr MacKewan's and Mr Dare's. A splendid day, very hot, the best day we have had this year, by far. No news. The Emperor and Empress of the French came up to London today from Dover by South-eastern railway to the Bricklayers Arms station. He then proceeded along the New Kent, to Westminster roads, over the bridge to Paddington, from which he went to Windsor Castle. The roads were crammed with people who went to see him, the houses were decked out with flags and the whole line through which he passed presented quite a novel appearance. He was escorted by the Life Guards and came in in an open carriage, in which were himself, Eugenie and Prince Albert. They all looked extremely well and bowed very graciously to the people. It is said that a number of French refugees who came over in '51, were imprisoned during the time he was here, in order to prevent any

attempt on his life. Splendid illuminations along the principal streets in London, in the evening.

17. Went on with 'Winter Palace', cut up some wood, cleaned some pictures, went errands etc. Another beautiful day, clearer than yesterday, not quite so hot. No news. The Emperor had a hunt today at Windsor. The blind boy has now 894 votes.

18. Went on with 'Winter Palace' and cut up wood etc. Fine day. Lord John Russell is on his way home from Vienna. It is now generally believed that Austria will (as it has often done before) play us false, and desert us instead of helping us. Important news is expected from Sebastopol, as something is supposed to be done. The Emperor did not go to the hunt yesterday. I do not know what he does today, but tomorrow he visits the city. All business is consequently suspended after 9 o'clock. The police seem apprehensive of an assassination of him, so a very sharp look out is kept by the detectives.

19. Drew 'Seal'. The Emperor went today to the city, where he received deputations, etc. In the evening he went to the Opera. He went in a closed carriage along with the Queen and Prince Albert and drove very fast (it is said because he was afraid of a stray shot finding its way near him). Enormous mobs were out in the evening to see him, and a number of accidents took place, arms broken, etc. A beautiful day. No news.

20. Finished 'wash stand', altered 'soup plate' and cut up wood; a very fine day. The Emperor went with the Queen today to the Crystal Palace at Sydenham. None but season ticket holders were admitted to the buildings while he was there, but he appeared to the people in the gardens, on the balcony with the Empress and bowed etc. It is said the sight was exceedingly grand as upwards of 20,000 people, well dressed, were assembled to see him. The fountains (some of them) were got by Sir J Paxton into play for the first time, but one of the pipes burst and spoilt the effect of some. The Empress was charmed with the Alhambra court. I saw them today for the first time, they looked remarkably jaded and knocked up, as I have not the least doubt they were. Today my father saw how his pictures were hung at the gallery, they were pretty well.

21. Began 'Tureen' and altered seal. The Emperor goes away today by the same route he came. I am not sorry nor do I believe is any one, for they made such a bustle and confusion. This was the private view today at my father's gallery; he sold 3. The blind boy has now 1016 votes. A fine day. The deficiency of the supplies in relation to the expenditure last year was 23 millions. There is going to be a loan of 16 mils. No fresh news.

22. Sunday. Went to chapel twice morning and evening. Mr Aldis preached in the morning and I don't know who in the evening. Fine day, with a sharp east wind . No news.

23. Went on with Tureen and cut up wood. Went out in afternoon to Watson's, Smithers' and Weir's at Peckham. Fine day. The long expected bombardment of Sebastopol has recommenced and continued for 2 days and nights continuously. There are 500 guns and mortars now in action against the town, each supplied with 600 rounds of shot. The Russians by their own accounts lost 850 men in the 2 days.

24. My father's birthday. He is 42 years old. Finished tureen and cut up wood. Fine day. A report today that the allies had destroyed the Mamelon tower at Sebastopol. There is going to be an extra amount of income tax this year, and the duty on tea, sugar and coffee is going to be raised.

25. Cut up wood, touched up 'Tureen,' went to H Weir Esq, and began 'Wall flower.' Cloudy day looks like rain. No news. The blind boy now has about 1250 votes.

26. Went on with 'Wall flower' and brightened 'Winter palace.' No news. Fine day. Henry's birthday. The Blind boy has now 1321 votes. Went to Mr MacKewan's in the morning.

27. Finished 'Wall flower,' touched up 'Vegetable dish' and 'Toast rack' and cut up some wood. No news. The electric telegraph now goes the whole of the way from London to the Crimea.[6] Dull day, rather. My birthday. I am fifteen years old. Made a resolution to get up earlier in the mornings, that being one of the best ways to success.

28. Cut up a great deal of wood, stamped the 'vocabs' and began 'Tureen' over again. No news. Dull day, rained a little. The Lord Mayor has been made a baronet on account of receiving the Emperor so well in the city.[7]

29. Sunday. Went to Maze Pond twice, morning and evening. Heard Mr Aldis both times. Fine day. No news. Today Mrs Wheeler came from Peckham to see us. Miss and Mr Leigh, Mrs Sowerby etc are all going to Devonshire next Tuesday, for one month.

30. Went on with Tureen, did a tracing, and went Mr Weir's at Peckham. No news. Today the Emperor of the French was shot at on the streets of Paris by an Italian. The shot missed and the man was taken. Dull day, raining a little.

1. **May**. Mr Leigh's birthday. Finished drawing Tureen and went some errands. No news. Showery day. Blind boy has now 1493 votes. The election takes place this day week.

2. Drew 'Sickle,' cut up wood and began 'Sieve.' No news. Fine day. The blind boy goes on capitally; he has now 1626 votes.

3. Finished 'sieve,' cut up wood and began Skein. Fine day. No news. Business beginning to look rather dull; my father and uncle consequently calling out, talking about turning off hands etc. I hope it very speedily gets better. A fire has taken place I think, tonight the sky looked very red. Blind boy 1650 votes.

4. Cut up wood, redrew 'skein' and rubbed it out. Began 'shower bath'. No news. A new illustrated paper is I believe to be started by Vizetelly, price 2[d]. Fine day. Blind boy upwards of 1860 votes.

5. Cut up wood, went to Mr Watson's and the Blind School and finished 'Shower bath.' One of the floating batteries for the Baltic fleet has been blown up by accident. It is now said the Emperor of the French will not go up to the Crimea. My father sold 40£s worth more pictures today, which cheered him up a little. Blind boy upwards of 2260 votes.

6.  The telegraph link from Varna in Bulgaria to the British base at Balaklava was completed on 25 April.
7.  Sir Francis Moon, Bt (see Appendix 1).

6. Sunday. Went to chapel twice, morning and evening. Heard Mr Aldis both times. No news. A fine day, despite all wishing for rain having had none for some weeks. One of our floating batteries intended for the Baltic was last Thursday accidentally set on fire at Millwall and was totally destroyed.

7. Tomorrow the election of blind boys and girls will take place at the London Tavern. We have 2403 votes to take in. The man who shot at the Emperor of the French is condemned to death, but it is expected the Emperor will pardon him. No news. Fine day. A fire took place tonight at Kennington, at a public house.

8. Today is the day of the election of pupils for the Blind School at the London Tavern. I was about all day. It was rather dull at the Tavern, not many people there. At the close of the poll we stood second on the list, having 3822 votes, the highest having 5588, and the one below us 2500. No news today. A very fine day.

9. Drew Skein again and began 'sink'. No news. Raining in the evening fairly sharply. It will do a deal of good. It is much needed. Tonight there was a fire in Vauxhall Walk. My father has sold some more sketches. Tonight a person came to know if he would teach painting.

10. Finished 'Sink'. No news. Fine day. The Crystal Palace have now nearly got all the fountains ready, so that they will be able to be used very soon. Another gentleman came tonight to look at my father's sketches. He is coming again to see them by daylight. There is a rather remarkable history going about regarding a young man, son of a rich merchant, who wished to become a painter, but his family were against it. He however prevailed on them to allow him to paint one large picture, which was to be exhibited and if it was considered successful, he was to go on, but if not, he was to bid farewell to painting. He did it and sent it to the Academy, it was admitted, the Queen saw it at the private view and bought it. Of course this success has made him.

11. Altered 'Sink', drew a 'gas jet,' cut up wood and began a 'siphon.' No news. A slight storm in the afternoon, plenty of rain and hail, with thunder and lightning. Business getting better.

12. Finished 'Syphon' and went to Mr Murray's. Fine day. The Russians have made 2 sorties to try and raise the siege, but have been unsuccessful.

13. Sunday. Went to chapel twice, morning and evening. Heard Mr I don't know who both times. No news. A very wet day.

14. Touched up 'Syphon,' cut up wood, went to Mr Dare's and began Spheroid. No news. Dull day. 2 boilers blew up this afternoon, in the Borough Road at the Atlas iron works, damaging and I think killing some men. The beams were splintered and lying in all directions, along with cogged wheel and broken machinery.

15. Finished Spheroid and drew Stalk. No news. Fine day. It was not an explosion at the Atlas works, but the weight of the shells for the government, was too great for the strength of the building, which was made for carpenters, and accordingly it fell in damaging but not killing 20 persons.[8]

8.  The Atlas iron works was making shells to be used in the Crimea.

16. Altered Sink, cut up wood and began redrawing Syphon. No news. Pianori, the man who shot at the Emperor, was executed yesterday, having been proved guilty and also was proved an escaped convict from the galleys. Dull day. My father went to the Book Society meeting tonight at Mr Galland's at Clapham.

17. Finished Siphon, cut up wood and began wicket. No news. Showery day. The French exhibition opened yesterday, but is not half finished I believe.

18. Cut up wood and finished wicket. No news. Dull day. An increase in our family took place, in the person of a young brother.[9] In the park at the back of the Horse Guards today, the Queen distributed the Crimean medals to the soldiers, great numbers of spectators, seats being erected all round the platform where the ceremony took place.

19. Drew 'Stick' and began 'Switch.' Fine day. Nothing is being done at Sebastopol, a most miserable state of things. General Canrobert has resigned his office of Commander in Chief of the French army, on a plea of ill health, but it is generally believed that he is not equal to the situation, although he is a good soldier, he is not a good commander. General Pelissier succeeds to him.

20. Sunday. Went to chapel twice, morning and evening. Heard Mr Aldis both times. No news. A very fine day.

21. Finished 'Switch,' altered 'Stick' and cut up wood. No news. Fine day. An emigrant ship, the John, was wrecked on the coast of Cornwall last Tuesday, through the obstinate perverseness of the captain, who when told they were approaching land, said contemptuously, pooh, pooh. Almost immediately the ship struck, 196 passengers drowned and none of the crew. The captain is arrested for manslaughter.

22. Began 'Twine,' cut up paper and cut out overlays. I went to Mr Weir's at Peckham. No news. Dull day. Tomorrow is the Derby day at Epsom

23. Whited 12 large mahogany blocks and went on with 'Twine.' No news. Today is the Derby day. Splendid fine day, plenty of people went to the race. The Wild Darell won it. Our new baby boy is fat and flourishing.

24. Finished 'Twine,' went to Mr Clay's and began 'Wafers.' No news. A fine day.

25. Drew 'Shuttlecock,' cut up wood and went on with 'wafers.' No news. The Baltic fleet is expected to do something soon!!! How often has that been said. A beautiful day. Fearfully hot. The Oaks day at Epsom today.

26. Touched up 'shuttlecock,' went to Mr Gibson's, altered Shaving brush and went to the new Society of Painters in Water colours. They have a capital exhibition; it is well supported by Bennett, Haghe, MacKewan, Corbould, Robins etc. The papers speak of something trifling having been done at Sebastopol, but the Russian accounts say nothing at them. Another hot day.

27. Sunday. Went to Maze Pond chapel twice, morning and evening, heard Mr Aldis both times. No news. Fine day, rain in the evening.

---

9. William Nathaniel Whymper (see Appendix 1).

28. Drew shrub. This morning news arrived that we had taken Kertsch (wonderful), which is a little place in the Crimea. But as I afterwards discovered we took it because they abandoned it and blew it up. A fine day, rather windy.

29. Went to Sparrow's and Gibson's and began 'Star.' We took upwards of 30 ships at Kertsch and some stores, it being one of the principal granaries for Sebastopol. A fine day.

30. Finished 'star' and went to Mr Prior's. My father went to Messrs Foster's and Gibson's. No news. A very showery day. I am reading Napoleon at St Helena, from the notes of Sir. H. Lowe.[10] With what liars he was surrounded to be sure, what a situation for a man to be placed in.

31. Altered 'Star,' cut up wood, finished 'Wafers' and went out errands. No news. A very wet day. Mr Gilbert has designed for papers a large drawing of the cabinet ministers (Aberdeen's) when they received the declaration of war from the Queen. This was to have been photographed, but the publishers not considering that the likenesses were sufficiently good (although most were easily recognised) have applied to the ministers separately to be photographed in the position Mr Gilbert determined, and all have been done excepting Lord Palmerston. My father is going to try and get him to sit for them through a gentleman's (Mr Beddome's) father whom we know, who is Lord Palmerston's physician and is intimate. If he does, this print will be among the most interesting that has ever been done, from its historical interest, truthful portraits, the room in which they sat has also been carefully copied, and the size photograph which is very large.

**June** 1st. Altered 'Wafers,' cut up wood, went out, began 'Worsted,' and stamped the vocabs. We caused the Russians to destroy at Kertsch 4 war steamers, and they have only one left now in the Sea of Azov. A dull day. Very unlike what June weather usually is.

2. Went on with 'Worsted,' cut out overlays and went to Fred Gilbert's. Fine day. Next Saturday, a new illustrated paper, called the Illustrated Times, will appear, price 2d weekly. They have an artist at Sebastopol, and profess to give a great deal for the money. Ingram of the 'News' says that it is impossible it can pay, whatever circulation it may attain; we shall see.

3. Sunday. Went to Maze Pond twice, morning and evening and heard Mr Aldis both times. No news. Very fine day.

4. Finished 'Worsted' and began Sucker, went to Gibson's etc, some further successes have been obtained in the Sea of Azov, a small town taken (which is the 3rd or fourth) and a very large quantity of grain. Altogether they have taken 240 ships. On Saturday the fountains played for the first time at the Crystal Palace, they succeeded admirably I am told. There was also a grand flower show there, which surpassed everything that has been seen before at Kew or Chiswick. My father has obtained (through the source before mentioned) the permission of Lord Palmerston to sit for his portrait.

10. William Forsyth, *History of the Captivity of Napoleon at St. Helena, from the letters and journals of the late Lieut.-Gen. Sir H. Lowe.* (London: J. Murray, 1853).

5. Drew an 'Idol.' Fine day. No news. Extremely dull day.

6. Finished 'Sucker,' cut up wood, and went to Mr Murray's. No news. This has been the hottest day this year. The thermometer 80 degrees in the shade.

7. Began 'Work bench' and went to Mr Gibson's. They have taken 10 more small forts in the Black Sea, but the most important thing they have taken is upwards of 17000 tons of coal, which were laid up for their war steamers, which they were unable to destroy. Why did they not do this earlier and of what use it would have been to the army. A fine day. My father went down today to Mr Gilbert's estate, along with him; his house he is building on it is furnishing now and will soon be ready.

8. Went on with 'work bench' and went to Mr Gibson's and Mr Weir's at Peckham. It was in the Times today, that the bombardment of Sebastopol recommenced last Wednesday. Fine day. The Baltic fleet is near Cronstadt.

9. Finished 'Work bench.' A report is current today that Anapa is taken, but it is not believed. No news for certain. Also a report the Mamelon tower at Sebastopol is taken; a very fine day. The 'Illustrated Times' came out today, price 2$^d$. Some very good stuff in it. It is well worth the money.

10. Sunday. Went to Maze Pond twice, morning and evening. Fine day. My father goes to Reigate tomorrow, to meet Mr McKewan and another gentleman. The report about the taking of the Mamelon Gallery seems believed and it is said another one called the 'White Tower' is taken.

11. Monday. Went to Mr Smither's and began 'wash stand.' The allies have taken at Sebastopol 400 prisoners and 64 pieces of cannon. My father went sketching to Reigate today. It was very fine.

12. Went on with 'wash stand' and went out, cut up wood and cut out overlays. No news. Elizabeth's birthday. Showery.

13. Went on with 'Wash stand,' went to Mr Ellis'. No news. Wet day.

14. Finished 'Wash stand' and cut up wood and began 'Water lily.' Showery day. It has been rumoured lately that Anapa (the last Russian fort on the Circassian coast) was taken by the Europeans, but today it was confirmed.

15. Went on with 'Water lily' and went to Mr Ellis', cut up wood etc. A very wet day. No news. Our going to the Isle of Wight this summer has been positively denied and going to Sevenoaks is, from different circumstances, almost impossible. (For which I am not sorry.)

16. Drew 'Skewer,' cut up wood, went on with 'Water lily' etc. No news. The assault of Sebastopol is anxiously expected. Very showery today. My mother went out today, the first time since her illness. Business rather slack.

17. Sunday. Went to Maze Pond House morning and evening. Heard Mr Aldis preach both times. The Russians have again been showing their ignorance of the laws of humanity by firing (at Hango in the Baltic) on a detachment of British sailors who were landing three prisoners under a flag of truce. They were attacked by 300 soldiers and fired on, notwithstanding the flag, and 23 out of 26 were killed.

18. Monday. Finished 'Water lily,' cut up wood etc. No news. Showery day.

19. Redrew 'Water lily,' altered 'Wash stand' and cut up wood. No news. Very fine day. This weather is about as unlike what June weather normally is, as can possibly be.

20. Drew some letters, touched up 'water lily,' went to Clowes and began Trimming. No news. Very fine. The fountains play all this week, shilling days and all, this being the first time they have done so. My father at the book meeting at Mr Brown's.

21. Went on with 'Trimming,' went to London Bridge station twice, to see him off and home again (to Dorking). No news. Some of the infernal machines which the Russians laid last year around Cronstadt in order to blow our ships up, have exploded, but have done no more damage than to tear the sheathing of the bottoms of the vessels.

22. Finished 'Trimming,' went to Rivington's and had a holiday. A London bank has failed (Strahan, Paul and Co) which has made moneyed men rather dull. They have debts to the amount of £750,000 and next to nothing to pay it with. How they have managed it, nobody knows, for the last partner brought in to the business 180,000£. They have made away with securities that were placed with them to keep (that is, stole them) and one clergyman has lost by this means, 22,000£. A couple of policemen in plain clothes went down to Sir J. Paul's residence at Reigate (where he lives in great state) to arrest him, late on Wednesday night, so late that they did not catch the train for that night. The next morning (Thursday) they went with him to station and arrived there just as the train was starting. Sir J Paul stepped into a railway carriage as the train was moving off. The officers attempted to follow him, but were stopped by the porter. They said to him "We are officers, resist us at your peril;" he answered them, "I am only obeying my orders, which are that no person shall get into a carriage when it is in motion," then shut the door to. The train went off without them. They immediately telegraphed up to London to stop him, and [by] the next train they proceeded up to London and arrived 10 minutes after him, and enquired whether he was stopped. The superintendent said that he did not know him, therefore he had not stopped him; so he got off, whether by accident or design, is not known; he however gave himself up in the course of the day. The trial is put off till next Wednesday.

Today the ministers received bad news which they publicly announced that 'they had no pleasure in telling'. It is reported that the Allies had assaulted Sebastopol but had been repulsed with a loss of 4,000 Englishmen and 3,000 French. It is, however, believed that they have known this some time but have kept it secret.

23. Began 'Vallence,' went errands etc. No news. Fine day, but appearance of much rain. The first shot has been fired (very lately) from Cronstadt at the British cruisers. We shall probably go in the country the latter end of next month.

24. Sunday. Went to Maze Pond twice, morning and evening. Heard Mr Aldis both times. No news. Uncle John came up to London today on account of bad health, and he and my brother Fred went to hear Rev Spurgeon, the preacher who had made so much noise lately.

25. Finished 'Vallence,' went to Mr MacKewan's etc. Fitting myself out lately in the painting way, intending to try to begin soon. No news. I heard today that the loss in the last affair at Sebastopol that we had, had been much exaggerated and that no more hundreds than was said thousands, have been killed.

26. Began redrawing 'Vallence.' No news. My father went to Sevenoaks today to try to get lodgings for us, but was (as I had predicted) unsuccessful, and I believe going there is finally abandoned!! A very fine day.

27. Finished 'Vallence' and went out etc. No news. Fine day. Wrote to Southend about lodgings. Lord Robert Grosvenor last week mentioned in the House of Lords that the aristocracy were setting the commoners a better example than they had before in such matters as driving in the parks on Sunday; which speech drew forth some handbills recommending an assembly in Hyde Park to see the aforesaid good example. A number of low fellows accordingly met and saluted the nobility with cries of 'don't employ y'r servants on Sunday', etc etc and they actually went so far as to compel the Duke and Duchess of Beaufort and several other noblemen and ladies to get out and walk, the police not interfering. This is a free country indeed when such things as these are allowed, and quickly passed over without much notice being taken of them.

28. Began 'Zodiac,' went to Mr Watson's etc. No news. Mr. Bennett will I believe sleep here tonight and my father and he and McKewan go out sketching tomorrow. A very hot day.

29. Went on with 'Zodiac' and went to London Bridge to see my father off to Betchworth Park. No news. 2 new papers started today, one daily and the other a $2^d$ pictorial weekly, in opposition to the 'Illustrated Times.' Very hot.

30. Finished 'Zodiac' and went to Mr B. Foster's. A very fine day. It was reported yesterday that Lord Raglan had been superseded, but the Ministers in the Lords in the evening denied that, but said he had temporally resigned on account of bad health; General Simpson taking the command. This evening it is generally believed that Lord Raglan is dead, and Sir G. Brown is very ill; the cholera has again broken out in the army before Sebastopol. This evening there was a fire at a tailors in the Westminster Road which afterwards extended to an oilman's, and caught the gunpowder in the shop, blew it up.

1. **July**. Sunday. Went to Maze Pond twice morning and evening. No news. A very fine day. The Head Superintendent of the police has done today what he ought to have done last Sunday, viz, prevented, as far as possible, the riotous meetings such as were in Hyde Park last Sunday. Today it is computed that at least 150,000 people assembled in the park and 600 policemen to oppose them. Upwards of 100 arrests were made of the ringleaders. Some of the mob were very desperate and wished to show off. For instance, one man got to the edge of the Serpentine into the water and swam half-way across, and then began to sink. He was rescued by the Humane Society and given up.

2. July. Touched up 'Zodiac,' finished 'worsted' and went out. Today authentic intelligence arrived, that Lord Raglan was dead. A loss to his

friends but a great benefit to the nation. It is said that the French Emperor again contemplates going to the Crimea. My father has now sold all his pictures but one.

3. Began drawing 'Smelling bottle'. No news. Some time last week the Allies in the Baltic fished up 4 infernal machines and were going to destroy them, but 2 of them exploded on the poop of a ship, severely wounding Admiral Seymour and some other officials. My father went to Richmond today with the Misses Hepburn.

4. Finished 'Smelling bottle' and cut up wood. No news. Fine day. My aunt at Moore Place goes to Ramsgate next Saturday.[11]

5. Altered 'Smelling bottle,' went out and began 'Work table.' No news. The movers of the Sunday Trading Prevention Bill have withdrawn, like asses as they are. (This is the bill which has excited so much attention lately.) What they have done (withdrawing it) of course only makes their opponents crow the more, with joy at it.

6. Went on with the 'work table,' cut up wood. No news. Very fine day. My father went to sketch at Richmond. Today we had an answer from Southend. Mr Madams said it was getting very full and was unable to procure us lodgings. We then thought of going to Eastbourne, but I don't think we shall go there.

7. Finished 'work table' and cut up wood. Business getting a little better, but rather slack still. There has been received a telegraphic despatch from the Baltic, to the effect that the fleet have been bombarding some place, the name of which I forget. A 1000£s has been voted for Lord Raglan's widow for life and 2000£ for the present Lord Raglan. Nothing of importance has been done at Sebastopol. A number of the Russian infernal machines that have been fished up in the Baltic, are on their way here. It is expected that there will be a more serious disturbance at Hyde Park tomorrow, as hints have been given out that the people will go armed.

8. Sunday. Went to Maze Pond twice morning and evening. Heard Mr Aldis both times. No news. Fine day. It appeared from what has been said in the papers and in the Houses of Parliament that the police used their staves rather too freely last Sunday; hitting indiscriminately. Today they were kept out of sight in Hyde Park but were in readiness. The mob finding nothing to be done there went down Piccadilly and in Belgrave Square breaking windows. This shows what kind of people they were. As Mr Peel said in the House 'they were mere canaille', and I quite agree with his suggestion that a few 6 pounders fired into them would do a deal of good.

9. Touched up 'work table,' cut up wood and went to Mr Smithers etc. Fine day but raining hard in the evening. This will do a great deal of good as it is much needed. I think it is most likely that we shall all go to Eastbourne as we are all in favour of it. Particulars have arrived of the attack on the 18th on Sebastopol, and it appears that it was agreed between Raglan and Pelissier that they should attack the Malakoff tower conjointly, as that commanded the Redan. The plan was afterwards altered that we should

---

11. Lydia, the wife of his father's older brother Ebenezer (see Appendix 1).

attack the Redan and the French the Malakoff. They attacked with 25,000 men, we took only 4000; what in the world we attacked such a formidable battery with such a small number of men I can't conceive. There was to have been an hour's severe bombardment before the attack, but Pelissier put it off and one of the French generals mistook a signal and began before the right time. Thus it was that a project well conceived was marked by mistakes and unaccountable alterations.

10. Drew diagrams for new apprentice, drew 'vent,' cut up wood and went to Mr Foster's. Fine day, raining hard in evening. Some despatches arrived tonight from the Baltic and also news that the Russians had made an attack on the allies before Sebastopol, but were defeated with great loss.

11. Went out, cut up wood and began the 'Ruins of Hougoumont.' No news. Raining hard all day. Where we shall go out of town is fluctuating between Eastbourne and Southend at present. Business very bad indeed.

12. Went on with Hougoumont etc. No news. Fine day.

13. Finished 'Hougoumont' and went out. A fine day. A telegraphic despatch arrived today, to the effect that we had silenced the Redan fort, it is not generally believed. Today Eastbourne is decidedly in the ascendant.

14. Began a 'Chinese merchant selling cats,' went to Mr Foster's etc. No news. A sharp thunderstorm at 6 o'clock this morning; after that a very fine day.

15. Sunday. Went to Maze Pond twice, morning and evening, heard Mr Davis of Portsea both times. It is whispered that the present government are trying to bring about a dishonourable peace, saying that the object of the war is accomplished, that we have prevented Russia from taking Turkey and have driven him back to his own ground. I do not think that this is stating the case fairly. It is true that we have prevented him taking Turkey etc but when the war began it was announced that it should not be ended without preventing the possibility of such an occurrence in future times. They have not done this. However I should not at all wonder if they did it. Such are the statesmen of England in these days. Tomorrow my father goes to Eastbourne to look lodgings for us.

16. Altered 'Spheroid,' went on with Chinese subject etc. A deserter from Sebastopol said that Admiral Nackimoff was killed by a cannon ball on the Great Bastion lately. A small place has been bombarded in the Baltic (near Helsingfors) with effect. Taganrog in the Sea of Azov has also been destroyed. A fire took place last night at the straw division of Hungerford market, from some boxes putting the lighted ashes from a tobacco pipe on one of the carts. It destroyed a great deal of straw but did not extend to the surrounding houses. Today my father went to Eastbourne and obtained us lodgings, paying however more than he had intended, which he only did from his unwillingness to come home a second time without obtaining us any. I am both glad and sorry at the same time. Glad that we are going to so good a place and sorry because it will cause so much expense. We go I believe next Saturday morning.

17. Drew 'Sum,' went out, cut up wood etc. No news. The days of old Smithfield are over. The new cattle market which seems to be a much

superior sort of thing, has been opened in Islington. No news. The Russians have been receiving reinforcements at Sebastopol. Fine day.

18. Touched up 'Sum,' drew some diagrams and began a large locomotive engine. No news. Fine day. My father went to the book meeting at Mr Such's.

19. Went on with locomotive. No news. Fine, with the exception of a little storm in the afternoon. I hope the weather will not be as it is now, when we go to Eastbourne.

20. Went on with 'Locomotive' and went twice to Mr Prior's etc. Fred's (my eldest brother's) birthday. Very fine day. No news. All mess bustle and hurry to get the things packed up tonight, as we start at 6 o'clock tomorrow morning for Eastbourne.

July 21 to **August** 9. I went to Eastbourne, which is a rather large country town on the south coast near Brighton. I did not like the place itself at all. I went from thence to Beachy Head, where I nearly broke my neck trying to climb the cliff, to Pevensey Castle, which belongs to the Earl of Burlington, to Hurstmonceux Castle, which is said to be the finest brick castle in England.[12] This latter belonged formerly to the celebrated Godwin, Earl of Kent, who farmed the land which is now swallowed up in the Godwin sands. I also went to Lewes Castle (while I was there, the Queen passed through the town), to Hailsham, Worthing, Seaford, Newhaven and Brighton. At Brighton I was in the pavilion and was disappointed with it (as everybody is). I liked the sea, and the sea front of the town much. The weather was rather rainy, but altogether I enjoyed myself very much. Lodgings and travelling are exceedingly dear in this part of England, as indeed is everything. During these 3 weeks there has been no news from the seat of war at all. It seems now that Austria leans towards Russia instead of the Western powers as before. Nothing or next to nothing has been done in Parliament because it is near the end of the season, and the Lords and gentlemen want to get away to their country seats, consequently when the most important things have been brought on, the house has frequently been counted out. The week before last my aunt at Moore Place was attacked with a fit, between paralysis and apoplexy. She lost the use of one of her arms several days, but is recovering it now. When I was at Lewes I went and saw the Russian prisoners. They have the appearance of worn out Frenchmen. I should not be able to tell the difference except by the language. Here endeth my holidays for this year.

---

12. At the end of his life Whymper wrote to a friend, 'as you are so close to it, do climb the dizzy heights of Beachy Head, and look down, with a coastguard Man holding each of your hands, upon the perilous cliffs where my mortal existence nearly terminated 56 years ago. Chalk and cheese are not good climbing material.' BL, Add. MS 63112, f. 100, Edward Whymper to Henry Montagnier, 8 March 1910. The chalk cliffs at Beachy Head have been climbed using modern ice axes and crampons, but not as conventional rock climbs.

From the 10$^{th}$ to the 17$^{th}$ I was very busy and was not able to attend to my diary. I must put down as well as I can remember the events. On Tuesday the 14$^{th}$ Parliament was prorogued till 23 of October next. The ministers were anxiously expecting some good news, which might gild this session a little, but it came too late as we shall see. On Wednesday morning news arrived, that the Baltic fleet, under Admiral Dundas, had bombarded Sveaborg, not like his namesake at Odessa, but had done the business completely. It is said, the shipping, forts, dockyard and town, are all a heap of ruins. The town was burning for 45 hours. This ought to have come a little earlier, to have cheered the hearts of the ministers.

On Friday evening news arrived that, on Friday morning, the Russians under General Liprandi, to the number of 50 or 60,000, had attacked the allies on the lines of the Tcherneya, before Sebastopol. They were totally repulsed, with the loss of 5 or 6000 men, killed and wounded, left on the field of battle. This is all very well, very good in its way, but, the great army that is before Sebastopol, is not there to defend itself, but to attack the others. All the delay that has occurred is very inexplicable to us. We suppose however that there is a reason for it.

18. Saturday. Went out and began 'Tea service.' The rest of family returned today from Eastbourne. A telegraphic despatch today, says that the English cavalry were pursuing the flying Russians, and that Generals Simpson and Pelissier, thinking that a fierce bombardment might do some good (help to finish up the effects of the battle) had agreed to begin this morning. Fine day, extremely hot.

19. Sunday. Went to Maze Pond twice, morning and evening. Heard Mr Aldis both times. Mr Eastty, one of the deacons and a member of the Book society, is very dangerously ill, and is not expected to recover; if he does, it is expected he will lose his intellect. No news. Fine day. Appearance of rain in the evening. I suppose tomorrow we shall have news from Sebastopol.

20. Monday. The Queen has gone to France, and in the words of the Times 'set the seal upon' the memorable alliance. She is to be fêted in a way that will, it is said, make even the Parisians open their eyes. All the fashionable world is gone after her and the consequence is, that the prices of provisions in Paris are the same as in times of famine. Fine day.

21. Altered the 'Locomotive.' No fresh news. Full particulars came this evening, of the bombardment of Sveaborg, but I have not yet seen them. Extremely hot. Mr. Jones a workman of ours, died today of bilious fever.

22 and 23. Finished 'Tea service,' and went out, cut up wood etc. No news from the seat of war. On the 21$^{st}$ the express train ran off the rails, a little way past Berwick on Tweed. The engine was the one that they usually draw the Queen with and yet they knew it was defective. The company will catch it severely, I expect, for allowing such a thing. Fine days. I have patronized the Lambeth Baths lately. The baths and washhouses and shoeblacks are, in my opinion, the greatest steps forward that England has made for many years.[13]

13. The baths on Lambeth Road opened in July 1853.

24. Began 'Sugar basin,' cut up wood, went out etc. No news. Last night there was a little storm, plenty of lightning but little rain. Mr Leigh preaches both morning and evening at Maze Pond next Sunday.

25. Went out, read a book and picked places for cuts, and went out; went on with 'Sugar basin.' The Queen is being fêted and lionized wherever she goes. When she entered Paris, as much as 40£s was paid for a single balcony and after all that they did not see her as she did not get to Paris until 8 in the evening, when it was getting quite dark. No news of the war.

26. Sunday. Went to Maze Pond twice, morning and evening heard Mr Leigh both times. No news. This is Prince Albert's 36th birthday. Very fine weather for the harvest.

27. Went out to Mr Wells' and saw Mr J. Gilbert at the Il. London News office, hard at work illustrating the Queen's visit to France. She returns today. No news. Rather warm.

28 - 29. No news. Fine days. On 29th my father went sketching at Cookham

30. Mrs Davies, next door neighbour, died this evening just as I was coming across the road from work, at ¼ past 9, My brother Fred went to a private exhibition of Mr Gordon Cumming's new entertainment of 'The hunter at home,' previous to his return to Africa. This extraordinary man (who is now not more than 35 years old) when he went to Africa was only 25, went in single handed to the interior of Africa to shoot lions etc. He killed 105 elephants and hundreds of giraffes etc which he considers very lame sport. The development of muscle in him is prodigious, his strength is enormous. It is said that he, every morning flourishes two large clubs about (one in each hand) before a large mirror, going with them as close as ever he can, in order to get his precision of arm as near as possible. These clubs are so heavy that one is as much as an ordinary man can lift. His exhibition will no doubt prove one of the most attractive that there are, as it is painted by Harrison Weir etc under his superintendence and described by himself.

31. Went on with 'Chinese cat merchant.' No news. My father went to Richmond Park and I went after him. We are very conveniently situated for getting to Richmond. Wind changed to due east. Fine day.

1. **September**. Finished 'cat merchants.' Fine day. When the Queen was in Paris, the Emperor it is said exercised a little piece of diplomatic art, on the future heir to the [throne] of England, in taking him out a drive by himself and instilling into his youthful mind such principles as will become useful to himself (the Emperor).

2. Sunday. Went to Maze Pond twice, morning and evening. Heard Mr Aldis both times. No news. Fine day.

3. Began 'The preparation of tea in China.' No news. It appears that in the battle of the Tcherneya, the English took no part, except in pursuing the flying Russians with their cavalry. They attacked the French, under General Gortschakoff, instead of under General Liprandi, as at first supposed. They left 3000 <u>dead</u>. The French and Sardinians killed and wounded did not amount to above 1000. The French and English batteries are now within a few paces of the Malakoff and Redan forts; an immediate assault is now expected. The papers are full of the Queen's visit to France,

since no English monarch has visited France since the time of Henry 8th and Francis the 1st.

4. Went on with preparation of tea and cut up wood. No news. Our business improving, but the book trade in general almost stopped. Partridge and Oakey the publishers in Paternoster Row have failed. Showery.

5. Went on with 'Preparation of tea.' No news. Bad weather for the northern crops which are not yet cut. Mrs Davies, next door to us, was buried today. Our friend Miss Brown of Clapham was turned today into a Mrs Hill. Poor girl? (of 38) unfortunate being.

6. Finished 'Preparation of tea' and cut up wood. No news. Fine day.

7. Began drawing a 'Choultry at Madeira'. No news. My uncle Ebenezer is I believe going to move from his house in Moore Place to a house opposite the new Vestry Hall, which house my father has bought, out of the produce of some railway shares which he has sold out.[14] The new gun which Nasmyth invented; which was to have done such wonders, has turned out a failure. It was to have thrown large masses of welded iron, which they have just found out, will not keep together when it leaves the mouth of the cannon.

8. Saturday. Went on with 'Choultry,' cut up wood, made a dabber etc. The bombardment of Sebastopol has commenced. The allies have sunk a Russian 74 gun ship at Sebastopol, of the enemies. Professor Anderson alias the Wizard of the North alias etc etc has taken the Lyceum Theatre and is exhibiting his tricks in conjuring, explaining table turning and spirit happenings etc etc. He exhibits (gratis) on the top of the portico, the electric light, and when I saw it, threw it on the government offices at Somerset House. It is a new extremely powerful light, but they cannot make it quite steady; it flickers a little.

9. Sunday. Went to Maze Pond twice, morning and evening, heard Mr Aldis both times. No news. Very fine day. Bad headache, I think from too much blood in the head.

10. Went on with 'Choultry' in the morning and in the afternoon went to Mr Clay at Muswell Hill (the printers). He has a pleasant son and daughter and a cross deaf wife. A good deal of ground surrounding the house with plenty of animals on it. Yesterday news came that the Malakoff tower was taken by the French on Saturday, also an attack on the Redan Fort by us has not succeeded. Alas, how have the mighty fallen! Nothing that we do seems to prosper and all this seems strange after the sieges of Lille, the storming of Badajoz and the battle of Blenheim. They also attacked the little Redan and another fort but were driven out. Our loss is stated as 2000. No general officer was killed, they having all kept out of the way.

In the evening as I was coming home from Mr Clays, it was placarded to the effect that Sebastopol was captured, but I consider the report as very doubtful, as I did not see that there was any official despatch. They consider the occupation of the Malakoff Tower as a great thing, as that will enable them to enfilade the Redan and other forts. The Russians

---

14. The Vestry Hall, Kennington Road, was built in 1853.

have been building a bridge from the north to the south side of the town, and have used it a good deal.[15]

11. Went on with 'Choultry,' cut up wood and went out. Fine day. The harvest being gathered in finely. But notwithstanding this the price of corn is actually rising, the reason offered by the farmers being that though the harvest is very good the corn in the ears is thin. Did ever anyone hear of such rascals? When one thing is good they say another is bad; for instance, they say that there is now not enough rain for the turnips so they will make them dear!

A large fire broke out at 2 o'clock this morning at the works of Mr Baker, timber merchant and saw mills, near the Archbishop's Palace. It was burning 6 hours. A good deal of damage done, but they were insured. Prince Napoleon yesterday visited Plymouth and saw the dock yards and a new frigate that is to be launched soon. Today all London was astonished by the announcement that Sebastopol (that is the southern side) had been blown up by the Russians and they had retreated by the raft bridge to the north side of the town. Of course there are many reasons for this, viz. the French having possession of the Malakoff they could sweep all the other batteries in possession of the Russians; they have also been running short of provisions for some time past, so that it appears they have done the wisest thing that they possibly could, in order to prevent a general capitulation. They have also burnt their fleet. We have destroyed their raft bridge. Prince Gortschakoff has demanded an armistice but I do not think it was granted. We did not at first dare to enter the town on account of the numerous mines that were continually being sprung, but another despatch came in the evening saying that we had done so, and that all the batteries were in our possession. Our unsuccessful attack on the Redan cost us upwards of 2000 men, that of the French on the Malakoff nearly 20,000. I hope that our generals will anticipate the routes the Russians <u>must</u> retreat by, and be prepared for them. I say <u>must</u> because they cannot get away by the sea because they have no fleet and we have, so that there are not above 2 ways for them to go by, either through Perekop, or throw themselves into Simpheropol, which is not expected they will, as they are not in a condition to stand another siege. If they try the former, we can, I think, stop them at Eupatoria and other places on that road.

Petropaulauski, the Russian capital in Kamschatka, was found to be deserted when our men of war steamers approached it. The Times comments very severely and to my mind justly on this. These steamers were sent out last year, to prevent the Russians escaping; <u>they</u> cruised about but the Russians escaped by some steamers up the River Amour, from which they will get into China and we shall not most likely take them.

12. Went on with 'Choultry' and went to Mr Murray's etc. My father is talking about going to Paris, with my uncle, in order to get up some book.

---

15. After the fall of the Malakhov Bastion to the French on 8 September, the Russians evacuated the southern side of Sevastopol, over their pontoon bridge, during the night of 8/9 September. The Allies occupied the town on 9 September, and the news reached Paris the next day.

This is a great undertaking for him, as he cannot speak French. Fine day. No further news.

13. Went on with 'Choultry,' went out, cut up wood. No news. It is believed nothing more will be done in the Baltic this year. Showery day, good for the parsnips.

14. Went on with 'Choultry,' went to Mr Murray's, cut up wood etc. In the last despatch from General Simpson, dated Sebastopol Sept 12 he says that the Russians have burnt their 3 remaining steamers which they might have preserved, therefore he thinks there will be a final evacuation of the northern as well as the southern side of the place. He thinks that they will retreat by way of Perekop, therefore they have done what I wished they would, and sent a division to occupy the road they must retreat by. They should strengthen this, perhaps when the bear is brought to bay it may become desperate. A railway accident took place the other day near Reading on account of a mad engine driver, driving his engine on a line (when he knew a train was coming) in the night and without any lights. He ran into it, killed himself and 4 or 5 others. General Pelissier has been made a Marshall of the French empire. My father goes to Paris on Monday most likely. Very showery day.

15. Went on with 'Choultry,' went to Euston Square etc. No news. My father has fixed upon going to Paris on Monday via Folkestone and Boulogne. Fine day. He went today to see my uncle John at Watford and Mr Johns at Kings Langley near there. More troops left today for the seat of war.

16. Sunday. Went to Maze Pond twice, morning and evening; heard Mr Aldis both times. No news. Dull day.

17. Went on with 'Choultry,' drew some letters, put in some figures in another block and went to Mr Dare's and Kearney's and saw my father and uncle go from the London Bridge railway station of the South Eastern Railway, through Folkestone and Boulogne to Paris. He will get there about 10 tonight. Mr Fenton, a photographist, has returned from the Crimea, where he has been taking photographs of the most interesting scenes that have been taking place. He has made an exhibition of them and has sent us a ticket. Dull day.

18. Went on with 'Choultry,' cut out overlays and paper up etc. Last Sunday and yesterday there were 5 or 6 fires in different parts of the metropolis, none of them large ones. The firm of Strahan, Paul and Bates are now going to take their trial for making away with securities confided to them. The Recorder said in his charge to the Grand Jury, that this offence did not come under the head of felony, so I expect they will get off far more leniently than they ought. The 'Times' in their leader today reviewed the condition of the Russian army in the Crimea, and said that there were only two courses for them to pursue, either to throw themselves into Simpheropol and stand another siege or to retreat through Perekop and abandon the Crimea. It is rumoured that they are ordered from Sebastopol to the latter, and they are to take their arms and baggage along with them. But I do not think that they can do this, as we have wisely posted divisions on their road. It is all very well to say 'do this' but how are they? I do not think

there is any truth in the rumour. This reminds me of an anecdote of Marshall Pelissier. The Emperor of the French ordered Pelissier through the telegraph to do a certain thing. Pelissier said it was impossible. But said the minister of war, 'The Emperor says it is to be done, so it must.' Pelissier replied, 'Then let him come and do it himself.' This shows what stuff their general is made of.

19. Went on with 'Choultry.' It is said, and confirmed through electric telegraph, that the Russians are leaving Simpheropol in large numbers and retreating through Perekop, thus giving some truth to the rumour of yesterday. We have sent some troops to watch Simpheropol. Today I went to the private view of the photographs taken by R. Fenton Esq in the spring and summer of this year in the Crimea. There were a great many portraits, including Generals, Raglan, Pelissier, Bosquet, Estcourt, Jones, Campbell, Brown etc, in fact of all the officers of any note out there. There were also many interesting groups, one especially so, of a council of war between Lord Raglan, Omer Pacha and General Pelissier on the morning of the successful attack on the Mamelon Tower. He had a good many pictures of Balaclava, and a series of 11 views of the plateau before Sebastopol, arranged panoramically. Altogether it is a most interesting exhibition and well worth seeing. They are to be published after the exhibition in parts, £2 2s each. Fine day.

20. Went on with 'Choultry.' We have been doing some damage at Riga with rockets, have dismounted a good many guns etc. This morning Mrs Davies junior died after a long and painful illness, both to herself and relations. We had a letter from my father yesterday at Paris. He gave us no details of his visit, but described Paris as the gayest, noisiest and finest city in the world. He said it was very hot and crowded. Fine day.

21. Finished 'Choultry' and drew some letters. Today the papers said we had taken at Sebastopol, 4000 cannons, 25,000 cannon balls, an immense quantity of powder, 250 anchors, 2 steam engines etc etc, which were not destroyed. This is something worth having. They also give a summary of what their fleet was in the Black Sea, and what it is now. It consisted of 17 sail of the line and a great number of steamers besides, corvettes, brigs etc, in all mounting more than 14000 guns, and now it is _ _ _ nothing. We have also received the Russian account of the affair. It is pretty correct, excepting of course, Prince Gortschakoff says that all that he retreated to the north side for, was to prevent the needless effusion of blood etc etc. This is quite in their usual style, it is stereotyped in fact, ready for the occasion. Very fine day. The funds, which have been very depressed lately, have risen a little.

22. Drew some letters and began tea service. No news. Fine day. My father came unexpectedly home early this morning (6 o'clock). He having been disgusted by the meannesses of my uncle (I thought that he would be), had some words with him which hastened their arrival at home. This journey home was very unpleasant. When he started from Dieppe the Customs House officers took 3 hours examining the luggage. He then went on board the steamer, a French iron one very low and narrow, at 3 o'clock in the afternoon. After having steamed 12 miles from Dieppe they perceived to

their intense annoyance a dense fog a little way ahead of them. On they went, not being able to see a dozen yards ahead of them. So they kept up all night a constant ringing of bells and firing of guns. They of course went on slowly (and once came across a great steamer doing the same as themselves) sounding constantly and looking out for the shore. At last they hailed a little boat and found that they were on the wrong side of Brighton for them, about a mile from the shore. They accordingly went back and kept on sounding. At last the man cried out 3 fathoms and immediately afterwards 2 ½. The captain was very excited and had the engines backed immediately as he knew they were close in shore. He then found he had overshot the mark on the other side and was very near Newhaven; at last to the infinite pleasure of all they got out of the fog and the scene was beautiful. The moon very bright, shining on the smooth sea, with fine cliffs and they steaming quickly into the harbour. When however he got to the railway station, he found that as they were 6 hours behind their time, that the railway officials had gone to sleep, not expecting them; and in consequence there was no train ready. My father went up to one of the sleepy guards and said, 'Is there going to be no train, if so, what are all these people to do (there were about 300 of them) for beds, there being but one hotel in Newhaven?' He replied: 'There will be none and as for the people, I don't know what they're to do,' adding, 'but I would advise you to go and secure a bed for yourself.' However, just at this moment, a gentleman came (who appeared to be a person of authority and known to them) and ordered them to make a train. They said it was impossible, etc., but they did make one after they had been about 2 hours over it. At last they started for London, but there was a fog on the line, so they proceeded but slowly, and once the pointsman mistaking the train, turned them on the down line instead of the up one. At last after dawdling through the streets home, he reached us at 6 o'clock in the morning, having been more than 7 hours on the journey more than he ought to have been. When in Paris, he went to the Louvre, Madeline, Nôtre Dame etc, and the Exhibition, paying of course most attention to the pictures. If we may judge by what are exhibited, English artists are by far the best. He liked the arrangement of the Exhibition very much, thought it was superior to ours. He however did not like Paris much, it did not agree with him; he thinks it like Bunyan's Vanity Fair, more than anything else. Coming home he went to Rouen, which he admired in all parts very much and would have staid longer if he could. He did not have a favourable idea of les Francais, as they always (almost) tried to cheat 'les étrangers.' He liked many things in their country, most especially their strong coffee and their architecture.

23. Went to Maze Pond twice, morning and evening. Heard Mr Aldis both times. No news. Fine day. A bad cold and cough I have caught, extremely disagreeable.

24. Went on with 'Tea service,' altered 'Choultry,' went out, cut up paper etc. No news. Fine day.

25. Went to Mr Murray's, went on with 'tea service.' No news. General Simpson's despatches have arrived containing the fall of Sebastopol, but they contain very little but what we have heard before, excepting we have

taken upwards of 100,000 projectiles. Fine day. Although there is such a plentiful harvest, bread is rising in price. Which circumstance excites strong remarks and great discontent and if I am not mistaken there will be unmistakable proofs of this on the part of the populace soon, in the shape of brickbats being sent through windows etc and other demonstrations of a like nature. They have put an extra duty upon sugar, cheese, candles etc and there is talk of salt becoming the old price again.

26. Drew a 'Silver shekel' and went to Mr Murray's. A very fine day. No news. My father went to Mr Gilbert's new estate at Dartford to sketch.

27. Touched up 'Shekel,' went out and drew an ancient parapet. No news. Very fine day, but raining in evening. My father went to Cashbury Park, near Watford, to sketch. Coming home he was startled by the whistle of the engine giving 3 shrieks, and then suddenly stopping, although it was an express train. After they had stopped some time (not at any station) all the people not being able to learn any information as to the why and wherefore of the stopping, got out of the train as they rather expected another train which ought to come soon after this, to run into them behind. After they had waited ½ hour, they found out that the guards of their train had perceived a body laying across the rails and had immediately acquainted the engineer of it. Then they went back and found that it was a young woman, lying across the down rails, quite dead but yet warm. They conjectured she must have been killed by a train which passed them just before they saw her. They brought her to their train and proceeded up to London, where it will wait most probably, until they get information about her friends. My mother went to the Crystal Palace and was charmed with the fountains, which now play in and outside the building. The Alhambra Court is now very magnificent. My brother Fred went to Mr Leigh's at Peckham.

28. Finished 'Tea service' etc etc. The list of killed and wounded in the unsuccessful attack on the Redan occupy a full page of the Times paper, closely printed. It is said that the places for the Russians to retreat into when our fire became too hot for them at Sebastopol, are very ingenious and very numerous, showing they must have felt our fire severely. Another thing that tells is that we found in their hospitals upwards of 1000 dead and many others still living, who they had abandoned to their fate, without anyone to attend to them, or without leaving them any provisions to keep them alive. Today there was a report accredited that the Russians had been defeated in a battle in the field near Eupatoria. No particulars. Very wet day. Price of bread rising. Talk of an extra income tax. Next Sunday is appointed as a thanksgiving day for the success of our arms before Sebastopol.

29. Quarter day. Alas one of my uncle's tenants runs away, but however he being of a polite turn of mind, sent the keys round with a note (not with the rent though). Went to Mr Prior's, drew some letters and began a 'Toledo sword' No news.

30. Sunday. Went to Maze Pond twice, morning and evening. Heard Mr Aldis both times. Raining very hard in afternoon and evening. Good for the turnips. No news. The Times of yesterday comments very severely on the

conduct of General Simpson, who it is said mismanaged the unsuccessful attack on the Redan almost wilfully and when it was going on, instead of looking about him to see what was doing, he was squatted in a ditch almost smothered in a cloak. This is most abominable, at least The Times says so, so it must be. The Times says he must be recalled; of course he will.

1. **October**. Monday. Finished 'Toledo blade' and drew some different kinds of lenses. No news. The German papers are full of a rumour of the evacuation of the Crimea, but I do not see the probability of it. The allied fleets have left Sebastopol but it is not known where they are gone. The Emperor of Russia has gone to Odessa, along with the 3 grand dukes. I hope he will like what he will see, for according to many accounts it is a ruined place. It is said that the Russian people are much enraged at the taking of Sebastopol. "Well let them be, it serves them right." There is going to be a general exchange of prisoners; those that we saw at Lewes they say are very glad, that they are going, though I really cannot see why, as it is said that they have nearly all been able to buy watches with the money they have by the making of the toys.

2. Began a 'Stereoscope' and a 'Tail of a horse.' No news. Dull day. Business not so good again.

3. Finished 'Tail' and drew it over again. No news. Wet day.

4. Went to Mr Clay's, cut up wood, paper etc, drew 'tail' a third time, which had to be altered. Very wet day. The Russians are fortifying the north side of Sebastopol and we, to our shame be it said, are, as I expected, not molesting them at all. We shall allow them to make it a pretty strong place (which indeed it is already, for they have some formidable forts there); we shall give them time to collect another army and threaten our rear; there will be probably another battle, and we shall have another barren victory and finally we shall make the assault of the place and will most likely lose six or eight times the number of men we should if we were to give it a vigorous bombardment and assault it now.

5. Finished stereoscope and drew an Archimedean screw. No particular news. Wet day.

6. Began drawing 'Farmer.' In the afternoon I went to Richmond. Fine day. Mr C. A. Johns came to dinner and Mr C. Smith (the painter) to tea; who by the by has nearly lost his sight. It is said that 6 English steamers have bombarded Riga, but it is not positive. 6 steamers indeed! It ought to have been 16, (if it is so), are we always to have things done by halves. It is known that the Russians are fortifying a place called Nicolaieff very much (it is situated between Odessa and Cherson, on the sea coast), indeed the Emperor himself has been superintending the works there himself. As we know this, our fleets ought to go and interrupt them, if there is sufficient depth of water to allow them, if not the gun boats can do it. I suppose however they will not do it and there will be another long bloody siege after we have turned them out of the Crimea. It was in the papers today that, after the French had taken the Malakoff (called by the Russians the Korniloff bastion) and we had entered the Redan, a sapper discovered a thick rope, leading into the Redan, which he cut in half with his axe and then showed it to his officer, who upon examination found that it was an

electric wire communicating with a large mine, immediately under the Redan. This was a most providential discovery, as, a number of mines were being fired by them, and undoubtedly, they would have fired that one very soon had it not been discovered. This was what I expected they would have done, when we attacked the Redan, and indeed this was very much feared among the men, as being blown up in the air is not one of the most comfortable things in the world. It is said that the allied generals at Sebastopol have formed some expedition, somewhere, but where, how, why or wherefore is not known. There have been 3 Field Marshals created, Viscount Hardinge, Viscount Combermere and the Earl of Strafford. The heir apparent to the throne of Prussia, Prince Frederick William, of the honourable! house of Hohenzollern (oh! oh!), brother of the present king, is now on a visit to the court at Balmoral; for what? to improve!! his acquaintance with the princess royal!!! It is said that at the time of the G$^t$ Exhibition, the fool had some nonsense with her and now he wants to put the finishing touch to it. The people are against the alliance, we wish to have nothing to do with German politics. The best thing he can do is to go back to Germany pretty quickly, and say what Punch says, 'That we have doubts if he can keep her and we don't like her relations.'

7. Sunday. Went to Maze Pond twice, morning and evening. Heard Mr Aldis and Mr George preach. No news. Fine day.

8. Monday. Finished 'Farmer,' went out, named blocks etc. No news. Fine day.

9. Tuesday. Went out, began Daniell's constant battery and began sugar beet. No news. My father went to Watford, and made a very pretty sketch. Fine day.

10. Drew 'tenterhooks,' cut up wood etc. It is reported our fleets are at Odessa and a bombardment is expected. I hope it may be so, and a better one than last time. If we were now to bombard Riga and Odessa (their 2 greatest ports), well, it would be a good finish to this year's operations. Fine day.

11. Went on with 'Sugar beet,' went out etc etc. No news. It is confirmed that the allied fleets are before Odessa. Showery and cold.

12. Outlined a view of Cawnpore etc etc. No news. Wet day. Mr Russell the Times correspondent at the seat of war, has had all his letters collected and made into a book, and a very interesting book it is; his powers of description being very great. It is a complete history of the fighting part of the war in the Black Sea. It is at present the book.

13. Finished 'Sugar beet,' went to Mr Clay's, Dare's and to Mr F. Gilbert's at Blackheath. No news. Charming day.

14. Sunday. Went to chapel twice, morning and evening. Heard a minister from Leeds both times.[16] No news. Very foggy day.

15. Monday. Cut up wood and paper, went on with Daniell's battery. No news. Muggy day. Prince Gortschakoff says that we are concentrating large masses of men in the valley of the Balbek (a little stream about 8

---

16. Alexander Stalker was paid £2 for preaching (MPAB, see Appendix 1).

miles north of Sebastopol) which looks like cutting them off from supplies. It is said also we are threatening Perekop. The Russians have been again defeated by the Turks in Asia, at Kars (a fortified place the Russians have been long attempting to take). This is gratifying, as the Turks have not done much lately to help themselves. It is reported in Russia that the disgraced Prince Menschikoff (who was said to be dead) has entered a convent, turned monk.

16. [Blank]

17. Began 'Tap,' went to Murray's, Clowes etc, cut out overlays and wood up etc. Nasty day. It is said on good authority that Marshal Pelissier is with 35,000 men in the valley of Baider, that Marmora has gone with 15000 to Simpheropol. These movements seem to indicate operations to the effect of cutting off the retreat of the Russians.

18. Began another Beet root, and finished a plan began by Mr Gibson. A place of the name of Kinburn has been destroyed in the Black Sea; nothing of importance, however, has been done. Mr Gilbert to tea with us.

19. Went to Mr Prior's and Penton's, altered plan, finished Tap etc. No news. Fine day. Business rather bad.

20. Went out, traced map, cut up wood and began diagram of stove. No news. Fine day.

21. Sunday. Went to Maze Pond twice, morning and evening. Heard strangers both times, both young men (boys). My uncle came up from Watford to see us today. Fred goes next Saturday in return. No news.

22. Finished diagram etc. It seems that what I had put down as a slight affair is something worth noting. Kinburn is situated at the mouth of the river Dnieper, and commanded the passage to Nicolaieff (which is the Russians principal arsenal now). We attacked it on the 17<sup>th</sup> and compelled the garrison of 2000 men to capitulate with 70 pieces of cannon and stores. This I suppose comes before an attempt on Nicolaieff. I hope that they may be quick and not lose valuable time in deliberations, allow the enemy time to fortify themselves and ourselves to be repulsed.

23. Began diagram map, went out etc. No news.

24. Went to London Bridge station, along with my father, who went to Mr Gilbert's, and finished map. The other fort on the opposite side of the Dnieper to Kinburn, has been evacuated. It was called Otchakov. It is said that the river is not deep enough for our men of war to go up to Nicolaieff, so we shall be obliged to content ourselves with sending our gun boats up there. Sir W. Molesworth died lately, suddenly. The seat in Parliament for the borough of Southwark is consequently vacant. Sir C. Napier has put up for it (in opposition to Messrs Scovell and Conyngham); his address is clear and simple. I sincerely hope he may get returned, for he is an honest old fellow whatever his other faults may be. He has been shamefully treated by Sir. J. Graham, who he has in consequence exposed most thoroughly as he deserved.

25. Cut up wood, went to Gibson's, and began 'beet root.' No news. Wind very high indeed. Strong gusts constantly blowing. According to the description of the Crimean winds, I should think that the wind blowing

now, is about 1/10 of their ordinary ones. Colder. An eclipse of the moon took place today, partly visible.

26. Went on with beet root, finished map etc. No news. Yesterday was the first anniversary of the battle of Balaclava. Windy day. Strahan and co were tried today, but I have not heard the result. The 2 new volumes of Macaulay's history have already upwards of 20,000 subscribers, although they have not yet appeared. A terrible railway accident occurred in the south of France, a little while ago, when an express train overtook and ran into a cattle train, killing 16 drovers besides wounding many others. Yesterday an engine ran off the Mitcham line; the engineer was killed on the spot, the stoker escaped unhurt. This is remarkable as the same stoker had escaped when his engine had tumbled over some arches near London Bridge into Bermondsey Street.

27. Went to Mr Clay's and went on with 'sugar beet,' etc. My brother Fred has gone to Watford to see my uncle John. No news from the seat of war. At last the commission for superseding Gen. Simpson in command of the army in the Crimea, has been issued. The only thing that can be said for him, is that he did not seek the appointment; he did not even wish for it. It is not officially announced who will take the command, but it is believed Gen. Codrington stands a good chance. The celebrated plate of the Waterloo banquet has been destroyed along with 11 other celebrated ones, in consequence of the publisher, Mr Boys retiring from business, and wishes to render some service to printsellers in general, by raising the price of impressions that they have, and also to hasten the sale of his stock. It is said that we now have 180,000 effective men in the Crimea. The Russians ought indeed to be powerful to stand against such numbers as those.

28. Sunday. Went to Maze Pond twice, morning and evening and heard both times curiously enough a Mr Hull from Watford, where Fred has gone. Yesterday the trial of Straham, Paul and Co came off (2nd day) and it really is quite refreshing to hear the sentence, which is 14 years transportation. I doubt whether any two ever deserved it so much as Messrs Strahan and Paul. As for Mr Bates, I don't think he was quite so guilty. Fine day.

29. Drew some letters, went to Mr Smithers and finished beet root. No news. Very wet day. Mrs Strahan has large property of her own, so ruin will not come on all of the family.

30. Began a Smee's battery, and began a coin, altered letters etc. No news. Raining hard. Several railway accidents have occurred from the rain, viz. a tunnel fell in, the lines got loosened etc.

31. Finished Smee's battery, went out and went on with coins. Major General Codrington is appointed to the command of the army in the Crimea. He has as yet shown himself a brave man, his division (the light) has always been first and most forward in the fight. Dr Blomfield, Lord Bishop of London, is now dying of paralysis. He is said to be rich. Very wet and very windy. Lord Dundonald's scheme for destroying fortresses is reported by Admiral Napier, to whom he showed it, to be quite practicable in his opinion. It will not however be tried.

**NOVEMBER**

1. A regular November day; piercing winds, dreary sky, uncomfortable. Finished one coin and began another. No news. Yesterday my aunt Bradlaugh fell down from giddiness and struck her head, bruising that and her arm badly. She is getting on all right.

2. Finished coin, cut up a lot of wood and began a Peruvian woman. No news. Particular account of the taking of Kinburn came today; this seems to think (as I suppose it must be) that the possession of it is a great point; for even if they build the ships at Nicolaieff, they must keep them there unless they can pass it. Cold day. The mortality and illness generally of London has, for the last few months, been much under the average, insomuch that the doctors are complaining that they have nothing to do. Illness, however, is not scarce in our house.

3. Finished Peruvian woman and went to S.P.C.K. No news. The contest for the election of member of Parliament for the Boro of Southwark, goes on very smartly between Napier and Scovell. Charles Dickens' new work is to be called 'Little Dorrit.' Cold, wet day.

4. Sunday. Went to Maze Pond, morning and evening. Mr Aldis both times. No news. Cold day.

5. Nov. The anniversary of the battle of Inkerman, Guy Fawkes day etc etc. The usual nonsense and waste of money took place today. No news. Altered Peruvian woman etc. Cold day, raining a little. Business improving, but not good.

6. Began Chinese soldier etc. No news. Cold day. My aunt Bradlaugh went to Watford today.

7. Drew a Vent peg and some nails, altered several blocks. No news. Cold day.

8. Began a 'Teal,' cut up wood etc. No news. Mr Scovell has retired from contesting the election of Southwark with Sir C. Napier, feeling that he had no chance. Fine day but cold.

9. Went on with 'teal,' cut up a lot of wood, altered a drawing etc. No news. Lord Mayor Salomons came into office today (on a Friday). I don't know how he will manage about the dinner, as it properly breaks into his Sabbath. Victor Hugo and his 2 sons have been making themselves obnoxious to the good people of Jersey, by sticking placards everywhere, about Louis Napoleon, of course very severe and violent, insomuch that the governor of Jersey gave notice to them to quit the island before the 2nd of December. This notice has given rise to an amusing squabble between the deputy and Victor, but go he must in spite of his protestations, if he insults the ally of our Queen although he may be a bad man, which he decidedly is. Public opinion is rather in favour of Hugo than otherwise, because they think that he has placed himself under our protection and we must give it him. So we must, or ought if he behaves himself, but not unless.

10. Finished 'Teal' and went out etc, drew diagrams. No news, as the campaign is really at an end. A fine day for November. Our cruisers in the Black Sea have captured 2 rafts of wood, proceeding to Nicolaieff, with 20,000£. They were upwards of 250 feet wide and 6 feet thick. There is to be another row at Hyde Park tomorrow. It is really a shame that the author-

ities allow such proceedings, but when they do go about stopping them, they do it in such a clumsy manner, that it makes the sovereign people cry out. There were some fine speeches made last night over the Lord Mayor's dinner it is said. O, that all these fine things were not all said, but some of them turned into deeds instead.

11. Sunday. Went to Maze Pond chapel twice, morning and evening. Heard Mr Aldis both times. I believe that he wishes to leave Maze Pond. There is going to be a special church meeting on the subject. No news. Very fine day.

12. Went out, cut up wood and drew 'Lapstone.' No news. Mr Aldis has determined to leave to go to Reading. I am rather glad, as there are other places I should like to go to better than Maze Pond. There was a letter today in the 'Times,' from a person in Russia, who says that we have no idea of the ideas (only) that enter their heads. One entertained seriously, and that they would do if they could, is, that the Grand Duke Constantine at the head of 20000 men, shall be embarked for England and sail for it direct if they can escape our cruisers in the Baltic. They are then to come to the mouth of the Thames, destroy our arsenals, come up the river, land the soldiers, who are to sack, plunder and burn London, and then to sail away. Such a mad idea is hardly possible to be conceived, but yet we are told that they really intend to try it when their fleet can get out.

13. Went on with Chinese soldier and cut out overlays, cut up wood etc. No news. Fine day.

14. Went to Drury Lane and went on with Chinese soldier. No news. Fine day.

15. Finished Chinese soldier, cut up wood and went out. No news. Very dark foggy day.

16. Drew 'Vent Peg,' 'Wristband,' went out etc. A telegraphic despatch came today announcing a victory that the Turks have gained by themselves over 20,000 of the Russians. Well done, Turks, help yourselves. Foggy day.

17. Cut out overlays and drew Whetstone. It appears that this victory was not gained over so many as was said, but that they were entrenched and defended by a river 5 feet deep. I have not learnt where it was fought. Mr Beddome the senior deacon came this evening and had a good deal of talk about Mr Aldis leaving us. This evening about 20 minutes to 8, a fire broke out in a linen drapers in Lambeth Walk and after burning with great violence for ¾ of an hour, was put out, when it had completely destroyed the shop and house and damaged several others. No lives lost I believe. Fine day.

18. Sunday. Went to Maze Pond twice, morning and evening. No news. Mr Aldis will preach his farewell sermon next Sunday. He is not thought by the people to have treated them well, leaving them in such a hurry, after he had been with them 18 years. Fine day. Cold.

19. Went to Mr Murray's and cut up, stacked and picked out wood. No news. Wet day. There has been a large meeting at Newcastle, to condemn the proceedings of the government, in turning Victor Hugo and the French

refugees out of Jersey, and arguments used at the meeting were both sensible and true.

20. Drew 'work table' etc. Fine day. My father went to Mr Gilbert's. No news. Sugar, has from the scarcity of ships to bring it over, from monopolists buying it up and keeping it out of the market, got to a price which has been unknown for more than 30 years.

21. Touched up 'work table,' cut up wood and went to Peckham. No news. My father went to his book society meeting at Mr Burroughs. Rained a little. Colder.

22. Began 'Saint Roch' at Paris. No news. Fine day.

23. Went on with St Roch, translated French, in afternoon went to Mr Leyland's reformatory at Wandsworth. No news. A rumour of a Swedish alliance being got up, General Canrobert has gone on an embassy. Fine day.

24. Went on with St. Roch and went out etc. No news. I heard that Sweden has joined, but I think that it must only be rumour. Drizzly day. The Home Friend will stop in Midsummer I hear.

25. Sunday. Went to Maze Pond twice, morning and evening. Heard Mr Aldis for the last time. The evening service was very crowded. No news. Fine day.

26. Went to Gibson's etc, cut out overlays etc etc. No news. Fine day. Mr Aldis came to bid us good bye. It is a good riddance.

27. Went on with St. Roch, cut up paper etc. No news. Fine day. Have been reading Huc's Travels in China[17], which are very amusing and interesting as we know so little about the interior of that vast country; and the Earl of Carlisle's diary, which is not bad, but after one has read it, you can not remember what it was all about.[18] This day next 4 weeks is Christmas day.

28. Went to Cox's, Clay's, Eastty's and Clowes, cut up wood etc. No news. Fine day.

29. Picked subjects for Home Friend, went out etc etc. No news. Fine day. Mr Dundas from Mr Murray's took tea and supper with us. This afternoon at 4 o'clock Cottons the firework place was set on fire and in 2 hours completely burnt to the ground. This makes the 4th or 5th time it has been destroyed. Mrs Cotton has had 2 husbands burnt and she has escaped every time. This is so remarkable that I think she must have something to do with their destruction, from interested motives most likely. If this is the case it is sure to be noticed by somebody.

30. Went out and on with St. Roch. No news. The King of Sardinia arrived today in England and in the afternoon at London, going through on his way to Windsor. He is going to be fêted in much the same way as the Emperor of the French was. A very fine day.

17. Evariste Huc, *Travels in Tartary, Thibet, and China, during the years 1844-5-6* (London: National Illustrated Library, 1852).
18. George Howard, *Diary in Turkish and Greek waters* (London: Longman, 1854).

**BOOK 2nd**

1. **December**. Saturday. Went to Clay's and Dare's. The King of Sardinia went to Woolwich today. Went to Gibson's and Taylor's etc etc. No news. The Emperor of Russia is supposed to be flitting about the Crimea, moving rapidly from one place to another. The fares of the Greenwich branch railway are now reduced, so that persons can go now from London Bridge to Greenwich for 2d. General Canrobert is on his way home from Sweden; the issue of the visit is not yet known. A fine day.

2. Dec. Sunday. Mr Trestrail of Baptist Missionary Soc. preached both times. No news. Fine day. Very cold.

3. Finished St Roch, made a dabber etc etc. No news. General J. Simpson has arrived in London, from the Crimea. The King of Sardinia visits the city tomorrow. Alexander Dumas the novelist has been, for simply saying that "although his body was in Paris his heart was in Jersey with Victor Hugo etc" imprisoned by the Emperor. If he does things like that at all frequently he will be turned out of Paris by another man as bad as himself in a very few years. Snow appeared this evening.

4. Went out, looked over trade blocks, touched up St. Roch etc. No news. The King of Sardinia went to the city today in a closed carriage, much to the disappointment of the sightseers who expected that he would have gone in an open one. When the aldermen were presented to him, he let them do the bowing etc, and did the king. He wears moustaches which come out about 1 foot on each side of his face. He looks much older than he is, supposed on account of the afflictions he has had, viz. losing mother and wife at the same time. Fine day.

5. Began the 'Catacombs of Paris.' A very cheerful subject. No news. The King goes away tomorrow. Fine day. Very cold. Freezing.

6. Went out, picked subjects for H. Friend etc. The King of Sardinia breakfasted with the Queen at ½ past 4 this morning and then left for Boulogne via Folkestone. Small fall of snow today.

7. Went on with 'Catacombs' etc. No news. Freezing. A bank at Odessa has failed and it is said that numerous patrols are required to keep the people in order. Parliament will not meet till the middle of January. There is some talk of the Sultan coming over here next spring. We are come in for visits with a vengeance.

8. Went to Mr Soper's, cut up wood, went on with Catacombs etc. No news. A rumour that the Russians had taken Kars. I should think it is too late for that. An accident on that fruitful (for them) line the North Kent. A number of people damaged. The other day there was a most stormy scene at a meeting of the shareholders of the Eastern Counties Railway at which they voted that the chairman was a rogue and that they should stop his salary, and I believe they are going to commence law proceedings against the directors for cheating and wilful mismanagement. A little snow. Very cold.

9. Sunday. Went to Maze Pond in morning and evening. Mr Hull of Watford preached again. A dreadful heavy hand at it. Very cold. No news.

10. Finished 'Catacombs,' went out etc. No news. Very cold. The Russians are fortifying St. Petersburg and Moscow. I suppose they apprehend danger. If we do not get on quicker than we did this year we shall not be at either of the above mentioned places for many years. Prices of all things rising.

11. Began the Cornmarket at Paris. Went to Mr Kearney and Mrs Gould's, cut up wood and cut out the overlay of a most ridiculous mythological outline drawn by Charles Kingsley. No news. Very cold. People are lying outside Whitechapel workhouse, huddled together, unable to get in.

12. Went to Mr Miller's, cut up paper and wood, went on with Corn Market etc. No news. Very cold.

13. Went to Prof. Bell, V.P.L.S. etc etc etc and went on with Corn Market. Alas! It is even so; a stupid government although warned 4 months ago that it would be so, (ample time to have sent supplies) have allowed the noble defenders of Kars to be starved into capitulation. What is to be said of this. It is treason and nothing else, to allow an ancient ally who is bound to us by many treaties to be defeated and trampled upon by an ancient enemy. Here is the ground to be gone over all again; more work to be done that might have been easily spared; but bribes and influence I suppose find their way to the great! men of this country as well as to those of our enemy Russia. Very cold day.

14. Went out and on with Corn Market; cut up paper and wood etc. No news. Rather warm; a great change in the weather. Fine day.

15. Went out etc. No news. The Crystal Palace Company are in a great rage as it is not succeeding, and they had a stupid, stormy meeting last night in which nobody could be heard, so it was adjourned for 3 weeks. They ought to have seen the difference between a temporary exhibition during the summer months and a permanent one, winter months as well. Warm.

16. Sunday. Went to Maze Pond in morning and evening. A Mr Peters (a very clever young man) from Rayleigh in Essex, preached. No news. Rather warm.

17. Cut up wood, went to Mr Dares etc, went on with Corn Market. No news. Very cold. Fine day.

18. Went to Clowes', made a dabber, mended a chair etc etc. No news. I hear that the roads in the Crimea are in a very wretched state. That is bad enough, but not so bad as last winter, when everything was in a wretched state. Mr Rogers the poet is dead. It is said that a young man prepared a life of him in expectation of the death of him, but the young man died first!! After all the fuss that has been made about them the 2 next volumes (3rd and 4th) of Macaulay's History of England have appeared. The public are in a rare way to get any new books and when they get them, they are generally disappointed. We shall see if it will be so in this case. A splendid edition of Longfellow's poems has just been published, illustrated by Gilbert, in a most magnificent style for wood-cuts.[19] Madame Rachel is reported to be dead. Very cold. Strong north east wind.

---

19. *The poetical works of Henry Wadsworth Longfellow* (London: Routledge, 1856); Gilbert's illustrations were engraved by the Dalziels.

19. Went out, drew a beetle etc. No news. Very cold.

20. Went out and on with Corn Market. The Turks have gained another victory under Omer Pacha, where I cannot say, beyond that it is in Asia somewhere. That is all the telegraph tells us, as if the continent of Asia was only one small province. Rogers the poet died at the advanced age of 93. The Queen's master in water-colour painting, Mr Corbould, was requested the other day by the Prince of Wales to allow his moustaches to grow. He pleaded that he could not as his wife did not like them. But at last his wife went into the country for a fortnight and he let them grow to the delight of the prince. The princess royal saw him so she requested him to cut off his whiskers, which he good naturedly did. What a pleasure it must be to him to be the royal doll.

21. Drew 'Twist,' cut up wood etc. No news. The shortest day. Fine day, weather very cold. Our school's annual recitations came off this night rather better than usual. The boys presented Mr Pinches with a handsome silver epergne.

22. Went to Blackheath, cut up wood etc and began 'Twelfth cake.' An appropriate time to draw it. This is the first anniversary of our midnight visit through the back window. We are safe from him for at least 3 months more. Very cold, but hardly as severe as it has been. The river is covered with blocks of ice. We are I see, at last in treaty with Sweden; the outlines of the treaty are in the papers.

23. Sunday. Mr Willey of Oxford preached. No news. Warm and very wet. Mr Green the potter, who is one of our few friends, is, I am afraid going to leave this neighbourhood. Went to Maze Pond morning and evening.

24. Went out, cut up wood etc etc. No news. Wet day. Christmas eve.

25. Christmas Day. I call this our grand feeding day; because we get up late and there is hardly an hour in the day but what we are eating something. Dull day. No news. Staid at home all day.

26. Went on with 'Twelfth cake', went out etc. No news. Showery.

27. Went on with Twelfth cake and drew a balance. Went to Gibson's etc, and cut up wood. Showery. I have been reading lately William Howitt's 2 years in Victoria. He went out there, I suppose, to observe and the result of his observations is this book which certainly would not draw anybody out there from a favourable description of the place. He says it is not a fit place for any decent person to go to. I wonder he went.

28. Finished 'Twelfth cake', drew 'stick,' cut out overlays etc. No news. Warm day. Here is a sudden change. A week ago it was below freezing point in the bedroom, and it is so warm now that we could do without fires.

29. Went out, cut up wood and began the interior of the Pantheon at Paris. No news. Fine day.

30. Sunday. Went to Maze Pond, morning and evening. Heard Mr Jones of Folkestone. In the evening it was a most admirable impressive sermon from the text, 'All souls are mine, saith the Lord'; and as Mr Jones said, it would be a great blessing if that text should be ringing constantly in the ears of all those despots who persecute for conscience sake to let them know, that though they can persecute the body, which they have some power over, they cannot alter or destroy the soul which is the peculiar

property of the Lord. No news. Warm in the morning, rather cold in the evening.

31. December. Went to Gibson's, drew letters etc, went on with Pantheon. No news. Another accident occurred the day before Christmas, on the North Kent line, from the switch man neglecting his duty. He has been taken into custody.

The last day of the old year! How many thoughts come into one's head.

## JANUARY 1856

1st. Went out, and on with Pantheon. No news. There seems to be a determined attempt to patch up a disgraceful and dishonourable peace, but nothing is known for certain about it. It is certain that the war has done us (the engravers) a great deal of harm, but we would not have a bad peace on account of that. Showery and warm.

2nd. Went to Soho Sq.; drew letters and went on with Pantheon. Went to the Polytechnic Institution. Amusing and instructive lectures. Warm and wet. My father went to Mr Cooke's to dinner and is not home now, 12 o'clock p.m. It is rarely he keeps out so late.

3. Went out, drew letters, cut up wood and went on with Pantheon. No news. Dull day.

4. Went to Mr Gibson's, Mrs Gould's, Mr Burton's, Mr Clark's, Mr Large's[20] and the stables, and went on with Pantheon. No news. They are putting on a most ugly termination to the clock tower at the Houses of Parliament; so bad that it spoils all the rest of the tower. The Victoria tower looks very grand now, as it is approaching completion. It is proposed to cart away that disgraceful National Gallery in Trafalgar Square. It would be enormous waste of money, but would be a great benefit if another was erected there worthy of the nation. Sir C. Barry wishes to extend the Houses of Parliament, but I think the outlay of money which it would cost is thought to be too great for it to be done at present. Mild weather.

5. Went out and on with Pantheon. No news. It is anticipated that Sweden will take an active part in the coming campaign. If they do, it will prove I should think of the utmost service to us, in many particulars. In forming depots in some of their ports, or they would be handy in case of storms. At all events Sweden is a good basis for operations against Russia. The board of works has commenced its sittings, and has commenced on the worst part of London, the sewers. How long they will keep on with it, no one can say. But to cleanse London and the Thames from them would be the greatest service they could render. If they pursue the subject diligently we shall have some chance of seeing the Thames that beautiful river again, which it used to be, instead of the nasty, filthy, sluggish, stinking, unwholesome

20. Ivall and Large were coach and harness makers in Tottenham Court Road.

river that it is now.[21] The second master of H.M.S.S. Lynx, Mr Deheny by name, has been condemned to be hanged by the neck until dead, on charge of cowardice, in the action before Kinburn. He pleads nervousness. Now I do not think that such a crime as that, should be made capital, unless he is an officer in command, and when it is obviously his duty to do such a thing, and he purposely or cowardly neglects doing so and by his conduct influences others. Because, a man may have been in action before (as Mr Deheny was) and not show any symptoms of it, but he may on another similar occasion be suddenly and unaccountably nervous or frightened without having any malicious intentions or without influencing others. And as Mr Deheny had been some time previously ill, I do not think that the law, if that is the law, should be put in force in his case. Fine day. Mr Jones' birthday. Rather warm.

6. Went to Maze Pond twice, morning and evening. No news. Mr Davies of Saltershall chapel in the city, preached, and as he was a very sleepy preacher I did not care to hear him. Wet and warm.

7. Went out and on with Pantheon. No news. Mild. A monster in human form has been lately discovered who insured the lives of (I think they have found out 4 cases certainly) people and afterwards poisoned them. He is suspected of having done this to no less than 16.

8. Went out and on with Pantheon. No news. As a prisoner (a thief) was being conveyed some short distance on the railway, he attempted to jump out of the window of the carriage. But the policeman managed to catch hold of his legs, and held like that until they arrived at the next station, (they could not for some reason get him in before) when they found he was bleeding from his ears, mouth, nose etc, and was in a most frightful condition. He had punished himself enough I should think.

9. Went on with Pantheon, cut up a great deal of wood etc. No news. Snowing and raining. Cold day. The children went to a party at Mr Eastty's and I fetched them away.

10. Went out to Mr Prior's and on with Pantheon. No news. Very cold.

11. Went out, cut up wood etc and finished Pantheon. No news. Very cold. Freezing hard.

12. Drew 'Trepan,' cut up wood and went out. No news. The docks at Sebastopol are now things which were, as they are all destroyed now. The army in the Crimea seems to be pretty comfortably lodged now. There are now no prospects of peace. Very cold.

---

21. The Metropolitan Board of Works was created by Act of Parliament in 1855, specifically to deal with London's sewers, and took office on 1 January 1856. The chief engineer, Joseph Bazalgette, developed detailed plans for a network of sewers with outfalls at Beckton on the north bank, and Plunstead on the south bank. However, the Board of Works had neither sufficient power nor money and nothing happened until 1858, when the great stink on the Thames caused by the unusual hot weather, made the smell in the Houses of Parliament insupportable. In July 1858 the Government passed a second act giving the Board of Works the necessary powers and the ability to raise £3,000,000, guaranteed by the Treasury. Work began immediately on Bazalgette's sewers, which were largely operational by 1865.

13. Sunday. Went to Maze Pond in morning and evening. Mr Williams from Lancashire preached. He is fit for the country and nothing else. Very cold. No news. I am thank goodness in good health without a cold or anything of the sort.

14. Went to Mr Clay's, Dare's etc and drew an architectural diagram. Very cold. No news. I am glad today that they have convicted that monster who has murdered so many people.[22]

15. Went out and began an Indian chief. No news. Very cold, snowing a little. I am reading the first articles I have seen of Thackeray's. He is very lively and amusing. The Persian Ambassador at St Petersburg had lately a son killed by charcoal, by the neglect of a servant. He was so enraged that he informed the government that he should have him flayed alive. But they would not allow it, so he has sent him to Persia to have it done. A nice man to deal with, that. The Rev. Mr Branch is dead. Last night I went to the 3$^{rd}$ annual exhibition of photographs in Pall Mall.[23] This art is now attaining a splendid degree of perfection. Some copies of prints, some landscapes and architecture were exquisitely natural. I bought several. This year's exhibition is a great advance on last.

16. Finished 'Indian chief' and went out etc. No news. Wet day. My brother went to another party.

17. Went on with Corn Market and began a Burmese temple and drew a 'Trefine.' Today news came that Russia (through the propositions of Austria) had accepted <u>our</u> terms for <u>peace,</u> <u>unconditionally.</u> It was proclaimed in the afternoon by the Lord Mayor, and the consequence is that the speculators on the Stock Exchange are almost out of their senses. The funds are rising rapidly. The conditions we offer I do not quite know, but I know one is that the Black Sea is to be open now to all vessels. I am not quite certain about the credibility of the information, as it was only a little while ago stated that Russia had refused some of the conditions. Let us not be too joyful, but remember the Sebastopol rumour. It may turn out false like that, or it may be a ruse on the part of Russia to gain time or something else. If we have peace, I suppose the prices of provisions which are so enormous now, will be lowered, which will be one great thing. Then the income tax will be reduced, that will be another, money will be more plentiful, which will be another great thing. It will do us an immense deal of good, and the newspapers harm. But if we get peace on an <u>honourable</u> and <u>solid</u> basis it will be a great thing. I should like (if it is true) to see the ministry get the cost of the war out of Russia; let them do it if they can. They can't and wont, as I have said before. If the emperor was charged at the same rate as we charged the king of Burmah, being more of course in

22. This was the case of William Palmer of Rugeley. After the death of his friend Cook, Palmer was arrested for forgery. Inquests were then held on Palmer's wife and his brother, who had recently died. Verdicts of wilful murder were returned. See Robert Graves, *They hanged my saintly Billy* (London: Cassell, 1957).
23. The Photographic Society

proportion to the number of men employed and killed, he would have to pay a bill of 50 or 60 millions at least. Let them fulfil their boastful brag. A very nasty day, very windy. Business at present very bad.

18. Went on with Burmese temple, went to Mr Harvey's at Richmond, and Mr Prior, cut up wood etc. No further news. Very rainy dirty day.

19. Went out, cut up wood and cut out overlays and went on with temple. No news. Warm and wet. This is not good weather for keeping in health, changing so constantly. I have not been well for the last 2 or 3 days, my inside being deranged somehow.

20. Went to Maze Pond in morning and evening. Heard the same man (Mr Williams) as last Sunday, but I liked him a great deal better today. In the evening sermon he launched a philippic against Dr Cumming. The reason which made him speak about it was, that his sermon was on prophets, and he said in reply to those persons who regard Mr Cumming and others as a sort of prophet, 'put such men to the test, compare them with the prophets; did they make money by their writing (like Dr Cumming) or did they flatter the rich and preach up the poor for the sake of popularity etc.' It came out in very fair style for him. Wet day. Dr Sandwith who was the surgeon to the English at Kars, has been liberated by the Russians for some kindness shown to their wounded (they are not total barbarians). Sharpe, the comic songster man, has just died in great distress, in Dover workhouse.

21. Went on with temple and went out. No news. Mr Murray has a book on Kars (Dr Sandwith's diary I believe) that is to be brought out in a week, illustrated. He wants to get it out before the peace is settled and Kars is forgotten. Showery day. Mr Eastty jun. and Mr Green to supper. The former is I think the best educated, most talented and pleasant man I know.

22. Finished 'Temple,' went out etc. No news, raining.

23. Altered Pantheon, went on with Corn Market and cut up a lot of wood. More prospects of peace, Russia especially wishes that Europe will appreciate her 'moderation and forbearance etc' in coming to terms! What humbug! As if there was no obligation in the case. In the evening went to Mr Brown's. Pleasant company and a very good supper. One young lady I noticed especially, a Miss Hivanry, a pretty and amiable little girl. Fine day.

24. [Blank]

25. Altered St Roch, drew diagrams etc. Went to Mr Kearney's and Mrs Gould's, cut up wood. The Nightingale subscription that was being got up does not succeed very well, as there is no definite purpose fixed for the money. No news.

26. Went to Mudie's, cut up a great deal of wood and cut out overlays. No news. Wet and fine.

27. Sunday. Went to Maze Pond in morning and evening. Mr Brewer of Leeds preached. A very fair man, and very odd. No news. Fine day.

28. Went to Clowes, Wells and Prior's, cut up wood etc etc. No news. Another sudden change in the weather. It froze last night. Business bad - very. It did not pay its expenses last year.

29. Went to Cox's, Clowes', Prior's and Well's, cut up wood and drew some letters. No news. Parliament meets on Thursday. They are getting on

with the Houses of Parliament very rapidly, in anticipation of it. A peace conference is going to meet in Paris in the beginning of next month. Murders are plentiful about this time of year; there have been several fresh ones lately. Very cold and dry.

30. Went out, drew letters, cut out overlays and cut up wood and began a map of Africa. I have bought some very nice stereoscopic views of buildings in Paris; all the details of ornament come <u>most</u> charming. No news. Very cold.

31. Cut up wood and went on with map. No news. Today Parliament met. I am invited to a party tomorrow night at Mr Hepburn's. A dull day. Cold.

1. **February**. Went on with map of Africa and went to Mr Dare's and Beddome's. No news. The Queen's speech had very little in worth talking about and it totally passed over the American quarrel. The funds fell 1 per cent yesterday in expectation of a war with them. It would be a very bad thing for them if we were to carry on a vigorous war against them, although if they liked they could make our West Indian colonies suffer preciously. Went to a party at Mr Hepburn's, at Clapham. Cold day.

2$^{nd}$. Went out, cut up wood and went on with map. No news. Cold day. A painter of the name of Glass has destroyed himself lately.

3. Sunday. Went to Maze Pond in morning and evening. Mr Jones of Newport, Isle of Wight, preached. Very ordinary sermons. Cold. No news.

4. Went on with map, drew some ornaments on a figure, went out, cut up wood etc. The peace congress meets at Paris on or about the 25 of February and the armistice has been agreed on until the end of March. It is thought if peace is not settled by that time, that we shall have to go to war again. The funds are rising again. Murders seem the fashion at the present time. A man on Saturday night killed his wife and 3 children (all young) with a chisel and on Sunday morning he gave himself up to the police. He says he was jealous of her. Very cold.

5. Finished map, cut up a good deal of wood and went out. No news. The adjourned meeting of the Eastern Counties railway was held the other day. It was, as might be expected, a stormy one, but the Chairman, Mr Waddington, appears to have cleared himself triumphantly of all accusations of dishonesty. I believe there is going to be a parliamentary commission on the state of the railway (especially the bridges which are said to be disgracefully rotten, quite unsafe), which no doubt will bring to light many disgraceful things. Murder certainly is the fashion. A young woman the other day (a servant) killed (as appears from the state of the child) her new born infant, and put it into a band box, as she did not wish it to be known that she had had it, where it was found by a fellow servant. She is committed for trial. Cold.

6. Began a map of Holland and Belgium and cut up wood. Mr Gilbert is engaged on a grand historical picture of the Crimean heroes before the Queen. He expects the Queen to sit for her portrait. No news. Very windy and cold.

7. Went to Gibson's etc and on with map, cut up wood. No news. My father took the chair at a meeting in the vestry of our chapel. The lecture was delivered by Mr E. Corderoy on the incidents of the war. Warm, and streets

very dirty. Have been reading Macaulay's 3rd volume of his history. I can't say I like his style very much, though many do. Rogers the poet left the 3 gems of his collection of pictures to the national gallery, where they have been placed.

8. Went to Clay's, cut up wood and drew 'Vane.' No news. There has been a new peer created; but only for his life the peerage lasts.[24] This is an innovation, but why should it not be? Some cry out that if that is done, the old families will become extinct. I should rather say, my lord may be a clever man and his son may be a stick; and is it any reason because the father is a clever man that the son should be rewarded for it? Not at all. But still I should not like to see the grandson of the Duke of Wellington starving, only on account of his grandfather. Or, in the case of a great man dying, without being rewarded for his services to his country, I should then say that his representatives should know that the nation is grateful, and they should have something to show that his services were not forgotten. I think this shows that we are getting more enlightened, and if this goes on (which I have no doubt it will) there will be some chance of the poor deserving man getting to be a great man. Very warm. Very dirty.

Saturday omitted!

10. Sunday. Went to Maze Pond in morning and evening. Heard Mr Jones of Newport again. No news. Very warm. Thermometer upwards of 70° indoors.

11. Went out, cut out overlay, went on with map etc. No news. Yesterday week a ship of 1000 tons was run down by a steamer off Folkestone, and there were upwards of 60 hands lost by it. Mr Rogers (the late) collection of works of art etc is to be sold off by auction. It is expected to realise a very large amount.

12. Went out, cut up a good deal of wood and went on with map. Rainy day. Went in the evening to Mr Brown's, Clapham Park, to a juvenile party. Should have enjoyed myself very much if we had not been scolded (deservedly I own) for coming home past 12 at night; which we did to oblige Mr Brown in carrying a friend in the carriage. No news.

13. Went out and on with map, cut up wood etc etc. No news. Rainy.

14. Finished map, cut up wood, cut out overlays and went to Mr Clay's, Well's etc. No news. Showery. Murray has just published a handbook of architecture. The price is rather large (36ˢ) but the writer is a good one, and the wood engravings are first rate; some of them are of the most elaborate description. This (as most of Murray's are) is a most carefully got up work.[25] Valentine's day.

---

24. Sir James Parke (1782 – 1868) was raised to the peerage on 16 Jan. as Baron Wensley-dale. In July following complaints about the creation of a life peerage the barony was made hereditary.

25. James Fergusson, *The illustrated handbook of architecture* (London: J. Murray, 1855); the two volumes contain over 800 wood engravings.

15. Touched up map, went to Mr Dare's, began 'Whistle,' cut up wood etc. No news. Baron Brunnow the Russian peace conference man, has arrived in Paris; the first one who got there. Fine day.

16. Went to Mr Cox's, stretched some paper for my father, cut up wood, altered map, went on with 'whistle' etc. No news. Mr Samuel Warren, author of 10,000£ a Year, has just been elected a member of Parliament for Midhurst, and Mr Black (the publisher) has been elected for Edinburgh in room of Macaulay, retired. Thus we see that literary are coming in for their share of the honours as well as others.

There have been some sharp debates on the subject of the Wensleydale life peerage (for Baron Parke) in the Houses, especially the Lords. All the young vagabonds of peers are trembling in their shoes, now they see something like peerages for merit <u>only</u> beginning. So the cry among them is that it is unconstitutional. What absurdity! However, the peerage being given is supported by the highest law officer in the Kingdom; I mean the Lord Chancellor, who declares that it is constitutional. The asses who say it is not, for the most part do not know the meaning of the word. It is referred to a select committee. Very fine day. Father went to Mr Gilbert's. A woman committed suicide over Westminster Bridge the day before yesterday.

17. Sunday. Went to Maze Pond in morning and evening. Heard a Mr Rosevere of Coventry preach. A very good preacher, and would have been asked to preach again, had not his congregation sent up by electric telegraph for him to come back. Another murder (at Portsmouth). No news. Cold.

18. Went to Mrs Gould's, cut up wood, drew some letters and went on with 'Whistle.' No news. The great project of uniting the new and old worlds together by telegraph seems about to be accomplished. It is I believe being done now. No news. Dr Vaughan of Brixton, who was charged with appropriating church fees, has been declared innocent. Very cold again. Among the good things that the board of works are about to do, is to make a road from Blackfriars to London Bridge on the Surrey side, clearing away all those dirty, small houses which make that neighbourhood in particular so bad and the banks of the Thames generally.

19. Finished 'Whistle,' cut up wood etc. No news. Sir J. Walmsley has attempted to introduce a bill (for desecrating the Sabbath really) but for Sunday recreation as he calls it. He would have the British Museum, National Gallery, and the Crystal Palace open on the Sunday, in order to improve the national mind (he says). Of course this has roused the religious world into action and they will do all they can (I have no doubt) to defend the Sabbath. There are numerous petitions being got up and there have been, and are going to be, numerous meetings held, against the bill. I went to a large one this night of about 4,000 at Exeter Hall composed exclusively of the male class, at which there were some pretty good speeches delivered though nothing very startling. Everything goes to prove that to destroy the Sabbath as a day of rest would be to damage England politically and morally. Taking it on the lowest grounds, viz. to argue that it is necessary to the health of the people, comparison with countries where it is disregarded, (France for instance) will show that they (the French) have

shorter lives on the average than the English. And would not our common sense alone tell us that? (of course I am speaking of those who have got any) Who will deny that a day of pleasure is not more wearisome and tiring, than a day of our ordinary work? It is to me, I will testify; and it is to others I know as well. Then taking the question on the highest ground, viz, that it was ordained and set apart by God himself for rest and is needed for religious purposes (of course this is not arguing with the atheist, but I regard him as the most contemptible thing on the face of the earth, for I think he can have no reason who denies the existence of a God). It was justly said at the meeting to-night, that for Englishmen who always regard liberty as one of our greatest blessings, to wish to deprive the largest body of people (the religious) in the country of their privileges, would be an act of the highest injustice and oppression; leaving out the absurdity of such an act. Many who are not religious would oppose the bill, because it is plain to them, it would injure instead of benefit them, in the end. The result we shall see shortly. I have not much doubt what it will be.

20. Drew some letters, went out, found names to trade blocks etc etc. No news. Cold day. Another murder in London (in Islington). There have been a good many failures among commercial men lately and others, but one most to be deplored is that of Messrs Scott Russell and Co., the shipbuilders who are building the monster ship on the Isle of Dogs at Greenwich. It would be a pity to put off such a great enterprise.

21. Drew some letters, cut up wood, went out and drew 'weather cock.' No news. Mr Pinches (my former schoolmaster) gave a lecture at the National schools, Lambeth Green. The lecture was pretty well attended and went off pretty well. Would have been very good if it had not been a little unconnected.

22. Went to Gibson's and other places, cut up wood and began 'Turn table.' No news. Hurrah!! Decisive victory over the infidels. The bill of Sir J. Walmsley was thrown out by a majority of 8½ to 1. This is a very gratifying proof of the state of the public mind on the subject. Only just think; that 3 whole columns of the Times newspaper was taken up with the titles of petitions presented last night! They are now going, it is said, to get up a bill for closing club houses on the Sunday (out of spite obviously) which will of course pass the Commons! (O yes, when probably every member belongs to some club) and after that the Lords. Ah ah it is too ridiculous to be thought about. A very cold day.

23. Finished 'Turn table,' went out, cut up wood, named blocks etc. Went in the evening to the Photographic Society exhibition. Bought some photographs. No news. The majority against the Sunday recreation bill would have been still greater if 4 members had not been shut out, who intended to vote against it. One of the members for Lambeth, Wilkinson by name, voted for it, and he will certainly lose his seat at the next election, and I should think the other one (Williams) will also lose his, for he abstained from voting.

24. Sunday. Went to Maze Pond in morning and evening. No news. Cold day. My uncle John came from Watford to see us today.

25. Began drawing 'Spider's Web.' No news. Cold day. Our friend Mr Brown of Streatham has been taken dangerously ill, and has lost his reason.

It was expected for a long time before. The London and N. Western railway has been persecuted and invaded on every side. By the G$^t$ Western, G$^t$ Northern and others, but it has been on peaceable terms with them. However, lately, the term of the agreement which the L. & N.W. had entered into with the G.N. expired (it had been settled by arbitration by W. Gladstone when they disagreed before) and they commenced under-working each other to all the places they went to. The N. Western began first and emptied the G$^t$ Northern so much, that on one occasion the express train started for the north with only one passenger. But the G$^t$ Northern commenced also, which turned the tables; the N. W. went still lower and lower, until it was evident at last that it was a useless contest, and now they are going to arbitration again. I shall try to take advantage of the competition by going to Peterborough a distance of 76½ miles for one shilling. They take persons to York now for 3$^s$6!!! The peace conference sits for the 1$^{st}$ time today.

26. Drew 'Twig,' squared a great number of blocks, cut up paper and began 'warp.' No news. Cold.

27. Finished 'warp,' went to Mr Clay's, squared blocks etc. No news. We have, I believe, now finished blowing up the docks at Sebastopol and they say, if the Russians wish to reconstruct them, they would find it twice as expensive as it was formerly. They have also blown up some of the forts there. An armistice is now known to be signed, but I don't know particulars. Cold. Several more murders. One in Walworth of a servant girl and some in the country.

28. Drew an architectural diagram, cut up wood, named blocks, went out etc. No news. The armistice has been agreed on till the end of March. I believe the plenipots sit again today.

29. Went on with 'Web', went to Cox's, named blocks etc. No news. Cold. Several more murders.

1. **March**. Finished 'Web', began 'Watch works', cut up wood etc. Rev. M Villiers is turned into Bishop of Carlisle. No news. Admiral Dundas has again the command of the Baltic fleet. Cold day.

2. Sunday. Went to Maze Pond in morning and evening. A Mr Crasweller preached. Cold. Mrs Bailey, wife of George, died a few days ago. No news.

3. Went to Mr Gibson's, altered a diagram and went on with 'watch works'. No news. It is said that the preliminaries of a peace are signed but I don't know on what foundation. Mr Sadleir M.P. has committed suicide (by taking the essential oil of almonds) in consequence of extensive speculations and forgeries which are almost unparalleled. In the Swedish railway company alone (of which he was chairman) he forged 50,000 shares of 5£ each. Of course he did not realise the full amount, but probably he got 200,000 by them. And also in many other companies etc, he confessed in a letter written just before his death.

4. Went to Mr Gibson's and Prior's etc, cut up wood and finished 'watch works'. Cold day. In the evening I went to a concert at the Horns Assembly Room, Kennington, where I heard Sims Reeves, Miss Dolby and others. Reeves did not have much in which he could show his powers and in consequence, although it was the first time that I had heard him, I did not think much of him, excepting that he had a clear and strong voice. Miss

Dolby sung some very pretty ballads, accompanying herself on the piano, and I was very much pleased with her style of singing, playing and also in her not being so affected as some of them (the singers) were.

5. Went numerous errands, cut up wood, touched up 'watch works', began 'whetstone' etc etc, drew letters. This morning I was woke up at ¼ past 5 (of course before it was light, considerably) by the bright light caused by the reflection of a conflagration at Covent Garden theatre. I went at 7 o'clock to see it, and the inside was then a mass of flames just like a furnace and they were as high as the roof had been. Mr Anderson, (the great Wizard of the North as he calls himself) after a long run upwards of 120 nights of his conjuring tricks at the Lyceum Theatre, took the Opera House to open a pantomime at Christmas. That appears to have been a loss in money to him and it stopped after about 40 nights; he then to finish up his engagement, began by acting himself in Rob Roy, Black eyed Susan and other things, which appear to have been all failures. He then went to operas, and to finish up the last two nights, he advertised a series of entertainments in number such as had never been seen before in this country. The second night (last night) was a bal masque. The following is the best account I can obtain of the fire. At a ¼ to five the company had dwindled down to about 200 of the dregs, as the newspapers express it, and Mr Anderson observing their flagging spirits, ordered the orchestra to strike up 'God Save the Queen'. They were all assembled on the stage singing the last stanza when one of the firemen of the theatre looking up to the ceiling saw to his horror a bright light through the chinks of the floor. It should be said that after the theatre was burnt in 1808, the fire officer refused to insure it again, so in case of fire the Duke of Bedford had built into the roof, a tank holding 40 tons of water with pipes from it leading all over the upper part of the theatre and 4 firemen to be constantly attending to it up above. Instead of doing that last night, they came on the stage. He flew upstairs to get at the pipes but found it was too late. The first announcement of it to the company was by a burning beam falling on the stage. Then a scene of the greatest confusion took place, gentlemen looking for their partners in vain, the officials trying to rescue property, the gas was turned off at the main, but the fire soon illuminated the theatre, finally the wretched masquers had to rush into the streets in their fantastic dresses, many of them fainting. Engines soon arrived but too late to save the theatre, only to preserve the surrounding property. When I saw it at ¼ past 5 it was at its height and the weight of the tank made the roof fall in at ½ past. I went at 7 o'clock to see it, and it then presented the appearance of a furnace, the stone walls standing, but inside it was a mass of fire. 85,000£'s worth of music and books, 100 complete suits of armour, are among the things destroyed, to which we must add 100,000£ at least for the superb building.[26]

26. The first Covent Garden Theatre opened in 1732, but burned down in 1808. The second theatre was designed by Robert Smirke and opened the following year. After the fire on Anderson's last night, a third theatre was opened in 1858. Designed by E.M. Barry, this was greatly extended in the 1980s.

6. Went errands and to Mr Weir's at Peckham and began some Indians fishing. No news. The Baltic fleet (advanced squadron) has already got into the Baltic. I am glad that they (the ministers) have not neglected war preparations, on account of the peace conference. To do so would be but false economy. Mr Gilbert expected to see Prince Albert today at the Palace about his picture, but I have not heard if he has. The fire at Covent Garden is not totally extinguished yet. Rained a little.

7. Finished Indians fishing, cut up wood, went out etc. No news. H. Ingram the proprietor of the Illustrated London News, has put up for the boro of Boston for M.P. There are doubts as to whether he can read and write!! The Queen visited the ruins of Covent Garden yesterday. Dull day.

8. Finished 'Whetstone', drew 'Truss' (for hernia), cut up wood etc. General Beatson who was sent out to get the Bashi bazouks into ship shape, has been deprived of his command, and sent home, with no notice taken of him. This, I think, from what I hear, is only a matter of caprice and dislike and will no doubt rouse one of the Roebuck school in Parliament to notice it. Fine day. No news.

9. Sunday. Went to Maze Pond in morning and evening. Heard Mr Crasweller. Very good in matter, but dreadful bad in style. No news.

10. Began 'Vizard', went to Mr Pickersgills, R.A. at Camden Town and to Mr Gibson's. No news. Mr Gilbert saw the Prince at the palace the other day and he appears to have been very gracious. Fine day.

11. Went on with 'Vizard', went to Gibson's, cut up wood and began the baths of the Samaritan on the Seine at Paris. No news. I believe that Covent Garden theatre is not going to be rebuilt, but the space is going to be covered by an extension of the market. Mr Ingram, the proprietor of the Illustrated London News, has by influence and as is generally believed by bribery, obtained a seat in Parliament for Boston! He is a notoriously vulgar man and some most absurd anecdotes are related of his vulgarity. It is said he cannot even read or write! I know he could not a few years ago. Fine day. We hear next to nothing of what is going on in the peace conference. I hear that Russia is still making large preparations for a renewal of the war, should the negotiations fail.

12. Finished the baths at Paris and went out etc. No news. Cold. Some more murders, and a fire occurred near us today, somewhere. A meeting of the Sunday League (for opening the British Museum etc on a Sunday) was held on Monday evening at St Martins Hall. It was crowded and some most absurd speeches, so far as reasoning went, were made. It was very riotous, in so much the chairman, Sir J Shelley, could not be heard. Such meetings as that will do no harm, but rather good.

13. Finished Vizard, drew letters etc. No news. Fine day, but very windy. My mother went to Peckham and my father to his conversazione with Miss Hepburns.

14. Began drawing the palace of the dukes at Venice, went to Apothecaries hall etc etc. No news. Very windy.

15. Went on with Ducal Palace, drew letters etc. No news. The Empress of the French is expected to be delivered of a child in a few days. Of course

great anxiety is felt as to whether it is a son or daughter. If it is a son it alters the French line of succession. Fine day.

16. Sunday. Went to Maze Pond in morning and evening. Mr Peters of Raleigh preached. He is liked very much and the choice will be between him and two others. No news. Windy and raining.

17. Went to Messrs Fauntleroy's and bought 720 lbs of boxwood, also to Mr Smithers and Mr Weir's. Went on with palace and cut out overlays. No news from Russia.. The Empress of the French was safely delivered of a **SON** at the Tuileries yesterday at 3 o'clock. This event throws Prince Napoleon the former heir out of the way, which aforesaid thing does not best please him. The Imperial infant has been baptized already, but it has so many names I forget them. Fine day and windy. Business very dull.

18. Marked box wood, named blocks, went errands, cut up wood and began some shields of heraldry. No news. Raining. I have long wished to compete for some of the prizes which are offered for the best designs and plans for building and I intend trying one at least soon. A new cathedral that is to be built at Lille, was put to public competition and there are so many plans sent in that they have been obliged to exhibit them in a large corn market, no other place being large enough. Competition is certainly the best way for getting new designs in architecture, and I should say, it was in many other things also.

19. Went out numerous errands, went on with shields, cut up wood etc. No news. We entertained the gentlemen of the Book Society this evening. Not a very large assemblage. Dull day.

20. Went on with shields, cut up wood etc. No news. Alas! Prussia has been invited to send members to the Conference. What nonsense! What good can Prussia possibly do? She can do this; give a powerful aid to Russia and do us harm. A man jumped from the whispering gallery in St Paul's the other day, and killed himself of course. Dull and rainy.

21. Good Friday. I went to Southend, per London and Tilbury railway. The concluding portion of it was only opened three weeks ago. It was an easy-made line and consequently a cheap one. No news. Drizzly day.

22. Went on with shields. No news. Fine day. 2 children murdered. War with America not an unlikely thing. Peace with Russia considered as certain. Business dull, but improving a little.

23. Sunday. Went to Maze Pond in morning and evening. No news. Dull day.

24. Drew some more shields etc. No news. It is expected peace will be proclaimed in a few days. Alas! it is too soon. Another year of war would have (if it had been carried on properly) done the business much better. It now and then oozes out that there have been some most disgraceful concessions made to Russia. I felt convinced when the conferences began that we should have all the work to do over again and I think we shall find that it will be even so. Dull and windy. Robberies have abounded lately and there is also, abundance of bad money being coined.

25. Drew some more shields, went to Gibson's and cut up wood. No news. I have written a letter to Great Grimsby to a person of the name of Adam Smith, who I saw advertise in the 'Builder' for the plans of some offices.

On his answer will much depend if I try for the premium which is given for the best design for them. It is rarely one meets with a joke made by a lady, but here is one that is worth repeating. It was remarked to a lady that it was a very desirable thing to have presence of mind in times of danger. 'Yes,' replied she, 'but I would much rather have absence of body.' Fine day. Cold and windy.

26. Went on with shields, cut up wood etc. No news. The Russian army in the south are so badly off for food that they are feeding on their horses. This, a colonel in the Guards told my father and he said he was quite certain of his information. Peace is expected to be signed today. If what I have just stated is true, the Russians have sufficient cause for wishing for peace. Cold and fine.

27. Went to Prior's and Mudie's, cut up wood and drew shields. No news. Great fire at Manchester, upwards of 15,000£ destroyed. Mr Smith came to supper. I made the acquaintance of a Mr Sandal, an architect, the other evening (his sons went to the same school as I did) and I have got a great deal of useful information out of him. Cold day, but very fine.

28. Cut up wood and drew shields. No news. Rumours of the signing of peace. Fine day. I have now in progress plans for some offices at Gt. Grimsby, Lincolnshire. I do not hardly expect to gain the prize, but I live in hope.

29. Cut up wood, went to Mr Scott's and Weir's and drew shields. No news. The Emperor of Russia has, I am given to understand, given a promise to visit Paris, before his coronation, if peace is concluded. The interesting fact is recorded that as the imperial prince (the child of France!) was being carried to his special apartments, his nurse stumbled, and he and she were precipitated to the ground. He was not hurt however. The Princess Royal has been specially confirmed in the Chapel Royal at Windsor. What dreadful mummery it is to be sure, as if they could go in an express train to heaven. The projected marriage of the princess with the muff of Prussia, is again talked about. It is said it will come off in two years. I should hope it would not. There has been a boiler explosion in Whitechapel, several killed, and there are several more murders. A very fine day.

30. Sunday. Went to Maze Pond in morning and evening. Heard Mr Price of Weymouth both times. Fine day. No news.

31. Went errands, cut out overlays, drew shields etc. Yesterday at 1 o'clock p.m. **PEACE** was signed in Paris at the hotel of the minister for foreign affairs. Immediately it was known in Paris they made splendid illuminations, opened the theatres gratis etc, and the news reached London at 10 o'clock last night, which set the bells ringing, the guns firing, people turned out of their houses to see what it was all about, great excitement etc, etc. It is, I believe, not an honourable peace; another year of war would have settled it much better. I do not know particulars so I cannot say what the terms are. A very fine day.

1. **April**. Fools Day. Finished all the shields, went to Mr Gibson's also to Mr Dare's and Corderoy's in Tooley St. No news. There was an execution in front of Newgate yesterday morning (of the murderer Bousfield who killed his wife and 3 children in Soho) and it is said it was the most horrible

and disgusting sight, for in the morning he had been thinking so much about being hung that he was quite powerless. So they had him brought (insensible) onto the gallows and put him in a chair. So in order to get the rope low enough to put it round his neck, they made the drop shorter. When the executioner withdrew the bolt, he of course ought to have been left suspended in the air, but instead of that his neck was merely jerked a little as his feet touched the ground and the shock brought him to his senses. Then commenced a fight, we might almost call it, with the hangman which lasted several minutes, but the end of it was that he was settled by the hangman hanging on to his legs. Beautiful day.

2. Altered a drawing of Notre Dame at Paris of Mr Prior's, went out and went on with ducal palace at Venice. No news. Mr Gilbert came in evening to tea. Fine day. A fire broke out last night in Fleet St at 8 o'clock, destroyed one warehouse and damaged several others. Business is rather improving. It had need for it is very different to what it was 2 years ago, when we were employing 7 more journeymen than we do now.

3. Went to Gibson's etc and went on with Ducal Palace, named blocks etc. No news. Another fire last night in a street out of Ludgate Hill, which destroyed a newspaper office. Very windy and rainy. Mr Pinches, my former school master, came to see my father's pictures this evening.

4. Went on with Ducal Palace, cut up wood etc. Fine day. Mr J Eastty came to tea, and staid the evening with us. He is without exception the pleasantest person I know. The French army are to come home from the East in detachments of 10,000 at a time. They should not I think send them home before the peace is ratified.

5. Went out to Mrs Gould's and went on with Ducal Palace. No news. The Pope has just blessed the Emperor and Empress of the French and the prince by electric telegraph. At a wake in Cork, so many people crowded into a room, that the floor gave way and 17 of them were killed. Nothing is yet known about the terms of the peace for Lord Pam is as silent as a post on the subject. Showery. April showers bring forth May floods.

6. Went to Maze Pond in morning and evening. Mr Drew of Newbury preached. Fine day. Our friend Mr Green the potter is just going to marry a person who is nearly blind. There must be strong affection between him and her to do that.

7. Finished Ducal Palace, altered map etc. No news. Several thousands of our seamen are already discharged. This seems rather absurd, when we have not got over our American quarrel yet, and as we are continually launching new gun-boats. The English will not learn wisdom in this particular. So often, as we have found it out to our cost I should think, they might remember by this time that it is not a cheap way to lower the army and navy in times of peace, but it is false economy. Probably in ten years or less we shall have proof of this. Fine day.

8. Had a holiday for going on with my competition plan. I would advise all those people who say 'Oh, I can do as well as that' just to try and design a building with ground plans and let them see if designing is so easy as they thought. I have found it a very different thing from what I expected. A fire in the Strand last night, a suicide of a banker and a loss of a ship of above

100 hands out of which only one was saved, are the only things worth noticing. Showery. My father sent his pictures to the Gallery today. This is his 3$^{rd}$ year.

9. Went on with drawing. No news. Mr Gilbert's large picture of the Queen receiving the wounded heroes at Buckingham Palace is now nearly finished. He is going to charge 530£ for it. A vessel arrived yesterday from Australia with 500,000 £s worth of gold. Fine day.

10. Went on with drawing. No news. Dull day. A murderess condemned to be hung. It will be by a new hangman, for it appears they are going to discharge Calcraft.

11. Went on with drawing. Showery and fine alternately. No news. Another woman condemned.

12. Went on with drawing. I have to send them in on Monday, but I think they will be in rather an unfinished state. No news. Fine day. It is expected the Emperor of Russia will come to London as well as Paris before his coronation. Does he wish to save himself being crowned?

13. Went to Maze Pond in morning and evening. Heard Mr Roseveer both times. He is more generally liked than anyone we have had. Fine day. This evening at ½ past 8 Vauxhall railway station was burnt to the railway, not to the ground. I went of course, as I always do when I can. The appearance of the wooden station and a very long one, being on fire all at the same time was very magnificent. No news.

14. Sent my drawings off this morning. I really don't expect to obtain the prize, for I sent them in in a very unfinished state. The fire began at the station in the booking office and drove the clerks away before they could telegraph to the other stations. Consequently an express dashed through it when it was on fire and an ordinary train actually turned the people out into the station. No news. Rainy and windy.

15. No news. Fine day. I think I shall compete for a design for a clock tower. It is an easier thing than the other, most decidedly.

16. Went to Clay's and Dare's etc. No news. My father's touching day at the picture gallery today. He thought that he was pretty well hung. He went in evening to Book Society meeting at Mr Dare's. My mother's birthday. She went to the Crystal Palace. I have been reading Dr Sandwith's account of the siege of Kars. I think all those who read it will come to the same opinion as I have, viz, that General Williams and his companions were brave men who were starved into surrender and death by the willful negligence and indifference of the Turkish pashas especially and by the English government partly. Also that the Russian General Mouriaveff behaved like an honourable and humane man. One cannot feel at all for the extirpation of the old class of Turks when we read such things of them as abound in this volume. Fine day, but cold.

17. Began a map. No news. I went with my father in the evening to his conversazione. It was densely crowded. A good many interesting pictures were exhibited but no first class things. Fine day, cold wind.

18. Went on with map, and to Mrs Gould's etc. No news. Fine day. The picture exhibitions are expected to be rather thin this year, but good.

19. Went to Murray's and on with map. No news. They are erecting places for letting off the fireworks in Hyde Park, when the peace is ratified. Today was the private view at my father's gallery. Sales were rather dull. Fine day.

20. Sunday. Went to Maze Pond in morning and evening. Mr Chown of Bradford preached. A very good preacher but a little too noisy. Fine day. No news.

21. Went to Gibson's etc, and on with map and named blocks. No news. My father has sold another picture, which thing so delighted him that on the joy of the moment, he bought one of the hanger's (Harrison Weir) pictures of ducks!!

22. Went out and on with map, drew a gimlet, ladle etc. No news. In the evening Mr Beddome, (the senior deacon of our chapel) came to see us. He has just arrived at the age of 69 and as he is a pleasant, very well informed man, who has moved in the upper classes, his company and conversation are at all times agreeable.[27] He has promised a long and romantic tale the next time he comes to see us of an elopement. Fine day.

23. Went out and on with map, cut up wood, etc. No news. My father esteems himself fortunate that he has just sold his remaining large picture. It was, however, only 30£. He went in the evening to Mr Gilbert's. Fine day.

24. My father's birthday, his age is 43 years.

25. Finished map, went to Mr Green's, Hepburn's etc etc. No news. Very hot. They (the Committee of the Board of Works) have at last decided, I believe, to have the sewage of London turned into the Thames a good many miles down the river, so that at the end of my life the water may be seen clear again.

26. Touched up map, cut up wood and went out. No news. Showery day. My father went to a dinner of the members of his picture gallery at Kingston today.

27. Went to Maze Pond in morning and evening. Mr Gotch, principal of Bristol College, preached in the morning (a very sleepy man) and Mr Chown of Bradford in the evening. He is very much liked by the congregation and is going to be asked to come on trial. Mr Roseveer of Coventry was asked but has declined. This is my birthday. I am 16. Time goes so fast, I never seem to be able to learn quick enough. And after all, what does the most learned know? In comparison with everything, nothing. No news. Very wet.

28. Went to Mr Gibson's and Smithers. Began a map. No news. Fine and showery. At the dinner on Saturday some of them got rather funny towards the close, Mr Fahey the sec. (who, by the way, does not enjoy a first rate reputation, on account of his keeping the artists out of their money after <u>he</u> has received it, and he doubtless pockets the interest of it) would persist that 20 sixpences made 5$^s$. It is very likely I think, that he has made 20 sixpences (of money received) only come to 5$^s$ in his accounts.

---

27. William Beddome was born on 13 April 1788. He was 68, but Whymper's practice was to refer to people just starting their twentieth year, for example, as being twenty.

29. Went to Mrs Gould and Mr Kearney's, began the House of Albert Durer at Nuremburg, cut up wood etc.[28] No news. Today with great (for us) ceremony peace was proclaimed at Temple Bar and other places by the Lord Marshal. Showery. The Queen held a drawing room today.

30. Went to Gibson's etc, cut up wood, went on with Durer's house. No news. I am in a very nervous state about my plans; my head has kept bobbing up and down so that I have done very little.

**MAY**

1. Went out and on with house. Had a half holiday. No news. The peace rejoicing is understood to come off on the Queen's birthday. I don't see anything to rejoice at, for we have <u>lost</u> about 130 millions in money and about 100,000 men in those few short years, and above all, we have done nothing, or left undone what we ought to have done.

2. Went on with house, altered a map of Mr Gibson's, cut up wood etc. No news. Fine day. Last night I took my plan to Greenwich. My own private conviction is that I shall not succeed.

3. Finished House, cut up wood, went out etc. No news. Wet day and cold, bad weather for May. My father went to Mr Hepburn's to dinner.

4. Sunday. Went to Maze Pond in morning and evening. Heard Mr Manning of Frome both times, an excellent conversationalist, but a bad preacher. We had him to dinner and he told a number of curious anecdotes. Here is one about himself. A friend of his (said he), said to him when he was first going to preach, "I suppose you would like to be handed down to immortality, now I will tell you the way. Every one writes books now in these days. Now do you take my advice and <u>not</u> write a book and you will be known as long as the world lasts as the man who never wrote a book."

I heard today that Mr Spurgeon lately preached a sermon on the occasion of the death of one of his oldest deacons, from the text 'and the beggar died'! The sermon must have been particularly pleasing to the deacon's relatives if it was in keeping with the text. Mr Chown, who preached at our chapel a little while ago, told my father of a very curious reason for a minister of his acquaintance preaching slowly; it was because his chapel had an echo in it and he found it very inconvenient sometimes to have two preaching at once, so he waited until the echo had done and then went on. Of course this grew to a habit.

There is an anecdote of Mr Gould the naturalist, not one of the most delicate. He is now engaged on getting up a book on the parasitical insects of birds alone, and of course in order to give their proper descriptions, he has to study them very carefully. He does it thus. He procures a fine specimen of the species, puts it in his stocking, puts it on, ties it up very carefully and tightly and leaves it on for a week!!! He then takes it off, counts the eggs, etc, how many are hatched, etc, etc. What will not men do in pursuit of science?

5. Began the Hotel de Ville at Paris, went to Castle's etc. No news. Mr Aldis came up today from Reading, came to see us and my father dined

---

28. Dürer's house in Nuremberg was then being repaired so that it could be opened as a museum.

with him at Mr Green's. Cold day. Rogers' (the late poet's) sale is now on. In one day 15,000£ were realized! Colonel Sibthorpe's collection has likewise been lately sold. The Royal Academy opened its annual exhibition today. It is I hear but an ordinary collection.

6. Went on with Hotel de Ville etc. No news. Dull day.

7. Went on with Hotel de Ville, cut up wood etc. No news. My father went to Gilbert's. He (my father) is going tomorrow to Ipswich to see my Grandfather.[29] This is rather remarkable because he has been talking about it for years and has not gone! Wet.

8. Went to Mr Gosse's at Islington and various errands and on with Hotel de Ville. No news. My father went today to Ipswich; he only stays a few days. My uncle Ebenezer's wife took tea and supper with us. Cloudy day.

9. Went out for my mother, went on with Hotel de Ville etc. No news. Fine day. I went to the Exhibition at the Academy. It was the 1$^{st}$ time I had been there, and the first time I had ever seen any good <u>oil</u> paintings. I was much struck with some of the marine and figure paintings, but did not think anything of the architectural and landscape departments. I might include sculpture in the latter class also. There is however no <u>very</u> striking picture this year.

10. Finished Hotel de Ville, went to Bishopsgate street station. No news. Very fine, very hot.

11. Sunday. Went to Maze Pond in morning and evening. Students preached. Fine day. Very hot.

12. Went on with map, cut up blocks, named them etc. No news. Business very bad, so much so that my uncle is going to Edinborough to see if any work can be got there. Wet day.

13. Went out, named blocks, and went on with map. No news. Fine day. Mario, the opera actor, has come over to England again and is now performing with Grisi and others at the Lyceum Theatre.

14. Went out, numbered blocks, packed up ditto and went on with map. No news. Wet.

15. Went to Mr Cook's at Marylebone and to the Strand. No news. This morning our old friend Mrs Warren was found dead in her bed by the side of her husband who was asleep. She had lived to the age of 84 or 5 and what is rather extraordinary, she came home to ours with some things she had been washing. "In the midst of life we are in death."

16. Went to Mr Murray's, Cox's, Prior's, also to Mr Weir's at Peckham, cut up wood and drew diagrams. No news. Fine day with showers. The bands playing on Sundays in the parks have been stopped by Lord Palmerston, at the urgent petition of the Archbishop of Canterbury. They were originally set going by order of Sir Benjamin Hall (who appears to be a thorough infidel and very obstinate) and has, he says, been attended by very large and orderly crowds of people. The religious part of the community consider, however, that by allowing them to be played, they are doing wrong and have put forth their strength to get them abolished, and have

---

29. Nathaniel Whymper (see Appendix 1).

succeeded. It is expected that those who have been deprived of hearing the music will assemble in large numbers in the parks and rows are expected in consequence. For my own part I do not consider that playing music (especially sacred which they did) is so criminal (in a religious light) as getting drunk or going excursions in the country on a Sunday. If they touch the small part they ought to touch the great part also. These matters have lately excited very much attention and will excite more, I think. The crisis is near.

17. Went out, drew diagram, cut up wood and went on with map. No news. Rainy. My cousin, Theophilus, is in want of a situation from his mother's second husband becoming a bankrupt.[30] My father has already assisted them and they want it again. My cousin ought to be helped; they ought not on account of their imprudence.

18. Went to Maze Pond in morning and evening. Not got a minister yet. Very windy and rainy. The showers must have cooled the ardour of the people who met in the parks today, if any did.

19. Monday. Went to Mr Gosse's, Clay's, and office of Bell's life in London etc, went on with map. No news. Showery. There was no disturbance in the park.

20. Went out, named the last of the Home Friend blocks, drew diagram, went on with map. No news. My uncle came home from Edinbro' last night. He brought a few blocks but his journey has not done much good. My father went to Mr Gilbert's and my mother to Peckham. Fine.

21. Went on with map etc. No news. Mr Green was married today. My father went to Book soc. meeting at Mr Edgar's at Clapham. I went in afternoon to the Kennington Oval to play at cricket. Fine until evening, then very wet.

22. Went on with map, cut up blocks etc. No news. Wet and fine. Young Mr Gale was married today. He takes possession of Mr Green's old house.

23. Went to Mrs Gould's and Mr Gibson's etc, cut up blocks and named them. No news. The government are having huge ugly frames of wood being put up all over the offices for next Thursday. Fine day. Fred went to a concert by the Italian Opera Company, at the Crystal Palace.

24. Went on with map. No news. Wm Palmer of Rudgely's trial for the murder of his acquaintance W. P. Cook has lasted part of last and the whole of this week and is not finished yet. The general impression is that he will get off from the want of direct evidence of his guilt. Showery.

25. Sunday. Went to Maze Pond in morning and evening. No news. Andrew Fuller's son preached. Showery. Disturbances are expected today in the parks. Democrats have been exerting their powers of mob oratory and to no good purpose.

26. Finished map, went to Gibson's, named blocks etc. No news. Fine day. Palmer's trial is still going on. Lord Campbell (the judge) is now summing up. The legal gentlemen believe Lord Campbell intends to hang him.

---

30. Theophilus's mother Sarah had married George Harding in 1850 (see Appendix 1). His bankruptcy was listed in *The Morning Chronicle* 10 May 1856.

Preparations are being made for next Thursday in the shape of tin flags, ugly gas stars and painted daubs which it is difficult to tell what they are intended for.

27. Went to Sparrow's, cut up wood, named blocks and cut them up. No news. Today at ½ past 3 the jury gave a verdict of guilty against Wm. Palmer. This celebrated case has excited so much attention that I shall rather briefly note down the chief circumstances. William Palmer is a native of Rudgely in Staffordshire. He was formerly a doctor but lately took to the pursuit of the turf and almost as a necessary consequence, gambling. Which latter involved him in pecuniary difficulties and he in trying to ward imprisonment off, forges a cheque of many hundreds in amount on his mother. He then insured his wife's life for 13,000£s and she dies under suspicious circumstances and saying suspicious things, but a few months afterwards. He claims the insurance money, but it is not paid him and he does not press it. Subsequently (lately) his wife's body is taken up and examined analytically and they come to the conclusion she was poisoned, the question is by whom. Palmer is suspected. I should have said that before his wife was examined he made the acquaintance of a person engaged in like pursuits to himself, of the name of John Cook, to whom it is stated he lost a large sum of money in betting. He (Palmer) becomes very fond of him, asks him to his home etc. Cook falls ill, but partially recovers, Palmer attends him, gives him as medicine some pills of strychnine which (whether strychnine or not) cause him to expire in horrible convulsions. Palmer is accused of having taken Cook's pocket book from underneath his pillow (by the chambermaid) which of course contained an account of his money transactions with him and he does not subsequently deny it. Palmer gets a doctor to draw up a statement of Cook's death, when he had not been present at it. (He had also had this done on the death of his wife, when he told the doctor to say she had died of excessive weakness caused by diarrhea.) Cook's body was also exhumed and the opinion come to, viz. that he had been poisoned by strychnine, and as these facts I have mentioned, came out in the inquest, Palmer was arrested on suspicion. [column and a half left blank]

28. Named blocks and cut them up, wood etc, went to Gibson's, drew figures. No news. Went to the Oval to cricket in the afternoon and got wet through from a tremendous shower during a thunderstorm. Today was the Derby Day at Epsom. The races are not so well attended, I think, as they were 5 or 6 years ago, although they collect an immense number now. The storm must have been particularly edifying to those who were on the open course. Poor Palmer was removed last night to Stafford jail. I hear that he intends appealing against the decision. He is not a man to die quietly. There will be a great number of places illuminated tomorrow night although it will not be a general one. Cheap excursion trains from the country are bringing great crowds.

29. Did sundry odd jobs and had a half-holiday given us on account of the celebration of peace. I went in the evening to view the illuminations and fireworks. I proceeded down the Boro, across London Bridge, along King William St, to the Exchange and the Bank. The former would have looked

very well if they had finished lighting it up. The pediment and frieze showing the letters "The earth is the Lord's and the fullness thereof" were finished and had a good effect. I then went along Cheapside, down Ludgate Hill, along Fleet St. These streets had very many houses in them illuminated, they were densely crowded and were extremely hot. From these, under Temple Bar, along the Strand. Somerset House had very large designs in the front that the wind prevented them being lighted at all. I then went to the Mall, and from thence I had a good view of the rockets etc let off from the Green Park. Of course I did not see the set pieces which were according to report afterwards very fine. I, after staying in the Mall 1 hour, went up St James St to Piccadilly, where I saw them better. At 11 o'clock I proceeded home through Pall Mall which was very brilliantly illuminated (especially the clubs) down Parliament St. The Admiralty boasted stars, crown, an immense anchor etc, the Horse Guards had about the same and the Board of Trade had immense letters forming V. PEACE. N. which was never completely lighted owing to its size, and I reached home at an early hour, thoroughly tired.

30. Went on with map, named blocks, cut them up etc, went out. The Oaks day at Epsom. Dull day. No news. Palmer will be hung at Stafford, where he was removed to, the evening that he was condemned. He professes innocence and I have great doubts as to his guilt.

31. Went to Clay's, cut up wood and blocks, named them etc. No news. Wet. The Bank has lowered their rates of discount and interest has fallen in consequence. The funds are falling in consequence of our unsettled relations with America. They (the Americans) still persist in giving an interpretation to a treaty that is obviously absurd.

**June.** 1. Sunday. Went to Maze Pond morning and evening. No news. Dull. A regular muff preached. So many occurrences that were in last week, rarely happen together, viz, the trial and condemnation of Palmer, the Derby races, the illuminations and fireworks, and the altering rates of discount. Altogether it was a very exciting week.

2. Went to Gibson's, cut up and named trade blocks etc. No news. Fine day.

3. Cut up and named blocks, began some 'Thugs.' No news. Fine day, but extremely hot. My father went with Mr Bennett to Mr Gilbert's.

4. Went to Gibson's and on with 'Thugs,' cut up blocks etc. No news. Extremely hot. Thermometer above 76 indoors in the afternoon. Already we are thinking where our country trip is to be. We (the boys) advocate Deal, my mother the Isle of Wight and my father Southend.

5. Went in the morning to Rowney's[31] etc, in afternoon to Murray's and in evening to Clowes' and Truscott's. Went on with 'Thugs' etc. No news. I saw placarded today that the American minister had resigned, which means, I suppose, our minister at New York, Mr Crampton. Whether it is so or not, in my opinion it would be the most prudent thing we could do, because a war with America, which seems by no

31. George Rowney and Co were suppliers of artistic materials, with premises in Rathbone Place, Oxford Street, who also acted as a publisher and printer.

means impossible, would be unpopular and the odium of it would in such case fall on his unfortunate shoulders and I do not see, that by resigning, he would precipitate hostilities, because he is not popular at New York. I have, I am happy to say, learnt a good deal of information on the Central American question from an interesting article in the Quarterly Review, which (although that was not their object) clearly demonstrates from a plain statement of <u>facts</u> that the Americans have not acted right in the affair and we I think, should be justified in commencing hostilities against them.[32]

6. Went to Gibson's and on with 'Thugs,' cut up wood etc etc. No news. I went to the Exhibition of the Painters in Water colours today and was disappointed. There were too many landscapes to suit me and the other pictures I was not particularly pleased with. Lewis' picture of a Frank encampment in Palestine however should be noticed as an instance of enormous labour and no effect. I also went to the exhibition at Suffolk St, but there was nothing in the 1000 pictures worth noticing.

7. Went out and on with Thugs. No news. The Americans having recognized that rascally General Walker, our relations with them are now very dangerous. Fine day. The Crystal Palace at Sydenham has got now a collection of modern paintings, English and foreign, in number about 800. The collection is as yet rather poor.

8. Sunday. Went in morning and evening to Maze Pond. Very fine, appearance however of rain. No news.

9. Went out errands, stacked box wood, named trade blocks, went on with Thugs etc. No news. Very fine.

10. Finished 'Thugs,' cut up blocks, went to Clowes etc, stacked wood. The report of the resignation of our minister Mr Crampton at New York, has been confirmed. The bill to remove the disabilities of Jews has just passed. It is a shame that it has met with such opposition as it has before now. Very fine and hot. Great and disastrous floods have prevailed for the last few weeks in the south of France. At Lyons from 3 to 500 houses were swept away.

11. Began Wreath, stacked wood etc. Went to the Oval to cricket in the afternoon. No news. Very fine. My father went yesterday and stayed today at Cashbury Park near Watford, with Mr Soper, sketching. He brought home two sketches.

12. Mounted an oilstone for my father, finished Wreath etc. No news. Wet day.

13. Went to Mr Warren's at Chelsea, Mr Gibson's and Mrs Gould's, altered Wreath and Thugs, squared blocks etc. No news. Restorations are being proceeded with of Westminster Abbey but they make the building look beastly. The beautiful old time worn and picturesque buttresses are being turned into spare new <u>Pusey-ite</u>, cold ditto and the splendid groined roof is now in parts gilded. What sublime taste to be sure! Surely this <u>is</u> an architectural age with a vengeance. Very wet all day.

32. *Quarterly Review* (June 1856): 235 – 286.

14. Went to Mrs Gould's, Mr Underwood's and Mr Watkin's. Named and arranged trade blocks. No news. Very showery. In afternoon I went to the reformatory school at Wandsworth to make sketches for view of it. William Palmer was hung this morning, or so said the electric telegraph through the papers. I am no more convinced now that he was guilty than I was before I had heard his name. If, however, he is innocent he will not suffer in the next world for it and if he is guilty ...

15. Sunday. Went to Maze Pond in morning and evening. Mr Lance preached. No news. Very fine. I am sorry to be obliged to record something that certainly would not please most who heard it. When my uncle went to Edinbro', among others he called upon a publisher of the name of Macpherson who last week as a fruit of the visit sent us a block to engrave. He wanted it done quickly, in fact sooner than we could do it, so to our astonishment in answer to our reply to that effect we had a letter in which he said 'As the block is for a religious publication, there would be no sin in working on the Sunday' (today). No indeed, Mr Macpherson, not to please you or anyone else will that be done. (We have let him know that, at the same time we shall get it done as soon as possible.) It is very strange that such an argument could be used from an educated person living in the 19$^{th}$ century. It would better suit the 12$^{th}$ or the 13$^{th}$.

16. Began an Indian Temple, arranged Gosse's and cut up wood etc. No news. Fine day.

17. Went to Warren's, Mrs Gould's and Mr Kearney's and various errands, packed trades and went on with Temple. No news. Went to Wandsworth. Fine day.

18. Went on with Temple, drew diagram, cut up wood etc. Went to Wandsworth. No news. My father went to Dartford to sketch and to Mr Gilbert's. My mother was presented today with a season ticket for the Crystal Palace at Sydenham and went today to witness the opening of the grand fountains and waterworks there. It was said that they (the fountains) were thrown to a height of 250 feet and many say that they surpassed the boasted one at Versailles. I shall try to see them. The Queen went today and got drenched by them being blown right over her.

19. Went to Gibson's twice, cut up wood, went on with Temple. No news. Wet.

20. Went on with Temple and went out errands to Gibson's etc. No news. About 60 or 70,000 £s have been collected in different countries and sent to the sufferers from the inundation in France. Today I learnt that my design for a clock tower was rejected among others. I shall try again.

In the afternoon there was a sharp thunderstorm that lasted about 40 minutes, with heavy showers of rain and hail. My drawing for the reformatory school at Wandsworth was seen yesterday by Prince Albert and most likely today by the Queen.

21. Went to Gibson's and various errands, cut up a good deal of wood, drew diagrams for gas fitter, trade block, and drew a fish. We this morning had a large order of above 60 fishes from Blacks, Edinbro, which will keep us busy for a month. No news. Showery. Longest day.

22. Sunday. Went to Maze Pond in morning and evening. Mr Trestrail preached this evening. He is rather too familiar for the pulpit. No news. Our friend John Brown of Streatham is not expected to live through this night, if he is not already dead. His complaint is apoplexy brought on from not enough exercise and partly constitutional and brain turned from excessive thought, which combined have worn him out.

23. Sorted Gosse's blocks, cut up blocks and parcelled them, began a fish. No news. My father wants us to go with him to Yorkshire and pay our own expenses! Would not he like it? Oh yes! But he won't get it. Fine day.

24. Finished fish etc. No news. My father went to Hayward's Heath, Sussex, to sketch. A journey of 80 miles to make a sketch is now thought nothing of, what would it have been thought of 30 years ago. Fine day.

25. Began another fish, cut up wood etc. Went to play at cricket at the Oval. No news. Very close. I expect there will be a severe thunderstorm this night from all appearances.

26. Went on with fish, etc. No news. My mother went to the Crystal Palace. My brothers, father etc went to Mr Hepburn's new house, nominally to make hay. The thunderstorm did not take place, so it has been awfully hot.

27. Finished fish and began another, sorted Gosse's and cut up wood. No news. My father went with the Misses Hepburns to Betchworth Park (near Dorking) to sketch. Very hot, the thermometer about 84° in the shade.

28. Finished fish and went to Paddington station to meet my cousin Theophilus, who we are trying to get a situation in London. No news. Fine day. Business is brisk, as it <u>will</u> be for a few weeks.

29. Sunday. Went to Maze Pond twice. Mr Thomas preached. No news. Fine day.

30. Went to Gibson's, cut up wood, drew letters etc, and began a 'Tunny.' No news. Fine day, but rainy in the evening. Our friend John Brown died last Thursday. His agony was extreme in his last moments, it arose from ossification of the heart as also of the veins, which was proved by a post mortem examination.

**1. JULY.** Finished 'Tunny' and went to Mr Foster's at St Johns Wood. No news. Fine day.

2. Began a fish and also a machine. Went to cricket in the afternoon to Kennington Oval. No news. My father went to Mr Gilbert's. My mother to Ham Common after lodgings. If they go there I shall not take my holidays.

3. Finished 'shearing machine' and fish. No news. My uncle John came on a visit to us today. Fine day, very nice and cool.

4. Drew 2 fishes, arranged Gosse's blocks, cut up wood etc. No news. I went part of the afternoon to the Oval to see a cricket match, between the Surrey and the Oxford Clubs. The batting of the former and the fielding of the latter was especially good. It is to be continued tomorrow. Fine day, rain threatening.

5. Touched up several fishes and drew another etc. No news. Fine day.

6. Sunday. Went to Maze Pond in morning and evening. Mr Aldis preached an excellent sermon on the death of our late friend Mr John Brown. In the evening a missionary from Jamaica preached. No news. Fine.

7. Drew a blast furnace and began another, went to Gibson's etc. No news. Rainy. We are now, I am glad to say, pretty busy and with a fair chance of keeping so for some time. I hope it may be so for many reasons.

8. Went on with 'blast furnace' and drew letters. No news. Rainy. The soldiers from the Crimea are going to make a triumphal? procession through London, or at least so say the papers! They are to be headed by the Queen!!!!!

9. Finished 'blast furnace,' went to Gibson's, began a fish etc etc. No news. The Guards from the Crimea walked about the town today, but it could not be called a triumphal entry or an enthusiastic reception. Showery. Accounts say that it will be a pretty good year for the crops. Apples will be scarce.

10. Finished fish and planed up blocks etc. No news. Fine day. My mother etc at the Crystal Palace.

11. Cut up wood, drew diagrams, altered fish. No news. My father went to Mr Gilbert's. Showery.

12. Drew diagrams, cut up wood, went to Kings Cross station etc. No news. Rainy. I went to the Oval, but did not play at cricket owing to the rain.

13. Sunday. Went to Maze Pond in morning and evening. A Lancashire man preached. No news. Fine weather.

14. Drew diagrams, arranged trade sheets etc. Mr Green came to tea. No news. Fine day.

15. Finished diagrams, began a fish, cut up wood etc. No news. My father went to Mr Clay's to dinner. It is now lightening very severely (sheet). My mother and brothers go to Ham Common this day next week.

16. Drew a machine and began another, cut up wood and arranged Gosse's. In the night the sheet lightening turned into fork ditto and it rained tremendously. No news. Thundering.

17. Finished machine and drew two others, cut up wood etc. No news. Fine day.

18. Drew a fish, squared 60 of Gosse's blocks, cut up wood etc. No news. I saw a large fire tonight, but I do not know its whereabouts. Fine. My father went sketching near Dorking.

19. Drew diagram fish and began another, went to the Oval to cricket, etc. No news. A very fine day. A cricket match has just come off which lasted 3 days between the counties of Surrey and Sussex in which the latter was beat by about 200 runs.

20. Went to Maze Pond in morning and evening. Mr Ashmead preached both times. No news. Fine day. Fred's birthday. His is 18.

21. Began a machine, went to Kearney etc. No news. Fine day.

22. Went on with machine. No news. Fine day.

23. Finished machine and arranged Gosse's blocks. A storm is approaching. It is now lightening. My mother and brothers went to Richmond today and will be away for a month. It is quite pleasant to have the house quiet for a few weeks. No news. My father went to Gilbert's.

24. Went to Paddington station with my cousin Theophilus who has had to return without getting a situation. No news. Began an air bladder of a fish. Fine day. My Grandfather completed his 70th year today.

26. Went in the evening to Ham Common.

27. Sunday. Went in morning to chapel to Richmond and staid at home in evening on account of rain. No news.

28. Came up to Lambeth. Went to Fred Gilbert's at Blackheath, drew fish etc. No news. Fine day.

29. Drew a fish, cut up wood etc. No news. Fine. Very busy in business.

30. Drew 2 maps, went errands, touched up blocks. No news. My father has gone to Richmond to sketch.

31. Drew letters, went on with Indian temple etc. No news. Fine day.

1. **August**. Went to Mrs Gould's, went on with Temple etc. No news. Fine day. A frightful accident has just occurred on an American railway. It was an excursion train of children and women, which had to meet at another spot, another train. When they got to the place, the train was not there, so the engine driver backed his train and in doing so he went smash into the other train which was coming round a curve. At the instant of the collision the carriages took fire and those who were not smashed were roasted without the bystanders being able to afford any assistance. About 60 or 70 were killed.

2nd to 14 inclusive. At home and at Ham Common. Having already lodged there two summers previously, there is but little in the neighbourhood that we are not acquainted with. Notwithstanding this, there are very many pretty and beautiful parts around. Richmond Park, and the river from Richmond to Kingston, have many nice views in them. While at Ham I did but little good, my time being principally occupied with playing at cricket and trying to catch fish who laughed at my vain endeavours. I tried to sketch in colours, but like my previous attempts it was a complete failure. During the time I was there my father went to Yorkshire taking with him my brother Fred, who has ambitions of being a painter. He has shown (considering his small practice) considerable ability in what he has already done, but greater things are expected of him.

News is rather scarce, newspapers consequently are dull. The weather has been rather variable, a good deal of fine, with a good deal of wet.

15. Began drawing a missionary block. No news. Showery day. My father has now gone to Richmond, Yorkshire.

16. Finished missionary block and went to Clay's etc. No news. Fine until evening. I go to Ham this evening. I went to the Oval this afternoon.

17. Sunday. At Ham. I went to chapel at Kingston morning and evening. Raining hard pretty nearly all day. A very good preacher at Kingston and the congregation sing better than any I have heard. The chapel has just been opened. I had the pleasure on Saturday of being driven down to Richmond by a drunken engineer who took us clean through stations we ought to have stopped at, much to the alarm, anger, etc., of the passengers.

18. Began a map and altered mission block, cut up wood etc. No news. Dull day.

19. Went on with map and went down to Ham, also returned. Very dull day. Raining incessantly. No news.

20. Went on with map. No news. Raining hard. My uncle has bought a new house for his own exclusive use. Hope he may enjoy it.

21. Went on with map, out errands, cut up wood for Skill, altered one of Skill's blocks etc. No news. Showery. My mother, brothers and sister came home today from Ham.

22. Went on with map, cut up a great deal of wood for Skill and Prior etc. No news. Showery.

23. Finished map and began another, went to King's Cross etc. Played at cricket in afternoon. Fine day. No news. Fred came home from York.

24. Sunday. Went to Maze Pond in morning and evening. A minister from Bath preached both times. No news. Fine day.

25. Went on with map, went errands etc. No news. Showery. There was a very large fire on the other side of the water this evening, which I did not see until it was nearly ended. A large number of the Crimean Guards were entertained today at a dinner at the Surrey music gardens. It was provided for by a public subscription which was liberally supported.

26. Went on with map, went to Butterworth's etc. No news. Very fine day. Played at cricket at Kennington Oval.

27. Went on with map. No news. Fine day. My father returned tonight.

28. Went on with map. Played at cricket at the Oval and went to Wandsworth. No news. Showery. My father has been rather unsuccessful in his sketching this season; he has not brought home any better and he has some worse than he did last year.

29. Went on with map, went to Mrs Gould's, errands, also corrected trade sheets. No news. Fine day with promise of better.

30. Went to Clay's, went on with map etc. No news. Fine day.

31. Sunday. Went to Maze Pond in morning and evening. A student preached both times. No news. Fine until the evening. My father in afternoon went to Peckham to see Mr Leigh who is now seriously ill from the effects of obstinacy in not seeing a doctor before.

1. **Sept**. Finished map etc. No news. Fine with a great deal of lightening.

2. Went on with another map. No news. Fine.

3. Went on with map etc. No news. Played at cricket at the Oval in afternoon. Fine day. My mother at Peckham, and my father at Mr Gilbert's.

4. Went on with map etc. No news. Fine day.

5. Finished map. Fine day. The Royal British Bank has just stopped payment, after sustaining a run on it of nearly a quarter of a million. It appears that the cause of its failing is because they have been unfortunate (the directors have) in some mining speculations and have lost by that about 200,000£s, being more than the whole of their capital. The depositors in the bank will most probably lose nothing by it, but it is the shareholders who will suffer. There has just been a call made up of 100£s on every share, and that with what they subscribed before, makes 150£s they have paid for 100£ share, and of this they will most likely never see a farthing of again, as of course the shares are of no value, when all the capital and credit of the bank are gone.

6. Altered and named maps etc, went errands. In the afternoon to cricket at the Oval. No news. Fine day.

7. Sunday. Went to Maze Pond in morning and evening. Heard a missionary from Jamaica both times. No news. Fine day. A large fire was

burning this evening near Blackfriars Bridge by the water side which must have destroyed many thousands in amount.

8. Went errands, named maps etc. No news. Fine day. My father goes out tomorrow for a second sketching excursion. I hope it may be more profitable than the first. He has just received a commission to paint a picture, however, of Richmond in Yorkshire where he has just been.

9. Arranged trades, went errands, began a map, cut up wood etc. No news. Fine.

10. Went errands, drew tool etc. No news. Fine. I went to Oval to cricket. At Baden at one of the gaming houses there was an officer (in the Prussian service I believe) who was playing deeply, and at last ventured and lost his all. He was so much excited that he blew his brains out at the table where they were playing. But did this interrupt the others going on? Not a bit, they had his blood etc wiped up and went on just the same. Almost precisely the same thing happened a few weeks back at the same place to an English officer. And it is the regent of that place we are now – no – the Queen is now entertaining and showing everything to. Enlightened man to allow and encourage such scenes as these! He has done worse than this however. He is a human brute of the first order.

11. Went errands, drew tools, cut up wood, looked over trade sheets etc. No news. Fine day. My mother at the Crystal Palace, Fred at Peckham and my father at Hastings.

12. Drew tools, went out etc. No news. Rainy. The Emperor of all the Russians is at last crowned at Moscow with great pomp and ceremony and also what is remarkable, without any accident to mar it.

13. Went on with map, arranged room etc. No news. Went to Oval, played a match and beat the other side by 42 runs. Drizzly day.

14. Sunday. Went to Maze Pond in morning and evening. Fine day. No news.

15. Went to Smithers and Dare's, drew a parrot, went on with map etc. No news. Very fine day.

16. Went on with map etc. No news. Fine day. My father returned today from Hastings, well satisfied with himself and bringing abundance of sketches.

17. Drew diagrams of irrigation, went on with map, cut up wood etc. No news. Threatening rain. Went to cricket in afternoon, played a match and were victorious as usual. 9 wickets to fall.

18. Drew diagrams, cut up wood and went out. No news. Fine day. Weather considerably colder than last week.

19. Went on with map and finished diagrams, cut up a great deal of wood etc. No news. Fine.

20. Went on with map, altered parrot etc. No news. A great fire broke out last night on Thames St near London Bridge and is burning still. I played a match at the Oval in the afternoon against the Merchant Tailors School 3$^{rd}$ Eleven and got beaten by one wicket. Pretty close work and was well contented. We play a return match next Saturday.

21. Sunday. Went to Maze Pond in morning and evening. Mr Cowdy of Leighton Buzzard preached both times. No news. Wet day.

22. Went to Smithers and [page corner torn off] places after photographs to illustrate 'Childe Harold.' Went on with map. No news. Showery. Business bad.

23. Finished map and began another, cut up wood etc etc. No news. Showery day. The game of last Saturday turned out not to be a defeat for us after all, as a mistake was discovered in the scoring papers, which made them have 4 more runs to get properly, so that it must be reckoned a drawn game.

24. Went on with map, went out, drew letters etc. No news. Rainy. Went to Oval in afternoon.

25. Drew signatures, went on with map, went to Gilbert's at Blackheath etc. No news. The late commander in chief of the army, Lord Hardinge, died yesterday morning at ½ past 11. Very wet. My mother at Crystal Palace.

26. Went on with map. No news. Very wet.

27. Went on with map, cut up wood and went to Blind School. My Father is endeavouring to make the Christian Knowledge Society start a new periodical. I hope he may succeed, but I am afraid he will not. Very wet. No news.

28. Sunday. Went to Maze Pond in morning and evening. Heard Mr Cowdy both times. He is a fine preacher I think. Wet day. No news.

## END OF BOOK 2

From 1st of December 1855 to 28 of September 1856, both dates inclusive.

**[Book Three]**

**September** 29. Went on with map, went out errands, cut up good deal of wood etc. No news. Fine day.

30. Went on with map, drew the autograph of a New Zealander, went out etc. No news. Our friend Mr Leigh getting worse, hardly expected to recover. Fine.

**Oct.** 1. Went on with map and went to Southend. 83 miles, 2$^{nd}$ class for 2/ 6. Enjoyed myself thoroughly. Indeed it would have been strange if I had not, for I had a beautiful day, country looked lovely, I rowed for 2½ hours and had a good bathe in the sea. No news. An accident on the North Kent railway, a passenger train ran into a coal train. Nobody killed.

2. Finished map. The last! Hurrah! The title for the paper we are trying to start is 'The Englishman.' That ought to succeed if properly conducted. No news. Fine.

3. Arranged and corrected 'trades sheets,' priced blocks etc. No news. Last Sunday was very disastrous for all shipping round the coast, a great many wrecks took place, especially on south coast at Shoreham, Hastings and Dover. Showery. Castle, one of our apprentices, treated the rest to a days pleasure at Richmond; a boat, cramming stomachs etc.

4. Cut up wood, revised trade sheet, began the Convent at Vallombrosa. No news. Wet.

5. Sunday. Went to Maze Pond in morning and evening. Mr Booth of Falmouth preached both times. No news. Wet.

6. Went on with convent, corrected trades etc. No news. The steamer 'Tay' has just been lost, but not any lives I believe. Showery and cold.

7. Finished convent, began Fontaine St Sulpice, Paris, went to Truscott's etc. No news. Wet.

8. Went to Blind School, cut up wood, began the Bridge of the Holy Trinity at Florence. No news. Wet. My mother went to Peckham.

9. Went to Butterworth's, Prior's and Clowes', went on with Bridge, looked over trade sheets etc. No news. Fine.

10. Cut up wood, began large diagram of seasons etc. No news. The disturbances or rather the war in Arkansas U.S. seems to be getting rather worse instead of better. It originated in the question should it be a free or a slave state? The majority of the inhabitants were for the former, but those of the surrounding slave states determined that it should be one, too, which of course was opposed; but many of their cities have been burnt, and men, women and children slaughtered in hundreds. The most savage acts have been perpetrated for a settlement of this apparently trivial question, which still is not decided. I went this afternoon to Primrose Hill and shall never (unless there is strong inducement) go there again on pleasure. Fine.

11. Went to Stephenson's the great engineer, cut up wood, went on with seasons etc. No news. I have turned over to the Peace Party not from love of them but from disgust of the way in which all our political operations are performed. Bomba (nickname of), King of Naples, has by various acts of petty tyranny and impertinence to foreign states provoked us to demand a cessation of the aforesaid acts and an apology, which Bomba refuses. We

68

bully, but Bomba is firm and is backed by Russia, upon which England is satisfied, and shuffles out of it, leaving the aforesaid tyrant to continue the petty acts of tyranny. Is the power of England declining? I think it is. Why? I am convinced as to the reason, as must all others who think about it.

12. Sunday. Went to Maze Pond in morning and evening and heard Mr Richards both times. No news. Fine.

13. Went to Mr G. Stephenson's, went on with seasons etc. Fine. No news. A total eclipse of the moon is, at the present time taking place, the moon has nearly disappeared.

14. Altered map and went on with seasons. No news. Fine.

15. Went to G. Stephenson's, cut up wood and went on with 'Seasons'. No news. Very wet. My father tempted by a sunny morning ventured to Reigate to sketch but returned in the afternoon with none but with a bad temper, which was expected.

16. Went on with 'Seasons', drew diagrams and went to G.R. Stephenson's. No news. Rainy. I have been reading the diary of Thomas Moore, poet. I have come to the conclusion that without having an over-abundant genius (or indeed intellect), he was most disgustingly conceited. One cannot get a better idea of a man, than by reading his diary (if he kept one), if at all carefully kept, detailing his actions and conversations. There is however a great deal of amusing matter in the volumes, worth perusal.

17. Drew diagrams, went on with 'Seasons' etc. No news. Fine for a wonder. Had Mr and Mrs W. Collingwood Smith to tea and supper, he as amusing and she as amusingly impudent as ever.

18. Finished season and went to cricket at Archbishops Grounds. Fine. Leaves falling fast now. Suicides are (as usual at this time of year), very numerous, no less than 21 being reported to the police last week. Another great vagabond has lately made his appearance in the world, in the shape of a Mr Robson, clerk in the transfer office of the Crystal Palace, who although in the receipt of only 150£ per annum, managed to keep 6 horses, (2 of which sold for 520£), several carriages and several houses at the same time, an instance not often met with, of how far a little will go, when one knows the way how. It is needless to say that he had other sources of wealth, which were the shares of the Crystal Palace and which he has it is supposed (it is not known at present) appropriated to the value of about 30,000£! He on being discovered fled to the continent, but was taken at Copenhagen, and will, it is hoped, meet with condign punishment.

19. Sunday. Went to Maze Pond in morning and evening. Mr Firow of Finchley preached both times. Very fine.

20. Began the solar system, cut up wood, went to Stephenson's, Prior's etc. No news. A house fell in Bishopsgate St on Saturday, burying 12 men in its ruins, some of whom were killed. We hear pretty regularly of one disgraceful row among the officers of the army in a year. This year's one has happened at Brighton, but has been promptly and justly punished. The malefactors were Lord Ernest Vane Tempest and 2 other young officers, who thought it becoming to themselves as officers and as was supposed of gentlemen, to annoy by all means in their power another young cornet in their regiment, because he perhaps had not the means and certainly had not the will, to join in their gallant exploits about Brighton. The climax of this

however was their, one night as he was leaving the mess table, taking him and shaving one side of his whiskers off and tying his hands, in order that they might feed him with pap, like a baby, which they did slapping him all the time. He took all this quite quietly and retired to his lodgings but he was disturbed in the night by having his door smashed open. He at last was aroused and reported their conduct to the Colonel, who referred the matter to the Duke of Cambridge who ordered them to deliver up their swords, and to be placed under close arrest; they have subsequently been tried and have been dismissed the service for ever and ever!! The Duke has given a decisive proof that he is fitted for his office.

I have mentioned before that Mr Spurgeon, who has turned a large portion of the religious world in London crazy, has been lately preaching in the large room of Exeter Hall for a considerable time, filling it in every part, but he has been refused the use of it by the proprietors and has consequently been obliged to take himself off. But Mr Spurgeon is not to be done in that way, so he hires the large music hall in the Surrey Gardens, (the concert season being over) and behold the result. He began last night and long before the appointed time of commencement all the hall and streets surrounding it were crammed with people, indeed they were estimated at 30,000 in number. They began the service and Spurgeon had got into the middle of his prayer, when all at once several persons were heard crying out, the roof is on fire, the building is falling, and other things, whereupon the greater part of the hearers rushed to the doors which were of course soon blocked up with their numbers, many were trampled on, and hundreds had their clothes torn from their backs. This spectacle, combined with the horrid shrieks of those unable to get out and who were terrified, combined with the groans of the wounded, formed one of the most frightful scenes that have ever been witnessed in London. According to the latest accounts, 7 have been killed (chiefly women) and hundreds wounded, numbers not known. The service had of course to be brought to a hasty conclusion and the shaking of the money boxes for contributions sounded not a little strange after such a frightful calamity. Mr Spurgeon has it is said, gone to the country to recover his senses, which he appears to have lost.

21. Went to Stephenson's, drew diagrams, cut up wood etc. My father and mother went to Smith's (the artists's) at Brixton. I saw today being hoisted out of the schooner and afterwards being conveyed over Westminster Bridge, the great bell for the clock tower of the Houses of Parliament. It is about 8 feet high and the same in diameter and was drawn by 16 horses. It has been christened "Big Ben" in honour of Sir B. Hall.[33]

33. After the Houses of Parliament burnt down in 1834, it was decided that the new building would have a large clock with four faces, but work did not begin on the clock tower until 1843. Tenders were invited for the manufacture of this large public clock, required to operate to a high degree of accuracy determined by the Astronomer Royal; E.J. Dent and Company began work on the mechanism in 1852. The bell, weighing sixteen tons, was cast in Stockton-on-Seas in 1856 and brought to London by sea. The clock tower was not finished until 1858, so the bell was suspended on gallows in Palace Yard, where it was tested for the next year. Benjamin Hall had been Commissioner of Works since 1855. Whymper's comment appears to remove the possibility that the bell was named after the heavyweight prize-fighter, Benjamin Caunt.

22. Finished the 'Solar system', drew diagrams and went to Watson's. My brother Fred went to Richmond to sketch. Very fine. A most murderous and cruel assault was made on Monday on the assistant of a jeweler in Parliament St as he was shutting up the shop. The assailant and 2 others wished undoubtedly to rob the shop and the assistant being in the way, he knocked him on the head with a life preserver. He was taken, but his 2 accomplices escaped. The assistant is expected to die from the blows.

23. Drew diagrams etc. Fine day. Had Bennett to tea. He has been to Scotland for 6 weeks, Kenilworth and Rievaulx Abbey 3 weeks, to Wales and to Hastings about a month, so that he has worked the season pretty well. He, as most of the artists, has had bad weather this year; he has however done about 60 sketches.

24. Drew a 'Whip', diagrams etc. No news. Fine. My father went to sketch at Richmond. It will be his last time this year I think.

25. Went to Stephenson's and to Gibson's, marked out blocks, drew diagrams etc. Fine. Had McKewan to supper and Gilbert to dinner. We know from reliable authority that Mr Spurgeon is delirious and insensible.

26. Sunday. Went to Maze Pond in morning and evening. Mr Booth preached both times. My uncle came up today a courting to Clapham. Fine but cold.

27. Went to Dover by an excursion train for $3^s6^d$, we did it in 3¼ one way and 3 hours the other. I thought the situation of Dover much finer than any place I have yet seen. I went through the castle (which is being extended), saw the submarine telegraph at the point that it enters the sea and other interesting things. Was altogether much pleased with the excursion which is as cheap as one could desire. I had a bathe and took a sketch of the S. Foreland with Dover in the distance, so that with this and travelling about 190 miles I did pretty well. Very fine.

28. Drew diagrams etc. No news. Fine but cold. My father went to Bennetts etc.

29. Drew diagrams, corrected proof sheets of atlas, drew a whip, funnel, and altered a block of Sir R. Murchison's. Foggy and very cold.

30. Drew diagrams. Fine. Mr Leigh has just had a physician to see him who says that his complaint was brought on by too much mental exertion which has acted on the spine, but has not touched the brain. It arose no doubt at the time that he had several millions of money at the Bank of England to take care of. He is not expected to live long. Fox and Henderson, the great contractors, have just failed. They built both the '51 and the present Crystal Palace. Their debts are about 350,000£s. So many of the eminent contractors have failed lately that it excites no surprise now, indeed after the exposures that have been made of the contract system, it would be strange if they did.

31. Drew diagrams, went to Mrs Gould's and booked blocks. No news. Very wet. My father went with Collingwood Smith to Gilbert's. Murders are again becoming the fashion. Last Sunday a mother murdered her child at Dover. Two children have lately been murdered in Cheshire. A man murdered his wife in Westminster this week, and so on for several others which I cannot specify.

**November** 1. Drew diagrams, went errands, drew graining comb etc. Fine. An accident on the Greenwich railway, which is a most rare occurrence. 7 persons smashed but none killed. The foggy weather on Wednesday was a cause of great inconvenience on the North Western railway, for by a collision in consequence thereof, the lines were destroyed and upwards of 20 trains were stopped, the people remaining in some of them for upwards of 14 hours without any refreshment.

2. Sunday. Went to Maze Pond in morning and evening. Mr Booth (our intended) preached both times. We had him home to dinner. He appears to be a sensible, plain man. Fine.

3. Drew diagrams etc. Fine. My father at Mr Beddome's. American affairs are looking very black. It appears to be all centred on the election of the president which comes off tomorrow. It is a curious fact that although the slave states contain 350,000 whites only, they rule the free states which contain 16 millions. The slave states contribute about 6 out of 7 of the leading men in the United States.

4. Drew moon diagrams and iron bridges diagrams, went to Clay's and Dare's, cut up wood etc. No news. Another railway accident with 50 people wounded. I went this evening to a 'political soirée' at St Martin's Hall held by Ernest Jones, the Chartist. I had expected to find a furious democrat railing at everything and everybody, but if he did I did not hear him, for I could not hear what he said. Once I began to catch a glimpse of what he was saying, but just as the climax was reached the interest was excited to hear, he suddenly dropt his voice and the people applauded. I am sure they heard no more than I did. On the whole I came away as wise as I went and 4$^d$ minus. He composed 2 pieces of poetry which he recited on the occasion, one 'the song of the living and the other the song of the dead' but they were very dead alive sort of things.

5. Drew diagrams etc, cut up wood. Fine and very cold. Guy Fawkes Day. It seems to me that the day is not thought so much of or kept like it used to be. My father went to Mr Green's to dinner. Last night at 12 o'clock our friend Mr Leigh died. He had been in the Bank of England 48 years and had risen there from being a common clerk to be one of the chief cashiers, with millions of money under his care. His library is very choice and worth at least 3000£. One of the kindest, and at the same time one of the firmest men I knew of. My mother saw him at 5 o'clock last night and went today.

6. Drew diagrams etc. Fine and colder. Business bad. My uncle gone to Edinburgh.

7. Went to Clay's etc, drew diagrams, named blocks. Fine and cold. In evening had Mr Booth to tea with Beddome and other friends who staid the evening.

8. Drew diagrams and went to Clay's and Dickes. Now we have got the weather very wet for the sake of variety, the streets are covered with mud. My father, mother and brothers went to Peckham to see the remains of Mr Leigh, but could not. Our friend Mr Exeter has just died at the advanced age of 85.

Among the numerous schemes of the present day, there is one for making a canal (for ships) from Shoreham to London, with a line of rail by the side of it for locomotives to tow the ships. It is proposed in order to save the time and more especially the expense of ships that are coming up the channel rounding the Foreland. It is said that the loss of insurance money to Lloyds alone is upwards of one million sterling, so that it would be exceedingly desirable to have the aforesaid canal. Time will show if it is practicable.

9. Sunday. Went to Maze Pond in morning and evening. Mr Booth preached. Showery and glass falling rapidly.

10. Drew diagrams and went to Regent Street. Mr Cope the assistant of the jeweler in Parliament St, who was assaulted, has just died. I hope they will hang his murderer, he is a ticket of leave man and must be a thorough brute. My brother Fred went to a musical soirée at Exeter Hall (smaller room).

11. Drew diagrams and began Britannia Tubular Bridge. Fine. Tomorrow Mr Leigh's funeral takes place. I am obliged to attend. Garotte robberies (that is, one man putting a rope round your neck and nearly strangling you and another or more picking your pockets) are becoming very common, several have occurred lately, so that people in some neighbourhoods are going to band together to exterminate them.

12. Finished Britannia Bridge. Went to Mr Leigh's funeral. He was buried in Nunhead cemetery exactly opposite the chapel. Mr Burnet of Camberwell officiated. Excessively cold day. Mr Baxter and son came in evening; took tea and supper with us.

13. Drew an elevation of part of Britannia Bridge. Truly this is a pleasant age to live in, what with swindlers, bankrupts, garotters, burglars, the German Legion, etc. etc., we are neither safe at home at night or day, (or in the streets either), nor are we safe in any commercial transaction. I am led to say this from the discovery of another gigantic fraud of upwards of 180,000£ on the Great Northern of England railway. I am happy to say the wretch has been captured. What punishment is sufficient for these men is a difficult problem to solve. I am also glad to say that the murderer of poor Mr Cope in Parliament St has been found guilty of willful murder and will be tried accordingly.

14. Drew diagrams, went to Clay's etc. Very cold. The last Quarterly Review has in it a very sharp article on the present mania for church building.[34] It is rather strange to see a Tory and high church review hitting right and left into their own side, and we must give them credit for doing it very cleverly. The great bell of Westminster was sounded yesterday for the first time and it rejoiced the ears of Mr Denison (the designer) to find that its note was the same as was predicted. It is said that St Paul's great bell was heard groaning at the same time, it is supposed that it was because it was no longer the king of bells for London. (They may believe it who like.)

15. Drew diagrams, cut up wood, began another tubular bridge over the river Aire. Very cold, last night ice appeared. Yesterday the river overflowed its banks in several places to the dismay of the surrounding

34. *Quarterly Review* (September 1856): 371 – 396.

neighbourhoods. It is a disgrace to our parishes that they do not raise the embankment a few <u>inches</u> higher to save all the discomfort arising from occasions like these. 1 foot would be sufficient and the cost would be exceedingly trifling. Turner, the painter, it is well known, left a large fortune to be appropriated in building artists' alms-houses, etc. He also left to the nation (National Gallery) a great number of paintings and drawings (it is stated in the Times), to the number of 20,000. Of the paintings 20 have been selected of the best and are now exhibiting temporarily at Marlborough House. The Times of last Monday had a very excellent sketch of his life and eccentricities.

16. Sunday. Went to Maze Pond in morning and evening. Mr Booth officiated. It is now pretty well settled that he shall settle down with us. Very cold and foggy.

17. Drew diagrams and finished tubular bridge. Cold and foggy. Mr Booth (it was determined this evening) is to be asked to come to us, with a view in the future to the pastorage.

18. Drew diagrams, went out, altered tubular bridge etc. Fine.

19. Drew diagrams, went to Blind School etc. Fine. Bogue the publisher has just died of suffocation. He was reputed rich and was full of his schemes to the last. He was preparing for publication an edition of Shakespeare's works, to bring out in opposition to one that Routledge is now advertising, which is to come out in shilling parts monthly, to contain 20 illustrations by Gilbert (each part). Gilbert is next year going to give up drawing for all periodicals. He is now almost entirely engaged by Routledge to whom he dictates.

20. Drew Life boat, cut up wood and began a volcanic range of mountains.

21. Finished Volcanic chain of mountains and cut up wood. Fine. The presidential election in United States is coming to an end. Mr Buchanan it appears is coming in pretty strongly.

22. Began a Lunar mountain, went to Gas Inspector's etc, cut up wood. Dull. My father went to Mr Hepburn's to dinner on Thursday.

23. Sunday. Went to Maze Pond in morning and evening. Mr Booth preached both times. He has accepted our invitation to be our pastor, but will not commence until the beginning of next year. This morning Mr Spurgeon recommenced preaching at the Surrey Music Hall again. It is said that the accident there has made him serious. I should hope it has for there is plenty of room for it. He has been compared by certain newspapers to the Hippopotamus at the Regents Park gardens, whom to see at first everyone flocked, but he is now deserted for more interesting things. The latter part has however yet to be fulfilled in his case. A most beautiful day, quite as good as our June usually is. Very warm.

24. Finished Lunar mountain and cut up wood. Cold.

25. Began another Lunar mountain, cut up wood, altered diagrams etc. My father went to Gilbert's. Garotting goes on more extensively than ever. They now strangle you at seven o'clock in the evening in the parks. Very cold.

26. Finished 'Lunar mountain' and began a third one, cut up wood etc. Very cold. Last night the first installment of snow appeared for this

season, but thawed directly this morning, so made the roads in a delightful mess.

27. Went on with Lunar mountain, altered diagrams and cut up a great deal of wood etc. Fine. All the snow having disappeared. Two more accidents have happened on the North western Railway, one a train running off the line, and the other a train running into a luggage train. I am happy to be able to record that two garotters have been sentenced to be transported for life. I hope many others may quickly follow.

28. Went to Mr Watson's, cut up wood and finished lunar mountain.

29. Named blocks, cut up wood, altered Lunar mountain etc. The engraving business appears to be very bad at present, there are great numbers of engravers out of work. We are not however nearly so bad off as some. I am happy (very) to record that the murderer of poor Mr Cope in Parliament St has been sentenced to death, and the public feeling is quite in accordance with the sentence.

30. Sunday. Went to Maze Pond in morning and evening, Mr Booth preached both times. He will go into the country for a fortnight before he enters on the ministry. Freezing hard.

**DECEMBER.** 1$^{st}$. Went on with Bridge at Florence, cut up wood, went out etc. Freezing. Accidents on the railways abound at the present time—one a day is about the average. Freezing.

2. Went to Mr Ellis', altered a grave in the Isle of Wight, went on with bridge etc. Freezing still.

3. Altered a picture of Edinburgh, cut up several pieces of wood, went on with bridge etc. Raining, snowing and hailing, thawing, freezing, such are the gradations of temperature today. The last named is the present state, which makes the road and pavement like glass.

4. Went to Truscott's and Gibson's, finished Florentine Bridge etc. Freezing and thawing.

5. Went to Wells' etc, cut up wood, touched up Bridge, altered a block of Sir R. Murchison's etc. Very windy. All the ice gone, a complete thaw. My father went to dinner at Whites the picture dealers and met a number of artists.

6. Began a railway map for South Eastern Company, went to Truscott's etc. Very windy. My father went to meeting of artists for arranging their conversazione for the ensuing season. They have made it quite a fashionable affair now and it is much sought after in consequence.

7. Went to Maze Pond in morning and evening. Dr Angus preached in the morning and a student in the evening. Very warm and strong S.W. wind.

8. Went to Gibson's etc, and began another railway map. Very windy. My school-fellow Gillman went to sea today as midshipman, he is going to Melbourne.

9. Went to Truscott's and on with railway map. Fine and warm but very windy. I expect to hear of numerous wrecks on the south coast.

10. Went on with Railway map. Windy. Mr Gilbert took tea with us today. Another garrotter has been sentenced to transportation for life! A few months back before these garotte robberies commenced it would have been difficult to have got such a sentence passed on an occasional one, but now

pretty well all are alarmed more or less about them and they are quite willing to do all they can to stop them.

11. Went on with Railway map. Windy and rainy.

12. Went on with Railway map. Very heavy rains. Windy. The greatest undertaking of modern times, viz. joining America to Europe by electric telegraph, is about to be an accomplished thing and a profitable undertaking also, for our Government guarantees 4 per cent per annum on the capital and it is reckoned that 40 per cent will be paid. All the shares were taken immediately the prospectus was issued and the work is being set about. Among the doings of this wonderful age a bridge a <u>mile long</u> for railway and passengers is not the least. One of this length is being executed in India. I expect an arrival to-night in the shape of a new relation; no one can tell what the night will bring forth.

13. Went on with Railway map. Fine. There have just appeared a large number of illustrated Christmas books (the engraving on wood) 3 of which we have helped in. Some are a great advance in the art and others are not, but taking them as a whole they are cheaper, more tasteful and better illustrated than any that have yet appeared.

14. Sunday. Went to Maze Pond in morning and evening. Fine day. Mr Richards preached.

15. Went on with Railway map. Very cold. The wretch Marley was hung this morning and it is to be hoped that his fate will deter others from following in his footsteps. In this case I think <u>severity</u> is <u>humanity</u>. At last it is decided that Geo Clowes (the printer) and my father are to start the new magazine, they taking the risk and profit (if any) and the Society for Promoting Christian Knowledge is to take 20,000 copies of it weekly in order to secure a circulation of that amount. It will however take more than 20,000 copies weekly to make it pay its expenses properly.

16. Finished Railway map, went to Mr Warren's, arranged blocks in draws. Foggy. My father went to dinner at Mr Green's and has kept me up till ½ past 12 (an unusual thing by the by).

17. Drew Moon diagram, began bridge at Sunderland etc. Fine and cold.

18. Went on with Bridge, cut up wood etc. Cold and fine. This day week is Christmas. We have heard very little about it this year, indeed I think, that this, as well as many other old institutions, are not thought so much about as they were in ages gone by. I have been lately reading Lord Bacon's essays and find that I cannot continue reading them for any length of time because there is more than sufficient to think about in one. They are, in fact, too good.

19. Went on with Bridge, began a Signature "Calvert," cut up wood. In evening went to Southwark Literary Institution to hear the annual recitations of my former school. Saw a great number of old 'chums' who are located in various places and different circumstances. Some are in the army, several in the navy, others in India, Australia, Cape of Good Hope, etc. I wonder how many will ever be celebrated men? What shall I myself be in ten years' time, are questions which only the future can determine.

20. Finished Signature, went on with bridge. Fine. The number of Christmas books that are published is really astonishing, one cannot

imagine how they can pay, but nevertheless our illustrated edition of the 'Book of Job' (illus. by Gilbert) can be compared with any of them without fear.

21. Sunday. Went to Maze Pond in morning and evening. Heard Mr Booth both times. Fine.

22. Finished bridge, drew letters, went to gas fitters etc. Fine.

23. Began Lunar mountain, went to Blind School, gas fitters, Truscott etc. Fine. In evening went to a party at my uncle's, played at Bagatelle, dancing and singing and so passed the evening and part of the morning for I did not get to bed till 2 o'clock.

24. Went errands, dusted and arranged prints etc, went on with Lunar mountain. Very wet. Christmas Eve. The bells of Lambeth Church have just been ringing their merry peal, and now all London is retiring to rest after a day's work of preparation for a day's work of piggery. Even at this time Lambeth Walk and other low streets are thronged with purchasers and sellers. I would write more but <u>must</u> leave off, for I am sleepy.

25. Christmas Day. Very foggy. Freezing. A thoroughly English day. I enjoyed myself at home in the quiet way very well, had no visitors and did not go out.

26. Finished Lunar mountain etc. Fine and cold. Our Persian quarrel appears to be going on towards war, neither we nor they knowing what we are quarrelling about very well. Prussia is at present getting warm with Switzerland and both are preparing for active operations. I do not know the precise reason of the dispute but it is very trifling I <u>do</u> know. It appears that Switzerland has a very good army when wanted, nearly 110,000 men in fact, and that, too, made of pretty good stuff.

27. Began Shells etc, went to Christian Knowledge Society etc. Fine and freezing. Our project of a new magazine goes on all right, the Soc. for P.C.K. is going to give a grant to the proprietors, (who will be Geo. Clowes and my father I believe). The title is to be settled next Monday. They are still however in want of an editor. They want to find a sensible, well educated and well read, yet of such a kind as to suit the lower orders, in fact he ought to have risen from them himself. They have been disappointed in different ways, viz. in Mr Quentin, who has just been appointed full editor of the Leisure Hour and so took him away; in Hugh Miller the geologist who was found but two nights ago shot in his bed room. He was an exceedingly nervous man latterly and was addicted to walking in his sleep; and it is supposed that he shot himself in one of his midnight rambles. He is indeed a loss, for he was both clever (though not originally well educated) and could write well, for instance his autobiography, which was highly interesting.

28. Sunday. Went to Maze Pond in morning and evening. Mr Booth preached. In evening several persons were baptized. Very cold. Fine.

29. Went to Gibson's etc, finished shell and went on with another. Fine. Our mags' title was settled today. It is "Far and near" or the Age we live in etc. Not a bad one, but not so good as might be found; but I would advise those who criticize titles to try and pick a new one themselves and then

they will be aware of the difficulty of the thing. Reade the author of "Never too late to mend" has consented to supply for us occasionally.

30. Altered and drew another shell, cut up good deal of wood etc. Fine. Today the news arrived that we have bombarded Canton. The cause of it was as follows. The feeling of the English and Chinese had been for a long time in a state of mutual irritation, which kept on increasing; but at last the governor of Canton took it into his head without the slightest pretext to seize a vessel which had been under the protection of the English flag, but was not actually under at that time. The commander of the ships of war stationed there (Sir M. Seymour) seized the opportunity to demand the admission of an English ambassador there, which was refused. He then seized a junk by way of reprisals and repeated his demand. Refused. Then he battered an old wall down, then took all the forts round about, which defended the city, and finally battered the governor's quarters, which had no effect at all. So now he has referred home for instructions. What they will be of course is not known, but it is the general opinion that we ought to assert our dignity before the most highly civilized nation of the globe??

31. Drew another shell, cut up wood, went to Mrs Gould's etc. Fine. Last day of the old year and the last hour. Poor old year! Our Wesleyan cook has gone to a service at her chapel, there is no knowing what time she will be home. This is the termination of the first half of my term of apprenticeship. If I do not get on better the second than I have in the first I shall not be worth much when I am out of my time.

**[1857]**

1 **Jan**. Cut up wood, began a map, began shells etc. Fine. Business improving a little with us.

2. Went errands, went on with map, altered diagram etc. Fine.

3. Finished map, went to Gas Inspectors, drew letters on railway map, cut up wood etc. There has just been opened for traffic a new branch of the North Eastern Railway (from Durham to Bishop Auckland) with 5 most splendid bridges on it, across the River Wear. Our railway works will now I think bear comparison with any of the roads and bridges that the Romans have left us. My father has been offering the editorship of the mag to Mr Reade. He has not answered us yet.

4. Sunday. Went to Maze Pond in morning and evening. Very rainy. This morning about ½ past 11 o'clock, I was blessed with another brother.[35] We are now 10 in number, 9 boys to 1 girl, which is rather out of proportion; but it is better, however, as it is for we know a gentleman whose brother has 13 daughters and I believe no sons; so that I should say we are the best off of the two.

5. Went to Mrs Gould's and the Times printing office, touched up map, made out lots of blocks etc. Very cold and snowing. The great Bell (big Ben by name) for the Houses of Parliament is now lying, so that it may be seen, in Palace Yard. That astonishing pile of buildings is now nearly completed, a monument of grandeur (combined with usefulness) to which it would be difficult to find an equal. It stands for the present and future ages to admire or envy. The ornament under the grand entrance of the Victoria Tower, veiled as it is by the gloom of the great archway, looks really magnificent, and speaks silently in the most forcible way the glory of Gothic architecture.

We had today an answer regarding the editorship of the new mag from Mr Reade. He is so excessively moderate that he asks for only a thousand a year for himself, which is 300£ more than the whole of the literary matter of the Leisure Hour (including 2 editors' pay) costs in a year. I need not say that his generous offer has been declined. My father thinks (and so do I) that 500£ is good pay for an editor.

6. Went to Gibson's and Covent Garden market, finished 2 shells etc. Fine. The Archbishop of Paris was murdered (I believe the day before yesterday) by a priest, in the church of St. Etienne de Mont. It appears that he had suspended the priest for preaching what they call heretical doctrine, but what we should call true doctrine. That however of course does not at all justify the act. From his conduct when examined he appears to be insane.[36]

There have been a good many wrecks lately, unfortunately; one which took place at Rhyl (Wales) a day or two back, in which a lifeboat and all hands were lost, was very distressing.

7. Cut up wood, looked over 'map', drew a shell etc. Fine and cold. My father took the chair at a meeting at our chapel, on the occasion of a lecture

---

35. Samuel Leigh Whymper (see Appendix 1).
36. The assailant, a disaffected priest named Verger, was executed one month later.

by our friend Mr Bailey, who afterwards told him that he had been down to Margate this week to look after an Indiaman of 1200 tons, which was riding off a place called Kingsgate near Broadstairs and was expected to go ashore; which he did the night that he arrived. It drove on the rocks perfectly helpless, (he says) completely at the mercy of the waves, and all on board must have inevitably perished if it had not been for the gallantry of the crew of two lifeboats belonging to Broadstairs (one of which went out twice to the wreck, the other once) who succeeded after several hours exertions in getting <u>all</u> the crew safe on shore, although they were in a very bad state from being exposed the greater part of the night to the fury of the waves and the blinding and freezing snow.

8. Drew a beetle, arranged diagrams, drew letters etc. Snow and rain.

The Times of today contained an account of the loss of the Northern Star (the ship I mentioned yesterday), written by a gentleman who resides at Broadstairs, who gives the crews of the boats the highest praise for the noble conduct in the affair. The mate of the American ship, said he felt proud of having descended from such men, and also that he felt sure that none but English would have risked their lives in such a manner.

9. Drew letters, proofed blocks, arranged diagrams. Very rainy and excessively gusty, which reminds one of the sea and of those who are on it. A subscription has very properly been set on foot for the families of the men who were lost by the capsizing of the Rhyl lifeboat. Upwards of 1200£s have already been raised.

10. Went to Gibson's, cut up wood, began two beetles, arranged diagrams etc. very heavy rain. Warm. Dr Ure and John Britton (the architect) have just died. So they drop off one by one.

11. Sunday. Went to Maze Pond in morning and evening. Mr Booth preached both times. Very rainy. Wind very strong from the north east.

12. Finished beetles, planed 12 blocks etc. Dull day. The American ambassador here has sent 50£ to the crews of the life boats at Broadstairs. There have been a very large number of subscriptions from others also sent to them. It is unfortunately true that a Margate lugger foundered with all hands (12 or 13) trying to assist the same ship. Several of those in the lugger are of the same name as those in the life boat and are probably relations. It must, notwithstanding the praise lavished on them for their noble conduct be a very melancholy time for them.

13. Went to S. for P.C.K., numbered and arranged diagrams, began an aquarium. Dull. Yesterday there was a meeting in Smithfield of (some say 25 and others only 10,000. Probably the latter is nearer the mark) bricklayers and others who are out of work. What the meeting was supposed to be for I cannot tell. Perhaps to raise the public sympathy and a public subscription.

14. Went to Mr Gibson's and on with aquarium. My father to dinner at Mr Green's to meet Mr Aldis. Dull.

15. Finished Aquarium, cut up several pieces of wood etc. Rainy. In evening I went to the 4th annual exhibition of Photographs. The progress they have made in portraits is very great (during the last year), but landscape and architecture is very little better, if at all. The art of

galvanography is perhaps the most important art yet discovered in connection with photography. It combines galvanism, photography and engraving on copper in one plate, and the product is very astonishing.

16. Began Roman Catholic diagram, drew letters etc. Dull and freezing. In evening I went to a party at Mr Hepburn's at Clapham. He has now a splendid house (I might say mansion) for which he pays a rent of 350£ a year, and he has also spent a sum of 3000£ over extra buildings, fittings etc. It is furnished in a very splendid manner, quite princely. There were about 80 persons at the party. He is by trade a tanner, having a very large place in Bermondsey. He is a most hospitable man, and his numerous family are very agreeable, considering circumstances.

17. Went to Gibson's, finished R.C. diagram, cut up wood, touched up aquarium etc. Fine and cold. The Swiss question is at last happily settled without bloodshed, or at least without much of it. Switzerland delivers up the prisoners and the independence of Neufchâtel is guaranteed. Thus both have settled it to the satisfaction of themselves and their neighbours without having to resort to the stupid and cruel means of violence.

18. Sunday. Went to Maze Pond in morning and evening. Heard Mr _ _ _ of Leicester both times. Very dirty.

19. Went to Mr Warren's and errands, cut up wood, drew a second aquarium. Rainy. Mr Read, our old apprentice, came to tea. He is just getting up a lot of painting to try and get in the Old Water Colour Society (for the 7 or 8th time), principally of Milan cathedral. I don't think he will get in, although his drawings display considerable talent. He has travelled in Europe a great deal and has just returned from a tour in Italy, principally undertaken for the Illustrated News. When he was at Naples, the late earthquake took place. He describes it thus, "I was woke up in the night by a violent heaving motion; I thought somebody was under the bed, but presently the glasses and windows began to rattle, so then I was convinced what it was and immediately jumped out of bed. I found the floor moving up and down so violently that I was in doubt whether I should run down stairs; but thought perhaps the house would come down before I did, so I jumped into bed again and fell into a sound sleep," which part I do not believe, especially as some thousands rushed out of their houses and passed the night out of doors. No lives were however lost through it.

20. Went to Paternoster Row etc, began aquarium no. 3, began an infirmary. Very heavy rain and windy. We are thinking about sending the late artist of the Illustrated News at Sebastopol (Mr Goodall) out down the Rhine etc to sketch for a new edition of Byron's Childe Harold. It will be a fine chance for him if he gets it. Artists who are worth anything are so much sought after now that it is difficult to get one good enough even for a brilliant offer like this.

21. Went on with Infirmary etc. Very cold. My father went in evening to Mr Green's at Clapham.

22. Went to Infirmary and finished drawing it, finished no 3 aquarium, cut up a good deal of wood etc. My father went in evening to Mr Hepburn's. Dull.

23. Began Aquarium no 4. In afternoon I went to Peckham to see the collection of prints, books etc of our late friend Mr Leigh. The books are nearly all choice, more than 3000 in number, extremely well bound; the prints and lithographs are of the rarest and best kinds, nearly 50 portfolio containing on an average more than 50 each. He had also several portfolios of photographs, of which they were kind enough to allow me to choose two for myself. Very rainy.

24. Cut up wood, arranged blocks and went on with Aquarium no 4. Rainy. The Chinese governor of Canton has been disgraced for his bad defence of the city, which looks as if they meant something.

25. Sunday. Went to Maze Pond in morning and evening. Mr – preached in morning and Dr Angus in evening. Rainy.

26. Finished Aquarium no 4, cut up wood and drew the fountain of St Sulpice at Paris. Wet. Very dull. Business pretty goodish.

27. Drew diagram, cut up wood and drew a plant for aquarium book. Freezing. Our new mag is expected to be ready in the middle of next month.

28. Cut up wood and began drawing Napoleon's tomb at Invalides, Paris. Snowing. Very cold.

29. Went to Soper's, cut up wood, went on with Napoleon's tomb. Freezing. There are at the present time great numbers of workmen unemployed in London. They have held several peaceable meetings in Smithfield at which some of them have enforced the opinion (not a bad one) that in times of scarcity the Government should employ them on public works.

30. Drew an Egyptian device, went on with Napoleon's tomb etc. Freezing.

31. Finished Napoleon's tomb, altered Egyptian device, did carpentering jobs etc. Snowed considerably in night. Freezing.

1. **February**. Sunday. Went to Maze Pond in morning and evening. Mr Fishbourne of Thaxted officiated. He is an exceedingly able preacher and I should not at all object to hearing him constantly. Freezing.

2. Went to Soper's etc, altered and improved catacombs, St Roch, Napoleon's tomb etc. Freezing.

3. Altered blocks, cut up lot of wood, began the Fountain Molière at Paris. Freezing. We are after all disappointed in the name of our mag, as a person has just advertised (of course before us) a poem of the same name. We foolishly neglected to register it, or we could by that means have prevented the disappointment.

4. Went on with Fontaine Molière, altered Infirmary, cut up wood etc. Freezing.

5. Went on with Fontaine Molière, altered Infirmary again, cut up wood, began a gallery in the Palais Royal. My father went to his first conversazione at Willis's Rooms (for this season). There are now exhibiting at Marlboro House, (free of course) about 100 of the Water Colour and sepia drawings of the late J.M. Turner R.A. and left by him to the nation. They are selected from the vast number he left, and are said to be very fine. He could hardly have been so avaricious as was made out, for these 20,000

drawings which he has left as a legacy to the nation, would have fetched him enormous sums, if he had chosen to sell them.

6. Went to Society (S.P.C.K.) and Mudie's, cut up wood, drew diagram. In afternoon I went to Peckham. Mr Leigh's copy of Roberts' Nubia and Holy Land is valued at 70£. A respectable price for one work!! Our troops have attacked Bushir (on the Persian gulf) and have taken it with about 20 killed on our side.

7. Went on with fountain, did odd jobs, cut up wood etc. Fine and warm.

8. Sunday. Went to Maze Pond in morning and evening. Mr Fishbourne of Thaxted preached both times. Fine.

9. Went errands, finished fountain, went on with Palais Royal etc. Rainy. The Chinese affair is at a stand still, Admiral Seymour waiting for instruction from home. The Persian affair is I believe going on briskly, conquering and to conquer (our army). All I wish in regard to it is, that the insane Shah may be brought to his senses.

10. Altered fountain, went on with Palais Royal, went to Rowneys, cut up wood etc. Fine. Mr S. Read, formerly our apprentice, was yesterday elected member of the Old Water Colour Society.

11. Whited wood, etc, went on with Palais Royal. Rainy. In evening my father went to a meeting of the Graphic at London University.

12. Went to Mrs Gould's, post, arranged blocks, went on with Palais Royal. Fine. No news.

13. Went errands, cut up wood, drew line round blocks, went on with Palais Royal. Fine. The budget (Chancellor of Exchequer) for this year was brought forward today. What it contained I do not know, but it was believed that the income tax would be lowered by one half. The Government pledged themselves to take it off entirely, the year after peace was concluded. Behold the state of affairs now! Comment is unnecessary.

14. Finished Palais Royal, went errands, removed cupboard etc. Fine. The income tax is to be taken off to the amount of two thirds on incomes below 150£ and in proportion on those above. It will make a considerable difference to us, nearly 30£ I think.

15. Sunday. Went to Maze Pond in morning and evening. Mr Hands of Salisbury preached. A solid Englishman. Fine.

16. Went to Covent Garden, cut up wood, began missionary block. Fine.

17. Went to Clowes and Covent Garden etc, went on with Indian postmen and began Kangaroo hunting. Fine. Alas! (and yet why do I say so) the magazine is not going to be started. The General Committee of the Society appointed a sub-com to see if it was advisable to be begun. They said it was and negotiations were entered into with Clowes and my father to undertake the responsibility of it, the Society advancing 2 or 3000£ to begin it with (to be repaid) and giving it their countenance and support. So far so good. But a (too?) busy member of the sub-committee found an editor in the person of a lawyer, a Mr Saunders, and would have him or none for principal editor. My father picked Mr Thornbury as under editor. The first number after much trouble was got together, but it was so flat (thanks to Mr Saunders) that when referred to the General Committee it quite disgusted them. That combined with the loss of the title (Far and near), together with

the long time the mag had been under consideration, which was their own fault, determined them to reject the idea altogether, which they have done.
18. Altered Fountain and Palais Royal, went on with Kangaroo hunting etc. Today I opened this year's cricket campaign at the Archbishops grounds. Very fine. My father went to an exhibition of pictures at Reigate, and afterwards to dinner at Mr Thornton's. Talking of Reigate, there has been a most abominable attempt at robbery and murder there lately. A young man was driving along the road near there, when he perceived a man lying in the road and as he came near him he heard him groaning for help. So the young man got out of the gig and went to help him. However, directly he got near him the man jumped up and putting a pistol to his breast called on him to deliver up a large amount of money, which he said he knew he had about him. The young man naturally resisted, when the ruffian shot him through, the ball lodging in the clavicle where it still remains. The ruffian then made off (I do not know if he obtained his booty) but it is believed by the police that they have a clue to him. A reward of 200£ is offered for his apprehension.
19. Went to Mudie's and Covent Garden, arranged Aquarium blocks etc. Went on with Kangaroo hunting. Fine.
20. Went on with kangaroo hunting, cut up wood, drew a leather bottle etc. Fine. My father went to tea at Peckham and supper to Mr Beddome's.
21. Finished Kangaroo hunting, drew a Water Scorpion, cut up wood etc. Fine. In evening I walked to Peckham. Mr Leigh's collection of books, prints and photographs will be sold by public auction in a short time as the person who was in treaty with the family for them refused to give 1000£ for them, which was the lowest they would take for the books only.
22. Sunday. Went to Maze Pond in morning and evening. Mr Hand preached both times. Fine.
23. Cut up wood, altered Indian postmen etc. Fine.
24. Began a second Napoleon's tomb, cut up lot of wood, altered fountain and drew hieroglyphic etc. Fine.
25. Made out list of cuts for Paris book, went on with Napoleon's tomb etc. Rainy. There has just been made a clever division of London into sections (somewhat like Paris in arrondissements) in order to facilitate the delivery of letters. It promises to answer well and has already it is said quickened the delivery considerably.
26. Went errands, cut up wood, made out another list, went on with Napoleon's tomb etc. Foggy. There has just been a dreadful colliery explosion (I think in Derbyshire) which has killed upwards of 120 men.
27. Went to Gibson's etc, cut up wood, finished Napoleon's tomb etc. Fine. My uncle Woods has come up from Swaffham and stops here until Monday. Disraeli and Gladstone have been very noisy in Parliament, the last few days, opposing the budget and other particulars, but they will not do any harm for the simplest person can see their wishes.
1. **March**. Sunday. Went in morning to Maze Pond where a minister from Aberdeen preached,[37] and in evening to Camden Road chapel

---

37. James Malcolm (see Appendix 1).

along with my uncle Woods, where he preached. And in order to go there, I committed what I believe to be a sin, (but which I hope may not be accounted so) viz. I rode in an omnibus, thereby keeping or helping to keep men unnecessarily on work, on the Sabbath day. I hope I may not do so again, for I believe it to be <u>wrong.</u>

That colliery explosion that I mentioned a day or two back, was at a place called Lund hill in Yorkshire and appears to have been most terrible in its effects, for out of 200 men who worked in the mine, not one quarter of that number have come out alive. The explosion resulted from the taking fire of fire damp (which the mine was subject to) from the flame of a naked candle which was un-prudently being used instead of the safety lamp. The proprietors of the mine seeing no other way of extinguishing the flames, agreed to stop the mouths of the colliery up, but they did not do so before calling a meeting of the neighbouring proprietors, who perfectly coincided with their opinion, although by so doing, they stopped the escape of any in the pit who might be living after the explosion.

2. Went on with 'Map', read book for places of cuts etc. Fine.

3. Went on with 'Map' etc, and had a half day holiday, went to Crystal Palace with my uncle Woods. It looks in a very miserable condition, as very few persons go to it now.

4. Went on with 'Map', went to Mudie's and Nosotty. Rainy.

5. Went to Mudie's, cut up wood, went on with Map etc. Fine. My father went in evening to conversazione with Mr and Mrs Green.

6. Went errands, on with Map, cut up wood etc. Fine. The Ministry was defeated last week (in trying to uphold the Chinese quarrel) by a small majority (16 out of 510) but sufficient to show the dangerous state they are in. There are it is usually considered but two steps open to them, to dissolve the Parliament or to resign. The former of these it is not thought they will attempt and <u>I</u> do not think they will do the latter either yet. The whole of the Palmerston Ministry has been a disgrace to them from beginning to end, for it has been characterized by the most abominable trifling with serious matters or by avoiding any sort of explanation of their conduct and turning the questions put into ridicule. Their love of <u>power</u> prevails over a love of <u>honour.</u>

7. Put screws in frames, pasted backs etc, went on with map and out errands. I was told tonight by a friend of ours, (who had it from good authority) of an instance of a very rapid rise in the world of 2 brothers. They worked as common stone masons on the St George's Roman Catholic cathedral, near us, within 15 or I think within 10 years and now last year their firm of Myers and Co, Builders, put by as clear gain the enormous sum of 40,000£. Fine.

8. Sunday. Went to Maze Pond in morning and evening. Mr Richards preached both times. We had today a very heavy fall of something which I cannot tell what it was. It was not snow or hail, but something between the two and in very large lumps. Very cold. Parliament is expected to be dissolved very shortly.

9. Went errands, to Peckham, on with map etc. Snowing.

10. Altered Corn Market and Catacombs, went to Gibson's etc, cut up wood and went on with map. Freezing.

11. Mending various articles etc, went on with map. Very cold. A house has been burnt down in the Clapham Road and 2 children in it. Mr Leigh's books are fixed to be sold next Monday and 2 following days at Messrs Sotheby and Wilkinson's. Those that will be sold are about 1700 in number and 42 portfolios of prints, photographs etc.

12. Went on with map, out errands etc. Very cold.

13. Went on with map etc and went for an afternoon's pleasure to Richmond, intending to have a row on the river, but was miserably disappointed in my expectations for as soon as I had got there, it began rainy and so continued all the rest of the day. Very windy.

14. Went to Mr Read's and to Wolff's etc, went on with map. Raining and the wind from the S.W. blowing at present with terrific force. The effect of which will be to strew the south coast with abundance of wrecks. Finally it is determined to dissolve the parliament, which will take place in about 3 weeks time. Lord Palmerston said that he should not resign (after the defeat of the Government) but should appeal to the people for support. In consequence thereof he has had second votes of confidence from large meetings in London and elsewhere. He is still rather popular although many disapprove of the Chinese quarrel. No less than 6 candidates have their bills out already in Lambeth, for the forthcoming election, but none of them are worth anything.

15. Sunday. Went to Maze Pond in morning and evening. A student in morning and Dr Angus in evening. We were favoured in the morning with a tremendous storm of hail snow and rain, which was very severe for a few hours. In the evening about 8 o'clock a fire broke out in our friend Henry Doulton's pottery, which destroyed a great deal of property before it was extinguished. It created considerable excitement in the neighbourhood from the great bell of Hodges' distillery being tolled for 10 minutes and guns were fired. He was I believe insured, so that he will lose little, if anything, from it.

16. Went on with map and for ½ an hour to Mr Leigh's sale. The books sold very badly considering their condition and splendid bindings and the prints etc rather so. For instance 4 vols of Lodge's portraits, which he had paid 120£ for, only brought 36£. Nash's mansions (four series) he paid 40 guineas, only brought 12 guineas. His Britton's Cathedrals and his Britton's antiquities however brought about 28£s.

17. Went on with map and to Mr Leigh's sale. Amongst the best works sold today was Roberts' Holy Land, Egypt and Nubia, a splendid original subscribers (and complete) copy, which brought 58£. There was rather a run after Turner's rivers of France (proofs) which was knocked down at £8 10$^s$. Today's and yesterday's sale brought each I think about 400£s. We bought only 9 books, among which my father got a very choice copy of Rogers' celebrated edition of his Italy and other poems (proofs) for the small sum of 29 shillings. The more recently published books such as Macaulay's history and Mahon ditto brought almost their full value, several times being sold above the trade prices..

18. Went on with map, cut up wood etc and began a coat of arms. Fine. The third and concluding portion of Mr Leigh's books were sold today and brought about 150£.

The Arctic explorer, Dr Kane (who has written a book which I am now reading) has unfortunately just died at Havannah. He was but 34 years old. This book, which gives an account of his second and last voyage in search of Sir J. Franklin, is exceedingly interesting as it describes a portion of Greenland which has never before been visited by any except the natives and by them but very rarely. He was a most indefatigable and gallant young man, and his loss is very much to be deplored.

19. Went on with map, to Gibson's, and finished coat of arms. No news. Showery and warm.

20. Went on with map etc. Fine. No news.

21. Finished map and began scene in Polar Regions, cut up wood etc. Very cold, the wind having shifted from S.W. to E. There are but three candidates for the election in Lambeth. They are, W Williams and WA Wilkinson (the present members) and Mr Rupell, a very wealthy young spooney.

22. Sunday. Went to Maze Pond in morning and evening. Heard a muff from Sydenham preach both times. Snowing. Very cold. I ought to have mentioned yesterday, but forgot (which shows how much I think of it) that my cousin John (my uncle Ebenezer's son) eloped the day before yesterday with a certain Miss Hewitt whom he became spooney on. (Let it be known that he is just 18, an apprentice to wood engraving, not yet out of his time.) He had all last week previous to it staid away from business on the plea of illness, which I believe was fudge, but on Friday morning came saying that although too ill to work, he thought that he might make himself useful in going about. So my father sent him with a message or parcel to one of our draughtsmen (Mr Skill). The morning went by – afternoon – evening - no John. Enquiries made, he is not found, but towards the end of the evening a little boy comes with a little note, which says that "he supposes his father will be very angry, and perhaps he deserves it (the sly dog), but he is very sorry (and won't do so again, etc), begs forgiveness and all that sort of thing, but does not tell where he is. He is, however, kind enough to say that he will give his parents an opportunity of writing to him in a week's time (how very kind). The commotion which this has produced among his relatives is, as it is said, more easily imagined than described. His father (my uncle) a screwish man, talks about duty, and although as he says he feels strongly in his miserable condition, yet he will never let that interfere with the proper course of conduct that ought to be pursued towards him, viz, sending him no supplies. The female part, talk about his cruelty to his maternal relation, who is subject to apoplexy. I do nothing but laugh!

23. Went on with iceberg, went to Mudie's etc. Very cold, slightly snowing.

24. Finished iceberg, touched up map, put a window in a church of Prior's etc. Rainy. The elections in Lambeth come off on Saturday next. Of the 3 now trying, I should say that Roupell is certain to be one of the selected

ones; the rejected one will be one of the two present members, (Williams and Wilkinson) it is difficult to guess which.

25. Went to Clay's, drew several diagrams (moon), made addition to map etc. Rainy. We had Mr Skelton in evening and to supper. He is brother in law to the president of the Royal Academy (Sir C. Eastlake), and has been travelling lately for many years on the Continent, and is therefore a capital talker, full of anecdote and very vivacious. He said that when he married Eastlake's sister, he expected to have a free entrée into his (Eastlake's) studio, but in that he was disappointed, for here the great painters keep their studios as close as the French ones do open.

26. Began drawing an ice-raft, arranged Fireside tales (2nd series) got out a set of plates to be coloured, cut up wood etc. Fine. Roupell has now made certain of being elected for Lambeth and he has addressed a circular to all the inhabitants to that effect. The poll takes place next Monday.

27. Went to Mr Cox's, finished ice raft etc. The elections are proceeding. There has been a society formed to try and keep Lord John Russell out of the representation of the City, but the little humbug is expected to get in nevertheless. Smith, the lessee of Drury Lane Theatre, is up for Bedford!!!

28. Cut up lot of wood, began a chapel in West Indies etc. Fine. Ernest Jones the Chartist put up for Nottingham, but has not got in, although he got more than 500 votes. Lord John is in for the City, in conjunction with Rothschild, Duke and Crawford. The Lambeth election comes off on Monday next.

29. Sunday. Went to Maze Pond in morning and evening. Mr Kirkland of Canterbury preached both times. We had him home to dinner and tea. The number of votes for the four City representatives were pretty equally divided; all of them, the unsuccessful one included, being over 6000 and under 7000. In Southwark as in Lambeth there are 3 trying, the 2 old ones Pellatt and Sir C. Napier and a new one, a lawyer, Locke by name. Fine.

30. Went on with West Indian chapel etc. Today the elections came off in Lambeth and Southwark and a rare fuss they made. Here Mr Roupell came off very triumphantly, polling the enormous number of 9066 votes, a number rarely attained anywhere. Williams the second member (now) obtained 7300 and odd votes, Wilkinson (unsuccessful) 3100. In Southwark the result was as expected, Sir C. Napier obtaining 4100, Locke 3600 and Pellatt (unsuccessful) 2500. The elections have in various parts been decided and have turned out many members well known in the House, viz. Sir W. Clay (the Church rate abolition man) Bright, Cobden, Layard and others. Bright and Cobden are, in my estimation, no loss at all.

31. Drew Esquimaux knife, cut up wood, went errands, named blocks etc. Rainy. There has been a frightful railway accident in Canada, in which a train ran off the rails, went over a bridge on to a frozen canal below, the engine broke through the ice and upward of 40 were killed.

**APRIL** 1st. Drew Arctic gloves and went errands etc. Darby's, the firework makers in Regent St, was destroyed (for about the fourth time) by fire last night, or rather this morning.

2. Drew Fox trap, cut up wood, went to Mr Skelton's etc. My father in evening at conversazione and my mother at Peckham.

3. Went on with W.I. chapel. My brother Fred is gone to Caterham, a newly-discovered part of the world within 18 miles of London. It is supposed to be very beautiful about those parts. Very rainy.

4. Went on with chapel, errands etc. Rainy.

5. Sunday. Went to Maze Pond in morning and evening. Mr Kirkland preached both times. Rainy.

6. Went on with chapel, read book for places, cut up wood etc. Fine.

7. Went to Gibson's and Clay's, cut up a great deal of wood etc, went on with chapel. Lord R. Grosvenor and Hanbury have just been elected for Middlesex in opposition to Viscount Chelsea. Lord Elgin has gone out to China as plenipotentiary there, to settle our quarrel. The Emperor of China appears also to be amicably disposed.

8. Began Basaltic Rocks, cut up wood, went errands etc. Fine. In evening I went to Mr Sandall's. Next Friday (Good Friday) I go most likely to Hastings.

9. Finished Basaltic rocks, cut up wood, altered block of Prior's etc. Fine.

10. Good Friday. Went to Hastings and back. Was not so pleased with Hastings as I ought to have been; but I have for an excuse, a bad headache and the burning sun. The view however from Fairlight I thought charming. I saw from it to Beachy Head on one side and beyond Dungeness on the other. The sea was perfectly still and looked very nice, but with Hastings itself, I must say that I was disappointed. Splendid day.

11. Went to Morbey's in Bishopsgate St and to Miller's at Islington etc, went on with chapel. Rainy.

12. Sunday. Went to Maze Pond in morning and evening. Mr Stalker preached both times, and both were very good sermons. Showery.

13. Finished chapel, went errands, planed up wood, pasted backs of pictures, cleaned glasses etc. Very rainy and snowing.

14. Rubbed up picture frame, cut up wood etc, began a diagram of coast of Norway, went to New Water Colour Society etc. My father sent his pictures (8 in number) to his exhibition today. Four of them are already sold.

15. Finished diagram and began another, arranged cuts, went errands etc. Yesterday afternoon at a ¼ to 2 o'clock another princess (the 9th child) was born to the nation. Expense! Expense!! Expense!!!

16. Went to Mr Brierly's (the artist who went to the Baltic to sketch during the war for the Illustrated London News) to Mr Skill's, and Skelton's, cut up wood, began some music. Rainy. My mother's birthday. She went to the Crystal Palace.

17. Finished 'music' and went to Mrs Gould's etc. Fine.

18. Went to Mr Wolff's and Skill's, traced a drawing of Dr Livingstone's etc. In afternoon went to Richmond and rowed to Kingston where had tea and returned – all serene – splendid day – enjoyed myself.

19. Sunday. Went to Maze Pond in morning and evening. Mr Williams of Accrington preached both times. Beautiful day.

20. Finished Coast of Norway and began an Esquimaux baby sledge. Very fine day.

21. Went to Mrs Gould's, on with 'baby sledge' etc. Very fine.

22. Went errands, also to Messrs Skill's and Wolff's, marked out wood, finished 'baby sledge', altered a diagram of Gibson's for Lord Dufferin etc etc. Rainy. Today was touching day at my father's gallery; he is pretty well satisfied with his hanging (as indeed he should be), 4 out of his 8 being on the line. This morning between 3 and 8 our friend Stephen Green's pottery was almost entirely destroyed by fire. He is a remarkably easy man, disliking the trouble of thinking excessively. He has said when people have waited on him for donations, 'what am I to give? I would rather give 5, 10 or 20£ rather than have to think what I have to give.' He will thus of course dislike the fire very much, not so much from the pecuniary loss, but from its trouble.

23. Went to Wolff's, Read's, Cox's and Weedon's, cut up 14 pieces of wood and began an arctic sledge. Dull.

24. My father's 44th birthday. My mother went to Mrs Gale's. Went on with arctic sledge etc. Very cold and smart showers of hail, all hail!

25. Cut up wood, went errands, went on with 'sledge' etc. Fine. In evening I tumbled flat on the pavement, scratched my hands and hurt my left knee considerably. Today was the private view at my father's gallery. He has now sold 5 out of his 8 but the 3 remaining are his largest ones. It was not thought a good day for selling.

26. Sunday. Went to Maze Pond in morning and evening, Mr Williams preached both times. Fine. My brother Henry's 12th birthday.

27. Finished sledge and began group of Esquimaux, cut up wood etc. My 17th birthday is today. Dull.

28. Went to Wells', Weedon's, Skelton's and Wolff's, cut up wood, dusted and arranged books and papers etc. Fine.

29. Drew some Egyptian diagrams, began a block of snakes, cut up wood, etc. Fine. The Chinese apparently are greatly excited about the present war. In Australia, outbreaks have been feared, although nothing of consequence has taken place, but at Sarawak, in Borneo, the kingdom of Rajah Brookes, an insurrection broke out and spread with the rapidity of a whirlwind, he had to flee for his life, and only saved it by swimming across a creek. He (the Rajah) however returned reinforced by a steamer and he soon suppressed the riots. He took for several days to slaughtering the Chinese, and when he had killed 3000, he thought he had done enough, so left off. Order is now restored. The Rajah is to be, and is, greatly praised for his promptitude and the vigour with which he acted; had he been less quick, he might not now have been Rajah of Sarawak.

30. Drew diagram, cut up wood and finished 'snakes.' Fine, slight showers of rain. I have commenced designing a new chapel for my uncle Woods at Swaffham, in the Italian style. I am very limited however in expense.

1. **May**. Improved snakes, went on with Esquimaux etc. Fine.

2. Went to Skelton's and on with Esquimaux. Fine and hot.

3. Sunday. Went to Maze Pond in morning and evening. Mr Malcolm of Aberdeen (late of) preached. He is now the man that is expected to be hooked. The fault I have to find with him is that he is too weak, but that is not his fault.

4. Cut up wood, wrote letters and began a silver claret jug, richly chased etc. Very fine and cool.

5. Cut up wood, went on with Claret jug etc etc. Fine. At the Lund hill colliery, where the explosion took place 2 or 3 months back, resulting in the deaths of 70 or 80 men, they let in water to put out the fire and have now just finished pumping it out again, and commenced clearing the pit. They have as yet only recovered 22 of the bodies, most of which were unrecognizable from mutilation and putrefaction.

6. Went to Aske's, post etc, cut up wood, and finished claret jug etc. Last night my father was elected a full member of New Water Colour Society (he was only an associate before) which will allow him to send as many pictures as he likes to the exhibition and he will only have to pay 5 per cent instead of 10 as before. Last Monday the Royal Academy Exhibition was opened, and from all accounts it appears to be a better exhibition than usual, one of the reasons being that nearly all the Academicians have contributed something. Yesterday the Great Art Treasures Exhibition at Manchester was opened by Prince Albert, with considerable pomp. The value of the property in that building is estimated at 4 millions sterling, or more than double the value of articles in the '51 show.

7. Went to Murray's, began an Egyptian drawing, and traced two drawings of Captain Need R.N. Last week I forgot to mention that the Duchess of Gloucester died in her 82$^{nd}$ year, being the last of the children of George 3$^{rd}$. My father and Fred went to the last meeting (this season) of the Artists and Amateurs Conversazione at Willis' Rooms.

8. Went out, cut up wood, finished Egyptian drawing, traced drawings etc etc. Fine. The bread which the Chinese endeavoured to poison the foreigners with at Canton, has arrived in England, been analysed, and found to contain considerably more arsenic than is sufficient to kill human beings. So much for John Chinaman.

9. Went to Murray's, traced drawings, went on with Esquimaux etc. Rainy. Had the pleasure to hear the voice of Big Ben today, for the first time, as I was crossing the parade ground, St James's Park. At that distance it sounded tremulous, not decided, but when I went afterwards close to it, that was lost and it then appeared like the roaring of lions. I was unfortunate enough today to receive a letter informing me that the people at Swaffham were rather partial to the elevation I have sent them for a chapel, which will necessitate my sending plans and sections also – all gratis.

10. Sunday. Went to Maze Pond in morning and evening. Mr Malcolm preached both times. Rainy. Wind – S. East.

11. Went to Aske's etc, cut up wood, went on with Esquimaux etc. Fine, but very oppressive, and lightening considerably. In evening I went to cricket to Archbishop's grounds. They have now recovered 82 bodies at the Lundhill colliery, most of whom must have been killed instantaneously.

END OF BOOK 3

Commencing Sept 29 1856 and finishing up to May 11$^{th}$ 1857 inclusive.

Diary. **BOOK 4.**
Commencing May 12 1857. Ending December 31 1857.

12. Went on with Esquimaux, to Aske's etc. Fine day.
13. Began a 'Lapp lady' (sketched by Lord Dufferin), cut up wood etc. The Grand Duke Constantine's visit to England is now fixed, and from all accounts, the Parisians will not be at all sorry to be rid of him, although through politeness he is fêted etc. General Todleben who defended Sebastopol so well for them, but so badly for us, is along with him, but will not I think pay his devotions here until September. The Royal Engineers are going to give him a banquet!! Fine.
14. Finished Lapp lady, went on with Esquimaux, went to Aske's, Sunter's etc. A storm which 2 days ago threatened us in London, passed over to Reading where its effects were severely felt. It damaged a church steeple, set fire to Railway station etc. Went in evening to cricket at Archbishop's grounds.
15. Went on with Jamaica chapel, cut up wood etc. In afternoon I went to Mortlake and after exploring Richmond Park, I arrived at Kingston and returned through Ham and Richmond to Barnes, tiring myself pretty well. Several of the deacons met tonight at our house, taking tea and supper.
16. Was walking about nearly all day, for I went twice to Mr Underhill's (the secretary of the Baptist Missionary Society, who has just returned from India after a 3 years absence, bringing with him a considerable number of photographs of the most celebrated and curious buildings in that country) and also to the British Museum. While there I looked into the new reading room, just completed and open this week to the public. I almost expected to be disappointed with it, from the doubtful praises of the press, but I came away astonished, amazed and delighted. It is quite sufficient to make the name of Sidney Smirke live for ever, if he died tomorrow.
17. Sunday. Went to Maze Pond in morning and evening. Mr Malcolm preached both times. Very fine, but although very pleasant for us, the agriculturalists are crying out for rain!
18. Went to Clay's, my uncle's, marked names on blocks and cut up wood. Went in evening to cricket at Archbishop's grounds. Fine.
19. Began a palace at Lucknow, finished chapel at Jamaica and cut up wood. Almost all the bodies of the unfortunates who were killed at Lund hill colliery explosion have been recovered and interred. It has been a most disagreeable and almost unnecessary duty that the jury have had to perform, in examining each body, and they are extremely glad that their labours are almost over.
20. Went on with palace. The marriage of the Princess Royal is now settled. Her lover is (as every one knows) Prince William, heir apparent to the throne of Prussia. The Queen has given notice to the Houses and they have pleased to acquiesce in the choice. They did not however, agree so readily to the amount and manner of giving her dowry. Long and sharp have been the discussions on the subject, some say that it is extremely undignified for her to receive a pension and that her husband must be but a poor spirited fellow if he would allow her to receive one. But that party I

think thinks more of the cost, than of lowering her dignity. It would never-theless be much agreeable to the nation to pay it at once and have done with it, but that probably will not be the way of settling the account.

21. Went on with Palace and to Miller's at Holloway etc. Fine.

22. Went on with Palace, cut up wood and to Miller's again. Lord Camp-bell has just been commenting on the sale of villainous publications (in the House of Lords). He said among other things, "that your Lordships are much troubling yourselves about the sale of poisons, I wish to bring to your notice, poisons of another kind. I mean, moral poisons." He then went into detail, bringing forward cases which he had punished lately and wanted to get additional powers for punishing such offences, but was unfortunately not able. He is much to be commended for his endeavour although unsuc-cessful, for some of these papers are abominable, one for instance, 'Paul Pry', is a perfect sink of iniquity.

23. Went on with Palace, went to Mr Murray's, Dr Livingstone's etc. We are still engaged on the latter's work, it seems as if we shall never be rid of it. It is a good job nevertheless. I have just commenced taking in Turner's 'Liber Studiorum' which is republishing in $10^s$ $6^d$ parts. Fine.

24. Sunday. Went to Maze Pond in morning and evening. Mr Malcolm preached both times. It is quite amusing to view the way in which the deacons of our chapel act. They (that is to say most of them) do not wish Mr M to come as pastor and therefore they talk somewhat in this style. Mr M is a very good, a very worthy man, but _ _ _ _ _, I admire him exceed-ingly, and _ _ _ _. They are afraid if there is only a decent majority in votes for him, that he will accept the place. And not unnatural either when a man has travelled 1700 miles to preach to you. Rainy.

25. Went to Rowney's etc, and drew diagrams (large) on paper. Mr Malcolm was elected tonight to the office of pastor of Maze Pond (if he will accept) by a majority of 29, the numbers being, 39 against him and 68 for him. Thus but a very small proportion of the members voted at all. Heavy showers of rain are falling, which all thankfully accept with grati-tude, for if it had not fallen, instead of the promise of a fine fruit year and an abundant harvest, we should most probably have suffered severely from scarcity of food.

26. Finished large diagrams, cut up wood etc. Tonight there are many illu-minations up in different parts of the town, as the Queen's birthday is kept today. Today was also the first day of the Epsom races. Very fine day, in the evening there was a most gorgeous sunset, the suns rays striking the edges of the numerous clouds made it very splendid.

27. Began Mr Booth's new chapel at Birkenhead, cut up wood etc.

28. Went on with chapel, cut up wood and drew more diagrams. Yesterday was the Derby day at Epsom; the betting circles were quite at fault with regard to the winner, none of the favourites being among the first three horses. The winner was 'Blink Bonny' who came in cleverly winning by a head. She was rode by Charlton.

29. Drew large diagrams. Exceedingly beautiful weather, but farmers and others are crying out for want of rain. All cannot be pleased at once. Today was Oaks day at Epsom, when 'Blink Bonny' was again victorious, as was

Ill.2 Village scene, engraved by Whympers' for Livingstone's *Missionary Travels and researches in South Africa*. Proof page with Livingstone's annotations. Reproduced with the permission of the Trustees of the National Library of Scotland.

indeed expected directly it was known she would run again, which thinned the attendance very much.

30. Drew diagrams, cut up wood etc. Fine. Another colliery explosion (in Wales I think), 12 people killed.

31. Sunday. Went to Maze Pond in morning and evening. A student preached both times.[38] Very fine. Glorious weather for us.

1 **June**. Whit Monday. Finished large diagram, went on with Mr Booth's chapel etc. Fine. The Grand Duke Constantine is come and gone. A good job, very few <u>wished</u> to see him. He only visited Osborne on Saturday and departed for Calais on Sunday (yesterday).

2. Finished B's chapel, cut up wood etc. Fine. 14 servants have just been drowned crossing the Lancaster sands, they got loitering about, drinking etc and the consequence was that they were caught by the tide and not one escaped. Went in evening to Mr Sandall's.

3. Altered and touched up B's chapel, also outlined a house at Canterbury. Fine. Occasional showers.

4. Went on with house in Canterbury, cut up wood and began a Catholic diagram. In evening I went to a sort of soirée at Mr Beddome's, met a good

38. Giles Hester (MPAB; see Appendix 1).

many friends (mostly female), and felt considerably awkward, not being used to female society.

5. Put in figures to chapel, cut up wood, began a diagram of phases of moon. The Eton Regatta came off yesterday with great éclat, the Prince of Wales being in attendance.

6. Went errands, on with moon diagram etc etc. In afternoon I went to Westminster Hall to finish my inspection of the competition designs for Foreign and War offices. It was my last chance for this evening they closed. While in the Hall I thought I might as well finish up with going for the first time to the Court of Queen's Bench. It must be hard work indeed for the judges to sit so long listening to dull barristers, if what I heard were a fair specimen. How I should like to be a lawyer, but I suppose I never shall. I fancy myself just suited to it and it just suited to me. We shall see. At last we have rain and promise of abundance of it.

7. Sunday. Went to Maze Pond in morning and evening. Mr Malcolm preached both times. Today he commenced his ministry with us. Pleasant showers.

8. Went to Rivington, cut up wood, finished Catholic diagram etc. Very heavy rain during the day and very nice sunshine, in fact as charming weather as can be imagined. The British Bank swindle having been fully exposed and great numbers crying for justice to be performed on the directors of it, the Attorney General has been compelled, if it is not a voluntary act, to proceed against them. Warrants of arrest have accordingly been issued and some have been captured and others have fled, among whom is the splendidly endowed (in the faculty line I mean) member for Tewkesbury, Humphrey Brown by name. 200£ is offered for him and all London is placarded with his name and description.

9. Finished moon diagram and went on with palace at Lucknow. Very wet.

10. Went on with palace and out errands. Slight showers, to refresh the flowers. As I was about to get in bed last night, my mother called and showed me what at first was not but afterwards became a very large conflagration. I find that it was the large goods station of the London and North Western Railway Co at Camden Town, belonging to Messrs Pickford. It must have been very fearful near, for to us at nearly 5 miles distance it seemed very great. There were more than one hundred horses in the stable, which fortunately a few men were able to turn out in time to save them, and they set off towards Hampstead, nearly killing an inspector of police who was coming in an opposite direction. The damage done (or rather the loss) is very variously estimated from 50,000£ to 250,000.

11. Went to Clowes, on with palace, cut up wood, and began some large houses. Went to cricket in evening at Archbishop's ground. Today there is a match on at the Oval, Surrey v. Kent; Kent is getting a confounded licking, of course. It will be finished I expect tomorrow.[39]

12. Went to Clowes, Joy's etc, on with houses etc. In afternoon went by rail to Richmond, walked through park to Kingston, took a boat, had 2 hours

---

39. Surrey won by seven wickets.

rowing and returned through Ham Common. Very fine. British Bank Humphrey Brown is captured, hurrah!! Also several other of the directors of that swindle. They will be prosecuted by the Attorney General, criminally.

13. Finished houses, went errands and on with Temple. Very fine, too good to last.

14. Sunday. Went to Maze Pond in morning and evening. Mr Malcolm preached both times. Fine. The Camden station that was burnt last week, was I find insured for 55,000£ so that the loss on Messrs Baxendale (Messrs Pickford nominally) will be but small if anything.

15. Put figures in block, went on with palace etc. Fine. Today is the first day of the great Handel festival at the Crystal Palace. The oratorio of 'Messiah' is to be performed, or rather I suppose has been performed by 3000 people, which is the largest number that have been congregated in England as yet and I think indeed in the world.

16. Altered and improved a drawing of 'Tuileries,' cut up wood etc. The first day of the festival (I take the account of the Times) went off most gloriously. The chorus were magnificent, the Hallelujiah being heard ½ a mile. How I should like to go, but it is too expensive. My uncle Woods paid us a short visit today.

17. Finished 'Tuileries,' on with palace etc. Very fine. Strawberries are beginning to get about, rather cheap in price. In afternoon went to cricket at Oval. The Queen went to the Crystal Palace today to Handel festival.

18. Drew an ancient gallery, cut up several pieces of wood and went on with Temple, altered antediluvian animal etc. Fine. A grand match at Oval today and tomorrow between Surrey and Cambridge.[40] Yesterday's performance at the Crystal Palace went off gloriously, and it is said that the Queen and Royal Family intend going tomorrow again.

19. Cut up wood, went errands, on with Temple and began the celebrated Taj Mahal at Agra built of white marble. Fine, but very hot and close, appearance of a storm.

20. Went to Miller's, Gosse's and Mudie's, cut up good deal of wood, went on with Taj Mahal etc. Last night or I think indeed this morning, we were visited by a rather severe thunderstorm and the rain fell in torrents. It beat against our front windows so, that they seemed as if they <u>must</u> come in, but they did not. It made our road look like a river which had overflowed its banks. There is now every appearance of a repetition of the above sort of thing again tonight.

21. Sunday. Went to Maze Pond in morning and evening. Mr Malcolm preached too [2] long sermons. Fine, sky heavy.

22. Errands, cut up 9 pieces of wood, read 3 books, went on with Taj Mahal. In evening to cricket at Archbishop's grounds. Fine, and very hot.

23. Went to Gibson's and Mackness, cut up wood etc, went on with Taj Mahal. Very fine.

---

40. Surrey beat Cambridgeshire by 36 runs.

24. Went errands, cut up lot of wood, went on with Taj Mahal etc. Fine and hot. The Manchester Art Treasure Exhibition is supposed to be now in full swing, but the numbers that visit it, I think do not come up to those anticipated. They rarely reach 12,000 in one day.[41] There have lately and indeed for a long time, been great complaints made as to the accommodation at the Queen's drawing rooms, the ladies especially have suffered from it; they have been penned in like sheep, kept waiting for hours and frequently have had to pass through the royal presence with dilapidated dresses (skirts torn off) and occasionally with bruised faces and black eyes. There was today in 'Times' an amusing description of the experiences of a lady of rank who was knocked down at the last one. The nuisance has at last been remedied.

25. Cut up wood, went to Bentley's and on with Taj Mahal. Fine, exceedingly. My father went sketching at Windsor with Miss Corderoy, 2 Miss Hepburns and Master ditto. Dr Fergusson and Mr Collambell held a consultation today on my mother. In evening I went to Oval to see the end of 1st day's play of Rugby School v. Marlborough College. The former will beat the latter, (who in my opinion are muffs) in one innings easily. Rugby boys fielded beautifully, considering what a frightful hot day we have had and that they had been playing 7 or 8 hours.

26. Went to Bentley's, cut up lot of wood, went on with Taj Mahal etc. Very hot.

27. On with Taj Mahal etc. In afternoon played a match at Oval. Yesterday the Victoria order of valour, manufactured out of Russian cannon, was distributed to 61 brave men in Hyde Park by Her Majesty in the presence of thousands of spectators, (galleries were erected for more than 7000). It is given for distinguished acts of bravery (at present in time of war) and will thus be open to merit and not to humbugs, as most of those decorations are. The great pity is that those who have most honourably earned this cross, are where they cannot receive it - in the grave.

28. Sunday. Went in morning to Boro Road Chapel, and heard Mr Harcourt for the first time. A man of moderate powers only but has the knack of commanding attention. In evening to Maze Pond. Mr Malcolm preached. Thermometer 85° indoors.

29. Went errands, on with Taj Mahal etc. Cloudy, looks like rain, of which we should be very glad. Thermometer is nevertheless 10° less than it was yesterday. Last night about ½ past 10, one of the most dreadful railway accidents that has happened near London took place. It was on the North Kent line near the Lewisham Station. A fast train from Strood had pulled up there on account of danger being signalled in front of them, and while waiting there, was ran into by a train which left only a ¼ of an hour after them. It totally destroyed the last 3rd class carriage, smashing the passengers in a most awful manner. Accounts vary as to number killed from 3 to 12 and of the wounded from 30 to 40.

41. Thomas Cook later ran special excursions, and the exhibition received one and a half million visitors.

In this morning's 'Times' there is a very long and for us very sad account of the mutiny in our Indian army. It has arisen apparently from a stupid quarrel regarding their cartridges, the manner of making and using which interfered with their religious scruples. This quarrel might no doubt by the exercise of a little common sense have been avoided. But such was not the policy of our Indian rulers and the spark broke out into a flame. I think at Meerut they first mutinied and those at Delhi quickly followed their example. The latter ones perpetrated a number of terrible crimes, murdering about 40 Europeans including some women and children which even insurgents might have respected. They will no doubt pay dearly for those crimes.

30. Finished Taj Mahal, cut up wood, made out list and began diagram of Egyptian stamp. Showery. The Times of this morning contained further particulars respecting the frightful accident on the North Kent. There are 11 killed on the spot or since died and about 35 seriously damaged. There is going to be, or is I think begun, an inquiry into the cause of it, but it will no doubt end in the usual unsatisfactory manner that all such inquiries do. Eyewitnesses state that most of those who were killed would have been saved if proper means had been promptly undertaken to rescue them from the frightful situation in which many were placed. One for instance, that they dared not move for fear of crushing him in the ruins of the carriage, was hanging by a thin strip of flesh which was all that connected his leg to his body, with his head downwards. Happily for him he died quickly.

**July** 1. Finished Egyptian stamp, read two tales, cut up wood and began ancient wood cut figures. Very wet and in morning was favoured with a sharp thunderstorm, perhaps a remnant of that one which astonished Liverpool yesterday. The Queen and family are gone to Manchester; they take up their abode at the Earl of Ellesmere's during their stay there. The enquiry into the causes of the accident on the North Kent Railway still goes on, and from it there appears to have been gross negligence of wilful carelessness on the part of the signalman at Blackheath (Griffiths) who reported having received a signal from Lewisham that the line was clear when none had been sent, and on the part of the stoker and engine driver of the train (9.30) who passed the guard of the 9.15 train holding up a red light and also drove past the distant signal post of the Lewisham station, which was at "danger." All three of them are in custody and have to take their trial for manslaughter.

2. Went on with wood-cut figures, etc. Dull and heavy sky. In afternoon I went to Royal Academy and was much pleased with Stanfield's sea pieces and landscapes and also with Halines and a few others, but with others, especially the Academicians, oh! - Millais' insanities, Maclise's crudities and cut out paper figures and some bad ones of Leslie, Redgrave (I think Ward also) Witherington, etc. I was horrified and disgusted. To finish up the afternoon I went to the Oval and saw part of a grand cricket match between the Gentlemen and the Players of England. The former will be beaten.[42]

3. Went on with woodcut figures, cut up wood etc. To cricket in evening at Archbishop's grounds. Last night in the House in the course of a debate on

voting money to British Museum, Lord J. Russell casually mentioned something about its being opened on Sunday, another took it up, another, another, until at last it became quite a furious skirmish, but the whole matter soon afterwards subsided and was forgotten. But this shows how strong the parties are on each side of the subject.

4. Went to Cowderay's, [Corderoy] cut up wood, and on with ancient woodcut, found cuts places in Hannah Lavender etc. The Belgian band of the "Guides" has arrived in London and is showing off at the Surrey music hall, and is creating considerable sensation.

5. Sunday. Went to Maze Pond in morning and evening. Mr Malcolm preached both times. He does not <u>draw</u>, nor do I think that he will; his usual effect on me is to make me slumber sweetly, at least in regard to all that he is saying. Rainy, sky stormy.

6. Cut up wood, began a ship at sea and went to Mr W. Goodall's, Skelton's etc. Very rainy. Mr Beddome, senior deacon of our chapel finished the evening with us. In today's paper there was an account of a very bad accident, arising from the breaking down of a bridge of boats, which was built to connect an island with the river bank at Shrewsbury. It was on the occasion of a fête of Jullien's and the people rushing away broke it down and 10 are known to be drowned (some more are also thought to be so) and many have dangerous fractures of limbs! Alas!

7. Finished ship at sea and began a funeral scene, etc. Fine. To cricket at Archbishop's ground in evening.

8. Finished funeral scene and began drawing a death bed scene, cut up wood, to uncle's etc. Fine. My father went sketching in Richmond Park, my mother visiting in Clapham Park and environs, Fred went to Crystal Palace with Uncle John who came up for a holiday and I went to help to conclude a cricket match begun last Saturday week.

9. Went with Uncle John to Euston Square before breakfast, to cricket at A.G. in evening. Finished death bed scene, went errands etc. Fine. There has been lately tried at Glasgow a rather celebrated poisoning case. It was of a young lady poisoning her young man. But after 7 or 8 days' investigation, the jury have acquitted Miss Madeleine Smith. And rightly, too, for as far as I can understand there were no grounds for proceeding against her for murder.

10. Looked out coins, began 2 ditto, went twice to Bucks, Mr Ellis etc. Fine. In afternoon I went to the newly built Educational Museum at Brompton. It is a frightfully ugly place outside, but quite the reverse in. It contains the late gift of Mr Sheepshanks to the nation and many beautiful art objects, architectural casts, models of machinery and is altogether a most interesting place.

11. Went on with coin, met my father at Fenchurch St station, went to Oval etc. Fine. The Lambeth petition against the late election (wishing to set aside Mr Roupell) was brought before the election committee yesterday (first day). By his own admission he had spent 2700£ before the nomina-

42. The Players did indeed win by 10 wickets. The match was completed the following day.

tion day and Williams spent about 760£, but out of the admitted sum he cannot or says it is impossible to account for many large sums being spent in an honest manner. All the evidence as yet is against him and so are the majority of the committee, I think, from the tone of their proceedings. Another woman has died from the effects of the accident on the North Kent Railway (last Sunday week) making twelve in all. My father went to Southend to finish his sketch and Fred to Richmond. A beautiful day.

12. Sunday. Went to Maze Pond in morning and evening. Mr Malcolm preached both times. My father went in evening to Mr Brocks. Very fine. In Essex they have already commenced cutting corn.

13. Finished coin, went out errands, began a plan of a Greek temple, read 'Roughing it in the Bush' for places for cuts etc etc. Still very fine. What a season we have had, and it still looks as if we should have this year. Farmers ought to rejoice, but I suppose they will not.

14. Went to Mr Weir's at Peckham, on with plan of temple, cut up wood etc etc. Fine.

15. Went to Clowes, errands etc, cut up wood, finished plan of temple and went on with coins. Very fine. Played a match at Oval in afternoon.

16. Went to Miller's (Holloway), cut up wood, on with coins etc. Cloudy, looks like rain. The petition against the return of Mr Roupell for Lambeth has been declared frivolous and vexatious (which means that the petitioners are to pay all costs) and Mr Roupell is now fairly fixed in his place in the parliament of the land. In afternoon I went to the Oval, to see a match between my county (Surrey) and Sussex. The play was splendid, but two blunders all the time I was there, one being a caught ball dropped and the other an overthrow. The dashing way in which the Surrey fielded is deserving of the highest praise, Mr F. Miller came out especially brilliant, for besides his beautiful fielding (during which I saw him make a splendid catch at long leg) he in one innings obtained as many runs as the whole of the Sussex men did in two innings, excepting 2. The scores were Miller 64. Sussex, 1st innings 35; 2nd innings 31, total 66. Surrey 1st innings 166, beating Sussex in one innings and 100 runs.

17. Went to my uncle's, cut up lot of wood, went on with coin, began drawing a Hindoo God, which I most certainly shall be exceedingly glad when I have done.

18. Went on with Hindoo God, went to Mr Weir's etc. As fine as ever. Went to Oval to cricket in afternoon.

19. Sunday. Went to Maze Pond morning and evening. Mr Armstrong (an impudent, smeary-faced old ass) preached in the morning, and Mr Watts, an excited, affected young donkey in the evening. Fine, weather oppressive.

20. Went to stables twice, to uncle's etc, cut up wood and went on with Hindoo God. My brother Fred's birthday, 19 years old. He went down per Great Western Railway to see my mother at Burnham. By the bye on that line the other day, the parliamentary ran into the express, or vice versa, no one killed but plenty damaged. On Saturday night and Sunday morning there was a large fire burning in Suffolk St, Boro, some very large workshops and other property were destroyed but too soon.

21. Went to Mr Skelton's, Goodall's, Mudie's etc. Finished Hindoo God. Very heavy rain in evening which will do immense good.

22. Cut up lot of wood, marked out and arranged abundance of ditto, began a large diagram (mechanical) etc. Dull.

23. Went errands, cut up wood, finished large diagram etc. Very fine. In afternoon I went to the Oval to see the annual match between Surrey and Oxfordshire. I only saw their first innings. It was a very good match, but Surrey is too strong in either players or amateurs, to be defeated. This is proved by the fact that out of all the matches they have played this year (and they are numerous) they have in every case been victorious. In the present match, Lockyer made a capital catch from a tip of Hon. W. Fiennes and Mr F. Miller threw up a ball from an enormous distance so beautifully that Hon. C. Leigh had to have 'run out' inscribed after his short score of 9. Stephenson made a fine innings of 73 or just as many as the 10 others put together, their total score being 148 (with byes). Oxford 101.

24. Began some more diagrams, cut up lot of wood, went to Mrs Gould's and Miller's etc. Very fine. The Atlantic submarine telegraph cable is manufactured and coiled in the holds of the Agamemnon (British 91) and the America (U.S.S. frigate) and is quite ready to be laid down. Before the ships set sail however they will make an experiment of laying about 20 miles of it near Sheerness.

25. Went on with diagrams, out errands etc. Fine but showery, the rain is everywhere very much needed, the grass especially is dreadfully parched. Last night I went to see, (although I did not put it down) a fire which broke out on the top floor of the left hand wing of Lambeth workhouse. There were a large number of engines speedily on the spot so that they were able (which is very seldom the case) to confine the fire to a small spot. The paupers were looking out of the windows near it, apparently not very much concerned.

26. Went to Maze Pond in morning and evening. A student preached in former and a West Indian missionary in the latter. Fine, and hot.

27. Went to Castle's and Hoddle's, errands, cut up wood, traced the rescue of a female at Shakespeare cliff, Dover, drew diagram etc. Fine but looks stormy.

28. Drew diagrams etc, went to Gosse's. Rainy early in day but very fine in latter part. In the afternoon I went to Lord's cricket ground and saw the first match that I have seen there viz. All England Eleven v. United All E. E. for the benefit of J. Dean. It is a very good match as the sides are the best that can be chosen, and are pretty even and is therefore exciting. All England kept in the whole day (today) for their second innings, getting the high score of 214, of which R. C. Tinley and A. Diver contributed 46 each and G. Parr 36. The U.A.E.E. have consequently to get 188 in their second innings to beat, as they beat A.E.E. in 1$^{st}$ innings by 27. I do not think they will get it, but they will from 150 to 160. The match is concluded tomorrow.

29. Went to Hoddle's, cut up lot of wood, drew diagrams etc. Fine. No news in particular. A report that the Emperor of the French is assassinated, but is not worthy of credit. By the by I have not mentioned the last conspiracy against his unfortunate life. It was discovered before it was attempted and perhaps before it was formed. But it was a favourable opportunity for him

to arrest some 'mauvais sujets' of his among whom we find the names of Mazzini and Ledru Rollin. I almost wish that he would execute them for they have given the world more than their share of trouble already.

30. Went to Paddington to see my mother, sister and 7 brothers off to Burnham. A peaceful house may be anticipated now. Drew diagrams etc. Fine. In evening went to <u>a sort of a spread</u> (as it is beautifully and elegantly termed in these days) at Mr Probart. Music, singing and feeding and excellent.

31. Went to Leicester Square, drew diagrams etc. The United A.E.E. got beaten at Lords, as I expected but by a much larger number than I expected they would. It was somewhere about 130 runs.[43]

1. **August**. Went to Rowney's, and various other errands, drew diagrams, read tales etc. Fine, almost too fine, for this weather makes one feel so precious weak. It is that if this weather lasts out but a week longer (and there seems every chance of its doing so) that all the harvest, and that a plentiful one, will be gathered in. In afternoon I went to New Water Colour Society Exhibition with Mr Sandall. I was as usual exceedingly pleased with Louis Haghe's pictures, his Italian letter writer of the time is admirable.[44] Mole I also like very much this year and several other artists, but there are many atrocious (shall I call them) pictures which are too bad to be looked at for a moment.

2. Sunday. Went to Maze Pond in morning and evening. Mr Malcolm again both times. Very fine. The latest accounts fix the number of men, women and children massacred at Delhi as 3,000. Alas! Alas! But it is almost deserved, so much has our power in India been abused.

3. Went to Castle's (tailors) and numerous errands, in fact was on my legs all day, helping my father to pack for his journey tomorrow. Was not in bed till past 12 o'clock.

4. My father and Fred went this morning (per North Western Railway) to Manchester, where they will stay a short time and then proceed to Scotland. I went today to Messrs White and Dalton's, Fred Gilbert's at Blackheath, Mr Corderoy's, Gibson's and Clowes. Packed up 6 parcels etc. In afternoon went to Oval to see the second day of Surrey and Sussex v. All England. My prepossessions were in favour of the counties, but when I got there I found they had only 150 in their first innings to All England's 203. Six wickets then fell of the counties (second innings) for about 57, until Lockyer and J. Lillywhite got in together and commenced pulling up the score and made 50 and 42 respectively, neither being out when time was called. This made the backers of the counties look up and restored the feeling in their favour. The game is continued tomorrow.

5. Got out wood for Skill, drew diagram, packed up blocks etc. Today we were favoured (I mean it) with some heavy showers, which after the preceding fine and dry weather, is a perfect Godsend. The rain stopped the

---

43. The United England Eleven were bowled out for fifty four and lost by 133 runs.
44. 'It is a picture with perhaps fewer faults than any other in the room, and one that is not only calculated to attract but to rivet the attention of the spectator.' *The Daily News* (28 April 1857).

match I spoke of yesterday, until 1 o'clock today, when Lockyer and J. Lillywhite again went in, their wickets falling for 62 and 46 respectively. The whole innings amounted to 221. England then went, played well, but Surrey and Sussex played better and got them all out for 59 runs, thus beating them by 110 runs. Hurrah for my native county and next door (although we could have done very well without them).

In India they are now hanging the sepoys in detachments of 12 or so. In Peshawar and other places, they have blown numbers from the barrels of the guns; at the former place they did 40 that way at once. Awful, but righteous. The thermometer is said to have been 110° in the shade last Monday. I know that today, when looking at the match, I thought that my brain would have been dried up so fierce was the sun's heat.

6. Went to Morbey's, the frame makers, cut up wood, drew diagram etc. Today my father leaves Manchester for Lancaster.

7. To Mr Ellis, cut up wood, drew scissors etc. Dull day. To Burnham tomorrow if fine, which I expect it will not be.

8th to 11th inclusive. At Burnham, where through eating too many apples, was violently taken with diarrhoea and was kept abed 2 days. I am now in consequences rather weak in body, especially in the legs, which is the only part that it has disagreeably affected. While at Burnham of course I saw very little of the country, owing to the before mentioned causes and the heavy rains which have lately been refreshing the earth after the long continued drought. Going down I saw Windsor Castle for the first time, but was not delighted with it, which most likely was owing to the unfavourable weather. At Maidenhead I saw the beautiful railway bridge over the Thames, and a very fine specimen of engineering it is. I have not before seen such a fine one and scarcely expect to see a finer.

12. Wrote letters to father and mother (who are more than 400 miles apart), went errands, on with diagrams etc. Fine after a fashion, that is to say very hot but rather dull. Had letter from father, who is now at Edinburgh. He as usual has had wet weather, indeed I think 10 to 1 against his having fine weather would not be a bad bet. He has been to Tantallon Castle (the sight of which I envy him) and is going to Dalkeith, but has not according to himself done much in the sketching way yet.

13. Drew diagrams, cut up wood, attended to general business etc. Fine day but is now (9 o'clock) lightening badly in the west. My uncle in the business is just about as much use as no one, so that now, my father and Fred being away, all the care and responsibility of the business is thrown on me. And very disagreeable I find it, for though I have to act in many things at my own discretion, I do not act as I myself should, but rather as I think others would. If I were left to do entirely as I thought proper, I make but little doubt that I should get on with it both quicker and better. Despatched the engraving of my uncle's (Woods) proposed new chapel at Swaffham to him, and I hope I shall see it no more, for it was no pleasure or pay.[45]

---

45. Nicholas Pevsner describes 'the terrible Baptist church, built in 1858, yellow brick, all round-arched, and with two tall corner towers with Italianate roofs.' *Buildings of England - Norfolk 2: North-West and South* (Harmondsworth: Penguin, 1999), 683. The foundation stone was laid by William Woods on 2 September 1858.

14 to 22. Partly at Burnham near Maidenhead and partly at home, but in consequence being busy in the superlative degree, unable to make any entry. During this time there has been a very large fire in Edinburgh that has turned upwards of 160 persons out of doors. But what effects us more than anything that has happened for years is the death of Mr Cox of the Christian Knowledge Society, who was killed in consequence of getting out of a Great Northern train, while it was still in motion. The wheels passed over his neck and literally cut his head off, severing it entirely from the body. I afterwards found out more particulars, which were as follows. He was going down to Colney Hatch station by an evening train, which instead of stopping at the station as it should, the engine driver took through for the distance of several 100 feet. He then allowed the train to be at rest for a considerable time (long enough to allow several other people to alight safely) and then suddenly reversed the engine and sent the train back to the station. Mr Cox it is believed from being rather short sighted, did not know the train was through the station, or else he would not have got out, but was on the steps when the engine was reversed, and the sudden jerk threw him off the carriage under the wheels, which passed over his eyes, dividing his head. Death was of course instantaneous but it was horrible. What makes the matter worse is that the engine driver actually laughed when Mr Cox went under the wheels, and on being indignantly reproved by a bystander for his carelessness and brutality, I believe swore at him. An inquest was held on Mr Cox when it was found that the station master of Hatfield was, in defiance of the company's rules, riding on the engine and talking to the driver. The jury expressed themselves very strongly on this and on some other things connected with the accident, but the coroner (Mr Wakley) did not agree with them. The family is going to try and get damages out of the Company, but I am afraid it will be without success. If Mr Cox's successor happens to be a very different man to <u>him</u>, it will probably fare hard with us, as we depend mostly on the Christian Knowledge Society's work.

[23-27 not described, nor space left]

28. Drew two diagrams of micrometer article for Encyclopaedia Britannica. The Surrey Gardens Company has come to grief and is in the Bankruptcy Court, which is by the doings of the directors and against the will of the shareholders. It now appears that the concern has never paid (and consequently no dividend of 10 per cent ought to have been paid, that being only a trick to sell the remaining shares) the building (concert hall) is deeply mortgaged and that they are 29,000£s in debt. Of course the shares (no doubt the shareholders congratulate themselves on their being limited) are worth nothing. Mr Jullien is pretty well ruined, having never been paid his salary, in fact it is a difficult job to find out where the money has gone to.

29-31 inclusive at Burnham. On last day went to Stoke Poges, the resting place of the poet Gray.

1. **September** Drew large mechanical diagrams, cut up 10 pieces of wood, went errands etc. Fine but showery, which is an advantage. Macaulay is going to be made a peer; how will Lord Macaulay sound?

2. Went errands, cut up wood, on with diagrams, began Oxford Cathedral for Society Almanack. Very wet. We are threatened with locusts, that plague of the East. My brother Alfred found one of the first that have been seen over here and forwarded it to Dr Gray at the British Museum, who returned a polite note. Many others have been found in different parts, several being in London.

3. Went to Paddington station to fetch the family home from Burnham, on with diagrams, and on with Oxford cathedral. Very wet. The latest news from India seems anything but satisfactory. The Sepoys have all now mutinied almost without exception, and none of them can be reckoned on to fight against the others. The Hindus still massacre Europeans wherever they find them.

4. Finished Oxford Cathedral, drew diagrams, etc. The latter is the most abominably uninteresting job that can be imagined. They are for lecturers, and as they are to be seen at a distance, the lines have to be made a sixth of an inch in thickness, doing which on boxwood is very tedious and disagreeable.

5. Went to Clay's, on with diagrams etc.

6. Sunday. Went to Maze Pond in morning and evening. Mr Malcolm preached flat sermons both times. The congregation sensibly (insensibly) diminishes, and I have no doubt that he will find his income do the same. Showery.

7. At the Crystal Palace, Sydenham, being the first shilling day on which the great fountains and the whole system of waterworks have played, I had determined that I would wait until such a day arrived, as I did not see the use of paying more for it. There were a great many people there, although not altogether of the choicest sort, but I was much pleased with what I saw, although it was so far windy that the fountains at no part of the time could be seen to much advantage. I admired the basket work surrounding them and some of the smaller ones most.

8. Drew diagrams, cut up wood etc. Very heavy rains.

9. Went errands, cut up wood, drew diagrams etc. Very wet. In this morning's 'Times' there was a very interesting account of a Mormon meeting on last Monday in Westminster (one of their conferences in fact) at which the proceedings were of an extraordinary and unprecedented kind. The elders made some peculiar statements, one of the favourites seemed to be that they (the elders) felt first rate. One from Reading told them that in his district, out of his parishioners 400 in number, over 250 were paupers!!

10. Drew diagrams, cut up wood etc Very wet. The North played the South at cricket at the Trent Bridge ground, Nottingham, on the first three days of the week. It was not finished, but the result if it had been played out, would probably have been the same as it usually is, viz. South victors, as they (the South) had only about 20 runs to get to beat and 2 wickets to fall, with Lockyer well in for 36 runs.[46]

[no entry for 11]

---

46. The South of England required fifteen more runs to win, when the game was drawn.

12. Drew diagrams, went to Mr Skelton's etc. Showery. The convict ship Nile has just left England for Australia; she takes with her a most valuable lot of articles, in the persons of Messrs Paul, Strahan, Bates, Agar, Saward, Robson and Redpath. Take care of them, cherish them by all means, if not nearly related by blood to each other, nobody can say that they are not in deeds. Seven greater robbers and general villains, it would be hard to find. There are large subscriptions being raised in different parts, for the aid of those who have suffered by the Indian rebellion. The Emperor of the French has just forwarded 1000£ from himself for it, while the names of the Queen and Prince Albert do not appear at all in the list.

13. Went to Maze Pond in morning and evening. Mr Malcolm preached both times. Rainy.

14. Drew diagrams, cut up wood etc, read tales for cuts. Showery. On Saturday a large Dutch steamer was run down off Dungeness Point, drowning about 19 or 20 persons. The reason of the accident does not yet appear. I had intended to have gone to Folkestone today, but was prevented by my father, and I am not now particularly sorry that I did not go, for it has been the most miserably drizzly day that we have had for a long time. I should also have seen very likely what I have not any particular wish to see, viz. some bodies washed ashore from the before mentioned wreck.

15. Went to Charing Cross, cut up wood, read tales, drew diagrams etc. Fine. My father has received an invitation from Mr Hepburn to go down for a few days with him to the place where he is now shooting. It is accepted and he goes tomorrow.

16. Cut up wood, plugged blocks, drew diagrams etc. Went to Oval and Archbishop's in afternoon. My father gone to Limpsfield, Surrey. My mother went in afternoon to Leyland's at Wandsworth. An exceedingly fine day.

17. Cut up wood, plugged blocks, drew diagrams etc. Very fine. Today the contents of the Overland Mail appeared in the Times. The chief event seems to be <u>another</u> of those horrid, barbarous massacres by Nana Sahib of a 150 more women and children at Cawnpore. It is known now that that wretch Nana Sahib has murdered on different occasions and in different manner upwards of <u>1000</u> Europeans, most of them being women. General Havelock discovered this last massacre when he took Cawnpore. He found the great courtyard two inches deep in blood and that they had stripped the women naked then beheaded them, torn their flesh from their yet warm bodies, forced it into their children's mouths then thrown the bodies down a well and the living children on the top of them. That villain has a large account to settle with us.

18. Drew diagrams, joined wood etc. My father returned from Limpsfield much pleased with his visit. The last news from India is not particularly encouraging, 2 regiments that had previously been staunch have mutinied and one other besides them has done ditto and killed its officers. General Havelock appears to be a thorough stick, one who is an ornament to the army; thoroughly devoid of all nonsense and red tapeism, although by no means rash. Lord Elgin has landed at Calcutta with his numerous staff.

19. Drew diagrams, cut up lot of wood etc. Rainy and fine. Our apprentice Cheshire gave his treat to the rest of the apprentices, previous to his time being up. We went to Kew, played at cricket, went on river, fed immensely etc etc.

20. Sunday. Day of rest to weary limbs. Went to Maze Pond in morning and evening. Mr Malcolm preached both times. He is expected to resign his office tomorrow evening.

21. Cut up lot of wood, drew diagrams, read tales etc. Fine. Mrs Hepburn brought us a brace of partridges. This evening Mr Malcolm resigned his office as Pastor of Maze Pond. I am glad of it. He is however to continue (unless he finds another place before) until Christmas. I am sorry for it. He complains of being badly used in the money department, but cannot prove it, in fact it is proved to the contrary. In price, he tried to act 'Scotch' and has made a mess of it.

22. Cut up wood. Drew diagrams, etc. Diagrams! Oh, sickening job. I have to draw lines frequently 1/6 of an inch thick and that for many weeks together. Oh, how I should rejoice to escape from this thraldom with scarcely any prospects of better times, to a seat in a civil engineer's office, where my head might be worked as well as my hands. I should not by any means object to getting into a bankers or a large warehouse if there were any decent prospects of rising after a time.

23. Named blocks of first canto of Childe Harold, altered a drawing board, cut up wood, drew diagrams etc. Fine, very fine and cool decidedly (with the spring) the pleasantest time of year. My father went today again down to Limpsfield, sketching. He admires the scenery of the neighbourhood, excessively.

24. Cut up wood. Drew diagrams, etc. etc. The same everlasting filthy round day after day. One day not varying at all from the other. Last night there was a large fire in Loughborough Road, Brixton.

25. Drew diagrams, cut up and joined wood etc. Showery. Yesterday there was a very bad accident on the Great Northern Railway. It happened to an express train from Manchester to London. When the train was near a viaduct over the Tuxford Road a snap was heard in the guard's break van, which was the last carriage. It immediately went off the line dragging 2 carriages off at the same time, which 3 of them separated from the train and rolled down the embankment. The rest of the train went on all right until it reached the viaduct, when the 2 remaining carriages then separated from the engine and tumbled over the viaduct turning a complete somersault in the air before reaching the ground. 4 people were killed, one gentleman (Hon Mr Clive) and 3 ladies. Almost all the others in the train were bruised, lacerated, had arms or legs broken etc, about 3 of which are not expected to recover. An axle breaking is thought to be the cause of the accident.

26. Drew diagrams, cut up wood etc. Very fine. Today my father returned from Limpsfield. An inquest has been held on the bodies of three who were killed on the Great Northern the other day, and an enquiry is being proceeded with into the causes of the accident. From the evidence that as yet has been given, my own opinion is that there was nobody to blame in the matter, as it arose from a cause or causes beyond their control, the

breaking of an axle or some equally important part. The line has been carefully gone over at the place where it occurred, and the rails have been
gauged and found to be perfect excepting where they are torn up by the
carriages going off.

27. Sunday. Went to Maze Pond in morning and evening. Mr Malcolm
preached both times. Showery.

28. Drew diagrams, cut up wood, altered a shell etc. One person more has
died from the effect of injuries received in the accident of Thursday last, on
the Great Northern Railway, making the 5th who has died.

29. Drew diagrams, joined wood etc. Fine. Mr Thornton the auctioneer at
Reigate, called today. He looked (on account of his dress and general countenance) more like the 'Putney Pet', or Nat Langham, than anything I have
any idea of.

30. Drew diagrams, joined wood etc. Very fine. The news from India is by
no means encouraging. By some it is thought much worse than any that we
have had; it is however most certainly worse than the last previous mail to
it. General Havelock, has been obliged to retreat to Cawnpore a second
time, when he advanced to relieve Lucknow, which latter place, although
well provisioned, is in a precarious and extremely dangerous situation.

1. **October**. Drew diagrams, cut up wood etc. Fine. Mr Cotsell junior came
to tea and supper. The jury appointed to inquire into the cause of the Great
Northern accident have in their verdict explained their opinion that sufficient control is not exercised over engine drivers in regard to the speeds
they travel at. It was proved in the evidence that there had been everything
favourable for the safety of the train; it was started by the superintendent,
watch in hand, most punctually, it was driven by a most unexceptionable
engineer, the carriages were in perfect order, as was also the line at the
place where the accident occurred (as was testified by the Government
inspector), in fact everything was all right and no one in blame. Therefore
there was only one thing that could have caused it and that is the speed,
upwards of 64 miles per hour.

2. Finished diagrams, planed blocks etc, began part of Horace Walpole's
library at Strawberry Hill. Exceedingly fine. There has been a murder at
Bramhall (in Staffordshire I think) under suspicious circumstances. It is of
a farmer. The family were aroused in the middle of the night by the eldest
son firing his gun off. His tale is as follows. He was, he says, woke by a
noise in the house, getting up and going out on to the stairs he saw several
men, at whom he fired, apparently without success. When he went to his
father's room he saw him shot in his bed. This is his tale, but from the
following circumstances I think the police authorities have been justified in
taking him into custody on suspicion. 1. A dog called a 'collie' was kept
which did not bark, and there are no foot marks found leading from the
house. 2. The house was in no place broken in, but if anyone out of the
house did the deed they must have been let in by some one secreted, which
is not a likely thing. 3. The son had quarrelled frequently lately on the
subject of the farm with the deceased. 4th And most damaging is that the
wadding of the gun which caused the old man's death, some leaves had
been torn out of a book in his room and exactly corresponded. Now it is not

likely that men would come into the house without loading their guns and it is likely that the son should use paper from the house.

3. Went on with library, blocked down several of the large diagrams etc. Dull. Fred and my father went sketching in Richmond Park. In today's 'Times' there was a telegraphic dispatch announcing the loss of the 'Central America' mail steamer under most awful circumstances. The ship foundered in a whirlpool sucking everyone in it down to a tremendous depth, and they then rose with the pieces of the wreck. About 620 were in the ship, out of which more than 500 were drowned.

4. Sunday. Went to Maze Pond morning and evening. Mr Malcolm preached both times, sermons in which error was mixed with truth, being beautifully calculated to lead those astray whose opinions are not settled.

5. Oh ye mountains fall on me and cover me, for this (the 8$^{th}$) is the fourth day I have not written in my diary. This day (the 5$^{th}$) I left my keys at our house of business, and so could not get at it; the next day, the 6$^{th}$, my uncle John came here and I had to sleep down stairs on the sofa so I could not get at it the second time. 7$^{th}$ The day <u>appointed</u> for humiliation and prayer on account of those suffering and who have suffered in India, but <u>I</u> did not see fit to keep the day so appointed, not recognizing the legality of the measure. I therefore took the early train down to Edenbridge (Kent) whence my road was through the village to Hever, where I halted to make a little sketch of the castle, thence to the quaint old village of Chidding-stone with its old gabled, carved wooden houses and capital old perpendicular church. From it I went to Penshurst, saw 'the Place' which I did not particularly admire (I thought it bald), and the church which I should have drawn if some people had not been going in to the morning service, then through Leigh to Watt's Cross, where the main road to Hast-ings is joined and on to Sevenoaks. There is a very long hill on the other side of Sevenoaks (near Tunbridge) which I had to go up, but the view from the top is very good, I might say fine, <u>especially so</u> as <u>I</u> saw it. From your feet downwards slopes a precipitous hill, with the road you ascended winding about it to break the ascent; at its feet is a most fertile plain, gently undulating, dotted over with villages and cottages, the thin blue smoke from them calmly ascending to the sky.

9. Mended blocks, went errands, cut up wood, went on with Walpole's library etc. 826 persons perished by the founding of the Russian 74 gun ship, which I have mentioned before. It heeled over in a gale of wind, as it was sailing from Revel to Cronstadt, and before any assistance could be rendered by the other ships which were close to it, it went down in about 30 fathoms water carrying every soul on board along with it

10. Mending blocks; positively morning, noon and night, no thanks or no pay for it either. Very fine. Last Wednesday was a disastrous one for ship-ping, on the southern coast more especially. Two were wrecked trying to get into Ramsgate Harbour, one on the Goodwins, two on the Isle of Wight, several at Portland, a large number on the Cornish coast, where it is said to have blown a hurricane, and one in Carmarthen Bay. When I was out walking on the seventh I found it quite windy enough, my straw hat <u>would</u> keep on blowing off much to my disgust.

Ugh! Is it enough to make one disgusted with humanity, (humanity?) to have to record such an event as is my lot today. But I suppose, alas, such things will happen almost to the end of the world. Yesterday morning about ½ past 5 o'clock, two youths, lightermen, were out on the search for any stray articles that especially are claimed by those of their craft. The scene is on the Thames, close by Waterloo Bridge. On one of the piers they perceive something – they draw near – it is a carpet bag. They take it, and perceive that there is a long piece of cord attached to the handles of the bag, it is very heavy so they put it in their boat and row to shore to open their prize and see what it contains. It <u>is</u> done in the presence of some other people, but when done what do they discover – why nothing but some bones with bits of flesh adhering to them, with a few articles of clothing stuffed in, on which are marks of blood. They do not know what to make of it, so by advice they take it to Bow Street police station, where when it is submitted to the surgeon, horror of horrors it is discovered to be the remains of a <u>human body</u>. On further investigation, it is decided to be a male, who has been stabbed and otherwise murdered and then salted, the body sawn up and here are some parts of it. The bag has no doubt been lowered over the side of the bridge by somebody with the cord, but instead of dropping into the water as intended, it stuck on the abutment. The head of the man is not found and the river is being dragged to discover it if possible. It is very much to be hoped that the authors (for there must have been more than one concerned in it) of this most infernal and diabolical murder will be brought to justice.[47]

11. Sunday. Went to Maze Pond in morning and evening. Mr Malcolm preached both times. In the evening, at the beginning of the service there were certainly fewer people present than I have ever seen before. They were not 30 in number, downstairs, where 600 can be accommodated.

12. General overlooking of the large diagrams etc etc. Fine, dull, that is to say it did not rain.

13. Finally (I hope) got rid of large diagrams. They are without doubt a great mistake. It is a filthy job to have to do them on boxwood. The bones found in the carpet bag under Waterloo Bridge have been examined by a jury, who as they did not know in the least how the deceased had come by his death, could give no verdict. Up to this morning no light had been thrown on and no clue obtained to the perpetrators of this abdominal atrocity. There has been a double murder and attempted suicide near Bath. Another Indian mail has arrived. It contains no news of great importance, one fortunate circumstance being that it contains no news of any fresh disaster. Therefore we may hope for the better, especially as Lucknow it is stated will (or has by this time) been relieved by the rascal Sir J. Outram. If he accomplishes this successfully we will forgive him some, at least, of his

47. 'But who will tell me what 'the Carpet-bag Mystery' was, which my Father and I discussed evening after evening? I have never come across a whisper of it since, and I suspect it of having been a hoax.' Edmund Gosse, *Father and son* (London: Heinemann, 1907), 128.

former delinquencies, though they be great. At Agra it appears that the imprisoned ones in the fort feel quite jolly for they have made two sorties in which they have captured several guns, done a great deal of damage to the insurgents, and been perfectly successful.

14. Went errands, also to Brown and Co's, on with Walpole's library etc.

15. Went to Brown and Co's, twice to Truscott's etc, sized large diagrams, made out list of newspapers for a spec of my father (I think a very promising one) of which more anon. Went to a lecture at Old Crosby Hall, Bishopsgate Street by S.C. Hall (Humbug Hall as called by engravers) on the art of engraving, copper, steel and wood. I heard several things I did not know and what I think no one else knew, in fact things 'as never vas.' He, considering he has lived his life with engravers, ought to have given a better lecture.

Another railway accident, this time on the South Wales railway. Two persons have died. Happened thus. A breakdown on down line, so they shifted a down train which was kept waiting by the break down on to the up line, and in proceeding, the down train met, when going round a curve, the up train, which was going faster than usual, as it was overdue. A frightful collision was of course the result, several carriages being smashed and the occupants along with them. Only one child was however killed. 300£ is offered for the discovery of the authors of the infernal Waterloo Bridge murder.

16. Coloured large diagrams, improved a drawing of Prior's, began a chimney piece at Strawberry Hill etc. Dull, fine. My father went to McKewan's in evening. The Indian mails have arrived, of which telegraphic messages had been previously received. They contain nothing of much importance. Two persons have died from the effects of injuries received in the accident mentioned yesterday on the South Wales Railway.

17. Went on with Chimney piece, cut up wood etc. Rainy. My father and Fred sketching at Richmond.

18. Sunday. Went to Maze Pond in morning and evening. Mr Malcolm preached in the morning and Mr Ward in the evening. Exceedingly wet, easterly wind, weather glass low and still falling, does not look as if we should have any more fine weather this year.

19. Went on with Chimney piece, cut up 9 pieces of wood, went to Gibson's etc. Rainy. My uncle has just returned from Ipswich; he proposed when there my father's spec to the first editor it has been to, but it was not favourably received. I myself am not so sanguine about it as I was; but still if we only get the editors to touch it, it will be a most capital idea.

In today's 'Times' there was an account of a drunken clergyman, who was found in a gutter, with yesterday's sermon in his pocket. The magistrate lectured and fined him, but he was impudent and unabashed withal, asked the magistrate to come and hear his sermon, as he was sure it would do him a great deal of good!

20. Cut up 10 pieces of wood, finished chimney piece, began a coin of Carausius etc. Dull, fine. In pursuance of his plan regarding us, my father sends my brother Alfred to Edinburgh next Friday to Clark's the printers. Thus, Fred engraver, Ted draughtsman, Alfred printer and so on; but shall

we finally keep to them. I think, in fact I <u>know</u> we shall not. Then what is the use of pursuing the plan of making us all those different trades? None whatever, if we could have got anything else that <u>we liked</u> and <u>should</u> keep to. In such a case, all the present time is being wasted.

21. Finished coin and began the Castle of St Angelo, Rome, cut up wood, went to uncle's etc. Wet.

22. Cut up wood, went on with Castle of St Angelo, mended latch and blind etc.

The 10<sup>th</sup> of November is the day of Mr Murray's annual trade sale, on which day Livingstone's journal and travels will appear. Were it not that many thousands of copies (I believe 12 or 15,000) copies of it, have been subscribed for, the sale would be seriously injured by so great a delay in the appearance of the work.

23. Went to Truscott's etc, made out lists of newspapers, on with Castle of St Angelo. It is at last decided at the Society for P.C.K. who is to have their superintendency, vacant by the death of Mr Cox. It is Mr Burt of the Tract Society. They had more than 100 applicants for the place, the principal of whom were Mr Cotsell, who has been brought up in expectation of having the situation, (and who is rightly much disappointed at not having it) and Mr Sharpe, the proprietor of Sharpe's Magazine, who was backed by Mr Clay and his party, but opposed by a great many and disliked by more.

24. Went errands, cut and marked out wood, went on with Castle of St Angelo. Fine. Sent two letters, one to S.C. Hall and other to Dr Mackay, about the former ridiculous lecture on the 15<sup>th</sup>. I wonder if they will insert them in their papers. I should think most likely not. Mr Clark came to ours today from Edinburgh. My brother Alfred's departure is now delayed to the middle of next week.

25. Sunday. Went to Maze Pond in morning and evening. Mr Malcolm preached both times. Very fine.

26. Went to Ramsgate by the South Eastern Railway. Soon after I arrived there, I had the unexpected pleasure of having the rain come down very heavily, which it continued to do almost the whole of the time that it was light, thereby lessening (I will not say stopping) my pleasure for the day. I followed the coast, sometimes on the shore, and the rest of the time on the cliffs to Broadstairs, Kingsgate and Margate, and there had my dinner, then taking the train back to Ramsgate. It rained incessantly (and by no means lightly) the whole of the time I was walking. At Kingsgate I saw the wreck of the Northern Belle, that is to say I saw one mast of her and four immense pontoons which they are going to try and raise the hull with at next spring tides, if it is fine weather.

27. Went on with St Angelo, out errands etc. I forgot to say yesterday that it was discovered (alas) on Saturday that Big Ben of Westminster is cracked, there is no help for it, it being a fact, and a stubborn thing, so that it will have to be melted and recast.[48] But in order to balance the

48. A four foot crack had been discovered in the bell, which was broken up and recast the following year in Whitechapel. The new bell was hung in the tower in October 1858, and the clock mechanism (which weighed five tons) was installed the following May.

sadness produced in the public's mind by the foregoing, today a tele-graphic dispatch appeared in the Times announcing the **FALL OF DELHI.** We have lost in the assault upwards of 5 or 600 killed and wounded, so that it appears the mutineers did not let our people walk in. Hurrah, brighter prospects appear. Lucknow and Agra will be immedi-ately relieved by Havelock and Outram, who has at last joined the former at Cawnpore, and we shall be able to pay back (although not possibly with interest) the debt we owe to the sepoys, the wretches. The General in chief has issued a proclamation in which he says that no quarter must be given, martial law must prevail. And he is quite right.

28. Went on with Angelo, cut up wood etc. It is great pity, but unfortu-nately is too true, that the so called king of Delhi has escaped for the present, with his sons, disguised as women. Fatalism it appears will not always answer. He does not covet death. In the evening saw my brother Alfred off from the Great Northern Station for Edinburgh. He is destined (fatal that) to be a printer, which I think I have said before. Showery.

29. Finished St Angelo, carried my father's bag to station, put figures in Taj Mahal etc. Showery. My father went sketching in Betchworth Park. The Great Eastern is rapidly progressing towards completion. She will be launched most likely, in the next month, or early in December. The launch will occupy 16 hours and will begin in the night time so that it may be completed in the day, before (no doubt) a great multitude. The electric light will be used during the launch in the night time.

30. Improved St Angelo, cut up wood, began basilica of Constantine. Fine, but cold. Tomorrow I go to Reading on business. We had a letter from my brother Alf this morning, announcing his safe arrival in Edinburgh. So far so good.

31. Went on with Basilica, cut up 5 pieces of wood and went to Reading to see the editor of Mercury, about my father's spec, namely the appearance periodically of good and large sized engravings in provincial journals. I did not however obtain an interview with Mr Cowslade until ¼ past 5 o'clock, and then at his private residence only. He gave no positive answer either way but will communicate with us. If pressed I think he will touch the scheme, but if not I think we shall hear no more about it from him. The amount of encouragement I received was about the same as I expected. Reading has several good churches, but although an ancient town does not show any old houses. I called on and took tea with Mr Aldis, there.

**November** 1. Sunday. Went to Maze Pond in morning and evening. A student from Bradford preached, and pretty well, but his pronunciation was horrible.[49] General Cavaignac is dead. A telegraphic despatch was in the Times yesterday announcing the event. It occurred very suddenly. Louis Napoleon is not sorry very probably. I cannot say I am. The weather is still extraordinarily fine, although gradually getting colder. I have heard several people remark that it is more like May than November. And indeed the appearance of the country warrants the

---

49. This was probably the first appearance of Charles Clarke (see Appendix 1).

remark, for the leaves have scarcely fallen at all from most and not at all from some of the trees as yet.

2. Went on with Basilica, planed blocks etc. Dull, fine. General Cavaignac was buried on Saturday with great pomp, in Paris. The general was out shooting when he died, the cause being a heart complaint. He died almost instantaneously. After numerous conjectures and contradictions, it is discovered that tomorrow and the following day are fixed for the launch of the Great Eastern. This is annoying to us as we wished to have a large engraving prepared of it before that event took place, which we have not been able to do, owing to the inconvenience we have experienced from the artist, Weedon.

3. Went to Miller's, Sunters', on with Basilica. Wet. One of the most prominent books of the day is Tom Brown's Schooldays. I am now reading it, and am very glad I am. It enlightens me as to the character of Dr Arnold of Rugby school. I previously, ignorantly hated his name, I shall now revere it. More I shall not say, but advise everyone to do as I am, read this book – and remember it.

4. Went to Miller's and Sunters', cut up wood, finished Basilica, began the baths of Caracalla. The attempted launch of the Great Eastern is what stares everyone in the face this morning. John Bull has to add this to his list of public failures this year, viz, the Atlantic telegraph, Big Ben, and the failures of our model Indian army. Quite enough, I think, for one year. The cause of the failure this time seems to be the insufficiency of the powers employed to drag it down to the water. By some means or other a capstan was whirled round with prodigious force, wounding and maiming a considerable number of workmen, one it is feared, mortally. The iron bars of it, 1½ inch thick, were doubled up by the force with which they struck the men. The launch will have now most certainly to be delayed for a month more, to get the next spring tides.

5. Went to Buck's and Sunter's, on with Baths of Caracalla, read book for cuts etc. Dull fine. Guy Fawkes day, on which account all the blackguards of the neighbourhood turn out and demand money in the day, hooting and yelling if they do not get it and hurrahing if they do, which money if got is spent in buying little machines which when let off make (as Mr Spurgeon says, 'a most unholy noise') but as I say a most infernal ditto.

6. Went errands, cut up 4 pieces of wood, finished Baths (no. 1), began Baths (no. 2). Foggy. Morrison the millionaire died last week, worth nearer 4 than 3,000,000£. Much good it did him, and much good he did with it, did he not, oh yes.

The Bank of England has again raised discounts. It is now 9 per cent. In consequence of the financial disturbances in America, most of our manufacturers, (in the Midland counties especially) are discharging their hands, or else employing them but 2 or 3 days a week. This morning a suspension of payment by a Sheffield house was announced, liabilities estimated between 6 and 7 hundred thousand pounds. It is however happily expected only to be a temporary suspension.

7. Cut up wood and went on with Baths of Caracalla (no. 2) etc. Fine. Cold. In afternoon I walked down to Richmond, on to Twickenham to see my

father sketching, and from thence to Ham Common, (Mr Warner's) where I had my tea and then walked direct up again, doing 25 miles between ½ past 2 and ½ past 9. I today walked the quickest that I have done yet, doing my first 5¾ miles in an hour and doing Richmond, 10 miles, in 1 hour and 50 minutes; which considering I am out of practice, had the roads bad, and had new shoes on, is good for <u>me</u>. The longest distance I have walked yet in one day is 35 miles (on the fast day), and the longest distance without a halt is 27 miles (down to Burnham, Bucks, when the family was there in the summer time.)

8. Sunday. Went to Maze Pond in morning and evening. Mr - - preached in morning very quietly but kept <u>my</u> attention fixed very well, and a student in the evening, who did not do that.

9. Went on with Baths of Caracalla (no. 2), cut up lot of wood, and began a large diagram on mahogany. Lord Mayor's day, Sir R.W. Carden being mayor. The show is this year shorn of some of its beauties? viz. the water procession and the usual attendance of soldiers. The latter it is said is owing to the great drain on them for the East. Mr. Murray's trade sale came off last Tuesday, and an unprecedented one it was. 13,500 copies of Livingstone's Travels were disposed of, with 1,500 copies of Lord Dufferin's yacht voyage (in addition to 2 editions previously sold), 1400 copies of Smile's life of Stephenson (in addition to 6 or 7000 previously sold), 6900 copies of Mrs Markham history of England of which about 70,000 copies have been got rid of before, and numerous other books. It has (wonderful event) actually made Mr Murray in good humour and tolerably amiable. Cold.

10. Finished mahogany block, and drew it over again, cut up wood etc. Fine and cold. Several large English firms have stopped payment, entirely owing to their American remittances being stopped. A Glasgow bank has also stopped which has 100 branches, whose liabilities range from 5 to 6,000,000£. This although the depositors' money is perfectly safe, owing to the great wealth of the shareholders, will cause the greatest trouble to all who are connected with it. The Bank of England has again raised its discount from 9 to 10 per cent and it is not improbable that they will even raise it higher.

11. Cut up wood, went to Mr Murray's, on with Baths of Caracalla (no.2) etc. Very fine and sunny. We had Mrs Baxter and daughter to tea and supper. I tried today and was unsuccessful, to get 6 copies of Livingstone's travels. The whole 15,000 copies although only published three days are disposed of, and they have orders to the tune of 4050 more, at least so I heard Mr. Cooke (Murray's partner) say. They go to press with it again for 5 or 6,000 copies which will doubtless be sold immediately. Murray's face today when I saw him was beaming with joy, although he never expresses it by word. The price of the copyright, Dr Livingstone left entirely with Mr Murray and although such an act would have been safer with the senior Murray, I have no doubt the junior will liberally recompense him.

News from India in this evening's papers. Lucknow is relieved by Havelock, and Generals Neill and Nicholson are killed, the King of Delhi, his sons and entire zenana taken, sons hanged but spared the King on account of his age (90). Poor old puppet.

12. Finished Baths of Caracalla (no.2), which is I think the only drawing which I have yet executed that my father has not complained of (no doubt generally justly) in some particular. Improved St Angelo, and Basilica of Constantine etc. Went in evening to Mr Pinches, my school master, showed him some of my drawings on wood with which he appeared to be pleased. We have November at last and no mistake, if it is not freezing it is pretty close on it.

Another large Scotch bank has failed to meet the run on it and has stopped, which accelerated the fate of Sanderson Sandeman & Co, the second discount house in London. They after having received a telegraphic despatch almost immediately followed the example. Their liabilities were believed to be about 4,000,000£. This will infallibly cause a number of smaller failures as they have bills lodged with them for discounting which they are unable to discount and must not return.

13. Touched up St Angelo, went errands, cut up wood and began some ruins at Palmyra. As sure as a gun, in this mornings 'Times' are a list of failures (resulting from Sanderson and Co) amounting to about 100,000£s. This evening I also heard that Messrs Fitch and Co, the large bacon merchants, were under the necessity of suspending payment, on the same account. The Bank Charter Act is abrogated by the Government. This will allow the Bank of England to issue notes until the pressure on the money market is relieved. Many it is said who were no safer than those who have failed are now perfectly so, and they are now jumping for joy in consequence. Parliament is expected to be specially convened in order to consider the best means of averting a panic and lessening the consequences of this commercial crisis, which is almost unparalleled.

14. Went on with Ruins at Palmyra, out errands etc. Imminent danger of a panic seems over. No fresh stoppages of any large houses are recorded, which is a fact we should be thankful for. A large French American house has however stopped, liabilities to the tune of 300,000£. Last week there were given away with the Illustrated London News four large coloured engravings of the Great Eastern (which is however now christened the 'Leviathan'). They were well-executed, and the number sold immensely. It is believed however that every copy of them sold was a loss to Mr Ingram. The number which is published at 5d. is already. selling for 2ˢ6ᵈ and is expected to fetch 5ˢ, or 12 times the price it was published at!!!

15. Went to Maze Pond in morning and evening. One of the editors of the 'Freeman' preached both times, and both very good sermons. Very fine, rather cold.

16. Went to Fred Gilbert's at Blackheath, to Mr Jones, cut up wood, on with ruins of Palmyra, began a Hindoo dhoolie etc. Fine, cold. This morning I caught a North Kent train very conveniently coming up from Blackheath owing to an accident on the line which delayed it 35 minutes. I believe it took place between the Dockyard and Arsenal stations at Woolwich. A train ran off the line. I heard no particulars and very likely we shall hear nothing about it for they try to hush up their accidents as much as they

can. There is a reported run on the London and Westminster Bank. I hope if true they may be able to stand it, for although I do not fall in love with joint stock banks, yet I think that is an honest one.

17. Went on with dhoolie, ruins at Palmyra etc. Cold. We are going to make an addition to our menagerie in the shape of a terrier dog, in order to persecute the rats, which at present persecute us.

18. Finished dhoolie, went to Truscott's and Jones' etc, cut up wood drew large diagrams etc. Fine and cold. Today the stoppage of the Wolverhampton Banking Company was announced, liabilities from 400,000 to 500,000£. It is they say principally owing to the stoppage of Messrs Sanderson, Sandeman and Co.

19. Cut up wood, priced blocks, drew large diagrams and on with Ruins of Palmyra etc. Colder. Today several minor stoppages are announced, generally on account of yesterday's failure. The worst seems now past. Large firms are getting more steady, which of course influences smaller ones in like manner.

20. Went errands, cut up wood, altered a drawing of Mr Skelton's, on with Ruins of Palmyra etc. The Great Eastern has been again attempted to be moved, some say it is moved, and others say it is not. I do not know which to believe.

21. Went on with Ruins of Palmyra, cut up wood and in doing so planed off the end of my left hand thumb to my great discomfort etc. Went in afternoon to Mrs Sowerby at Peckham, where I had tea and staid the evening. I looked over for the first time 'Hakewill's Italy' with Turner's plates in it. I admire the whole work very much.[50] Fine.

22. Sunday. Went to Maze Pond in morning and evening. Mr Walker (the quiet preacher who we had a few Sundays ago) preached both times. Fine, but rain threatened.

23. Went to Gibson's, cut up 8 pieces of wood, plugged diagrams, drew ditto etc etc. Very windy and rainy. The barometer has fallen more than an inch since yesterday.

24. Cut up wood, began a hut at Bangkok, Siam etc. Rain, fog etc in abundance.

25. Cut up wood, out errands, on with Siamese hut, etc. Rainy. The world at present is very dull and will be so I suppose until the meeting of parliament, which takes place very shortly.

26. Went to Truscott's, altered and improved French blocks, made a list of ditto. Getting very cold, and my brother Alfred writes that it is getting awfully cold at Edinburgh, there being plenty of ice already.

27. To Truscott's again, improved French blocks, out errands etc. The mails are announced by telegraphic despatches but they contain no news of much importance. Rainy.

---

50. *A picturesque tour of Italy from drawings made in 1816 - 1817, by James Hakewill* (London: J. Murray, 1820). A large folio volume of steel engravings, which included eighteen of watercolours made by Turner from sketches by Hakewill. Turner first visited Italy from August 1819 to January 1820, probably after this commission.

28. Improved French blocks etc. We have just got lent to us from one of my brothers schoolfellows, a small working model of a locomotive, about 18 inches long and 6 inches gauge. It acted very well at first but afterwards <u>would not</u>. The cause of it was I think a leak leading from the boiler, which when the steam got up with any force, allowed the water to pour out very quickly, and also I am afraid pour water in the cylinders. I hope I may not have to pay dearly for my amusement.

29. Went to Maze Pond in morning and evening. Mr [space] of Arlington preached both times. My father officiated as clerk tonight at chapel, for the first time, the deacons who usually fulfil that office being away. Mr Clark of Bradford will commence his ministry among us for the space of one month. I hope it will not be preparatory to his settlement with us.

30. Went on with Siamese hut, out errands etc. Fine but very cold. The Great Eastern has been moved at last and although only 24 feet, yet it must be satisfactory to the Company to know that it will move at all. It appears that on Saturday they broke several immense iron cables, the links of which were the thickness of a man's arm and also several other pieces of machinery before they got it to move an inch. But when it did move, it went at about the rate of 1 inch per minute. On Saturday they moved it altogether about 9 feet, and Mr Brunel seeing plainly that if it was not moved yesterday it would probably not be moved at all, gave orders that the work was to be resumed on Sunday morning. So when the morning came, at it again they went, but without the least success, indeed for a long time it seemed as if they would not move it again. The ship groaned and creaked, but there were no signs of its moving. After using all their strength for nought, Mr Brunel has several large battering rams rigged up and appointed I think about 30 men to each, but when these were tried with the usual powers still there was no success. They then collected all the screw jacks and hydraulic machines from the neighbouring yards, and applied them in addition to all the others, but it was not until the very last ounce of pressure had been got out of them and they thought that they would have burst or broke, that the ship condescended to move. The whole movement is now about 24 feet 6 inches since the commencement of the launch.

**December** 1. Cut up wood, went errands, began a careful drawing (from a photograph) for a specimen of Peterboro' Cathedral, altered French blocks etc.

2. Went to Gibson's, cut up wood, made list of Indian subjects for blocks, on with Peterboro. Fine. We have lately had some beautiful moonlights, too good for us.

3. Went to uncle's and other errands, improved a drawing of forum by Read, put figures in blocks etc. Very heavy rains and very windy from the S.S.W.

4. Went to Truscott's, Brown and Standfast's, cut up wood, improving Madeline etc.[51] Dull.

---

51. Brown and Standfast were newsagents in Little George Street, Westminster.

The Leviathan has again been moved. Yesterday it was about 14 feet, making the whole distance it has yet been, about 48 feet. It has however 250 more to go, so that if it continues only at the present rate of moving, it will be launched at the beginning of June next year.

5. Improved French blocks, cut up wood etc. Fine but colder. Went with my sister and brother Jo, to the Educational Museum at Brompton. It was very crowded, at least in the Sheepshank's collection rooms, but not in other parts.[52] I hear that the Great Eastern has been moved about 10 feet more today.

6. Went to Maze Pond in morning and evening. Mr C Clarke preached both times. His pronunciation is vile, and yet he has just passed his Bachelor of Arts examination at the University of London. Drizzly, thoroughly English weather, streets very muddy.

7. Altered French blocks etc. Dull. The Leviathan has only been moved 6$^{ft}$ 8$^{in}$ instead of 10 feet, as I stated on Saturday, and that was only accomplished with the very greatest difficulty.

8. Altered French blocks, out errands, began Black Gate at Treves. Very foggy, the only day we have had so, this season. Telegraphic despatches have been received announcing that Lucknow is again in danger, and Generals Havelock and Outram are surrounded by rebels. The danger is thought to be great. General C. Campbell has left Calcutta on account of it, to direct the operations in person.

9. Went to Truscott's, cut up wood, on with Porta Nigra, Treves.

10. Went to Truscott's, cut up wood, coloured large diagrams again, on with Porta Nigra etc. Young Mr Glennie came this evening. He is a clever caricaturist and is probably going to try to turn his talent to some purpose by drawing on wood. There are silly reports flying about the town to the effect that Havelock is defeated, wounded or killed. Now much as I should lament such an event, yet I do not feel in the slightest degree uneasy about these reports, because the mails have just been telegraphed to London and it is not likely <u>fresh</u> mail should arrive 3 days after the others.

11. Went errands, cut up wood, named stories of the Beatitudes, on with Porta Nigra etc. Fine.

12. Cut up wood, on with Porta Nigra. Failure of large firms still continue about the rate of 2 millions per week. They do not seem to excite much alarm or even distrust, but on the contrary confidence is being restored in the money market. It is said on good authority that the 100 feet which the Great Eastern has been moved has cost to the company 70 thousand pounds sterling. If I were a shareholder, I think I should do anything rather than bless Brunel. Between the Great Eastern and Western this genius? has wasted no small sum of money.

James Henderson has been acquitted of the murder of his father, at Bramhall. I have fully read the details, but cannot see how the jury can get over the facts alleged on the coroner's inquest.[53]

---

52. Opened in the middle of 1857, this original South Kensington Museum, had been built with profits from the 1851 Great Exhibition, and was open two evenings a week, until ten o'clock.
53. See 1 October 1857.

Lucknow is the great topic of the day. Yesterday afternoon telegraphic despatches were received announcing that it was in the greatest danger, being surrounded by 50,000 sepoys, against whom there were only 2 or 3000 men with Havelock. Still later in the day, further despatches were received, telegraphed from a vessel which had nearly caught up with the previous mail, and announced that General Sir Colin Campbell had already arrived at Cawnpore, collected 7000 men and had marched to the relief of Lucknow. We are now of course on tiptoe to hear the result. There is scarcely any doubt but that when Havelock and Campbell unite, they will if not destroy, at least decisively rout <u>any</u> force that could be brought against them.

13. Sunday. Went to Maze Pond in morning and evening. Mr C. Clarke <u>B.A.</u> preached both times. Hoh! The h's. It is perfectly orrible to ear, eaven, ope, eart, etc. etc. etc. for they are legion. Without this, to say the least, Mr Clark <u>may</u> be a very clever young man; but with it ----- I think no man should attempt to speak in public.

14. Went various errands, cut up wood, began a diagram on pear wood, on with Porta Nigra etc. Fine, but cold and windy.

15. Went errands, cut up and whitened wood for Mr Glennie, finished Porta Nigra and on with large diagrams. Beyond my daily work list, I seldom say anything about myself, but today I shall. I, when I first came to business (drawing on wood), did not like it at all, and wished myself, to go to sea. This wish wore off in course of time and I settled down to my fate (after a fashion) but very discontentedly. I had ideas floating in my head that I should one day turn out some great person, be <u>the</u> person of <u>my</u> day, perhaps Prime Minister, or at least a millionaire. Who has not had them? They have not left <u>me</u> yet: time will show if they be true or false. But I can now settle down to whatever my lot in life is to be, much more contentedly than I thought I should then. I then went on misanthropically, not much caring about anything and not thought at all about <u>by</u> anybody, until my father went to Paris in 1855. When he returned from thence, he brought with him a very nicely illustrated guide to Paris, which he showed to our work people as containing examples of the way they should cut, but bemoaning however that no one in England could draw architecture like they were. I instantly thought, this should not (if true) be so, so I will try <u>myself</u>, and I did. The first block I did, I copied from the book and it was thought well of, but I did not particularly persevere, so I was forgotten, and was again neglected for a considerable time, until the 21st October, 1857, when I began the Castle of St Angelo, and the 6 of November, when I began Baths of Caracalla (no.2) for Mr Brown's history of Rome, when a new era began, I began to draw architecture decently, and was again brought into notice. I hope I may not fall into neglect again, for there now seems a lead opening which I will follow as hard as I can, and with God's help, not only draw well, but will draw better and better and, if possible, <u>better than all</u>!

16. Out errands, cut up wood, finished no.1 diagram. Very fine for an English December.

17. Cut up wood, drew no.2 large diagram. Another case of strictly illegal torturing in the Times. The case was of a prisoner at Dartmoor prison, on whom the jailers fitted a kind of belt with handcuffs, the effect of which is supposed to be to make the prisoner very uncomfortable, to say the least. The prisoner was naturally very indignant at such treatment and after a time became savage, managed to partly set himself free and assaulted the jailer. The trial was brought on by the prison authorities to decide whether the assault was with intent to murder or do bodily harm or not. It was heard before Mr Justice Willes, who seems to have acted very fairly and impartially in the matter. He, before he would have anything to do with the matter, wished to know if this belt (that is the application of it) was legal. They said it was permitted by the Secretary of State and was generally ordered to be applied by the Visiting Justices. Justice Willes said that he knew of no statute permitting the use of it and that therefore it must be illegal. (They could not get over this.) The judge was of course obliged to submit the case to a jury, who took a different view of the matter to what I do, and found the prisoner guilty. The judge then sentenced him to be transported, I forget how long. The prisoner implored mercy, urging that great violence had been used towards him. The judge said that if he were assured such was the case, he would most certainly not sentence him, but he said that he now thought it was not and therefore, etc. I think however that he should find out if the belt is illegal and if it were used, for that was not denied.[54]

18. Cut up wood, drew no.3 large diagram etc. This evening Mr Pinches' (our school) annual recitations etc came off at the Southwark Literary Institution, Boro Road. It was about as good a show as usual, but they have never come up to what I should like to see them. I should try to impart a higher tone to the acting and make the boys feel what they say. It has always appeared ridiculous to me for them to act in white waistcoats and kid gloves, and I wonder as Pinches is so fond of imitating the public school customs that he does not approximate more to Westminster School, which at Christmas has a whole play acted in costume.

19. Went to Miller's etc, cut up wood, and began no.4 large diagram etc. Nice day. Blue sky seen and sun shining pretty brightly.

20. Went to Boro Road Chapel in morning, Mr Harcourt preached and in evening to Maze Pond, Mr C Clarke preaching, who we had to dinner and tea. Rainy.

21. Finished no.4 diagram, cut up wood, out errands, and began Diocletian's Palace at Spalatro .

This evening about ½ past 10, we were disturbed by being informed that a couple of men were promenading on the top of our business house, but although ours and the adjacent premises on both sides were thoroughly searched by us and several policemen, we failed to discover anything, and

54. The unfortunate prisoner, Joseph Weaver, was sentenced to another fourteen years penal servitude.

came to the conclusion that it was a cock and bull story. Shortest day. Drizzly and dull.

22. Went on with Diocletian's Palace, out errands etc. Another accident to the Great Eastern is posted up tonight. We do not have much to interest us at this time of the year, in the way of news, so that any occurrence of this sort is quite a blessing. My brother Alfred seems comfortably settled at Edinburgh, but whether for any good, remains to be proved. His letters to us came at first at the rate of 1 a morning, but they have dwindled down already to about 1 every 4 or 5 days. It will after a few weeks certainly be unreasonable to expect him to write more than once a fortnight.

23. Went on with Diocletian's Palace etc. In afternoon I went to Marlborough House to see some of the sketches and pictures which Turner left to the nation. <u>Many</u> of the sketches I like, some of them exceedingly, especially those in the 'Liber Studiorum' series, which are wonderful. They are finished with a delicacy and carefulness that I did not expect to find, so much so, that I feel quite disgusted with the copies of them which I am taking in. The same I cannot say for his pictures, that is to say, those which are exhibited there, for with the exception of 'Crossing the brook' there is I think not one which I can as a whole, say that I like. They are misty, foggy, foolish, glaring, hideous, unnatural and senseless. But, there is a fine specimen of his genius at the Brompton Museum; its title is I think a 'Vessel in distress off Yarmouth pier,' <u>that is</u> fine, the sea being splendidly painted, painted as I have never seen it before, dashing, roaring on the beach, animated - lifelike. Undoubtedly he was a great genius who lived too long, as his later work testify.

24. Went on with Diocletian's Palace, cut up lot of wood etc. Very fine and quite warm, we are able to do without fires quite comfortably. Christmas Eve. Some people think and say a great deal about this time of the year; we do not. For my own part I think no more of it, and see no difference in it, from any other time. There was a large fire in some part of London tonight, I heard it was in Shadwell.

25. Xmas day. Staid at home all day. We managed to enjoy ourselves pretty well, in the quiet way, and I daresay that our recollection of the day will be more pleasurable than those of such as have enjoyed themselves in a noisy or riotous way. Remarkably fine and mild. Such a Christmas day has not been seen in England for many a year. The sky is a summer one and the feel of the air, as if it was spring.

26. Finished Diocletian's Palace, cut up wood, went to Mr Ellis' etc. In evening I went to the South Kensington Museum, and enjoyed myself very much, although there were a great number of people there as it is free today and next week.

27. Sunday. Went to Maze Pond in morning and evening. Mr Clarke preached both times. Fine, but much colder. I have not I think mentioned before that Dr Ashwell the well known physician, (who was at Mr Beddome's this day week) died last Monday morning suddenly of disease of the heart, and was buried yesterday. Only six days between being out visiting and burial. Quick work and solemn. He is doubtlessly supposed by many to be a wealthy man, but the reverse is the case; he is in fact

insolvent. Several years ago he put in a claim to some property, value 20,000£, after a hard struggle he was victorious, at least he got 13,000£, but had out of that to pay 6000£ costs; so that he only actually netted 7000£. He then discovered that by a previous career of extravagance he had accumulated private debts to the amount of 20,000£, so now he thinks that he will reform and commences paying them off, but finds that to get into is easier than to get out. He at his death still had debts to the amount of several thousands. People who know nothing of him very likely thought that he was a very happy, jolly man, but could he have been happy under such circumstances. Other of our friends and acquaintances have died under different circumstances to what we should have expected, for instance Mr Cox, S.P.C.K., and Mr Watson of the Deaf and Dumb Asylum (from whom we had the splendid job of the 'Vocabulary'). The former has actually died insolvent, the creditors accepting 15$^s$ in the £ in order to allow the widow to retain a little house property for a subsistence; and the latter who on good authority it is stated ought to be worth 50,000£, has died comparatively poor. Such is life. My father has gone to supper at Mr Beddomes' and has not yet returned.

28. [left blank]

29. On with Peterboro Cathedral, cut up wood, drew large diagram on boxwood etc. The direction of the Crystal Palace Company, is exciting the disgust of the more respectable and sober part of the community by their absurd and (for such a place) indecent proceedings. They advertise as the present attractions of the Palace, Punch and Judy, a dancing Bear, Dog Toby, a Ballet, a Twelfth cake, and dances, roundabouts, etc. The proceedings in the dances and under the mistletoe have been of the most riotous character.

30. Went to Mr Cowie's twice, began some Assyrian thrones, cut up wood etc. My mother and Fred went this evening to hear the renowned Christy's minstrels, who have now performed in London 150 times.

31. Improved pear wood diagrams, cut up wood, finished 'thrones,' on with Peterboro' Cathedral etc. In evening went to Mr Sandall. In the Kingdom of Naples there have been some most tremendous and awful earthquakes. It is estimated that at least 13,000 people have perished in them (some think a much greater number), several large towns being wholly destroyed. It is far preferable to have England's climate and England's advantages than Italy's sky with its calamities.

Diary. **BOOK 5.**
Jan. 1st 1858 to Dec 4th 1858 inclusive.

**Jan.** 1. 1858. Cut up wood, put figures in block, on with Peterboro' Cathedral, etc. Fine. This last year has certainly been for us, an unparalleled one for fine weather. It is most opportune, for if we had had a bad season, with the heavy taxes arising from the late Crimean and Persian, and the present Indian and Chinese wars and to crown all, the commercial crisis arising from American speculation, all at once, there must inevitably have been the greatest distress among all classes in all parts of the country. Let us try to be proportionably grateful.

2. Went to Rowney's, cut up wood, on with Peterboro' Cathedral etc. Weather still remarkably fine.

3. Sunday. Went to Maze Pond in morning and evening. Mr Clarke preached both times. He has improved much, both in matter and manner, since he has come amongst us. Fine, but rather cold.

4. Went on with Peterboro' Cathedral, out errands etc. Fine but cold. In this morning's Times I see that it has been snowing at Paris, so that we shall probably have it very soon also. Prostitution is carried on in some parts of London to a shameful extent, and the parishes in which those parts are situate are getting alarmed and scandalized at their proceedings. Meetings have been held and government is to be memorialized on the subject, and solicited to try and legalize their prosecution. Dr Guthrie of Edinburgh has written a book almost entirely on that subject and the Times has taken it up, so that we may expect to have the abominable profligacy now so much abounding openly in the streets at least diminished, if not eradicated.

5. Went on with Peterboro Cathedral, cut up wood etc. The railway shares are getting up very high, that is to say to what they have been lately. They must fall again, so look out ye speculators. Very, very cold.

6. Went on with Peterboro Cathedral, cut up wood etc. There has been another attempt to launch the Leviathan, which resulted in moving one end 8 feet and the other 3 feet.

7. Cut up wood, named Herodotus blocks, on with Peterboro Cathedral. Death, the destroyer, has been making his ravages among the great ones of the earth. This morning's Times contained the sad intelligence that the brave Havelock is no more. Alas, at the time when the whole nation felt that he was a hero indeed he was lying dead. Honour be to the brave. He was one of 'nature's gentlemen' truly religious, fearless and honourable, not being afraid to say what he thought and felt and therefore preached the gospel to his regiment. The effect was visible in time, for it was found that no regiment was like his, and so well known was this, that it extorted the expression from a Governor General, that he wished General Havelock would conduct the whole army. Field Marshall Radetsky (age 92) and Madame Rachel the French actress (age 37) are also announced to be dead.

8. Went on with Peterborough Cathedral etc etc. The weather has now almost returned to its former salubrity. It suits me better than the cold weather, at least that is to say when I am at work. I hope this year may be as good as the last, but I have my fears about prematurity.

9. Went on with Peterboro' Cathedral, out errands etc. Fine and quite warm again. Mr MacKewan came in evening.

10. Sunday. Went to Maze Pond in morning and evening. Mr Cowdy of Leighton preached both times. We have had him before, but I liked him today much better than before.

11. Went on with Peterboro Cathedral, both morning, noon and night.

12. Finished Peterboro' Cathedral, made list of newspapers etc. The Leviathan has (for it) been moved very considerably in the last few days. Yesterday it was moved 20 feet, and I have heard that today its progress has been very considerable. Cold again.

13. Touched up Peterboro, cut up 12 pieces of wood, drew a gas meter etc. The Leviathan is expected to be afloat today so yesterday afternoon it had only 15 feet more to go. In evening I went to Mr Sandall's and father to the 'Graphic' Artists Club, held at London University, Gower St.

14. Touched up Peterboro Cathedral. This block I have been engaged on for a long time past, not so much as a specimen of my talent for effect, but for minuteness and correctness of detail. I may say without vanity that in the former of these two last, I have succeeded, and have probably put as much work in, as there has ever been put in a block of the same size before. Mr John Gilbert looked at it yesterday and did me the honour to say that it was as good as that kind of drawing could possibly be, and although that is an excess of compliment, yet I cannot but feel flattered by so great praise, from so great a master of his art. The drawing was merely done as a specimen, but on its being shown by my father to Mr J. Murray (the publisher) today, he ordered him to engrave it, as he said he could make use of it. I hope this may be a means of bringing my name before the public as a correct architectural draughtsman, which if I once get, I will do my best to keep. Drew large diagrams on paper etc, went errands.

15. Was occupied all day writing a prospectus to each of the principal country newspaper proprietors, about a plan which my father has had under consideration for a long time, and which I think I have mentioned before, viz, supplying provincial papers with casts of engravings. We are preparing a cut of the marriage of Princess Royal, and hence my writing the circulars.

My drawing of Peterboro was shown today to Weale the publisher, and at the office of the 'Building News' they said they liked it, but no good has yet come of it.

The Leviathan yesterday went 13 feet at one end, and three at the other; it will now be left until the 30th when the spring tides are expected to float it.

Yesterday at ½ past 9 in the evening, the Emperor Napoleon was attempted to be assassinated by some grenades being thrown into his carriage as he was proceeding to the Opera. He was not hurt but several people were wounded. All such attempts, besides being barbarous, are impolitic, as they invariably fail in the end sought, if the act itself succeeds. If the Emperor had been killed, he would in all probability be canonized as a saint, the acts of 'December' being forgotten. No, turn him out by a legitimate revolution if you will, heap infamy on the savage murderer if you will, execrate his memory if you will, but do not assassinate him.

16. Wrote and despatched more circulars, cut up wood, began La Fontaine St Sulpice. It appears from further telegrams (I fall in with custom but protest against it) that the attempt against the Emperor's life was of the most savage character. Upwards of 60 persons, have been seriously hurt by the explosions, several of whom are not expected to live. The authors of this infamous deed were principally Italians 27 of whom have been arrested. The projectiles they used were hand grenades between 3 and 4 inches diameter, three of which only exploded, though many more were thrown.[55]

17. Sunday. Went to Maze Pond in morning and evening. Mr Cowdy preached both times. I like him very much and cannot but hope that he will settle amongst us. I think he will fill the chapel, for he seems a very hard-working, determined man in the cause of his Master. He is moreover a civilized man, which is more than all preachers are.

18. Went on with Fontaine St Sulpice, touched up F -- Gaillon etc etc. Fine, but cold.

19. Wrote circulars, on with Fontaine St Sulpice etc. The Duke of Devonshire is just dead, as is also the Archdeacon Venables.

20. Went on with Fontaine St Sulpice, began our large block for the Provincial papers of the marriage of the Princess in the Chapel. I do the architecture only. Went to Gibsons etc. Very fine.

21. Finished St Sulpice, went to Gibson's, Prior and F Gilbert's, cut up wood etc. Fine but very windy and very cold. Today there was a grand review at Woolwich in the presence of the King of the Belgians, Prince of Prussia etc etc. This evening the second grand performance took place at her Majesty's Theatre; the wind blew nearly all the illuminations out.

22. Touched up St Sulpice, wrote a number of circulars, cut up wood, out errands, read tale books etc. Fine but still very cold.

23. Began the Renaissance court of the Louvre, cut up wood, made some additions to our block of the marriage of the Princess Royal, went to Regents Park hunting after Hinds Observatory, which I did not find till dark owing to no one being able to tell me, also to Wolf's etc.

24. Sunday. Went to Maze Pond in morning and evening. Mr Millard of Huntingdon preached both times, who I could not fix my attention on at all, though I am told they were very good sermons.

25. Went on with Louvre etc etc. Today the Princess Royal was married and tonight there were and <u>are</u> a great number of illuminations up in the streets with a greater number of gabies gaping at them, so I am told. Cold.

26. Went on with Louvre, named French blocks, went errands etc. It appears that there was quite a scene in the central and most interesting part of the marriage ceremony yesterday. The Princess threw herself back into the arms of her mother who it is said was very much affected, hugged and kissed, etc., etc. Oh, humbug, bosh and foolery.

---

55. This attempt on Louis Napoleon's life was apparently carried out by people based in Britain, prompting strong French protests, which led to Palmerston's bill, making conspiracy to commit murder outside British jurisdiction a felony instead of a misdemeanour (see 20 February 1858).

27. Went on with Louvre, out errands etc etc. Very cold, and as a consequence thereof chilblains trouble me on my feet, which is almost as bad as if they were on my hands, for when they begin to itch I cannot work or do anything else.

28. Went on with Louvre, out errands, cut up wood etc. Very cold. Signor Lablaches' death at Naples, is announced by telegraph.

29. Went on with Louvre, cut up wood etc. Slightly rainy with promise of much more.

30. Went on with Louvre, cleared up my father's rooms etc. He today made me a present of some sketches of his own and W.C. Smith's, which it strikes me, I can make something worth having out of. Wet. Today was to be the final floating day of the Leviathan, it is said that yesterday she displayed unmistakable symptoms of liveliness.

31. Sunday. Went in morning and evening to Maze Pond. Mr Best of Ramsgate preached both times. Dull and dirty.

1. **February**. Finished Louvre, cut up wood, went out errands, began an American Railway car etc. The Leviathan was at last launched on Sunday and towed down to Deptford where she still is. This evening my father went to meeting of the N. Water C. Soc. He has been elected a member of the hanging committee. This evening I and my sister went to hear the well known Christy's Minstrels who amused us very satisfactorily for two hours. Cold.

2. Went on with American car etc etc. Last night by the appearance of the sky I predicted a heavy fall of snow, and this morning it began at 11 o'clock and has continued falling until now. Today the Princess Royal left London for Berlin. She passed through the city, over London Bridge to the Bricklayer's Arms railway station. Although but a very short notice was given, the City authorities prepared the streets in a suitable manner. Very cold.

3. Finished American Railway Car, went to Messrs Corderoys etc, drew diagrams on paper. A thorough thaw, which has made almost all the snow disappear. Warm.

4. Drew diagrams on paper, went out errands etc. Wet. My father in evening went to a meeting of Artists Conversazione.

5. Finished diagrams on paper, went to Mr Weale's, Wolf's and Tenniels etc. Fine day.

6. Began an American locomotive, went to Camden Station etc etc. Fine. Some months ago (I don't know if I mentioned it at the time) there were 10 pictures, all of the highest class, valued at 10,000£s stolen from Charlton Park, the seat of the Earl of Suffolk. They were taken out of the frames, rolled up and carried off in the coolest manner imaginable by a man who was known to have arrived at Swindon Station (15 miles distant) the previous evening and who was seen the same morning going off with 2 parcels, no doubt containing the pictures. After that however he was lost sight of, until a few days ago. He has confessed his guilt and most fortunately the whole of the pictures have been recovered. The thief had been several years previously butler to the Earl and lately had been a messenger in the War Office.

7. Went to Maze Pond in morning and evening. Dr Angus preached in the former and a student in the latter.[56] Rather cold. On Friday night there was a little passage of words between Mr Roebuck and Lord Palmerston, very amusing, but what would have been thought unparliamentary a few years ago.

8. Went on with American locomotive, cut up wood etc etc. Cold.

9. Went on with American locomotive etc. Fine and cold. In evening I went to a lecture at Exeter Hall on 'Progress,' exemplified particularly in George Stephenson, by Edward Corderoy. It was a good subject for one, but it also became a difficult one, from having been so well worked lately. Mr Corderoy nevertheless treated it very well, although I scarcely heard anything that was new to me.[57]

10. Finished American locomotive, and went to Mr Corderoy's and the Camden locomotive works, having had an order obligingly forwarded to us by Mr J McConnell the general loco superintendent. I received a considerable amount of attention from Mr Henderson and others on the works who showed me all I wanted. I sketched one of those magnificent monuments to the name of Stephenson, I mean one of the most modern of our express locomotives, and as Mr Henderson said it was one of the finest machines in the world. Amongst the latest improvements in them are the steam brake and india rubber springs, both of which are capital inventions or applications of knowledge.

11. Began one of MacConnell's locomotives, went to Camden again and to Mr Watkins. Freezing. We have taken Canton, but I do not know that we are the better for having done so, at present.

12. Went on with MacConnell's locomotive, cut up wood etc. Rainy. This evening there was another disturbance with that pest of ours, my father's sister, Mrs Bradlaugh. The cause of it need not be narrated here, suffice it to say that I think this time we shall be rid of her. I lay the decline of our business principally to her coming to Canterbury Place, for I believe that she has had more influence than any other single cause.

13. Went on with McConnell's locomotive, cut up wood etc. The British Institution exhibition is just opened. It is said to be a much better one than usual. A large picture of the new Palace of Westminster by Mr Dawson is attracting considerable notice, as is also Mr Gilbert's picture; they are both 420£ in price.

14. Sunday. Went to Maze Pond in morning and evening. Mr Millard of Huntingdon preached both times. Very rainy.

15. Went to William (Railway Carriage builders), Goswell St and to Mr Corderoy's. Finished McConnell's locomotive, drew title to missionary map etc. The state of the London barracks is attracting public attention. Some of them are so filthy that when the sergeant calls the men in the morning the windows have to be opened 5 minutes before he can put his head in the room, so horrible is the stench. This and other causes produce much greater mortality among the men than should be.

---

56. A Mr Walker preached in the evening (MPAB).
57. Corderoy's lecture was published by the Young Men's Christian Association.

16. Went to Truscott's and to Goswell St, also to Waterloo Station to sketch railway carriages. Raining slightly. Our old friend Mr Watts (of the firm Doulton and Watts for 41 years) died last Tuesday, aged 73, and was buried today in Norwood Cemetery. His liberality was exceedingly great, many of the poor of Lambeth will lament his death from that cause alone. There was a rather numerous attendance of friends at the funeral, but not a single relative, for the good reason, that he has <u>none</u> living.

17. Went to Waterloo Station, cut up wood, drew railway carriage etc.

18. Went to Cords etc, cut up wood, finished 1$^{st}$ and 2$^{nd}$ class carriages etc. My mother went this evening to the Blue Coat School to see one of their Easter suppers, at which they go through a considerable amount of mummery and bosh.

19. Drew 3 diagrams for article 'Optics' in Encyclopaedia Britannica, cut up lot of wood etc. Freezing again.

20. Drew 2 diagrams, cut up wood, went out errands etc. Very cold. Business rather improving; <u>I</u> am very busy. Last night the ministers were defeated by a majority of 19. The occasion of it was Lord Palmerston's 'conspiracy to murder bill,' which he moved to be read the first or second time (I don't know which), but Mr M. Gibson moved in opposition an amendment to the bill, which was carried after some sharp work by a majority of 19 in a house of 450 members. It seems hard, but also, unavoidable, Lord Palmerston must resign.

21. Sunday. Went to Maze Pond in morning and evening. Mr. Millard preached both times. I am afraid that he will stick to us, if we do not to <u>him</u>. He is an exceedingly pleasant man in company, literary, and has a taste for art, which will make him acceptable at our house, but these are not, I think, the proper qualifications for a minister. Freezing.

22. Drew 2 optics and began 2 others, cut up a lot of wood, out errands etc. Freezing still, winter seems reluctant to leave us. In this morning's 'Times' it was confidently stated that Lord Palmerston had resigned, but although that step seems unavoidable, it has not yet been officially announced, and it was also stated that that deadly old Tory Lord Derby had been entrusted with the formation of the new ministry.

At a church meeting this evening at our chapel, the people seemed almost unanimously in favour of Mr Millard, so that I suppose nolens volens I shall be compelled to hear him.

23. Drew 2 diagrams for Optics, cut up wood, went errands etc, put in figure and improved block of Prior's. The announcement in the Times yesterday, although premature was perfectly correct. Lord Palmerston last night announced his resignation, adding that Lord Derby had been entrusted with the formation of the new cabinet; whether he will succeed remains to be seen. The House are meanwhile adjourned until Friday next.

24. Went to Truscott's, Corderoy's, John Watkin's, Dalton's, to get a glass lamp, in King William Street, to Fosters in Pall Mall to see the collection of pictures belonging to the late Mr Leggatt, and to the Architectural and Architectural Photographic Societies[58] exhibitions in

---

58. Architectural Photographic Association.

Suffolk St. The latter society numbers me among its members, and I purchased at the gallery a number of photographs which I hope to turn to good practical purposes.

25. Cut up lot of wood, went out errands, on with Delhi etc. Today we had Mr Watson (Nisbet) and Gilbert here to dinner. The object was, I believe, to get Gilbert to illustrate and Nisbet to publish a new edition of Bunyan's Pilgrim's Progress, the designs for which we would of course engrave. Mr Bennett also came in in the evening. Very windy and cold.

26. Finished Delhi, cut up wood, began more optics diagrams. My father and mother went to a dinner at Mr Green's. In today's papers is the official announcement of the formation of Lord Derby's administration, and the names of the members of it.

27. Cut up wood, finished 7 diagrams for Optics etc. In afternoon I went to the first annual meeting of the members of the Architectural Photographic Association. It now numbers upwards of 950 members, out of which only 17 were present at the meeting. Professor Cockerell RA took the chair and the proceedings were of an exceedingly uninteresting nature. Very cold, but dry and fine.

28. Sunday. Went to Maze Pond in morning and evening. Mr Sheridan Knowles (late actor) preached both times. I do not like dramatic preaching; I would rather hear a quiet sermon, but others seem to like it and the consequence was that the chapel was, contrary to custom, very full.[59] Fine, but likelihood of rain. Last night there was a partial eclipse of the moon visible, which took place at the time predicted to a minute.

1. **March**. Went various errands, cut up wood, drew Optics 4 diagrams, etc. Very cold and snowing. The British Bank Directors trial is at last concluded, and they are sentenced, much too leniently I think, but it is a good and pleasant thing to see justice at last dealt out to villains. The manager of this horrid swindle (Stapleton) has been fined only 1 shilling, but that of course is a disgrace, and the directors he directed to be imprisoned for spaces from 3 to 12 months in the Queen's Prison. 4 of the wretches who attempted to take the life of the French Emperor have been found guilty of the crime, Rudio, Pieri and Orsini are to be guillotined and Gomez to be perpetually imprisoned. They I think richly deserve their fate.

2. Went errands, to Christian Knowledge Society etc, cut up wood, drew 2 diagrams. Freezing still, though not snowing.

3. Went to Murray, Mudie's and Christian Knowledge Society to return Paris blocks, cut up lot of wood, drew optical diagrams etc. Young Mr Glennie came in evening and took supper with us.

4. Went errands, cut up a lot of wood, drew optical diagrams etc. My father went in evening to a meeting of his conversazione at Willis' Rooms. The

---

59. Years later, Edward's older brother Frederick, a devotee of the theatre, remembered the occasion. 'How well does he recall the breathless interest and curiosity of the congregation … at one juncture, Knowles stopped short, and said, slowly and solemnly, "Read your Bibles, - and William Shakespeare." It was a daring act in that somewhat rigid and frigid congregation.' J. Panton Ham, *The pulpit and the stage: four lectures, with illustrative notes by Fred Whymper* (London: C.H. Clarke, 1878), 98-99.

heavy snow which was falling almost all yesterday, is now fast disappearing and I hope we may see no more of it this winter. The North Western and Great Northern Railways are mad again. They now take one, by their fast trains, to Manchester and back third class for 5ˢ or to Peterboro and back for 3ˢ second class, allowing 7 days at the places. I shall if possible take an early opportunity this time of using them.

5. Went errands, cut up wood for Miller, drew 2 optical diagrams etc. Rainy, the snow disappearing fast.

6. Cut up lot of wood, drew an optical diagram etc. We had D. McKewan to tea. He is about setting out for Smyrna. His purpose in going is to paint some pictures for the contractor of the Smyrna railway who is going to present them to the Sultan to carry favour. A very nice job it is for McKewan and a good paying one too. Snowing again.

7. Sunday. Went to Maze Pond in morning and evening. Mr Evans late of Manchester preached both times. During the evening service someone or some persons got into the chapel vestry window through a window and eased the place of a watch that was lying about. Nothing else is missed at present, but it is suspected that the thieves were after the communion service, which is a very handsome one of solid silver. Very windy.

8. Went to Miller's at Camden Town, drew optical diagrams etc. My father has just concluded an agreement with Mr Watson (Nisbet) to engrave an edition of Pilgrim's Progress, which is of course to be the edition of editions, illustrated by J. Gilbert. We are also at present engaged in illustrating a work of Rev. Mr Ellis on Madagascar, for which we have some most interesting photographic portraits of the Crown Prince and Princess etc etc. These and several other things which we expect will happily make us busy for 6 months, and restore us to something like our former status among engravers. Snowing at intervals throughout the day.

9. Went to Anelay's at Blackheath, cut up a lot of wood, drew optical diagrams etc.

10. Cut up a lot of wood, named blocks, finished Optical diagrams etc. Still snowing at times although it does not lay upon the ground. There has been another insane attempt at revolution in France by about 40 persons at Chalons; after parading the town, making a considerable disturbance and telling a considerable number of lies in saying that the Republic had been proclaimed at Paris etc, they were all taken and will no doubt be severely punished. These attempts, conspiracies etc though of small importance in themselves, show the temper of the French people, and the small cloud which seems so insignificant now, will probably brew into a gust tempest which will destroy the present government, with the murderer at the head of it.

11. Went to Scott's at Peckham, cut up a great deal of wood for Gilbert's Pilgrims Progress, arranged optical diagrams, began more pear wood diagrams etc. Fine, but still freezing.

12. Went to Truscott's and St Mark's College, Chelsea, cut up wood, looking over optical diagrams, went on with large pear wood diagrams etc. Fine and cold.

13. Went on with pear wood diagrams, cut up wood, screwed up a block, looked over optical diagrams etc. Warmer but very wet.

14. Sunday. Went to Maze Pond in morning and evening. Students preached both times, and very good sermons. Very wet. Tomorrow D.V. and weather permitting I go to Peterboro' for the first time.

15. Got up at ½ past 4 and went to Peterboro. I went principally to get a sketch of the spiracles on the tower of the great west front, and I succeeded. My minor object in going, was to see the annular eclipse of the sun, Peterboro being almost on the central line. I was in the cathedral at the time of the sun's greatest obscuration, or when the annular ring was perfect, but I saw quite as much of the eclipse as I wanted. The darkness however at the worst (astronomers would say best) part was not great, I have frequently seen it darker before a thunderstorm. Peterboro cathedral I consider splendid, I only regret I could not stay and sketch it thoroughly. The west front is very grand (but it did not make the same impression on me that it would if I had not drawn it most carefully from a photograph tolerably lately) and the central tower as well as the north one I admire very much, but the interior of the choir struck me as being remarkably splendid, the carvings in wood are most magnificent. There is some glorious old Norman stuff in the building and the greater part seems to me to be <u>pure</u>, which is not often seen. I must try to revisit it this year if possible but there are many parts of it which I feel confident I might put to use in picture times. The ride down was not so interesting although there are a good many pretty parts on the line.

In this morning's 'Times' there was a most capital article on the French spy system (or rather the spy system of Louis Napoleon) which is now so abominable. <u>France is on the eve of a revolution</u>. On Saturday last Orsini and Pieiri were executed and though it was but just it will not in the least add to the popularity of the 'unconvicted felon' whose life they attempted to take.

There has been a great row at Dublin on the occasion of the new Lord-Lieutenant making his entry into that city, between the students of the university and the police and soldiers, which promises to attract considerable attention. It appears that the students with the usual Irish love of fun (doubtful fun nevertheless) had before the procession passed, pelted everyone within their reach, indiscriminately, with oranges etc, including the police. Everyone for a long time put up with it with good humour, until all at once a Colonel Browne (who has hitherto been a favourite at Dublin) gave the soldiers orders to charge on the students, which they did along with the police. The dragoons used their sabres pretty freely, cutting and slashing about in all directions, and the police were not less sparing with their staves. Many of the students were severely hurt, some dangerously.

16. Looked over and planed optical diagrams etc. Very fine. From all accounts, my view of the eclipse yesterday was as good as anyone's, so that I ought to esteem myself very fortunate.

17. Looked over and planed optical diagrams, out errands, cut up wood, on with large pear wood diagrams etc. Rather rainy, but weather nevertheless

looking remarkably fine. We had young Glennie and Mr. Mole the artist to supper this evening.

18. Went to Nisbet's, to get a sea gule, to St Mark's College, and to Mr Garbett's, drew pear diagrams, looked over and arranged optical diagrams.

19. Walked to Blackheath (Anelay's) and back, cut up wood, looked over and arranged optical diagrams, on with pear wood diagrams etc. Fine.

20. Went errands, got off Optical diagrams, cut up wood and on with pear wood diagrams. Fine.

21. Sunday. Went to Maze Pond in morning and evening. Mr Richards preached both times. My uncle John came this afternoon and returns to Watford tomorrow morning. Very fine.

22. Went errands, on with pear wood diagrams etc. Fine.

23. On with pear wood diagrams etc. In evening went to Mr Sandall's. An accident occurred yesterday morning to the early express from Birmingham on the North Western. Several carriages were smashed though no lives were lost.

24. Cut up wood, went to Well's and Vokin's, on with pear wood diagrams etc. In evening I went to the Lambeth Ragged Schools, built by H. Beaufoy, Esq., to witness the presentation of a testimonial to W. H. Miller for his great exertions in promoting the happiness and welfare of the lower classes, especially in his late endeavours to provide a novel and cheap entertainment for the poor, to counteract the bad influences of the penny theatres, etc. Lord Shaftesbury took the chair, and presented the testimonial, which consisted of 100 sovereigns, a handsome time-piece and an emblazoned testimonial on vellum. Mr Miller returned thanks in rather an egotistical speech, and afterwards gave a portion of his entertainment entitled 'A Journey from the North Pole to the Equator'. The proceedings were conducted in a 'Lambeth' style, which I must confess I expected. Very fine.

25. Went to Mr Murray's, cut up 11 pieces of wood, finished pear wood diagrams, began some plans of Italian palaces (which have come most opportunely) etc. Rather cold.

26. Went to Mr Browne's, cut up wood, drew plans etc. Fine. Tomorrow (D.V.) I intend to go to St Albans.

27. Went to St Albans, by the way of Watford. The exterior of the Abbey certainly disappointed me, as it is neither picturesque nor architectural (with the exception of one charming window which I sketched) but the interior was far above my expectations. I sketched the choir and stood doing it 5 hours, which considering I had walked to Euston Square (3 miles) and from Watford (7½), besides having to walk the same back again, was not bad. The screens and some other architectural ornaments of the abbey are splendid; the interior on the whole delighted me, as did the courtesy of the Rector, who gave me a ticket to sketch in it. I must visit it again some other time as there is much that will I am sure be very useful to me in it.

28. Sunday. Went to Maze Pond in morning and evening. The well-known Andrew Fuller's grandson preached both times. Though young, he is a very good, spirited (though not noisy), thoughtful preacher, and I have little

doubt when matured will be a very useful one. Showery, exceedingly beautiful weather.

29. Went to Miller's, Waterlow's, Cords etc, drew plans, began a sketch on paper of principal doorway of St Mark's, Venice. My brother Fred was disappointed today, to find that out of 5 pictures which he had sent to Suffolk Street, only 1 had been hung, and that one, badly. Such are the chances of an artist's life, and such the disappointments. I should not wonder if I meet with a cross in some of my plans by and by. Very fine.

30. Went to Scott's (Peckham) cut up wood, went on with sketch of St Mark's, began a pear wood diagram. Rainy. On Sunday last there was a fire in Bloomsbury, in which 14 persons were burnt and one jumped out of a window and smashed himself. There was yesterday (I think) a large conflagration in Manchester.

31. Finished sketch of St Mark's, went on with pear wood diagram etc. Rainy.

1 **April**. Touched up sketch of St Mark's, on with pear wood diagram, etc etc. Mr Gilbert came and stayed to dinner. In evening my mother and father went to a meeting of the Artists and Amateur Conversazione at Willis Rooms. My Uncle John came up from Watford this evening and goes with me to Hastings tomorrow (weather permitting). Rainy.

2. Good Friday. Ugh! Away with your vacillating, uncertain, changeable people who take a long time fixing a thing and equally long unfixing it. Of this description of article is my Uncle John. Rather showery.

3. Finished pear wood diagrams, went numerous errands, cut up wood, began plan no.10 etc. Rainy. Today I was told by a schoolfellow of mine, who is now articled to a lawyer, that in their office there are some writs ready to be served on the Eastern Steam Navigation Company, who own the Leviathan.[60] They have raised all their capital, and as the company is not 'limited,' someone will have to pay dearly for their shares. My Uncle Ebenezer, who is always hoping to make clever specs (and not near so often succeeding), has just bought a few 20£ shares in the concern, for 5£ each and thinks that he has got a good bargain, but he may find it a horrid bad one.

Mr Burt (S.P.C.K.) came to dinner.

4. Sunday. Went to Maze Pond in morning and evening. Mr Robinson preached both times. My father went with him to Mr Hepburn's to dinner and tea. Fine.

5. Finished plan no.10, began no.11, cut up wood etc, helped my father to prepare his pictures (14 in number) for his Societies Exhibition, etc. Rainy. Last week the South Western Railways station at Salisbury was burnt down; they have been exceedingly careless or unfortunate in losses by fire. Mr Millard has accepted the offer made to him to come as pastor to Maze Pond, and will commence in the middle of May. I hope he may turn out to be a better article than our late dear departed - Mr Malcolm.[61]

---

60. Possibly this was Thomas Roffey, who became Whymper's solicitor (see Appendix 1).
61. James Millard was formerly welcomed to Maze Pond by William Beddome, the senior deacon, John Eastty and others on 2 June. (*Baptist Magazine* 1858, 445.)

6. Went errands, cut up wood, finished plan no.11 and began no.6; helped my father with his pictures etc. My father got his pictures sent in this evening, 3 of the 14 are already sold. Fires are numerous in London lately, there were 2 on the south side of the Thames on Sunday night, and 2 on the north side last night. Dull. Mr Read called in in the evening.

7. Touched up Peterboro Cathedral and Palace at Lucknow, cut up wood, finished plan no.6 and began large plan of Vatican. Very wet. My brother Fred and Will Farnfield went tonight to a concert at the Surrey Music Hall in aid of the Female Orphan Asylum.

8. Went on with large plan of Vatican etc. My Father went to New Water Colour Gallery for the first days hanging of the pictures. Very wet.

9. Went on with Vatican, out errands etc. Dull. My father at the gallery again.

10. Went to New W. Colour Society, on with Vatican, got out 19 pieces of wood etc. The disgraceful competitions between the London and N. Western R$^y$ on the one hand and the Great Northern and Manchester, Sheffield and Lincoln on the other, have this day by agreement been ended; it was high time they did; I know if I were a shareholder I would let the direction know it.

11. Sunday. Went to Maze Pond in morning and evening. Rev. Mr. Davies, the secretary of the Tract Society, preached both times.[62] We had him home to dinner, and although I have the strongest hatred and disgust of the Tract Society's way of doing business, yet Mr Davies left a very favourable impression on my mind. He seems a very able man and is a pretty powerful preacher. Very fine.

12. Finished Vatican, began Mappin's diagrams etc.

13. Went to Murray's, Colnaghi's, Illustrated News and Illustrated Times offices, also to Camden Town, cut up wood, on with Mappin's blocks etc.[63] Very fine. Today my father finished hanging the New Water Colour Gallery and although there are only about 310 pictures, he is pretty well tired of it.

14. Marked wood, drew Mappin's blocks etc. Fine.

15. Went to Society, Vizetelly's etc, cut up wood, on with Mappin's blocks etc. Today was touching day at my father's gallery. What is rather remarkable, almost all the artists seem satisfied with their hanging. Very warm and fine.

16. Went to Scott's (Peckham) on with Mappin's blocks, out errands etc. My father went to dinner at Mr Green's. Today the Queen sent notice to the gallery that she would visit it at 4 o'clock. She is seldom a buyer at exhibitions, excepting the Academy. There was a short and sharp thunderstorm this evening, which we were prepared for by the excessive heat of the last two days. Heavy rain. Today is my mother's birthday, she is 39. She went today to Richmond and Ham.

---

62. This was George Henry Davis, who also preached the following week (see Appendix 1).
63. Colnaghi's was a fine art publishing firm in Pall Mall. The Mappin Brothers were a cutlery business in King William Street.

17. Finished Mappin's blocks etc. Today was the private view of the New Water Colour Gallery. Although the exhibition is but an average one, yet the sales have been good. My father sent 15 pictures in, 3 of which were sold previously and 5 more have been sold today, so that he has done pretty well. The Queen went yesterday with the Prince Consort and 3 of the children, besides 6 or 7 others.

All this week has been taken up with the trial of Dr. S. Bernard, who was charged with conspiracy to murder the Emperor Napoleon and with actually murdering several people outside the Opera house at Paris. The Crown prosecuted, and Mr Edwin James most ably led the defence. The speech of Mr. E.J. produced so great an impression, that the spectators cheered, and the Attorney General fearful of the result replied to it, in a very warm and unnecessary speech. He hoped the jury would not be led away by Mr E.J.'s speech and got so very spiteful about it, that even partial Lord Campbell, was obliged to pull him up and tell him that the jury would be directed to give their verdict on the evidence and not on the speech. The jury took a considerable time in coming to verdict, which when arrived at was - not guilty. This, considering all things, was a correct one, because it was obviously absurd to charge a man with the murder of people who he had never heard of, and had no intention of hurting, but as the charges against him were coupled together, they were it appears obliged to find him guilty of both or else of neither. The verdict has given great satisfaction here, and will no doubt give the reverse to many in France. The judges on the trial were evidently much disconcerted, for they did not even pass the customary vote of thanks to the jury, for their long attendance, but precipitately left the court.

18. Sunday. Went to Maze Pond in morning and evening. Mr Davies preached both times. Very fine, with beautiful skies.

19. Began a view of Benares etc, went errands. My Father had today in the 'Times' an exceedingly laudatory notice of his Bass Rock – The Home of the Sea Fowl. He was also praised in the 'Standard.'

In evening I went to Photographic Societies exhibition at the Kensington Museum. It does not I think exhibit any marked improvement over that of last year, although there are many photographs in it both large in size and charming in detail.

20. Finished Benares, cut up wood, and began what is to be a very elaborate view of St Mark's church, Venice, from a photograph. In evening I went to Peckham.

21. Went on with St Mark's, touched up etc proofs of plans of Rome etc. In evening I went to a meeting of the Hampstead Conversazione at which there were a very large number of David Cox's paintings and sketches brought together showing the great variety and brilliant nature of this fine old fellow's drawings. Fine.

22. Went on with St Mark's, drew in 9 plugs, cut up wood etc. Fine. My Uncle Woods came up from Swaffham today. In evening I went to a meeting of the Lambeth Ragged Schools.

23. Went on with St Mark's, drew a physiological diagram etc. In evening I went to Mr Sandall's. Yesterday morning the celebrated clipper ship 'James Baines' was almost totally destroyed by fire at Liverpool.

24. Went to Mappin's to sketch tea and coffee pots etc. In afternoon I went to Richmond and walked by river side to Kingston, returning from thence to Richmond by the road through Ham, calling on the Warner's. Very fine. The notices of my father's pictures in this year's exhibition by the newspapers and journals have been on the whole exceedingly flattering. The Times spoke very well of him, the Athenaeum, Illustrated News, Builder and Standard have all done the same and we have in no case heard of an adverse criticism. Today is my father's birthday; he is 45.

25. Sunday. Went to Maze Pond in morning and evening. Mr Sheridan Knowles preached both times. I do not like his styles but the matter of this evening's sermon I liked very much. Very wet.

26. Cut up wood, went to Barton's (Oxford St.) and sketched there, drew a tea pot etc. Fine. Hurrah! I have got a nice commission. It is to go to the north of England to sketch for a new illustrated edition of Smiles' life of George Stephenson. My father proposed it some months ago to Mr Murray who spoke of it to Smiles and ergo – I go. Today is my brother Henry's birthday.

27. Went errands, on with Mappin's tea and coffee pots etc. Dull. This evening there was a very large conflagration in St Katherine's Docks, to which (as is my usual custom when possible) I went.

28. Went to Fleet Street, Stanfords and to Mr Smiles twice at London Bridge, to arrange for my journey to the north; on with Mappins tea pots etc. This time next week, I shall I suppose be in Newcastle or Darlington. Fine.

29. Went on with Mappin's blocks, went to Smiles' at Blackheath etc. Mr Smiles is a most gentlemanly and polite man; besides being well up in his own profession, he is well informed on artistic matters. He has given me every information in his power that I needed for my journey and has promised to obtain 'passes' on the lines I shall have to pass over, which I shall wait for. Very rainy.

30. Went to and had interview with Mr Murray, cut up wood, on with Mappin's tea pots, began Burton's bedsteads etc.

1. **May**. Went to Gibson's etc, cut up wood, drew one of Burton's bedsteads etc. Very rainy.

2. Sunday. Went to Boro' Road in morning, Mr Harcourt preached, and to Maze Pond in evening, Mr Green preached. Very wet. Tomorrow if fine (which is extremely improbable) I go to Liverpool, commencing my journey for Smiles' life of Stephenson.

3. Went to Mr Smiles at London Bridge Station and got my passes for my journey, 6 in number, but it is postponed until Wednesday morning, when I hope the weather will be favourable; cut up wood, drew coffee pot, began the Basilica of St Paul at Rome etc. Today the exhibition of the Royal Academy opened its doors to the public. It is said to be a very good one.

4. Went numerous errands, cut up wood, finished Basilica of St Paul at Rome etc. Showery. My departure is fixed for the second time tomorrow morning, which I hope will be fine.

5. [Left blank. No entry until May 18][64]

18. Left Leicester at ½ past 1 this morning, so as to get up to London to breakfast, which I did with plenty of time to spare. Finished up some of my sketches, waited on Mr Dixon CE in one of the Railway Committee Rooms of the House of Commons etc.

19. Went to Mr Brown's at Paddington, finished up some of my sketches, wrote letters etc.

20. Finished up sketches etc. I have been fortunate enough to please my father with my sketches, and today Mr. J. Gilbert looked at some of them, and praised them, though I think it is doubtful if he is sincere in what he says. Tomorrow I see my principal, Mr Smiles; if I please him I care but little for anyone else. Fine.

21. Finished up sketches etc, waited with them on Mr Smiles. He appeared to be pleased with them, anyhow I think he was satisfied, which is a great blessing.[65]

22. Touched up sketches finally and called on Mr Murray with them. He did not criticize them, but on the contrary praised a few of them, which is a great thing for him to do.

23. Went to Maze Pond in morning and evening. Mr Millard preached both times. He is now regularly installed in his place. May he remain there long and do much good.

24. Marked out and cut up 20 pieces of wood, drew a Davy's safety lamp etc. Very wet, being Whit Monday.

25. Drew G Stephenson's safety lamp, half lap joint etc, put up blind. Rainy. My father bought yesterday a very beautiful drawing by Cook, member New Water Colour Society, (which was exhibited at last year's exhibition) at a sale at 'Fosters,' for the very small sum of 15£. Its actual value is probably nearly 3 times that amount. The title is Bocastle harbour, pilot boat going out.

26. Cut up 8 pieces of wood etc, drew Stephenson's signature, outlined lime works etc. A porter (yesterday I think) was completely cut up on the North Kent line at Blackheath station, by a train which stole upon him without him perceiving it. Very showery.

27. Drew Frances Henderson's signature, began High Street house Wylam, etc. I am in luck (in the matter of the life of Stephenson), for in addition to having pleased my father and satisfied Mr Smiles, I have – to say the least – satisfied Mr Murray also. It is a great thing when one has 3 employers for one job to satisfy them all. Rainy.

28. Went on with High Street House, began the High pit, Killingworth etc. In evening went to cricket at the Archbishop's grounds.

---

64. 'The illustrations to this volume are from sketches made on the spot by Mr. Edward Whymper.' Samuel Smiles, *The story of the life of George Stephenson, railway engineer* (London: J. Murray, 1859), vi. One can therefore assume that Whymper visited the Sankey Viaduct on the Liverpool to Manchester line, Stephenson's birthplace at Wylam (on the Tyne), various pits around Newcastle, railway and industrial workings at Clay Cross and Ambergate, near Derby, and Trinity Church in Chesterfield.

65. 'Young Whymper has done his part of the work exceedingly well.' Samuel Smiles to John Murray, 6 July 1858, NLS, John Murray Archive, Acc.12604/0295.

29. Went on with High Street House, cut up wood, went to Mr Harvey's at Richmond etc. In afternoon went to Oval to try to discover a cricket club that I can get into, but was unsuccessful. Try, but again. Very fine.

30. Sunday. Went to Maze Pond in morning and evening. Mr Millard preached both times. The weather has all at once, set in intensely hot, which is very trying.

31. Finished High St House, went on with Lime works at Ambergate etc. Very, very hot, but we are almost roasted wherever we are, and whatever we do. My Aunt Woods came on a visit from Swaffham via Tring. In evening went to Archbishop's to cricket.

1. **June**. Cut wood, finished Lime works, on with High pit at Killingworth etc. Very hot. The 'Times' was yesterday excluded from France, for exercising too great liberty of speech.

2. Went on with High pit at Killingworth, out errands etc. It is hot, hotter, hottest today, of all the days this week. The heat is tremendous, considering the sudden manner in which it has come upon us.

3. Finished High pit, began Sankey Viaduct, near Warrington. Fine etc. I have resolved that my face shall not be seen on the Oval or any other cricket ground this year at least. It is far too expensive in time and money for me at present. May God aid me in keeping it.

4. Went on with Sankey Viaduct, out errands etc. In evening I visited for the first time Mr Albert Smith's entertainment of Mont Blanc, etc., which closes this season finally, previous to Mr Smith going to China for a new entertainment. People often go to these sort of things with exorbitant expectations raised by previous descriptions which have been told them; I however found myself quite satisfied and more.

5. Went to uncle's, on with Sankey viaduct etc. This morning there was a very sharp thunderstorm, which has not however had much effect in clearing the air. My father went yesterday to Guildford, etc, sketching, and fell in with a brother of Millais on the same errand. Millais is a queer fish. His brother said that he had been painting an apple blossom 3 years. Art (in this case at least) is long and life short.

6. Sunday. Went to Maze Pond in morning and evening. Mr Millard preached both times. Beautiful day.

7. Finished Sankey Viaduct, touched up High St House, cut up lot of wood, went to Scott's, H Weir's, Anelay's and Mr Smiles'. The latter is a very agreeable and pleasant man, and I have another journey in prospect from him, to illustrate the life of Watt. Fine.

8. Cut up wood, traced the 'Rocket,' began a Whimsey etc. What fools men do make of themselves. Why here is H. K. Smithers, a member of the Southwark Book Society, supped frequently here, the secretary of the Commercial Dock Company, has been found guilty and committed for trial for stealing 250£, the property of the Company. How he has come to do it is a mystery to us, but I suppose wonder will never cease. He has a large family and a wife, all of whom will no doubt have to pay the penalty of their father's guilt. Thundery.

9. Went to Mr Smiles at London Bridge, to Scott's etc, cut up wood, finished Whimsey. Very hot.

10. Went to reading room of Brit. Museum, to Willis and Southerans, traced monastery of St George, cut up wood, began Jumma masjid at Delhi, began a coat of arms for Mr Murray etc.[66] Very fine and very hot. My father and mother are gone to Mr J. Brown's to spend the evening.

11. Went out errands, cut up wood, began House at Willington Quay, on with Jumma masjid at Delhi. Very hot. Smithers' defalcations are said to be between 7 and 12,000£. There can be no doubt now but that he is an accomplished swindler and nothing else, and it is mortifying to us, as well as many others, to find ourselves so taken in by a man we believed honest.

12. Went to Mr Garbett's, cut up wood, on with jumma masjid etc. In evening we had D. MacKewan, who has not long since returned from Smyrna and is consequently full of the tales of his travels.

13. Sunday. Went to Maze Pond in morning and evening. Mr Millard preached both times. Very fine. It appears from what MacKewan said last night, that he has been let in pretty extensively by that rascal Smithers, who it also appears behaved with the greatest effrontery when he was arrested.

14. Finished jumma masjid, out errands, on with House at Willington Quay etc. Very hot.

15. Went to Scott's, Anelay's and Smiles, cut up wood, touched up blocks of Harvey's, on with House at Willington Quay. Very hot.

16. Went various errands, cut up lot of wood, touched up Harvey's Bull Bridge, on with House at Willington Quay etc. Very hot. My father has gone to Shere near Guildford sketching. I am very glad to say that our business is much brightening up, not I think that we much deserve it, for we do not get the work done nearly so quickly as I think we should.

17. Went errands, sketched factory, cut up wood, drew factory, on with Willington Quay. Our late acquaintance Smithers has got transported for 6 years, which is not so much as he deserves I think.

18. Cut up wood, on with House at Willington Quay etc. Very fine. We had the rare pleasure of having Mrs Sowerby and Miss Leigh today to dinner. The late very hot weather made the Thames stink exceeding great, insomuch that if it had lasted a few days longer, we should doubtless have had some act of Parliament passed for pumping it and for settling the great drainage question, but unfortunately yesterday the temperature fell 10°. It had previously been 93° in the shade, or hotter than it had been for 43 years.

19. On with House at Willington Quay, and out various errands etc. In afternoon I went to New Water Colour Society's exhibition which I did not like, and evening to the Photographic Society's ditto at which there were many interesting and useful subjects. I bought a few which I shall I hope turn to good account

20. Sunday. Went in morning and evening to Maze Pond. Mr Millard preached both times. Very rainy although hot.

21. Went errands, redrew partly factory block, redrew almost entirely Harvey's Summit Tunnel etc. Fine. An accident occurred on the South Western Railway yesterday to the excursion train returning from Port-

---

66. Sotheran and Willis were publishers located in Little Tower Street.

smouth in Bishopstoke Station at about 8 o'clock. The 3 last carriages of the train ran off the lines as they were crossing some points killing 1 man and wounding dangerously a great number of others.

22. Went errands, finished redrawing Harvey's tunnel, finished factory, finished House at Willington Quay etc. This morning my brother Alfred arrived from Edinburgh. He will stay with us about a fortnight.

23. Improved Anelay's chat moss, went to Smiles etc etc. Very fine.

24. Waited on Mr Robert Stephenson, C.E., M.P., etc. etc., and was treated very civilly by him. I showed him his father's portrait which he thought very good and some others of the illustrations we are doing for Mr Smiles, all of which he liked. Went to Robertson's, began West Moor pit etc. In evening I went for second time to Christy's Minstrels (who are as amusing as ever) with my brother Alfred.

25. Drew Sparrow's signature, cut up wood, went errands, went on with West Moor pit etc. Went in evening to cricket at Archbishop grounds and to the photographic institution in Leicester Square.

26. Went on with West Moor pit, packed parcels, out errands etc. In afternoon went to Kingston and had a row on the river.

27. Sunday. Went to Maze Pond in morning and evening. Mr Millard preached both times. The river Thames is stinking frightfully at present and is alarming almost everyone in consequence. I hope the hot weather will continue, and we shall at least have it tried to be remedied.

28. Marked out and cut up lot of wood, went errands, drew tea pots etc. Fine.

29. Finished the tea pots, cut up wood etc. Had Mr and Mrs Millard to tea and supper. Pleasant people. Tomorrow I go to Blisworth, Kilsby Tunnel, Rugby, Coventry, Kenilworth and Warwick, mostly for the first time.

30. Went to Blisworth, Crick, Kenilworth and Leamington, but was not able to go to Warwick, owing to my being taken ill from remaining about 12 hours without any food. Fine.

1. **July**. Went to Walker in Cornhill, sketched watches, touched up yesterday's sketches etc. The day before yesterday there was a great fire in the London docks, which has done immense damage. There was it appears a considerable quantity of saltpetre in the portion of the building on fire, which blew some walls down killing it is feared several persons.

My excursion yesterday terminated very unfavourably; I had intended to have had a moonlight stroll round Warwick and perhaps to have gone as far as Stratford on Avon and to have come up by a night train, but my imprudence put an end to it.

2. Went errands, cut up wood, finished up sketches, began a railway watch etc. Slightly showery.

3. Went to Smiles, Sparrow's, etc, cut up wood, finished watches, finished West Moor pit etc. In evening had Mr Skelton to supper.

4. Sunday. Went to Maze Pond in morning and evening. Mr Millard preached both times. Wet in evening.

5. Touched up watches, West Moor pit, on with Clay Cross works etc. In evening went to cricket at Archbishop's ground. Rainy, pretty considerably during the day.

141

6. Went on with Clay Cross works, cut up wood etc. Showery.

7. Went on with Clay Cross works etc, cut up wood. In afternoon we were favoured with a sharp thunderstorm and abundant rain.

8. Finished Clay Cross works, out errands, cut up wood, began a boy driving a gin horse, touched up various blocks etc. Very showery. My father went to Clapham, mother to Brixton. The friends of the late Mr Cox commenced an action against the Great Northern Railway Company to recover damages for the widow on account of his death. They had a large number of counsel for the prosecution, including Mr Edwin James, and they finally obtained 1000£ which is a good present to the widow, though not heavy damages, everything considered.

9. Went various errands, finished Gin etc. There was a short time back a bad accident on the South Eastern Railway near Chilham, owing to the driver going too fast round a very sharp curve, which threw the carriages off the rails. Three have already died, more are expected and a great number are wounded.

10. Went to Mr Smiles, cut up wood, touched up Gin, altered and improved Dickinson's Coalville etc. Very wet. My father went to Gilbert's. I am intriguing to get an illustrated edition of 'Tom Brown's school days' which I feel sure would prove successful if done.

11. Sunday. Went to Maze Pond in morning and evening. Mr Millard preached both times for the 'Special India Fund.' He is about taking to open air preaching. Very fine.

12. Altered Peterboro Cathedral, went to see Mr Smiles at London Bridge and did not see him, cut up wood, went errands etc. In the evening Mrs (or Madame) Cottons (or Cotons) was burnt down for the third or 4th time. The explosions of the fireworks in the house were very severe. In evening went to cricket in Archbishop's grounds. I am afraid that I am about to be laid up with scarlatina or measles or something of the sort. I have as yet mentioned it to nobody, but I must tomorrow.

13. Went errands, cut up lot of wood, began a map for Mr Millard etc. My father has gone to stay the night with young Glennie at Richmond. Fine. The fires last night and the consequent explosions are said to have damaged nearly 100 persons. I should think that number was gainsaid, but it is certain a great number were injured.

14. Finished Mr Millard's map, cut up wood, began the no.1 engine at Darlington, went to Mr Smiles at Blackheath and Mr Scott's etc.

15. Had the great pleasure, (which I have now had for several months) of looking after Master Clint, who is supposed to be a genius, but I cannot see it. (I can see that he is a very troublesome, ill-behaved boy.) Went on with no.1 engine etc.

16. Went on with no.1 engine at Darlington, out errands, wrote long letter for Smiles etc. Went in evening to Archbishop's to cricket. Tomorrow we get rid of the principal portion of the family to Gomshall, a small place on the Reading and Reigate branch of the South Eastern Railway.

17. Went on with no.1 engine, did various odd jobs, out various errands etc. In afternoon went to Richmond, rambled through the park to Kingston,

rowed on river for 2 or 3 hours, returned home calling at Mr Warner, and young Glennie's who is now staying in Petersham. Very fine.

18. Sunday. Went to Maze Pond in morning and evening. Mr Millard preached both times. Had very heavy rain in the morning, but turned out a beautiful day afterwards.

19. Went to Mudie's, errands, finished no.1 engine, cut up wood, began the Literary and Philosophical Institute at Newcastle on Tyne.

20. Went to Cord's twice, Wormull's twice, watchmakers twice etc, cut up wood, drew one signature (Cliff) and began another, went on with Literary Institution. In evening went to cricket at the Archbishop's grounds. Very fine.

21. Went errands, cut up and whitened a lot of wood for Gosse, packed it, sent it off, wrote letter, finished signatures, packed them and sent them off, on with Literary Institute etc. In evening walked round to see the new Chelsea suspension bridge. I do not like the outline of it, as seen from a distance, I think it looks like an affectation of the Russian style, but when on it I think it looks exceedingly well and appears to harmonize with the surrounding scenery.[67]

22. Went on with Literary Institute, out errands, packed parcels etc etc. In afternoon I went to the Oval to see the match between Surrey and all England. All England got over their $1^{st}$ innings for 62, then Surrey took the bat and at the close of the day but five wickets had fallen for 184, out of which Mr Miller obtained 24, Lane 4, Caesar 4, Burbridge 35, H Stephenson 25, Caffyn 74 and Lockyer 10, the last two not being out. The game is resumed tomorrow.

23. Went to Barlow's in King William St, marked out wood, went to Mr Millard and Gibson's twice, on with Literary Institute etc. Very fine. In afternoon I went to see the conclusion of the match I spoke of yesterday. As I prophesied, England got a most tremendous licking, being beaten in one innings and 28 runs. Hurrah! for my county.[68]

24. Went on with Literary Institute etc. Rainy. I am now all alone at home and am very glad to have a little quiet and freedom. In afternoon went to the Royal Academy and Old Water Colour exhibitions. I thought them both very good. The Academy was crowded to excess.

25. Sunday. Went to Maze Pond in morning and stayed at home to keep house in the evening, being solus – alone. Fine but excessively windy.

26. Went errands, cut up and marked out lot of wood, finished Literary Institute etc. Fine. Today my father returned from Gomshall, where he has been staying for the last few days.

27. Drew a sword (for Bentley), cut up lot of wood, went to Barlow's etc, began Kilsby Tunnel. My father went down to Gomshall again today, taking with him 2 Miss Hepburns. Very rainy.

28. Went errands, cut up wood, on with Kilsby Tunnel, wrote letter to John's, general business etc. Tomorrow D.V. I walk down to Gomshall,

---

67. The first Chelsea Bridge was a suspension bridge with cast-iron towers, designed by Thomas Page. It was replaced in 1934.
68. Surrey scored 244, with Caffyn making a century. England were bowled out for 154.

27 miles and a hilly country. I intend if I wake to leave at 3, it is now ¼ past 10 …

29. Walked down to Gomshall, but was unfortunately stupid enough to miss my way twice. The route I adopted through Ewell, Epsom, Leatherhead, Great Bookham, Effingham and Horsley was (with my miles) about 30 miles if not several miles more. I however accomplished it in 7 ¼ hours.

30. I intended today to have walked up through Cobham and Kingston, but owing to the lies of a man who directed me, I again missed my way, and after leaving Cobham I found myself at Weybridge. Walked on to Walton, where I had to wait 1½ hours for a train to Clapham, and in the park was again misdirected by a postman, which made me feel exceedingly savage. In evening I played cricket in Archbishop's grounds, and I got my old school rival George Canham to come, for the first time. Very hot.

31. Went various errands, cut up wood, on with Kilsby Tunnel, to British Museum library, Windsor's and Newton's etc. Very fine.

1. **August**. Sunday. Went to Maze Pond in morning and evening, Mr Millard preaching both times. The congregation does not improve much yet, though some are sanguine that it will presently.

2. Went to Symons (Vauxhall), Gibson's, cut up wood, out for change, to Clowes, to watchmakers etc. Very fine. In evening I went to the Archbishop's to cricket. My father went to a meeting of the New Water Colour Society. In this morning's Times, I saw, I must say with regret, that Mr Edward Pease who I waited on for his portrait (which we have just engraved) died at Darlington. He was in his 93rd year and I am sure no one from looking at him would have thought so, or have thought that he was so near death.

3. Went to New Water Colour Society to fetch my father's unsold pictures (3) away, also to Suffolk St, to watchmakers etc. Cut up wood, went on with Kilsby Tunnel etc. Rainy. In evening went to Archbishop's grounds.

4. Went to Mr Smiles, finished Kilsby Tunnel etc etc. Windy and rainy.

5. Began the Rocket, cut up wood, planed 11 Stephenson blocks, went to Clowes, Clays and Barlows, etc. The Atlantic Telegraph cable after 3 or 4 failures has at last been laid. The effect of this on the 1000£ shares was immediate; yesterday they might have been had for 350 but today they are selling at 800.

6. Went on with Rocket, wrote letters, managed business etc. In evening went to Archbishop's grounds and to Mr Skelton's.

7. Wrote letters, went on with Rocket etc. In evening went to Archbishop's ground to cricket.

8. Sunday. Went to Maze Pond in morning and evening. Mr Millard preached both times, and in afternoon to Westminster Abbey, the service of which made me think more of man than of God. All the fine flourishes in music, walking before the preacher, fine dresses and ornaments, are not at all well calculated to promote the glory of God. The walking about and talking and laughing during the service I think abominable.

9. Began Clay Cross village and Middlesbro on Tees, cut up wood etc. Fine. The great Cherbourg fetes which are just over, do not appear to have been anything very tremendous. The most amusing thing I have heard in

relation to them, is the water getting into the new dock before it was blessed, inaugurated etc etc.

10. Went errands, cut up wood, went on with Clay Cross village etc. Went to Archbishop's grounds in the evening and formed the nucleus of the North Lambeth Cricket Club, which I hope may last many years. My father came up from Gomshall today, but returns there again tomorrow.

11. Went on with Clay Cross, cut up wood etc etc. Fine.

12. Finished Clay Cross village, cut up wood, went to Mudie's, British Museum to compare corals etc with the originals, wrote letters to Anelay and father, got out list of cuts for 'Cherry stones' etc. Went in evening to Archbishop's grounds. Had a good deal of thunder and lightning at intervals during the day. Excessively hot.

13. Touched up Clay Cross, the Rocket etc, cut up and whitened wood, on with Middlesboro etc. Still very hot, the expected thunderstorm not arrived. The formation of the North Lambeth Cricket Club seems to be going on quite prosperously, we add members daily. I do not however wish to get more than 25 members for some time to come.

14. Cut up lot of wood, went on with Middlesboro', wrote letters to father and Macmillan. Today the first fete of the early closing movement took place at the Crystal Palace. It has been a most unfavourable day, as it has been raining tremendously.

15. Sunday. Went to Maze Pond in morning and evening. Mr Millard preached both times and in afternoon to Westminster Abbey, Dr Wordsworth as usual preaching a very ordinary lecture - not a sermon. Fine.

16. Went on with Middlesboro' etc. Today my father and brother Fred returned from Gomshall. My father is going at the end of this week to Cornwall for his "grand go."

17. Finished Middlesboro', cut up wood, went to Waterloo Station, began Alton Grange etc. Went in evening to Archbishop's, and after that to Notting Hill or rather Shepherd's Bush to look after Jos. Scott one of our old apprentices, but did not find him.

18. Went errands, cut up wood, on with Alton Grange, began Mr Gubbins House at Lucknow etc.

19. Went to Gibson's etc, cut up wood, went on with House at Lucknow etc. Fine and disagreeably hot.

20. Went on with Gubbins' house at Lucknow, went various errands, attended to business etc. Fine day. My father went to Plymouth today, en route for Cornwall.

21. Went to Clays (with Tenniel's blocks), Hogarth's etc, cut up wood, on with Gubbins' house, on with Alton Grange etc.

22. Sunday. Went to Maze Pond in morning and evening, Mr Millard preaching both times, and in afternoon to Westminster Abbey, Dr Wordsworth preaching. Very fine.

23. Went to Clowes and Blackwood's, wrote numerous letters, packed parcels, finished Alton Grange, began the 'Experiment' etc. Fine. Tomorrow I disappear to Gomshall till Thursday.

24<sup>th</sup> and 25 at Gomshall, Surrey.

26. Went to Clay's and Truscott's, on with Gubbins' house at Lucknow, wrote lot of letters etc. Fine.

27. Went to Murray's and Butterworth's etc, cut up wood, packed parcels, went on with Experiment, finished Gubbins' house etc. In evening went to Archbishop's grounds.

28. Went to Miller's (Camden Town) twice, also to Smiles and Scott's, finished Experiment, wrote letters etc. Today all the family returned from Gomshall. Rainy.

29. Sunday. Went in morning and evening to Maze Pond, Mr Millard preached both times, and in afternoon to Westminster Abbey, Dr Wordsworth preaching. Rainy.

30. Cut up wood, touched up blocks, began a church after an earthquake. Had Edward Burchall [Birchall] up with us today and stays the night, he is a nice lively good tempered fellow and it would be a good job if more were like him.

31. Went to Lambeth County Court to get out summons, cut up wood, went to Aske's, on with ruined church etc.

1. **September**. Went on with ruined church etc.

2. Went to Tomlinson's and Skelton's, planed blocks, finished ruined church etc. My father is now at Boscastle, Cornwall and is expected back on Tuesday next.

3. Went errands and on with title to Useful Arts etc. Rainy.

4. On with title to Useful Arts, made additions to a map of Gibson's etc. In afternoon went to Kew Gardens and all the time I was there had to stand under the trees to escape the drenching rain, and then hurried home again.

5. Sunday. Went in morning and evening to Maze Pond. Very heavy rains during day.

6. Began a map of the railway in the Midland counties etc.

7. Went errands, on with map etc. Fine. Today my father returned from his "grand go" in Cornwall etc.

8. Went errands, cut up wood, finished map etc.

9. Went to Clowes, Morrell's and Broden's, on with St Mark's, Venice.

10. On with St Mark's, and in evening to cricket at Archbishop's grounds. Dull.

11. Went on with St Mark's, packed blocks etc. In afternoon we went to Richmond, played at cricket, rowed to Kingston, fed and returned, Fred giving the usual treat to celebrate his being out of his time. Rather dull.

12. Went to Maze Pond in morning and evening. Mr Millard preached both times. A brilliant day, but excessively hot. Our friend Mr Beddome is supposed to be dying and is not expected to live through the night.

13. Went on with St Mark's, also with Mappin's blocks (a fresh batch) etc.

14. Went on with St Mark's. In evening to cricket at Archbishop's. My father went sketching at Gilbert's. Brother Fred has gone to Maidstone for 3 weeks or a month. Very fine and very hot. Said to be owing to the comet. Fudge![69]

---

69. Donati's Comet, first seen in June 1858, was one of the brightest of the nineteenth century. It came nearest to the earth on 9 October, and developed a prominent dust trail.

Ill. 3 St. Mark's, Venice, drawn on wood by Edward Whymper for Byron's *Childe Harold.*

15. Went on with St Mark's, cut up wood, touched several of Mappin's blocks, went to Scott's at Peckham, etc. Fine. Last night at 20 minutes to 9 our old friend Mr W. Beddome died. I do not know his age exactly but it is somewhere about three score and ten.

16. Went to Scott's, cut up wood, wrote letters etc. Mr Beddome was in his 71st year. Fine.

17. Went on with St Mark's, to Scott's etc. Had Mr Millard and a pair of deacons to tea and supper. Some very heavy rain fell suddenly in the evening.

18. Went on with St Mark's etc. Very fine. Went in afternoon to Crystal Palace. It was an 'Early Closing Movement' day, on which there were the extra attractions of a concert, wrestling, hurdle racing etc. Saw Mrs Clara Novello for the first time; cannot be said to have heard her, as the place is much too large for any human voice. When you do hear them any distance off, it is only from their unnaturally straining their organs of screaming!

19. Went to Maze Pond in morning and evening. Mr Millard preached both times; in the evening it was the funeral service of Mr W. Beddome, who was buried this afternoon at Ilford. Very wet.

20. Finished and touched up St Mark's, (with which I had again the good fortune to please Mr Murray), touched up and redrew some of Mappin's blocks, went to Hoddle's etc. Fine. The comet has again been visible lately. I saw it on Saturday night, but it was not then very distinct. There have been also a great number of meteors seen lately.

21. Went to Mappin's, touched up, planed and packing their blocks (27), cut up and whitened 25 pieces of wood for Mr Gosse, drew letters in Almanac title etc. Fine. Went to cricket at Archbishop's grounds in evening. Tomorrow I intend if possible to go to Norwich and have a little tour in Norfolk, with an ultimate eye to business however.

22 of September to 1st of **October** [blank]

2. Went errands, cut up wood, began a drawing of Lincoln Cathedral. Fine.

3. Sunday. Went in morning and evening to Maze Pond. Mr Millard preached both times. Rainy.

4. Cut up wood, went on with Lincoln Cathedral etc. Rainy.

5. Went to Mudie's, on with Lincoln Cathedral etc. My brother Fred returned this afternoon from Maidstone where he has been disporting himself for about 3 weeks. This evening the star was visible through the tail of the comet and in close proximity to the nucleus, which it almost put out by its own brilliancy. It attracted a great number of gazers to the streets, and 1$^d$ peeps through telescopes were very numerous.

6. Cut up wood, began Bangor Cathedral etc.

7. Went errands, cut up wood, went to Lambeth County Court, on with Bangor Cathedral. Very windy and very rainy.

8. Went errands, on with Bangor Cathedral etc. Fine.

9. Went to Lambeth County Court, on with Bangor Cathedral, drew a Windmill etc. In afternoon went to British Museum, Mudie's etc. Fine.

10. Sunday. Went to Maze Pond in morning and evening. Mr Millard preached both times. In the evening he preached a very good sermon to medical students and drew a numerous audience to hear it. My uncle John came up today and stays the night with us. Very wet.

11. Went to Anelay's and Smiles, marked out wood etc, finished Bangor Cathedral etc. Fine. There has just been received news of a most awful fire and shipwreck at sea of the "Austria" German and American steam packet. It had on board a very large number of passengers, amounting with crew to nearly 600 people, out of which I think 87 have been saved.[70]

[space left]

12. Went errands, touched up Bangor Cathedral, went on with Lincoln Cathedral etc. Fine.

13. Went errands, did various odd jobs, wrote letter etc, went on with Lincoln Cathedral. Fine.

---

70. The steamship *Austria* left Hamburg on 4 September 1858 for New York, but caught fire ten days later in the Atlantic. Sixty seven passengers were saved and 471 died.

14. Went errands, to Society, Sangster's[71] and County Court, went on with Lincoln Cathedral, began a Comet Lucifer match label, stowed away paper, oil and string etc. Fine.

15. Finished Comet label, wrote 3 letters, went on with Lincoln Cathedral etc. Fine. My father has just returned from a two days sojourn at Gomshall, where he has been sketching.

16. Went on with Lincoln Cathedral, to Mr Skelton's etc. Very fine, as warm and pleasant as a day in June. In afternoon went to cricket at Archbishop's, which I should think will be the last time I shall be seen there this year, unless the autumn is unusually fine.

17. Sunday. Went to Maze Pond in morning and evening. Mr Millard preached both times.

18. Drew letters in St Marks, went on with Lincoln Cathedral etc. Rainy and very cold again.

19. Altered 'Comets,' went errands, on with Lincoln Cathedral etc. Very wet.

20. Named a number of Gosse's blocks, went on with Lincoln Cathedral etc. Fine.

21. Wrote letters, went errands, went on with Lincoln Cathedral etc. Fine.

22. Cut up wood, went errands, improved Skelton's 'wolf of the capitol,' finished Lincoln cathedral etc.

23. Cut up wood, went to Murray's etc, named Childe Harold blocks, etc. Very fine day. Went in afternoon to cricket at Archbishop's.

24. Sunday. Went to Maze Pond in morning and evening. Mr Millard preached both times. Fine.

25. Went to Mudie's and the British Museum, cut up wood, touched up Lincoln Cathedral, stacked 150 rounds of wood etc. Fine.

26. Packed parcels, stamped blocks, cut up wood, began Pool of Hezekiah etc. Fine.

27. Went to Museum, uncle's, Mr Sandall's and various publishers etc, on with Pool of Hezekiah etc. Fine but getting colder.

28. Altered or almost redrew Skelton's 'Pantheon' etc. Very wet.

29. Finished altering 'Pantheon,' went on with Pool of Hezekiah etc. Dull and cold.

30. Went on with Pool of Hezekiah etc. In afternoon went to cricket at Archbishop's.

31. Sunday. Went to Maze Pond in morning and evening. Mr Millard preached both times. In the evening he baptized 11 persons. Very cold.

1. **November**. Finished Pool of Hezekiah, got Mr Ellis' photographs etc into shipshape, began door in Ely Cathedral etc. Very foggy.

2. Went to Railway office, Spooner's etc, went on with door at Ely. Fine and cold. Business is very, very bad, although we expect shortly to be much better, but we have expected that so long and so often that I almost despair of ever seeing it so. My father's painting interferes sadly with his

---

71. Sangster and Fletcher were booksellers and publishers in Paternoster Row.

share of it, and my uncle is more incapable than ever. There is plenty of work doing, that I know to a certainty, but how to get it I do not know.

3. Went on with door at Ely etc etc. It is a curious fact that the less we have to do in the way of business, the busier we are, that is to say the heads of the place. In the last few months I have been excessively busy, yet have made but little money.

4. Made more alterations to Pantheon, began St Peter's church at Colchester, on with door at Ely etc. My mother has gone to stay a few days at Burnham, Bucks.

5. Finished St Peter's, went errands, on with door at Ely, coloured maps etc. Rainy.

6. Went numerous errands, on with door at Ely. Today my mother returned from Burnham.

7. Went to Maze Pond in morning and evening. Mr Millard preached both times. Rainy.

8. Went to Gracechurch after photographs, marked out wood, altered St Peter's Colchester, on with door at Ely. Fine.

9. Went to Uncle's, Oakly St, cut up wood, on with door at Ely etc. Fine. My father went to dinner at Mr McKewan's. Lord Mayor's day. Today Alderman Wire became Lord Mayor of London. I remember being frequently told, when a small boy, by those who knew, that I was very like him at that time. I certainly am not now and should be very sorry to be so, for he is (if the portraits are correct) an exceedingly gluttonous looking man. I have heard a saying in regard to his becoming Lord Mayor, which though not quite according to Cocker I will relate.
[space left]

10. Went to Beddome's, Truscott's and Watkin's, began a view of Hebron (the oldest city in the world) etc. Mr J. Watkins the eminent photographer called in, in the evening.

11. Went to Truscott's, finished Hebron etc etc. David Cox junior called in in the evening. Fine and cold.

12. Went to Uncle's (twice) and Chester St (stables, twice), on with door at Ely etc. Fine. My father and mother went to dinner at Mr Hepburn's. Fred went to Jullien's concert at Lyceum theatre.

13. Went to uncle's, railway office, etc, got out and whitened wood for Gosse, packed parcels, wrote letters etc, on with door at Ely.

14. Went to Maze Pond in morning and evening and to Westminster Abbey in the afternoon, where Dean Trench preached. Dry but very windy and cloudy.

15. Went on with door at Ely etc. Very very windy.

16. Finished door at Ely, cut up wood, went errands, began title to Missionary Quarterly Herald etc. Very windy still with slight rain.

17. Finished designs for letters, went errands, named proofs etc. Fine and cold. Young Mr Glennie called in the evening. He is already a very fine sketcher and will, I have little doubt, make a good artist.

18. Went errands, finished title to Missionary Herald, began a flower (Daphne Indica), made pencil sketches from S. Cook's 'Boscastle' also

from my Father's 'Boscastle.' Went in evening to a lecture at the boys school room, Lambeth Green.

19. Went errands, cut up wood, sketched my father's view Boscastle village, went on with Daphne Indica etc. Fine and freezing.

20. Finished Daphne Indica, went errands, wrote letters, packed parcels etc.

21. Went in morning and evening to Maze Pond, Mr Millard preached both times, and in afternoon to Westminster Abbey. Very cold.

22. Went to G. Godwin's at Brompton (the Editor of the Builder) to show him two of my drawings on wood. Could not see, but had the answer as usual, 'the drawings are very nice, but we have nothing today.' All this is very discouraging, but if we did not have discouragement we should not know what encouragement was. Went also to city to look after photographs, cut up lot of wood, began 'Cawnpore,' began 'Gaza' etc.

23. Went errands, on with Gaza, began a drawing of Bethlehem etc. Mr Mole (the artist) came in evening and stayed to supper.

24. Finished Gaza, went on with Bethlehem, cut up wood etc. There will be some smart skirmishing in parliament between some of the great railway companies the next session, I reckon. Several of them have given notice to enter several bills which are sure to be opposed. Work for lawyers!

25. Finished 'Bethlehem,' began drawing an ornamental alphabet etc. Yesterday Lord Lyons died. Another brave man gone to his last resting place. M. Montalembert has just been arrested, tried and condemned to an imprisonment of 6 months and to pay a fine of 3000 francs for writing a little pamphlet in praise of England (in France). What a fool Louis Napoleon is; this act is but placing a few more stakes on the fire to make the pot boil in which he is. Rainy; a total change in weather from freezing hard to quite a warm temperature.

26. Cut up wood, began another Bethlehem etc. Fine and very warm.

27. Finished Bethlehem (no.2) etc. Went in afternoon to try and get in St Paul's to make a sketch of the preparations for the evening services, which commence tomorrow, and found it as might have been expected, closed. Very rainy.

28. Sunday. Went in morning and evening to Maze Pond, Mr Millard preached both times and in afternoon to Westminster Abbey. I went to St Paul's after leaving the abbey to endeavour to get in to the evening service, which commenced at 7 and although I was there at 5 o'clock and waited more than an hour, yet the cathedral was filled before I could get in. The crowd outside was enormous, I should think that there were probably from 15 or 20,000 people there.

29. Went on with Ornamental Alphabet etc. Rainy. The 'Times' this morning said that the arrangements in the cathedral for the service were very complete and very comfortable; that might be so, but at the exterior they were most certainly very bad.

30. Went on with ornamental alphabet etc. Fine. Mr Wolf the animal painter came in evening and took tea and supper with us.

1. **December**. Drew a coat of arms, went on with ornamental alphabet, cut up wood etc. There has been a proposal made and I believe a subscription

already begun at Oxford and Cambridge to defray the fine imposed on M. de Montalembert. <u>He</u> however does not wish it. I wish it may reach a good round sum, just to show our sympathy with and our feelings towards the felon who sits on the throne.

2. Cut up wood, drew a Greek inscription for 'Septuagint', began title to Quarterly Missionary Herald etc. Fine. Father and mother out to tea etc at Mr Soper's.

3. Went on with title to Quarterly Missionary Herald, on with alphabet, cut up wood etc. This morning's Times contained the extraordinary intelligence that Napoleon the little had reversed the sentence of M. de Montalembert, in remembrance of the 2nd of December. The motive it is not easy to divine whatever the pretence may be. Rainy.

4. Began a design on paper for a cover to S.P.C.K.'s publications, went to Sulman's at Islington etc. Rainy.

**[Book 6 ]**

**Dec** 5. Sunday. Went in morning and evening. Mr Millard preached both times, and in afternoon to W. Abbey. Fine.

6. Went errands, marked out lot of wood, finished designs on paper for Soc. publications etc, went on with title to Q.M.H. Fine, streets most filthy. The two great railway companies, the L. & N.W. and the G.N., which have for the last year and a half, been trying in all manner of ways to cut each others throats, have at last come to an agreement, and have raised their prices accordingly. I am heartily glad of it, for it has been a most disgraceful contest throughout, especially on the part of the Great Northern Railway. Neither side can plead 'not guilty' but certainly the palm of iniquity must be awarded to the Great Northern. The bulk of their shareholders seem to be sick of the proceedings of their directors, but do not seem to be able to get rid of them, owing to the extraordinary system of profits which the railway companies adopt, by which means the directors can always carry a motion, although the majority of those present at the meeting may be against them.

7. Sorted a great number of old blocks, went on with title to Qu.M.H.

8. Cut up wood, finished title to Q.M.H. etc. There have been for the last few days some very heavy fogs in London, and yesterday there was a bad collision on the North London Railway as the effect of the same. About 30 persons were wounded, several dangerously, but none are dead yet.

9. Made fresh designs on paper for Societies publications etc. In evening went to a concert at St James' Hall, at which almost all of the principal English artistes were employed. The piano forte fantasies of Miss Goddard were particularly good.

10. Went errands. Went to S.P.C.K., British Museum, etc. Went on with ornamental alphabet.

11. Went various errands, went on with ornamental alphabet etc. We are contemplating going into colour printing. 3 or 4 of the principal engravers have already tried it, with success, and as the demand is great for it, almost now greater than for ordinary wood blocks; it would be almost suicidal not to enter into it. Fine.

12. Sunday. Went to Maze Pond in morning and evening. Mr. Millard preached both times, and in afternoon to Westminster Abbey. Fine and very cold.

13. Went to Scott's (Peckham) on with alphabet, began the Tadpole Fish etc. Business still very bad. It is very annoying to find others getting plenty of work when we have next to nothing to do. We must however endeavour to repress our envious feelings and work harder, and perhaps one day we may have our reward.

14. Went errands, finished tadpole fish, went on with alphabet etc. Rowbotham the artist came to tea and supper.

15. Went to Gibson's, Sunters' etc. Packed parcel, went on with alphabet etc.

16. Marked out 14 pieces of wood, went errands, on with alphabet etc. In evening I went to the 2$^{nd}$ annual exhibition of the Architectural Photo-

graphic Association. The exhibition includes some very good specimens of photography and is on the whole about as good as the first one.

17. Went on with alphabet etc etc. In evening went to the annual recitations of Mr Pinches' school. Saw a considerable number of my old school fellows and familiar faces. Fine.

18. Went errands, pierced a block, went on with alphabet etc. We have had in the last few days almost the only rain of any importance that has fallen during the whole of this year. Many crops have suffered severely from the drought.

19. Sunday. Went in morning, afternoon and evening to Maze Pond, and in afternoon to Westminster Abbey. Very wet.

20. Went errands, cut up wood, drew a Bible for S.P.C.K.'s covers, went on with alphabet etc. In evening went to North Brixton to hear a lecture by Rev. MᶜConnel Hussey. Fine.

21. Went errands, on with alphabet, put letters in Bible etc. Rainy. In evening went to Mr. Smiles', took him from my father a copy of 'Childe Harolde' as a present. He professed to be highly delighted and I think he was pleased. Met a young man there of the name of Walker, who is a draughtsman at Scott Russell's the eminent shipbuilders. He told me that they have now working in their yard a grandson of Lord Byron's whose title is Lord Oakham.[72] In appearance (I am told) he is as common as a navvy!

22. Went errands, altered Bible, on with alphabet etc. To-night Mr Albert Smith re-opened his exhibition at the Egyptian Hall. His new entertainment is entitled, 'From Mont Blanc to Canton'. Fine.

23. Went errands, cut up wood, drew letters, on with alphabet etc. Very windy.

24. Went on with alphabet etc. Wet. My father and uncle have lately been investing their money in 2 smacks, one a cod fisher, the Comet, 75 tons, and the other a trawler, the Liberty, 50 tons. They do not seem to be at all a bad spec, the cod fisher especially, which has brought up 60£ worth of fish.

25. Xmas day. Did much the same as usual. Spent our Christmas by ourselves. I manufactured some weights for exercising with, to try and improve my strength. Very wet.

26. Sunday went to Maze Pond in morning and evening, Mr. Millard preached, and to the Abbey in afternoon, Dean Trench preached. Mr Cadman of St. George's in the Boro, Southwark, who is one of the popular preachers in London, preached at St. Paul's this evening, so I called at St. Paul's on my way to chapel to see if I could get in to hear him, but finding it hopeless, I went on my way.

27. Went on with alphabet and commenced getting up a new scrap book for the shop. I hear that tonight there has been a very serious accident at the Victoria Theatre, in which 12 boys have been crushed as they were going up the staircase. We shall doubtless hear more about it tomorrow. Fine.

---

72. This must be an error. There was no such title.

28. Was all day making out a list of books for our book on wood engraving of which more anon. The accident which I briefly mentioned yesterday is alas too true. Instead of 12 there are 15 dead, with a very considerable number also who are seriously wounded. The account in the Times of this morning is as follows. Owing to the attractions of the pantomime, the manager thought it advisable to have 2 performances, one in afternoon and the other in evening. The afternoon performance was nearly over and the mob was leaving the gallery when a slight explosion of gas took place on the staircase and then the accident occurred. Those who were waiting [blank space left]

29. Went on with book on Wood Engraving, put a great number of cuts in a scrap book of my father's etc. Fine. Brother Fred has gone to a sort of a 'spread' at my uncle Elijah's. I was asked but have shirked it. Another unfortunate one is found to have been killed at the Victoria, making 16 deaths in all.

30. Drew a block for Gosse, went to museum and traced another for him. Collected material for book on engraving. Rainy.

31. Drew a block for Gosse, went on with alphabet etc. Fine. They are off, they are off! Who say you? The South Western and the Brighton R$^y$ Companies I reply. And truly a very pretty quarrel it is, history as follows. [blank column left]

**[1859]**

1. **January**. 1859. Went on with alphabet, out errands etc. The new Portsmouth Railway was opened today.

2. Sunday. Went to Maze Pond in morning and evening. Mr. Millard preached both times. Very foggy.

3. Went on with alphabet, out errands, stamped blocks etc. Oh, what a world it is. Or at least what a strange world of creatures we are. My father came in this evening and in conduct acted in a perfect manaical manner. It resembled the conduct of Frederick the Great's father more than any other example I can give.

4. Marked out wood, finished alphabet, etc. Fine, but streets in a filthy state. Last night I was told, one of the staircases at the Polytechnic Institution fell down injuring upwards of 30 people. I am not at all surprised, for the crowding there at Christmas time is something terrific.

5. Went to Underwoods (Grosvenor Square) cut up wood, went on with alphabet etc. There was one person killed and between 30 and 40 injured in the accident at the Polytechnic.[73] It was as I stated, a spiral staircase fell from overcrowding. Rainy.

6. Finished alphabet, went errands, touched up blocks, went on with the History of the Virgin, drew in a cottage from a Gilbert etc. In the evening I went to St Martin's Hall to hear Charles Dickens read his Christmas Carol and the Trial from Pickwick, as Mr Green had kindly left us 3 tickets for the stalls. The hall was crowded with a highly respectable audience.[74] [almost complete column left blank]

9. Sunday. Went to Maze Pond in morning and evening, Mr. Millard preached, also in afternoon to the Young Men's Soc, the subject being the temptation of Christ. Very cold. I anticipate snow tonight. The first fall this winter took place yesterday morning.

10. Went on with History of the Virgin, cut up wood etc. Cold.

11. Went to Museum, traced cuts, wrote, looked over works etc, marked out wood, went to Gibson's. Fine and cold. Barometer much higher than it has been for a long time. It now stands at 30.7.

12. Went to Gibson's, on with History of the Virgin, made out lists, looked over and named cuts etc.

13. Went to Museum, traced cut, wrote and read etc. Fine and colder. Mr Gilbert came in evening.

14. Finished the cut from the History of the Virgin, etc. Cold.

15. Touched up History of the Virgin from the original block book at the British Museum, traced a cut, went to S.P.C.K., mended a block, commenced filling in our new scrap book, etc.

16. Sunday. Went to Maze Pond in morning, afternoon and evening. Mr. Millard preached both times. Very cold.

17. Drew some more ornamental letters, cut up lot of wood, read White's history of Selborne for cuts etc. Very wet and very windy.

---

73. The person killed was a child, Emma Pike, aged 10.
74. St Martin's Hall was in Long Acre.

18. Went to Museum, traced cuts etc, cut up wood, went on with letters, began writing out a list of birds. Wet.

19. Finished list of birds, marked out 30 pieces of wood, began the Temptation of Christ from the Speculum Humanae Salvationis. My father has, I think, at last got one of the jobs settled which we have been looking out for a long time. It is a book of birds and will probably have 150 or 200 cuts in it. This will keep us going briskly for some months. Fine and very warm.

20. Made list of fishes, went on with Temptation, went to Museum etc. We have now every prospect of being busy this year as I think we are certain of yet further jobs amounting to 200 or 250 blocks. I sincerely rejoice, more for my father's sake than my own, as it is very dispiriting to a man with 10 children and no great fortune not to be able to obtain work to do. Very windy.

21. Finished list of fishes and learnt thereby a little of Ichthyology, finished the Temptation etc. The Brighton R$^y$ Company applied at the end of last month for an injunction from the Court of Chancery to prevent the South Western R$^y$ running trains over their portion of railway running from Havant to Portsmouth, but from the decision of the Lord Chancellor the S.W.R. have recovered their privileges. This evening I commenced drawing from life (at home). I have picked up a very good boy model about 12 years old who will suit my purposes pretty well at present.

22. Cut up wood, drew the Anglesey Morris, began mouth of Sturgeon etc. Fine.

23. Sunday. Went to Maze Pond in morning and evening. Mr Millard preached both times. It was windier today than I have ever known it. The rain also fell copiously.

24. Cut up wood, went to Museum, made out a fresh list of fishes, finished mouth of Sturgeon etc. My father is painting a small picture from a sketch of Miss Hepburn's of the Castle of Chillon, which will, if I mistake not, be one of his most attractive subjects. Fine. Hallam, the historian, is just dead, at the age I believe of 83. I must own with shame that I have not yet read a single volume of his writings, but hope to do so ere long.

25. Went to Museum, S.P.C.K. etc, began the head of the Hammer Headed Shark etc, cut up wood. I have just read a book in the style of Tom Brown's Schooldays, (which I have before spoken of). It is not so good as Tom Brown, but still is very good. I cannot tell how it is but such books as these affect me more powerfully than any others. I feel convinced that a simple style, natural and unaffected, not too minute, but describing with power, will produce more effect and affect the mind more than the loftiest or grandest matter written in the most magnificent manner. This evening I made my boy model strip (not having previously done so) and found that he is very well formed. His legs are a defect at present being too thin, but that may perhaps be got over. My father went to dinner at Mr Hepburn's. Today a Burns Commemoration Festival was held at the Crystal Palace. The directors have given a prize of 50 guineas to the successful candidate in a competition got up for the occasion. It was to be a poem, not less than 100 and not more than 200 lines in length.

26. Finished Hammer headed Shark etc, cut up wood, drew a block for Gosse's book and began the roe of the sturgeon. Fine. This evening we had the deacons of our chapel to tea and supper (with Mr Millard). The prize poem was read by Mr Phelps yesterday at the Crystal Palace. The successful competitor is a lady. The proceedings generally yesterday at the C.P. were on a miserable scale according to the Times.

27. Made out fresh list of fishes, finished roe of sturgeon etc. Fine: indeed it is wonderful weather for this time of the year. I heard it suggested the other day (in joke) by an acquaintance of mine that the calendar must be wrong, that the years in fact were too short, as the seasons are becoming now quite transposed. But seriously, there seems something in the suggestion.

My father and mother went to a church meeting at our chapel.

The name of the lady who has gained the Crystal Palace prize for her ode is Ida Craig. She is already known in the literary world.

28. Cut up wood, began Internal organs of Myxine, began reading a history of England for cuts etc. Fine.

29. Finished internal organs of Myxine, went on making list of cuts for new history of England etc.

30. Sunday. Went to Maze Pond in morning and evening, Mr. Millard preached, and to Westminster Abbey in the afternoon, Dr. Wordsworth preaching. Wet.

31. Finished list of subjects for History of England, marked out 20 pieces of wood, went to Museum. etc.

1. **February**. Cut up wood, went errands, drew a mackerel (a stinking job), wrote out list for history of England, etc. Very windy.

2. Began a skeleton of the Perch etc. Parliament I believe opens today. By the by, I have quite forgotten to put down that the Princess Royal (late) of England was safely delivered of a son at Berlin last week. It has been doing very well since. The telegraphic message arrived at Windsor from Berlin in 6 minutes.

3. Made lists of birds, cut up wood, went to Wolf's and British Museum, corrected engraving blocks, began Wolf fish etc. Fine but freezing. My father and Fred went to the first meeting of the A. and A. conversazione.

4. Went to Museum and Lewis' the auctioneer's twice, finished Wolf fish etc. Rainy. Parliament opened yesterday and not the day before, as I stated. There seems every probability of this session being an exciting one, reform in some shape or other will be accomplished, church rates will most likely be abolished and other measures of importance will come on.

5. Cut up wood, went to Vizetelly's, began a statue of Magister John Schow. Rainy.

6. Sunday. Went to Maze Pond in morning and Salters Hall chapel in the evening. Fine, very windy.

7. Went on with saint, cut up wood, went to Gibsons, began a large map for a new Quarterly Review of Bentley's etc. Rainy.

8. Went to Gibson's and errands, cut up wood, on with map for Bentley etc. Rainy. We shall, I think, be nicely busy this year, for we keep on having little jobs come in, as well as the big ones. Thanks be to our Father in

Heaven from whom all blessings flow, and may we strive to deserve them, so far as we may be said to deserve anything.

9. Went errands, cut up wood, finished Bentley's map, finished statue of John Schow etc.

10. Put up blind, touched Gudgeon and Loach of Gibson's, went on with skeleton of perch etc.

11. Cut up wood, began a perch etc. In evening spent a pleasant evening at Mr. Roffey's. Met an old schoolfellow, Chester Foulsham, who I was always partial to, though I am not sure if the liking is reciprocal.

12. Marked out a lot of wood, finished perch, went to Gibson's etc etc. In afternoon went to Kew, but there being no boats there for hire, walked on to Richmond, from thence rowed to Twickenham, round the island and back again to Richmond. I then walked to Ham Common, took tea at Warners and from thence home again.

13. Sunday. Went in morning and evening to Maze Pond, Mr. Millard preached, and in afternoon to the Abbey. Fine.

14. Went to Raffles and various errands, cut up lot of wood, packed parcels, on with skeleton of Perch, began Lump sucker etc. My cousin came today from Yeovil.

15. Went to Brit. Mus., also to Butterworth and to Spooner, cut up lot of wood, went various errands, on with Skeleton of Perch, on with lump sucker etc. In evening Frank Dillon came with D. M$^c$Kewan to see my father, Vacher also came in. I went in evening to the Old Water Colour Rooms to hear a lecture, Venice by G.E. Street (architect) at which [blank space left]

16. Went errands, cut up wood, went on with Lump sucker and on with Skeleton of Perch. John Cassell has offered some premiums for the best tales for his journals, to be sent in by next August under certain conditions. I am at present trying to concoct a story, getting material, etc.

17. Went to Museum, traced some plates from Britton's Lichfield, went on with Skeleton of Perch etc.

18. Went on with Skeleton of Perch, cut up wood, went errands etc Mr Gosse came up from York early this morning and will stay with us about a week.

19. Finished Skeleton of Perch, cut up wood, drew a rush-holder etc. Went to tea at Peckham and had a pleasant evening there. Wet.

20. Sunday. Went to Maze Pond in morning and evening. Mr Millard preached, and to Westminster Abbey in the afternoon, Dean Trench preaching. Fine. I like Mr Gosse exceedingly. Besides being a clever and learned man (and the conversation of such must always be pleasing to me) he is an excellent Christian, brim full of his Bible, and very apt with his texts. He is a Plymouth brother, which is the same as saying that he is no sect, and his opinions and views on religion coincide almost perfectly with my own. The stay of such a man in one's house is, I think, almost sure to do one good.

21. Went to Museum, traced a number of fishes, corrected proofs etc. Dr Hook, vicar of Leeds (whose High Church and almost Pusey tendency is

well known) has just had the vacant deanery of Chichester offered to him and has accepted it.

22. Went various errands, cut up wood, began a Lancelet, the Butterfly fish and the Beardless Ophidium. The ministers last night asked for leave to bring in their bill on church rates. Leave was granted after a long discussion. Fine.

23. Finished Lump sucker, cut up wood, went errands, began the Forked Hake, Basking Shark and the Gymnetrus Hawkinsii. In evening I went to Pimlico to hear Mr Gosse give a lecture on "the wonders of the sea." He is a nice lecturer on those subjects and I should like to play the showman to him during the summer season at the watering places, where I have little doubt that he would draw well..

24. Went to Museum, traced diagrams for Tomlinson, finished Lancelet, Beardless Ophidium and Basking Shark, cut up wood etc. Fine. In evening went to a spread at Mr R. Taylor's next door. Dancing all the evening (24 dances) and broke up only at 5 next morning. I left at 12.

25. Went to Tomlinson's at Camden Town, cut up wood, drew 2 diagrams etc. Today Mr Gosse left us for his home at Marychurch near Torquay. He is an exceedingly nice Christian man, and I like him all the more since his stay with us.

26. Touched up a drawing of Skelton's, went to Walbrook (British Orphan Asylum) etc.[75] There will, I think, be no war as was feared. In answer to a question last night by Lord Palmerston, it was stated by the ministers that they had intelligence that Italy would very shortly be evacuated by both Austrian and French troops; and it was also stated that Lord Cowley's mission to Vienna was entirely pacific.

27. Sunday. Went to Maze Pond morning and evening. Mr. Aldis preached for the Baptist fund. The sermon in the evening on the humanity of Christ was most admirable. In the afternoon I went to the Abbey. Fine.

28. Went to Gibson's, finished touching up sheet of Skelton's, cut out sizes of 60 fish and pasted them in manuscript etc. The Ministerial Reform Bill comes on this week. It is generally understood that if there is any serious opposition to it that the ministry will resign.

1. **March**. Went to Museum, out errands, finished Forked Hake and Gymnetrus Hawkinsii, traced lot of fishes etc. Last night the ministers introduced their reform bill, but I have not had time to read it yet.

2. Went errands, marked out 80 pieces of wood, also cut up some, went on with Ocellated Blenny, began Cornish sucker.

3. Went to Blind School twice and sketched, finished it at home etc. My father went to 2nd conversazione at Willis' Rooms. I went in evening to Mr. Sandalls.

4. Touched up sketch of Blind School, also sketched central tower of ditto, went to Museum, made sketches of Lichfield Cathedral, finished Ocellated Blenny, touched up 2 others etc.

75. The British Orphan Asylum was at 12 Walbrook, in the city.

5. Went to Museum, made an elaborate tracing of choir of Lichfield cathedral from Britton etc.

6. Sunday. Went to Maze Pond in morning, Mr. Millard preached, but had to stay at home in evening on account of illness; very severe headache and cold. Fine.

7. Altered silvery hair-tail and began a large block of some fort in New Mexico. I am considerably better today but Collambell says that unless I take care of myself and do not work quite as hard, I shall probably bring on a fever. Pleasant news.

8. Went on with Fort in New Mexico, put a number of cuts into scrap book, altered a block of Skelton's etc. I feel better.

9. Finished Fort, went to Butterworth's, put cuts in scrap book etc. Today I feel worse again.

10. Went to Ward's and Pewtress', marked out wood, corrected 5 fishes of Gibson's, packed parcels etc. The Government church rate abolition bill was defeated last night by a respectable majority. It was a most ridiculous and if entertained seriously might be called a most iniquitous bill, for the purpose and intent of it was, to compel everyone to pay them still, or else if you did not, it would deprive you of your parochial privileges.

11. Went errands, drew the Angel fish, began 10 spined stickleback etc. Very windy.

12. Went errands, on with Stickleback, counted out and parcelled 200 min. atlas etc

13. Sunday. Went to Maze Pond in morning, afternoon and evening. Mr. Millard preached both times. Very wet. I am very much better indeed, though not strong yet, I may say quite recovered.

14. Went to Barbe's (for pencils) and to Museum, corrected fish of Gibson's, cut up and marked out wood, finished stickleback and began Tench etc.[76] Rainy.

15. Went numerous errands, marked out and cut up great deal of wood, went on with Tench etc.

16. Marked out lot of wood, finished tench, finished a block for Bentley of the valley of the Rio Grande etc. There was a few days ago a most remarkable squadron of Italians landed at Cork.[77] [space left]

17. Went to Clowes etc, touched various blocks, marked out wood, began interior of Lichfield Cathedral etc. Very windy. Today my father had the bad news that one of his smacks [space left]

18. Went to Evans, on with Lichfield Cathedral etc. Today the 'Comet' was towed up the Thames and my father learnt the extent of the damage that was done to it. [space left blank]

---

76. Lechertier Barbe and Co. was a supplier of artists' materials in Regent Street.
77. King Ferdinand of Naples had released from prison sixty-six political opponents who had been held since 1848, and sent them into exile on a steamer to Spain, from where they were to be taken to America. Placed on board an American ship at Cadiz, the Italian exiles, who outnumbered the crew, prevailed upon the American captain to take them to Cork.

19. Went errands, on with Lichfield Cathedral etc, read the 'Gentile World' for cuts etc. Fine.

20. Went in morning, afternoon and evening to Maze Pond, Mr. Millard preached both times. Fine but very windy.

21. Cut up wood, packed parcels, wrote upwards of 30 letters, went on with Lichfield Cathedral and in evening went to Mrs Sowerby at Peckham. A good day's work. Fine.

22. Went on with Lichfield Cathedral etc.

23. Went on with Lichfield Cathedral, wrote letters etc. I have just managed to get myself into rather a queer position, as follows; [1 column left blank][78]

24. Went on with Lichfield Cathedral, went errands etc

25. Went on with Lichfield Cathedral etc, and went several errands. There have been some severe debates on the Government Reform Bill during the last few nights which will probably end in the defeat of the said bill, and the resignation of the Derbyites or a dissolution of Parliament, either of which things we do not wish to come to pass at present. Fine.

26. Went on with Lichfield Cathedral etc. Fine. Held a committee meeting of my cricket club at our house of business this evening when some important business was transacted.

27. Sunday. Went to Maze Pond in morning, afternoon and evening. Mr. Millard preached both times.

28. Went on with Lichfield Cathedral etc. Fred has got one of his pictures hung at Suffolk St out of 2 which he sent. The exhibition is I believe slightly better than usual. Rainy.

29. Finished Lichfield Cathedral, marked out wood etc. Mr and Mrs Pewtress came in evening.

30. Touched up Lichfield Cathedral, touched 2 blocks of Gibson's, went to Heaths, cut up wood, outlined fishes etc. A great deal of snow fell during the day, so much so, that in the afternoon it laid thickly on the ground.

31. Marked out and cut up lot of wood, went to Well's, and British Museum, went on with Viviparous Blenny and Rainbow Wrasse etc. The Brighton and S. C. R^y and the South Western Railway are at it hammer and tongs, as I expected they would be. We can now be taken to Portsmouth and back in 3½ hours for 3/6, or by the Brighton R^y to the Isle of Wight and back, by the special expresses for the same money. I suppose they will continue at this fun until next June, when they will suddenly learn wisdom, by discovering that their half-yearly meeting is approaching. The powder mills at Hounslow have again blown up, destroying 6 people. In a building 3 miles away, 100 panels of glass were broken by it. I have risked my guinea in the Art Union for this year and of course confidently expect a prize; perhaps 20,000 besides expect the same.

---

78. On 19 March 1859, a small notice appeared in *The Times* under the names of Miss M. Wilson of Kennington Lane, and Mr Edward Whymper of Lambeth Road, asking for financial contributions for a Richard Apps of Jonathan Street, Lambeth, who had been attacked by ruffians and left unable to support his family.

1 **April**. Awful day to be born on. Went to museum, on with Rainbow Wrasse and Viviparous Blenny, touched up drawings of Gibson's and went to Mr Smiles.

2. Finished Rainbow Wrasse and went to the museum, where when I was leaving I saw the Queen and Prince Albert who had also been just paying it a visit. Very wet. Mr Burt and Mr Smith (the author of the autobiography of a journey man printer) came today to dinner. My father went in evening to Frank Dillon's to meet some artists.

3. Sunday. Went to Maze Pond in morning and evening, Mr Millard preached both times. Fine.

4. Drew Garfish, went to museum, went to Gibson's, helped to get my father's drawings ready for the exhibition etc.

5. Went to museum, arranged fish, corrected proofs, wrote titles to father's pictures etc etc.

6. Went errands, cut up wood, cut out cuts, began the centre of the Blind School. Fine, very hot; the heat being exceedingly oppressive from the very great change in the temperature. This day last week it was freezing.

7. Went to museum, drew Rough tailed stickleback, began Basse and Grey mullet, wrote letters, packed parcels, etc etc.

8. Went on with Centre of Blind School, packed parcels, wrote letters etc. Had another committee meeting of my cricket club (the N.L.C.C.). We have lately been delighted by receiving formal permission from the Archbishop to play in his grounds. We can now go ahead confidently.

9. Went on with blind school etc. The New Water colour exhibition will be rather over the average this year. I am afraid my father will not sell so well as usual, owing chiefly to three things. 1. This being a better exhibition, 2$^{nd}$ on account of the dissolution obliging many who would have purchased to spend their money in elections, 3$^{rd}$ to his subjects not being quite so good as usual, although I think the painting on them is better.

10. Went to Maze Pond in morning and evening, Mr Millard preached both times. Rainy.

11. Went errands, to Gibson's, on with centre of Blind school, finished Basse, went on with Grey mullet. Several very heavy showers of rain and great quantities of hail fell during the day, in one of which storms I got a severe drenching. The difference of temperature between last week and the previous one, was 58°. The highest last week was 78° and the lowest in the week previously was 20°. A very great change even for a changeable climate.

12. Drew 'John Dory' arranged fishes, wrote letters and packed parcels etc. In evening went to a meeting of the Peckham Rye Albion Cricket Club of which I am a member, at the Edinburgh Castle Tavern. I am afraid that they are a rather queer, beery lot and I must mind that I am not drawn into their bad habits. Very, very wet, and I managed to get fully my share of moisture.

13. Cut up wood, finished Grey Mullet, went on with centre of Blind School etc. Vulgar Frederick Doulton (the potter) is putting up as a member for Lambeth. I hope he may not get in, but am afraid he will.

14. Arranged fishes etc, packed blocks for and wrote to Mr Kelke, went errands etc, on with centre of Blind School. Very wet.

15. Named proofs, cut up wood etc, went on with centre of Blind School, began general view of Blind School, began 3 fishes etc. Very cold. In evening had another cricket meeting; we are going on pretty prosperously.

16. Went to museum, Dobbs Kidd and Co[79], Blackwood's etc, cut up wood, went on with fish etc. The Oxford and Cambridge boat race came off yesterday, between Putney and Mortlake, which resulted in the Oxford eight winning.

[space left]

The Queen went yesterday to the New Water Colour Gallery and bought 4 pictures, one of Edward Warren's, one of Mole, one of Richardson and one of somebody whose name I forget. In the evening there was a severe snowstorm.

17. Went to Maze Pond in morning and evening, Mr Millard preached both times. Fine.

18. Went errands, finished sketching and began drawing Blind School. My Father sold 5 of his drawings on Saturday at the New Water colour private view but has not sold any today. Strange to say, all those which are sold are the worst and the ones which he (and I also) considered least likely to sell.

19. Went to Society, cut up wood, went out hunting for photographs, finished 3 bearded Rockling, went on with Blind School etc. Parliament was prorogued today. Sir W. Clay, I believe, intends putting up for Lambeth. I hope he may succeed in keeping the ignorant, radical Fred Doulton out.

20. Went to museum, Gibson's, Askes', photograph hunting etc, cut up wood, went on with centre of Blind School etc. Mr. W. Williams has at last again put up for Lambeth and unless Mr Doulton makes greater efforts than I or others think him capable of, he will stand but a poor chance of being returned. My father went to Gilbert's. Skelton came in evening. Fine.

21. Went on with centre of Blind School etc etc. Had a cricket meeting in evening and afterwards went to the Victoria Theatre to a meeting of Doulton's in the hopes of making or helping to make a disturbance. There was, however, quite row enough without my assistance, the groaning and hissing was tremendous; although I was within a few feet of the speakers I could not hear a word they said. I got fortunately on the stage; being the first time I was ever in a theatre.

22. Good Friday. Finished centre of Blind School and cut up wood, although it was a holiday. War between the Austrians, and the Sardinians and French seems now certain; the first blow will probably be struck next Sunday.

23. Went on with Blind School, cut up wood etc.

24. Easter Sunday. Went to Maze Pond in morning and evening. Mr Vince of Birmingham preached in the morning and Mr – of Bradford in the evening. They were both excellent sermons, the best however was most

79. Dobbs, Kidd and Co. was a stationers in Fleet Street.

undoubtedly the former. And yet he was only a carpenter originally which shows that it is by no means a necessary thing to be educated (as it is called) for the ministry. Very wet, which drives all thoughts of cricket into the distance. Our opening meeting was to have been next Tuesday.

25. Went errands, marked out wood, worked on a picture of my father's etc, and on with Blind School. Very wet.

26. Went errands, cut up wood, made lists, went on with Blind School. My brother Henry's 14th birthday. Fine. Young Glennie came in evening and stayed to supper.

27. Went errands, went on with Blind School etc. The Times reviewed this year's exhibition of the New Water Colour today. My father in common with a number of others, got but a very brief notice. Fine. My 20th birthday.

28. Went to Clowes' etc, on with Blind School. Very wet. Today we had the sad intelligence that the Austrian army had declared war by crossing the Ticino, numbering 120,000 men, and also that the French were pouring their troops into Sardinia as fast as possible, 8 regiments left Paris for Lyons yesterday. Where this miserable war will end it is impossible to conjecture, but I think if it does not end within a twelve-month's time it will involve all the nations of Europe and then - - it is dreadful to think of. I forgot to mention on Tuesday (which was a great omission, as I am mightily rejoiced thereat) that Fred Doulton had - in spite of his protestations that he was going to the poll – resigned, or rather retired from the contest. Roupell and Williams, will therefore walk the course. All I can say for them is, - bad is the best!

29. Finished Blind School, marked wood, wrote letter etc, began temple at Baalbec.

30. Went on with temple at Baalbec, went photograph hunting etc. In afternoon went to museum to carry on a life of Handel which I am compiling; with the intention of trying to get it published for the Handel commemoration which takes place in June. I think however it is very doubtful if it will be finished in time.

1. **May**. Sunday. Went to Maze Pond in morning and evening, Mr Millard preached both times. Fine.

2. Went to S.P.C.K., to Hogarth's, museum etc, photograph hunting, touched up large block of Blind School, began the house at Delhi in which Mr Mackay was murdered etc. Fine. Today the Royal Academy opened its annual exhibition. My brother Fred succeeded in getting a picture hung which he sent. The exhibition is said to be a very fair, average one. Telegrams have arrived of accounts of skirmishes between the Austrians and the Sardinians.

3. Wrote letters, packed parcels, went on with Temple at Baalbec etc. I did not (as might be expected) get a prize in the Art Union, and there is likely to be somewhat of a disturbance from the fact, that out of 15,000£ subscribed, only 2,500£ was given away in prizes. Query. Where has the rest gone to?

4. Went on with House at Delhi, cut up wood etc, drew Gilt-head, went to Stockwell and South Lambeth to sketch schools etc. Very fine, but cold from an easterly wind.

5. Finished house at Delhi, marked out and cut up wood, went on with Temple at Baalbec, made a finished sketch of Springgrove schools etc. Fine.
6. Drew Springgrove schools, cut up wood, went on with Temple at Baalbec etc. In evening had my first spurt of walking of this season and find that at present I cannot walk faster than I did last year though doubtless I can walk further. Very fine.
7. Went on with Temple at Baalbec, cut up wood, arranged fish etc. Fine, though raining in evening.
8. Sunday. Went to Maze Pond in morning and Regent St, Lambeth in evening. Mr Clark preached at the former and Mr Lancaster at the latter. Very fine.
9. Went on with Temple at Baalbec, marked out wood, etc etc. The Archbishop of Canterbury who had forgotten to give orders for our admission to his grounds, has been reminded of it and has at last done so, so that the North Lambeth CC will meet for the first time (weather permitting) tomorrow evening.[80]
10. Finished Temple at Baalbec, marked out wood, went errands, went photograph hunting, to museum etc. In evening went to the first meeting of the North Lambeth Cricket Club. I hope it may continue many years in existence and I in it, but I have my fears about it.
11. Touched up fish of Gibson's, wrote letter, marked lot of wood, arranged photographs, began a general view of ruins at Baalbec etc. My father went today to Selborne in Hampshire, to make sketches for a new edition of White's Selborne. He will stay in the neighbourhood a day or two.
12. Went errands, marked out wood, went on with Baalbec etc.
13. Finished Baalbec, cut up lots of wood, began a plan of Delhi etc. In evening went to Archbishops' grounds. The old gentleman has behaved very kindly; he has signed our 20 members tickets with his own hand and appears to take some little interest in the affair. Very fine. My mother went down today to Haslemere to look at a house which my father saw and liked yesterday. They have been for a considerable time talking of a move and now perhaps we shall have it.
14. Was almost the whole day at my paper to be read to-morrow to the Young Men's Christian Association at Maze Pond. Got on but slowly with it. Very fine.
15. Sunday. Went to Maze Pond in morning, afternoon and evening. In afternoon, read my paper on 'Ought Christians to resist tyrannical governments?' Rainy. Mr Millard preached both times.
16. Went on with plan of Delhi etc. Raining. The war in Italy does not make any progress, one way or another. The Austrians adhere to the character that they have always had, viz, of being extraordinary slow in all their movements. The Emperor of the French has left Paris and has arrived at Genoa.
17. Finished plan, began a view of Damascus etc. Very wet; went to Archbishop's in evening, but as only one but myself was there, we had no meeting.

80. John Bird Sumner (1780 – 1862) Archbishop of Canterbury from 1848 to 1862.

18. Went on with Damascus, cut up wood, began several fishes, altered fish of Gibson's etc.

19. Went to Miller's etc, cut up lot of wood, drew Argentine, began Flying fish etc. My father has just sold two more of his pictures (value 52£) so that altogether he has done pretty well. It is however strange, that the whole of his best pictures in the exhibition remain unsold. Very wet.

20. Went to museum, cut up wood, finished flying fish, went on with Coal fish, Torsk and Trout etc. My father and mother went in evening to Mr Hepburn's.

21. Went to Gibson's, cut up wood, went on with trout, altered blocks of Green's and Skelton's etc.

22. Sunday. Went to Maze Pond in morning and evening, and to the Abbey in afternoon. Mr Millard preached both times at former place and Dean French at the latter. Fine.

23. Cut up wood, finished 'Trout', altered Pike of Gibson's, ditto a block of Green's etc etc. Fine. This morning were telegraphed two accounts of a battle between the Austrians, and the French and Sardinians. The two accounts were very dissimilar.

24. Went to museum and S.P.C.K., marked out wood, touched up Pike, went on with Torsk etc. In evening went to Archbishop's grounds and had a meeting of the club afterwards, which latter performance was rather riotous. Very fine.

25. Finished Torsk and Coal fish, touched up Trout, began marking sizes of blocks for Gentile World etc. Very fine. My father went sketching at the old pond at Southend, the only pond he says in England that he has heard of, that is worth much.

26. Marked sizes of Gentile World cuts, and made a list of them, went to Clowes, the museum, and the Society, began a Salmon etc. In evening went to Peckham to a practice night of the C. Club I have joined there. I do not like [those] fellows much, and consider their bowling on the whole very bad; many can hit very hard but that is doubtful qualification.

27. Finished Salmon, began Cod, marked wood etc. In evening went to Archbishop's to cricket (N.L.C.C.). Very fine.

28. Made another list of Gentile World cuts, finished Cod, touched up fish of Gibson's etc In afternoon went to Richmond and from there rowed with Fred and Walker to Kingston and back. Sultry day.

29. Sunday. Went to Maze Pond in morning and evening; Mr Millard preached both times. Very wet.

30. Went to Hungerford Market for Haddock, drew it, cut up wood, touched up fish of Gibson's etc. Rainy. Today my Aunt and Uncle Woods from Swaffham came to stay the night with us, bringing a friend. My grandfather, grandmother in law and another aunt also came up from Ipswich.[81]

31. Arranged fish etc, went to Dickes, and to Maze Pond chapel to make plans of it etc. Today my brother Alfred came up from Edinburgh, much

81. Edward Whymper's grandmother-in-law was Charlotte; the aunt must have been Theodosia Whymper, his father's youngest sibling (see Appendix 1).

grown. My uncle and aunt etc, have also left us for the Isle of Wight, where they will pass a month. My grandfather today learnt from the surgeon that he came up to see, that his days were numbered and that he could not hope to recover from his bad leg. This is rather sad news for him, but at his age (72) he could not reasonably expect otherwise.

1. **June**. Derby day at Epsom. Arranged and got off another batch of 43 fish, marked wood, began a lion surrounded by 13 stars, etc. Walked in evening with Alfred and Thomas Roffey to the Morden turnpike on the Epsom road. The company returning I thought rather more numerous than usual, and although we walked more than 16 miles, yet we did not see a single accident.

2. Finished Lion surrounded by stars, drew letters in 2 blocks of Skelton's, began Gilbert White's house at Selborne etc. Very wet. Father went in afternoon with Gilbert to the Regent Park Zoological Gardens.[82] There was another battle on the 31st between the Austrians and Sardinians, in which the former are said again to be beaten.

3. Went on with White's house at Selborne, made list of and cut out sizes of the cuts for the first part of White's Selborne, put cuts in scrap book etc.

4. Went on with plan of Maze Pond chapel, marked wood etc. Decided that we are to leave London and take up our permanent abode at Haslemere (at least for 3 years). I have had nothing to do with this step but have always opposed it, as I think that it will bring many troubles. My grandfather etc left here today for Ipswich. Very rainy, and in afternoon had a small thunderstorm.

5. Sunday. Went to Maze Pond in morning and evening. Mr Millard preached both times. Heavy rain, and snow, thunder and lightning this afternoon.

6. Finished plan of Maze Pond, went on with White's house at Selborne, etc. Fine day. Father and mother went to a social tea meeting at our chapel this evening. I hate tea meetings.

7. Cut up and marked out a lot of wood, went on with White's house at [space left]

8. Went to museum to meet Mr C. Tomlinson and went on with Picked Dog fish, cut up wood, commenced cleaning out room in Canterbury Place for my future bed room etc. Very fine. Cherries were being sold today in the streets.

9. Drew some of Tomlinson's diagrams, marked out wood, cleared out rooms. In evening went [to] Peckham Rye intending to have an evening with the Albion Club, but they however did not play so I played with the Standard, and had a very pleasant evening. I bowled and caught 7 or 8 and managed to stick at my wicket pretty well. My father went in afternoon to Hayes Common, Kent. Very fine. In today's 'Times' there was announced the death of David Cox who is, as they said the greatest of English water colour painters.

---

82. The Zoological Gardens – London Zoo – had opened in 1828.

10. Drew more of Tomlinsons' diagrams, wrote letter, packed blocks etc. Today I heard that one of Christy's Minstrels has just died. It was Mr Pierce, the inimitable singer and actor of the now world-wide song "Hoop de dooden doo". I am very sorry for them and for myself. Mr Soper supped with us.

In evening I went to Archbishop's Ground and had a pleasant game in spite of the wet evening. The Brighton Railway [space left blank]

11. [Left blank]

12. Sunday. Went to Maze Pond in morning and evening, Mr Millard preached both times. We had a severe thunderstorm and heavy rain in the afternoon, for which I was very glad, and it now looks (11 p.m.) as if we are going to have a continuation of the same.

13. Went to Skelton's, Wolf and Tomlinson's, finished diagrams for the latter, cut up lot of wood etc. Prince Metternich died on Saturday. [space left]

14. Went on with Picked Dogfish, improved fish of Gibson's, and arranged 3$^{rd}$ and final batch of 53 fish. David Cox is buried today at Harborne Church, Birmingham. Very fine. Went in evening to Archbishop's Grounds to cricket. Heard a rumour of the death of Cook the water colour marine painter. Lord Palmerston is entrusted again with getting up an administration, and Lord John Russell has accepted office under him as Secretary for Foreign Affairs.

15. Drew an Eel, went on with White's house at Selborne etc. The rumour of Cook's death has resolved itself into a certainty. He was a charming painter, wonderfully facile and simple in his style and at the same time very true to nature. Very fine.

16. Cut up wood, touched up fish of Gibson's, went on with Picked dogfish. Went to museum, made tracings etc. In evening went to Peckham and played with my club. Was not so fortunate in either bowling or batting as I was last Thursday with the Standard club. Tonight I only got 3 or 4 wickets. By the bye I paid our sec E Bower my subscriptions last Thursday which he has not given me a receipt for. Father went to Southend.

17. [Blank]

18. Finished Sand eel, touched drawing of Gibson's, began Skate etc. Father went with our apprentice C. Green sketching in Holwood Park.

19. Sunday. Went to Maze Pond in morning and evening and to Westminster Abbey in the afternoon. Mr Millard preached both times, at the former place and Lord John Thynne at the latter. Very fine, though some call the heat oppressive..

20. Went to museum, arranged fish, corrected and touched up proofs, finished Skate etc. Very wet.

21. Touched up proofs, marked out wood and got into the very dirty operations of cleaning out rooms which have not been used for several years etc. Wet in evening. Went in evening to Archbishop's grounds; we keep up attendance pretty well, 14 being present.

22. Got off 3$^{rd}$ lot of fish, 56 in number, went on with White's house at Selborne etc. In evening rowed from Bishop's walk (Renshaw's) to above Putney Bridge in company with 2 others in a gig, which was pretty well, as

we did it all the way up against tide, and the whole distance there and back in 3 hours. Rainy, sky looking tempestuous.

23. Finished White's house at Selborne, cut up wood, drew a diagram for Tomlinson, touched up a diagram of Green's etc etc. In evening went to Peckham to practice with Albion C.C. Got only 2 wickets and did not stick very well. Played very little time.

24. Drew some of Tomlinson's diagrams, cut up wood, cleared out rooms etc. In evening went to cricket at Archbishop's grounds. Very fine.

25. Went on with Tomlinson's diagrams, cut up wood, wrote letter, packed parcel etc. Father went to Haslemere to see how the house is getting on. Very fine and very hot.

26. Sunday. Went to Maze Pond in morning and evening, Mr Millard preached both times, and to Westminster Abbey in afternoon, Dean Trench preached. About ½ past 7 o'clock this morning we had a very sharp thunderstorm, during which a man was instantaneously struck dead by lightning on Clapham Common, who had taken shelter under a poplar tree.

27. Began a map of environs of Selborne etc. There has been another great battle fought between the Austrians, and French and Sardinians. One account states the Austrians hors de combat at 35000, and prisoners 15000 men. There were 300,000 Austrians engaged in it and their positions stretched to a distance of 12 or 15 miles. Exceedingly hot, with heavy rain in evening. My aunt and uncle Woods today returned here from the Isle of Wight.

28. Went errands, marked wood, went on with Damascus etc. The Emperor of Austria has left his army for Vienna. Why? This looks queer. Very wet.

29. Finished Damascus, marked out wood, went on with White's map of Selborne. Aunt and uncle Woods left today for Swaffham via Tring and Northampton. My mother went down to Haslemere and brought back an immense hamper of garden produce.

30. Cut up wood, touched up Damascus, went on with map of Selborne, made out new list of Gentile World cuts, wrote letter etc. Fine

---

On Tuesday morning at 3 o'clock my uncle Ebenezer's wife died at Debenham in Suffolk, in great pain. She had previously been attacked several times by apoplexy and paralysis, the cause of her death was however I believe neither of these, but I have not heard particulars.

---

1. **July**. [Blank]

2. [Blank]

3. Sunday. Went to Maze Pond in morning and evening; Mr Millard preached both times. Fine, but is now lightening considerably and raining heavily..

4. Cleared up rooms, went on with map, parcelled wood, marked out ditto etc. Mr Stephen Green came to tea. Very fine. In evening went to Battersea Park, then over the old bridge to Chelsea, thence over the new bridge to

West end Railway and by that to London Bridge. The West End and C.P. Railway was enormously expensive to construct, costing upwards of £100,000 per mile, and must be an expensive line to work, as I noticed two gradients of 1 in 95 and one of 1 in 85.

5. Went on with map of Selborne, marked wood etc. In evening went to Archbishop's grounds.

6. Went to museum, on with Tomlinson's diagrams, marked wood, finished map of Selborne and its environs etc.

7. Went to Gibson's, on with Tomlinson's diagrams etc. In afternoon went to the match at the Oval, Surrey v Oxford (16). The Oxford went in first and got 166 runs. The Surrey had 1 wicket down for [space left] when I left. Very fine and very hot. Went in evening to the P.R.A.C.C. at Peckham Rye and had a pleasant evening.

8. Began St Asaph Cathedral for Almanac, marked wood etc. Went in evening to Archbishop's Grounds and was very successful in bowling; getting 8 or 10 wickets, but in batting, alas! 0.

9. [Blank]

10. Sunday. Went to Maze Pond in morning and evening. Heard Mr Millard in morning and Mr Stokes in evening. Excessively hot.

11. Finished Tomlinson's diagrams, packing for removal, cut up wood, wrote letter, packed block etc, on with cathedral. The big clock at Westminster has at last (today) commenced striking the hours. It is too slow to suit my taste.[83]

12 to 16. Busy moving to Haslemere. [space left]

17. Sunday. Went to Maze Pond in morning and evening. Mr Millard preached both times. Very fine.

18. Finished Cathedral of St Asaph, cut up wood, went errands etc. My father returned today from Haslemere. We are just now in the midst of a very severe thunderstorm. The lightening is very blinding.

19 to 23. [Blank]

24. Sunday. Went to Maze Pond in evening, Mr Millard preaching, and to Westminster Abbey in morning, Dean Trench officiating. My father went yesterday to Haslemere, and I am going to try to walk down next Wednesday.

25. Went to Tomlinson's, museum, Mudie's, S.P.C.K. etc, cut up wood, packed parcels etc. Fine. Today I learn the conclusion of the great cricket match between England and Surrey. Unfortunate Surrey got beaten by 430 runs; a thorough defeat.[84]

26. Finished Memmonium at Thebes, marked out lot of wood, wrote letter etc. Fred returned today from Haslemere. Very fine.

83. The clock had been started on about the 31 May, but not until 11 July were the hours struck on the great bell. The four quarter bells were first chimed on 7 September, when Whymper was in Haslemere.

84. The game was played on 21, 22, 23 July. Surrey lost by 392 runs. V. E. Walker, for England, scored a century then took all ten Surrey wickets.

27. Finished Pyramids and Sphinx, cut up lot of wood, began East Gate at Damascus etc. Fred in evening went to the conversazione at the Royal Academy.

28. Finished East Gate, cut up lot of wood, went errands etc. Tomorrow I with several others go to Haslemere. Very hot indeed.

[No entry or date notation for July 29 to **August** 6. Blank space left.]

7. Sunday. Went in morning and evening to Maze Pond, Mr Millard preached, and in afternoon to Westminster Abbey. Fine.

8. Cut up wood, began some architectural drawings for Mr Murray etc. Very rainy.

9. Began the Colosseum, Rome. My father returned from Haslemere this morning, where he has been since Thursday. Exceedingly wet and rather windy. Yesterday there was a trial of the engines of the Great Eastern, [which] was perfectly satisfactory.

10. Went on with Colosseum, marked wood etc. Very wet. My uncle Ebenezer is going to the Shetland Islands shortly.

11. Went on with Colosseum. Went to Peckham in afternoon to see a match between 22 of Peckham Rye and district and the new All England Eleven. This latter lot are I believe got together by Sherman, and it will, like his other specs, not have I expect very great success. Went on to the Rye in the evening. Fine.

12. Finished Colosseum, got out wood, went on with architectural view etc. In evening went to Battersea Park to cricket; the 3 grounds are now getting in very respectable order. Very fine.

13. Went on with architectural tomb etc. Fine.

14. Sunday. Went to Maze Pond in morning, and to Bloomsbury Chapel in the evening. Rainy.

15. Went to Skelton's and Wolf, marked wood etc, went on with architectural tomb. Father returned from Haslemere, I met him at Waterloo Station. Rainy in morning.

16. Went on with architectural tomb, altered block of Green's, marked wood, went errands etc. Fine. Went to Archbishop's Grounds in evening.

17. Went errands, marked out and cut up wood, went on with architectural tomb etc. Fine.

18. Went to Waterloo Station and to Mr Murray's to meet Dr Thomson, an army surgeon who is going to write a book on New Zealand which we are to illustrate. Marked out lot of wood, went on with architectural tomb, packed parcels etc. Fine, but very close and steamy.

19, 20. [Blank]

21. Sunday. Went to Maze Pond in morning and evening. Mr Edwards agent of the Grand Ligne Canadian mission, preached both times.

22. Went to Bennetts, Greenfields and Gibsons, whitened wood for Walker and Green, finished Architectural Tomb etc etc. Fine.

23. Marked out lot of wood, wrote several letters, packed parcels etc, began 5 storied Pagoda. Fine. Father has gone again to Haslemere. I went to cricket to Archbishop's Grounds.

24-27. [Blank]

28. Sunday. Went to Maze Pond in morning and evening. Mr – sub editor of the 'Freeman' preached both times, and as usual most excellent sermons. Very fine.

29. Went on with old arch at Jerusalem, marked out wood, packed lot of parcels etc. Very wet. Father returned today from Haslemere. I learn now that the fire there was a much more serious affair than I had anticipated. [Blank space left]

30. Went to Anelay's, marked out wood etc, went on with old arch at Jerusalem, altered a block of Miller's, etc. Fine.

31. Finished old arch at Jerusalem, marked out wood etc. Fine. Today the North Lambeth C.C. played under my direction a match with the North Brixton C.C. The scores were 22 and 43 and 38 and 48 (with two wickets to fall), respectively. My share in the former scores was 2, leg before wicket, and 19 not out. It was my first match and the N.L.C.C.'s ditto; it should however be said that we were one man deficient all through both in batting and fielding.

1. **September**. Went errands, cut up and marked out great lot of wood, wrote letter, packed parcels, went on with architectural view no. 1 etc. Fine.

2. Went to Skelton's and Mudie's, packed parcels, marked wood, and went on with architectural view no. 1. Very wet.

3-14. at Haslemere [blank space left]

14. Returned today from Haslemere. Went to Skelton's, marked out lot of wood, packed parcels etc, began N.W. angle of wall at Jerusalem. Today's papers contained a detailed account of the barbarous treachery of the Chinese.

[space left]

15. [Blank]

16. [Blank]

17. Sunday. Went to Maze Pond in morning and evening. Mr Millard preached both times. Fine but chilly, autumn comes on apace.

18, 19. [Blank]

20. Finished N.W. angle of wall, began Christ Church, Jerusalem, wrote letter etc. Fine. Went to cricket at Archbishop's in evening.

21. Went on with Christ Church, wrote letter, cut up wood and attended to general business.

22. A busy day. Wrote to father and MacKewan, packed parcels etc, went to S.P.C.K. etc, went on with Christchurch, Jerusalem. In afternoon went to Peckham, and called on 8 people afterwards, and most fortunately found them all at home. Wet. The day before yesterday Tom Sayers, champion of England, fought Bob Brettle of Birmingham for 400£ to 200£ and won in 6 rounds, the chief reason of winning so easily was by Brettle's shoulder being dislocated in the 5th round.

23, 24. [Blank]

25. Sunday. Went to Maze Pond in morning and evening, Mr Millard preached both times. Rainy.

26. Marked wood, wrote some long letters, finished Church at Samaria, altered several drawings etc. Very rainy indeed and has been exceedingly queer weather for some weeks past.

27. [Blank]

28. Wrote letters, finished Wall of Jerusalem and began the Valley of the Kedron etc etc. In today's Times there was a letter from Dr Livingstone; announcing the discovery of another large lake in central Africa. This one which he calls Lake Shirwa is about 20 to 30 miles broad by 50 to 60 long. Fine.

29. Went errands, went to museum for Tomlinson's diagrams, marked wood, drew remains of ancient Tyre, went on with Valley of Kedron etc. Fred came up from Haslemere after a ten days sojourn there; he has just completed and sent a picture to the Winter Exhibition.

30. Went on with Valley of Kedron, drew a diagram of overhead motion, cut up and marked out wood etc. My father returned after a somewhat long sojourn at Haslemere. Very wet.

1. **Oct**. [Blank]

2. Sunday. Went to Maze Pond in morning and evening. Mr Millard preached both times. Fine. My father went to dinner at Mr Green's.

3. Went to Mudie's, Wolf's, Skelton's and Tomlinson etc, finished overhead motion, cut up, marked out great lot of wood etc. Yesterday we noticed that the Westminster clock did not strike the hours and now today we learn that the great bell, Big Ben no. 2, has cracked.[85] [space left]

4. Began Smyrna, marked out wood, wrote letter, put up safe etc etc. Excessively hot.

5. Went on with Smyrna and Tomlinson's blocks, planed lots of blocks, wrote letter, packed parcel, named 35 blocks, touched proofs etc. Very fine.

6. Named blocks, finished Rose engine, went on with Smyrna, cut up wood and out errands etc.

7. Went on with Smyrna, general business, wrote several letters etc. Father went today to Haslemere.

8. General business, wrote letters etc etc. In afternoon went to cricket at Archbishop's Grounds. Rainy. The cracking of the second great bell has of course given rise to considerable talk, everyone who has had anything to do with it is blaming everyone else and altogether it is a pretty scene.

9. Sunday. Went to Maze Pond in morning and evening. Mr Millard preached both times. Fine.

10. Marked out lot of wood, wrote letter, finished Smyrna, began a pinnacly iceberg etc etc. Father returned from Haslemere. He has just made a very nice sketch of a rather celebrated bridge at a little village called Eashing near Godalming. It is very picturesque and has been previously painted by Creswick, Soper and other artists.

11. Finished Pinnacly Berg, marked out and cut up lot of wood, wrote letter, began ice belt etc etc. The Great Eastern has arrived without further

---

85. A vertical crack one foot long had appeared. With the thirteen and a half ton bell now 200 ft up, suspended above the clock mechanism, it was decided not to recast the bell, but to turn it ninety degrees and fit a lighter hammer. The original chimes restarted in 1862, and have, with some interruptions, continued ever since.

accident at Holyhead. In today's Times was an account of the first match that the England eleven have played in America. They played at Montreal, Canada, against 22 Canadians, and beat them easily; having 8 wickets to spare. Bravo! Old England. May they go on conquering and to conquer.

12. [Blank space, then] Father went to dinner at Mr Green's and kept out till nearly 12 o'clock.

13. Marked out wood, went on with Ice belt, named blocks etc. Today's Times contained the sad announcement of the death of Mr Robert Stephenson. Our two greatest engineers have thus died within a few days of each other.[86] They can be ill spared, for although there are men, many men, of very superior intellect in this profession yet theirs over-topped all. Their conceptions were so brilliant and the execution of their ideas so well carried out, especially in the case of Robert Stephenson who in his long career can scarcely reckon a single failure. He died at his residence in Hyde Park yesterday aged 56 years.

14. Went errands, cut up and marked out wood, finished Ice belt, began Ice foot etc. Fine.

15. Went to SPCK to meet Mr Isaacs, waited until the place was shut up and he did not come. Fine. Went in afternoon to Archbishops.

[End; note book filled up]

86. Isambard Kingdom Brunel had died on 15 September.

# Appendix 1    Persons referred to in the diary

**Aberdeen, George Hamilton-Gordon, fourth Earl of** (1784 – 1860) Peelite Prime Minister in a coalition with the Whigs, from December 1852 until January 1855.

**Agar, Edward** (c.1825 – aft. 1857) Responsible for stealing £12,000 worth of gold bullion from the South Eastern Railway in May 1855, Agar was sentenced to transportation for life for forgery, and turned evidence against his accomplices in the bullion robbery.

**Aldis, John** (1808 – 1907) Baptist minister at Maze Pond from 1837 until 1855, when he moved to Reading. He was President of the Baptist Union in 1866.

**Anderson, John Henry** (1814 – 1874) Popular conjuror and magician, who originated the trick of pulling a rabbit from a top hat.

**Anelay, Henry** (1817 – 1883) Draughtsman and landscape painter who lived at Eyre Cottage, Blackheath; an unsuccessful candidate for the NWCS.

**Angus, Joseph** (1816 – 1902) Baptist biblical scholar, and president of Stepney Baptist College (which moved to Regent's Park in 1856).

**Armstrong, William King** (1822 – 1896) Baptist minister in Ashton under Lyne, Lancashire. Born in Scotland, Armstrong finished his career in Sussex.

**Ashmead, George** (c.1803 – 1883) Baptist minister, born in Gloucestershire.

**Ashwell, Samuel** (c.1799 – 1857) Physician.

**Aske, William Henry** (c.1825 – 1863) Wood engraver, a neighbour of the Whympers at 10 Barkham Terrace, Lambeth Road.

**Bailey, Eliza** (c.1812 – 1856) Wife of **George Bailey** (c.1815 – ?) a haberdasher, of High Street, Southwark. The Baileys were members of Maze Pond chapel, although their name is usually spelt 'Bayley' in the MPMB, where Eliza Bayley's death is recorded on 29 February 1856.

**Baker, George** (fl. 1855) George Baker and Sons were builders in Lambeth, next to the Archbishop's Palace

**Barlow, James** (c.1824 – 1887) Ironmonger in King William Street, who later moved to Leatherhead.

**Barry, Sir Charles** (1795 – 1860) Architect who won the competition, held after the fire in 1834, to design the new Houses of Parliament.

**Barton, James** (fl. 1858) Iron founder at 370 Oxford Street.

**Bates, Robert Makin** (fl.1841 – 1857) Partner in the bank of **Strahan, Paul** and Bates, sentenced to fourteen years' transportation.

**Baxter, George** (1804 – 1867) Wood engraver who developed and patented a process of colour printing, using oils. **Harrison Weir** was a pupil of Baxter's.

**Beatson, William Fergusson** (1804 – 1872) Army officer experienced in working with irregulars, he offered his services to the Turks during the Crimean War, but after some conflict with his British officer, returned to England.

**Beaufoy, Henry** (1786 – 1851) Manager of the family vinegar brewery in South Lambeth Road, and founder of the Lambeth Ragged School, with which Whymper's parents were involved. His father, Mark Beaufoy (1764 – 1827), was the first Englishman to climb Mont Blanc, in 1787, when he made the fourth ascent of the mountain, a few days after de Saussure.

**Beddome, Edward Smith** (1821 – 1884) Underwriter who lived at Trinity Square, Newington, Southwark. The son of **William Beddome** (1788 – 1858), a warehouse manager and wool merchant for Favell, Beddome and Co, of Gresham Street. William Beddome was a senior deacon at Maze Pond, and on the committee of the Stepney Baptist College.

**Bell, Thomas** (1792 – 1880) Zoologist who contributed to many popular works on such subjects as crustacea, reptiles and quadrupeds. He was president of the Linnean Society from 1853, and chaired the meeting in 1858 at which Alfred Wallace's letter about evolution, sent from the East Indies, was read alongside Darwin's initial paper.

**Bennett, William** (1811 – 1871) Member of the NWCS, possibly a pupil of **David Cox**.

**Bentley, Richard** (1794 – 1871) Printer and publisher, based in Shoe Lane. *Bentley's Quarterly Review* first appeared in March 1859, but the map drawn by Whymper, 7 – 9 February 1859, was not used.

**Bernal, Ralph** (1784 – 1854) Lawyer and MP, whose inheritance of a large West Indian estate enabled him to amass a vast collection of glass, ceramics, plate, armour and pictures. On his death the government declined to buy the collection for the new South Kensington Museum, and the consequent auction raised £70,000.

**Bernard, Simon Francis** (1817 – 1862) A French revolutionary resident in London from 1853. Despite his acquittal he was probably involved in the attempt made on **Louis Napoleon**'s life in January 1858.

**Best, William** (1826 – 1875) Baptist minister in Ramsey (not Ramsgate as Whymper thought), then Leeds.

**Black, Adam** (1784 – 1874) With his nephew Charles, Black established the publishing house of A and C Black in Edinburgh. He succeeded **Macaulay** as MP for Edinburgh.

**Blomfield, Charles James** (1786 – 1857) Bishop of London from 1828 until his death.

**Bogue, David** (c.1808 – 1856) Publisher, at 86 Fleet Street.

[Bomba see **Ferdinand II**]

**Bonaparte, Charles-Louis Napoleon** (1808 – 1873) Nephew of the first **Emperor Napoleon** (1769 – 1821), Louis Napoleon was elected president of the French republic in 1848, but in 1851 he staged a coup d'état and declared himself Emperor Napoleon III.

**Booth, Samuel Harris** (1824 – 1902) Baptist minister in Birkenhead, and later Islington, who turned down the offer of being the minister at Maze Pond in January 1857. He succeeded **James Millard** as secretary of the Baptist Union.

**Bosquet, Pierre François Joseph** (1810 – 1861) French general during the Crimean War.

**Bousfield, William** (c.1824 – 1856) French polisher in Soho, hung on 31 March 1856 for the murder of his wife and three children.

**Bower, Edward Skillington** (1840 – 1885) Son of a blacksmith, Bower became a cabman in Southwark. He was secretary of the North Lambeth Cricket Club.

**Boys, Thomas Shotter** (1803 – 1874) Watercolour painter and lithographer who also worked as a print-seller.

**Bradbury, William** (1800 – 1869) William Bradbury and **Frederick Mullett Evans** (1803 – 1870) were printers who ran a large firm in Lombard Street (with offices also in Bouverie Street) which specialised in high–quality production of illustrated periodicals. Bradbury and Evans were the proprietors and printers of *Punch*.

**Braidwood, James** (1801 – 1861) Celebrated superintendent of the London Fire Brigade, whose step-son Thomas Jackson was killed in a fire at Blackfriars, 16 /17 February 1855.

**Branch, John** (c.1807 – 1856) Baptist minister at Waterloo Chapel, Lambeth.

**Brewer, Robert Kitson** (c.1813 – 1875) Baptist minister at Great George's Street chapel in Leeds.

**Brierly, Sir Oswald Walters** (1817 – 1894) Painter of marine scenery and a naval engineer. After ten years in Australia, Brierly was commissioned by the *London Illustrated News* to accompany the fleet to the Baltic when war broke out with Russia in 1854. The following year he went to the Black Sea.

**Bright, John** (1811 – 1889) Radical politician and MP for Manchester from 1847 to 1857, then MP for Birmingham from 1858.

**Britton, John** (1771 – 1857) Antiquary whose multi–volume *Beauties of England and Wales* was illustrated with steel engravings.

**Brock, William** (1807 – 1875) Baptist minister at Bloomsbury Chapel from 1848, many of whose sermons were published.

**Brooke, Sir James** (1803 – 1868) Army officer and adventurer appointed consul–general for Borneo in 1847. He declared himself rajah of Sarawak, but was forced to flee in 1857 after a rebellion by Chinese mine–workers.

**Brown, Sir George** (1790 – 1865) Lieutenant–general, Brown led the light division in the Crimea under Lord Raglan. He fell sick after the abortive assault on Sevastopol in June 1855, and was invalided home immediately after Lord Raglan's death.

**Brown, Humphrey** (1803 – 1860) MP for Tewkesbury in 1857, and a director of the Royal British Bank, from which he borrowed £70,000. Brown was convicted of obtaining credit by falsely presenting the bank's accounts and sentenced to a year in prison, of which he served five months in 1858.

**Brown, John W.** (c.1791 – 1856) Banker and a member of Maze Pond chapel, resident at Oakland Lodge, Streatham Hill. His daughter, **Emma Ann Brown,** (1825/6 – 1904) married Henry Hill, a clerk in a life assurance company, at Clapham Congregational Church on 5 September 1855. On her marriage certificate her age is given as twenty-seven, but the census returns indicate that she was thirty, although Whymper thought she was thirty eight.

**Browne, Robert William** (1809 – 1895) Ordained deacon, and Professor of Classical History at King's College, London, Browne was the author of *History of Rome* (1859), for which Edward Whymper supplied the illustrations.

**Brunel, Isambard Kingdom** (1806 – 1859) Engineer responsible for the SS Great Eastern, the largest ship of her time, built between 1854 and 1857.

**Brunnow, Philipp von** (1797 – 1875) Russian diplomat, who had been the ambassador in London.

**Buchanan, James** (1791 – 1868) US president from 1857 to 1861, Buchanan's failure to deal with secession led to the civil war.

**Buck, William James** (c.1820 – 1897) Painter, born in London.

**Burnet, John** (c.1790 – ?1871) Baptist minister in Camberwell, born in Scotland.

**Burt, Thomas** (b. c.1814) Publisher and bookseller, superintendent of the SPCK from 1857.

**Butterworth, Charles** (c.1831 – 1907) Butterworth and Heath were a wood engraving firm in the Strand. Born in Camberwell, Butterworth was still listed as a wood engraver in 1901.

**Cadman, William** (1815 – 1891) Anglican vicar of St George's, Southwark.

**Calcraft, William** (1800 – 1879) Hangman from 1829 until 1874, Calcraft was notoriously incompetent (see entry for 1 April 1856).

**Campbell, Colin** (1792 – 1863) Army officer; a major–general in the Crimea, he was appointed commander–in–chief in India on the outbreak of the mutiny.

**Campbell, John, first Baron Campbell of St Andrews** (1779 – 1861) Lord chief justice from 1850 to 1859, then lord chancellor. He presided in the trials of **William Palmer** and the Royal British Bank directors.

**Canham, George** (1839 – aft. 1901) School friend of Whymper's, who became a banker's clerk, married, had two daughters and eventually moved from Brixton to Malden in Surrey. His father was a timber merchant's clerk.

**Canrobert, François** (1809 – 1895) Commander of the French forces in the Crimea until his resignation in May 1855.

**Carden, Sir Robert Walter** (1801 – 1888) Banker elected Lord Mayor of London in 1857.

**Carlisle, George William Frederick Howard, seventh Earl of** (1802 – 1864) Liberal politician who was travelling on the continent during 1853-4, before appointment as lord lieutenant of Ireland by **Palmerston** in 1855.

**Cassell, John** (1817 – 1865) Publisher who started in the 1840s with popular newspapers and periodicals. From 1885 to 1888 Edward Whymper worked as a general manager for the firm that Cassell had founded.

**Castle, Charles** (c.1838 – ?1907) Son of an engraver from Holborn, apprenticed to the Whympers. He is subsequently listed as a photo miniature painter, and in 1891, as an artist and a sculptor.

**Castle, John William** (1825 – 1889) Tailor in Lambeth, near to the Whympers.

**Cavaignac, Louis Eugène** (1802 – 1857) Republican general who stood against **Louis Napoleon** in the election of 1848.

**Chelsea, Henry Cadogan, Viscount** (1812 – 1873) MP for Dover from 1852, he unsuccessfully contested Middlesex in 1857 and succeeded as fourth Earl Cadogan in 1864.

**Cheshire, William** (1837 – 1915) Wood engraver who served his apprenticeship with the Whympers. His family were neighbours of the Whympers at 12 Canterbury Place. Cheshire settled in Sutton as an artist and engraver.

**Chown, Joseph Parbery** (1821 – 1886) Baptist minister at Sion chapel, Bradford, who moved to the Bloomsbury chapel in 1875.

**Clark, Robert** (1825 – 1894) R & R Clark were an important printing firm, founded in Edinburgh in 1846, where **Alfred Whymper** served his apprenticeship. Clarks printed Edward Whymper's books, *Scrambles amongst the Alps* and *Travels amongst the Great Andes of the Equator*.

**Clarke, Charles** (fl. 1858 – 1864) Baptist preacher from Bradford, who succeeded **James Millard** as pastor at Maze Pond in 1864.

**Clay, Richard** (1790 – 1877) Printer with offices in Bread Street Hill. He lived at the Avenue, Muswell Hill, with his wife Susan. Clay printed the edition of Aesop's Fables for which Josiah Whymper engraved the illustrations by **Tenniel**, as well as **Dufferin**'s *Letters from high latitudes*.

**Clay, Sir William** (1791 – 1869) MP for Tower Hamlets from 1832 to 1857, and chairman of Southwark and Vauxhall water companies.

**Clint, Alfred** (c.1844 – aft. 1858) Son of Alfred Clint (1807 – 1883), a marine painter. The younger Clint trained as a painter.

**Clowes, George** (1814 – 1886) William Clowes and Sons was the country's largest printing firm, based at Duke Street, Blackfriars. They were an early user of steam–powered presses in the 1820s, worked with Charles Knight on the *Penny Magazine*, and printed for many of the publishers for whom the Whympers worked (**John Murray**, William Longman). After the death of their father in 1847, William Clowes (1807 – 1883) ran the firm with his brothers, Winchester (1808–1862), and George. George Clowes was an early member of the Alpine Club.

**Cobden, Richard** (1804 – 1865) Industrialist, politician and social reformer, Cobden lost his seat as MP for Rochdale in 1857.

**Cockerell, Charles Robert** (1788 – 1863) Architect and professor, whose work included the Ashmolean Museum, Oxford.

**Codrington, Sir William John** (1804 – 1884) Army officer appointed commander–in–chief of British forces in the Crimea in November 1855.

**Collambell, Charles** (c.1813 – 1890) The Whymper family doctor and their neighbour at 15 Lambeth Terrace. Collambell was a fellow of the Royal College of Surgeons.

**Combermere, Stapleton Cotton, first Viscount** (1773 – 1865) Army officer.

**Coningham, William** (1815 – 1884) Unsuccessful candidate for the constituency of Westminster in 1852, he was elected MP for Brighton in 1857.

[Conyngham see **Coningham**]

**Constantine Nicholayevich, Grand Duke** (1827 – 1892) Son of the Emperor Nicholas I, Grand Duke Constantine was in charge of the Russian navy.

**Cook, Samuel** (1806 – 1859) Painter of marine scenes, and a member of the NWCS from 1854.

**Cooke, Robert Francis** (1816 – 1891) Partner of the publisher, **John Murray**.

**Corbould, Edward Henry** (1815 – 1905) Member of the NWCS, appointed as drawing master to the royal children in 1851. A draughtsman on wood, Corbould provided illustrations for many books and periodicals.

**Corderoy, Edward** (1811 – 1865) J. and Edward Corderoy and Co. were provision agents in Tooley Street. Edward Corderoy was involved in local politics and lectured for the Young Men's Christian Association. Edward Whymper drew some illustrations for his published lecture on **George Stephenson**.

**Coton, Frances** (fl. 1855 – 1858) Firework maker in Westminster Road.

**Cotsell, William** (c.1794 – ?) Royal Navy purser, whose son **John Thomas H. Cotsell** (1820/1 – 1903) was an officer of the SPCK. They lived in Camberwell.

**Cowdy, Samuel** (1817 – 1900) Baptist minister in Leighton Buzzard.

**Cowie, Frederick** (c.1832 – 1885) London painter.

**Cowley, Henry Richard Charles Wellesley, first Earl** (1804 – 1884) Ambassador to France from 1851, Lord Cowley was sent to Vienna in 1859, to mediate between Austria and France.

**Cowslade, William W.** (1818 – 1915) Proprietor of the *Reading Mercury*.

**Cox, David** (1783 – 1859) Painter. His son **David Cox** (1809 – 1885) was a member of the NWCS.

**Cox, George** (1795 – 1857) Bookseller and publisher, with premises at Bedford Street, Covent Garden, and superintendent of SPCK until his death.

**Craig, Ida** (1831 – 1903) Scottish poetess, who won first prize (out of 621 candidates), for her *Ode on the centenary of Burns* at the anniversary celebrations at the Crystal Palace on 25 January 1859.

**Crampton, Sir John Fiennes Twistleton** (1805 – 1886) British representative in Washington from 1852 to May 1856, when he was recalled to London at the insistence of the American government, due to his involvement in the illegal recruitment of mercenaries for the Crimean War.

**Crassweller, Harris** (1827 – 1905) Baptist minister in Leominster.

**Crawford, Robert Wigram** (1813 – 1889) City merchant, who was MP for the City of London from 1857 until 1874.

**Creswick, Thomas** (1811 – 1869) Landscape painter and member of the RA.

**Cumming, John** (1807 – 1881) Minister of the Presbyterian Church of England, who preached in London and prophesied that the second coming would occur in 1867.

**Cumming, Roualeyn George Gordon-** (1820 – 1866) Army officer and sportsman who achieved great popularity lecturing, displaying his trophies and through his book, *Five Years of a Hunter's Life in the Far Interior of South Africa.*

**Dalton, William Henry** (fl. 1857) Publisher, 28 Cockspur Street.

**Dalziel, George** (1815 – 1902) George Dalziel, along with his brother **Edward Dalziel** (1817 – 1905), started London's largest wood engraving firm. They worked principally for the publisher Routledge, but also supervised the illustrations for the Great Exhibition catalogue in 1851. The Dalziels engraved the Pre-Raphaelite illustrations to Moxon's edition of Tennyson's *Poems* in 1857, and also **Tenniel's** illustrations to *Alice's adventures in wonderland* (1865). Most of the engravings of **John Gilbert's** illustrations to **Nisbet's** edition of *The book of Job* (1857) were shared between the Dalziels and Josiah Whymper (see 20 December 1856).

**Darby, Henry** (c.1806 – 1870) Described in the census as a 'pyrotechnist,' and in the Post Office Directory as 'artist in fireworks to Her Majesty,' Darby's premises were at 98 Regent Street, near Lambeth Walk.

**Dare, Charles William** (c.1819 – 1898) Barrister who practised in Lincoln's Inn. He lived at 4 Andover Street, St Giles, Camberwell.

**Davies, Ann E.** (c.1798 – 1855) Neighbour to the Whympers in Lambeth Terrace, married to William Davies, a secretary.

**Davis, George Henry** (c.1812 – 1876) Baptist minister, who was Secretary of the Religious Tract Society from 1855.

**Davis, Joseph** (c.1808 – aft. 1855) Baptist minister at Portsea.

**Dawson, Henry** (1811 – 1878) Landscape painter who worked in London from 1850.

[Deheny See **Dennehy**]

[Denison, Edmund see **Grimthorpe**]

**Dennehy, Philip James** (fl. 1856) Second master in the navy, court-martialled and sentenced to death for being absent from duty while his ship was under fire. The sentence was commuted to transportation for life, but after considerable indignation in the press, this was reduced to a year's imprisonment.

**Derby, Edward Stanley, fourteenth Earl of** (1799 – 1869) Prime Minister for a brief period in 1852, Derby formed a Conservative administration in 1858–9.

**Dickens, Charles** (1812 – 1870) Author whose public readings were extremely popular. His usual performance was the whole of *Christmas Carol* and the trial scene from *Pickwick Papers*.

**Dickes, William** (1815 – 1892) Illustrator, engraver and publisher. Licensed to use Baxter's process, Dickes did all the colour printing for the SPCK.

**Dickinson, William Robert** (fl. 1836 – 1882) London artist.

**Dillon, Frank** (1823 – 1909) Landscape painter, resident in Montague Place, Bloomsbury, who made many visits to Egypt, starting in 1854. He travelled widely in Europe, also visiting Morocco and Japan.

**Disraeli, Benjamin** (1804 – 1881) Tory politician who was chancellor of the exchequer during 1852, but in opposition from 1853 until 1858, when he returned as chancellor under **Derby**. Later Prime Minister in 1868 and from 1874-80.

**Dolby, Charlotte** (1821 – 1885) Contralto singer.

**Doulton, Frederick** (1824 – 1872) Member of the Doulton pottery family, he was elected MP for Lambeth after the resignation of **Roupell** in 1862, and sat until 1868. Doulton and his wife were members of Maze Pond chapel until becoming Unitarians in 1852.

**Doulton, Sir Henry** (1820 – 1897) Older brother of **Frederick Doulton**, he managed the family pottery business in Lambeth High Street.

**Drew, Joseph** (c.1821 – 1905) Baptist minister in Newbury.

**Dufferin and Ava, Frederick Blackwood (later Hamilton-Temple-Blackwood), first Marquess of** (1826 – 1902) Dufferin sailed his yacht to Iceland, Jan Mayen Island and Spitsbergen in 1856, and the resulting popular account, *Letters from High Latitudes*, was illustrated with engravings by the Whympers. From 1884 to 1888 Dufferin was Viceroy of India, where he knew Edward's younger brother, **Henry Josiah Whymper**.

**Duke, Sir James, Bt,** (<u>d</u>. 1873) MP for City of London from 1849 until 1865.

**Dumas, Alexandre** (1802 – 1870) Popular French author and a friend of **Victor Hugo**, whom he visited on Guernsey.

**Dundas, Edward William** (c.1800 – 1866) Bookseller, who became an assistant to John Murray.

**Dundas, Sir Richard Saunders** (1802 – 1861) Admiral, appointed to command the Baltic fleet in February 1855.

**Dundonald, Thomas Cochrane, tenth Earl of** (1775 – 1860) Popular naval officer, who, during the Napoleonic Wars developed a plan to bombard French ships in their harbours, using poison gas from burning sulphur. By now an admiral, Dundonald suggested it would work against Sevastopol, but the town fell before the government could make use of his idea. Much of Thomas Cochrane's career provided the basis for the character of Jack Aubrey in the novels by Patrick O'Brien.

**Eastlake, Sir Charles** (1793 – 1865) Artist who had spent fourteen years in Italy, before supervising the interior decoration of the new Palace of Westminster. President of the RA, he became the first director of the National Gallery in 1855.

**Eastty, Nathaniel** (c.1793 – 1859) Beer merchant and shipping agent, with premises in Upper Thames Street. Born in Ipswich, Eastty was a member of the same Baptist chapel there (Stoke Green) as Josiah Whymper, and was a deacon at Maze Pond chapel for sixteen years. His son **John Eastty** (1823/4 – 1896), a provision agent connected to **Corderoy** and Co, was also a prominent member of Maze Pond chapel, who lived at 86 Grange Road, Bermondsey.

**Edgar, William** (c.1790 – 1869) Silk mercer with Swan and Edgar of Piccadilly, who lived in Clapham.

**Elgin, James Bruce, eighth Earl of** (1811 – 1863) High commissioner and plenipotentiary in China from 1857 to 1859.

**Ellis, Thomas** (c.1803 – after 1861) Letterpress printer in Lambeth. [Whymper could be referring to a naturalist painter, Thomas Ellis (fl. 1842 – 1856) who lived at Peckham, and exhibited at the RA.]

**Ellis, William** (1794 – 1872) Missionary who started a series of visits to Madagascar in 1852, where his proselytizing efforts failed but he made valuable botanical collections, and took many photographs. The Whympers engraved the illustrations to his book *Three visits to Madagascar during the years 1853-1854-1856*, published in 1858.

**Estcourt, James Bucknall Bucknall** (1802 – 1855) Major-General, who died of cholera in the Crimea.

**Evans, David** (fl. 1858) Baptist preacher from Manchester

[Evans see **Bradbury, William**]

**Exeter, John** (c.1771 – 1856) Landed proprietor, resident in Lambeth.

**Fahey, James** (1804 – 1885) Watercolour painter and secretary of the NWCS from 1838. He resigned in 1874 due to financial irregularities.

**Fariner, Thomas** (c.1835 – ?) Engine smith in Bermondsey.

**Farnfield, William Henry** (1838 – 1897) Neighbour of the Whympers in Lambeth Terrace, who became an articled clerk to a solicitor. Farnfield's father was an artillery officer (on half pay).

**Fauntleroy, Thomas** (c.1797 – 1870) Ivory merchant and box wood supplier in Tooley Street. His daughter Jane Fauntleroy was a witness at the wedding of **Emma Brown** and Henry Hill.

**Fenton, Roger** (1819 – 1869) Lawyer whose inheritance allowed him to follow an interest in art, then photography, Fenton was instrumental in setting up the Photographic Society of London (from 1894 the Royal Photographic Society). He was commissioned by Thomas Agnew to take photographs in the Crimea, where he stayed from March through June of 1855.

**Ferdinand II** (1810 – 1859) Bourbon King of the Two Sicilies from 1830, responsible for the heavy-handed suppression of liberal opposition in 1848.

**Fishbourne, James Culbert** (c.1827 – 1875) Baptist minister in Thaxted, then Hastings.

**Foster, Myles Birket** (1825 – 1899) After early training as a wood engraver, Birket Foster became a widely admired watercolour painter and illustrator. He provided illustrations for many books of poetry – Scott, Milton – and *Birket Foster's Pictures of English Landscape*, engraved by the **Dalziels**, was a showcase for his work. At Josiah Whymper's suggestion, he moved from St John's Wood, to Witley, near Haslemere, in 1863.

**Foulsham, Chester** (1837 – 1904) Schoolfellow of Edward Whymper's, who became an architect. Foulsham's father managed the Clayton Arms in Lambeth.

**Franklin, Sir John** (1786 – 1847) Naval officer and arctic explorer, who left London in May 1845, commanding *Erebus* and *Terror*, on his second attempt to find the north west passage. After leaving Greenland in July they were never seen again. Many expeditions went in search of Franklin, and in 1854 John Rae found evidence of bodies from the two ships on King William Island. In 1859 Leopold McClintock confirmed the disappearance of the ships' entire crews.

**Fuller, Andrew** (1754 – 1815) Baptist theologian and first secretary of the Baptist Ministry Society. His son, **Andrew Gunton Fuller** (1799 – 1884), and grandson **Sir Thomas Ekins Fuller** (1831 – 1910), were both members of Maze Pond chapel, but left there to become ministers elsewhere. Thomas Fuller later became an important political figure in South Africa.

**Gale, Joseph** (c.1832 – 1891) Sign and ticket writer, born in East London.

**Galland, Robert** (c.1826 – 1896) Solicitor with Edwards, Frankish and Galland of New Palace Yard, Westminster, who lived at Larkhall Lane, Clapham.

**Garbett, Edward** (1817 – 1887) Church of England minister of St Bartholomew's church, Gray's Inn Road, and editor of *The Record*.

**George, Jonathan** (d. c. 1860) Born in Glamorgan, a Baptist minister in Camberwell.

**Gibson, Edmund Stanley** (1820 – 1895) Draughtsman on wood, who lived at 3, Henry Place, Kennington Lane.

**Gibson, Thomas Milner** (1806 – 1884) Radical MP for Manchester from 1841 to 1857, then for Ashton under Lyne from December 1857 to 1868. His amendment to the Conspiracy to Murder Bill caused the defeat of **Palmerston's** administration in 1858.

**Gilbert, Frederick** (c.1828 – ?1896) Water colour painter and draughtsman, resident in Lewisham then Greenwich.

**Gilbert, Sir John** (1817 – 1897) Prolific illustrator and painter, Gilbert lived all his life at Blackheath. A member of the Old Water Colour Society, and later a Royal Academician, Gilbert was knighted in 1872. In an un–credited article written while on the boat to Ecuador, Whymper drew attention to his astonishing facility as a draughtsman on wood. 'As a boy, the writer of this notice has often waited whilst Gilbert has made a drawing for some magazine or other publication. The MS has been read, the composition determined upon, and the drawing executed in less time than most artists would find necessary for the reading of the MS alone.' Whymper marvelled at Gilbert's completion of his full page illustration of the Charge of the Light Brigade, for the *Illustrated London News* in only three hours, while the newspaper's messenger waited for the block. ("Sir John Gilbert R.A." *Leisure Hour* 1880: 183–185.)

**Gillman, James** (b̲. c.1842) Schoolfellow of Whymper's who went into the army. His father was a clergyman, and his mother from New South Wales.

**Gladstone, William Ewart** (1809 – 1898) Chancellor of the Exchequer under **Aberdeen** from 1853 until his resignation in February 1855. He remained in opposition until re-accepting this post under **Palmerston** in June 1859. He was subsequently Prime Minister on four occasions: 1868-74, 1880-85, 1886 and 1892-4.

[Glennie see **Glenny**]

**Glenny, William Joseph** (1838 – 1886) Born in Battersea, Glenny worked as a drawing master, before becoming Professor of Drawing at King's College.

**Goddard, Arabella** (1836 – 1922) Pianist.

**Godwin, George** (1813 – 1888) Architect and writer who edited *The Builder*, a popular weekly professional journal.

**Gomez, Antonio** (b̲. c.1829) Neapolitan sentenced to life imprisonment for the attempted assassination of Napoleon III on 14 January 1858.

**Goodall, Walter** (1830 – 1889) Watercolour painter resident in St Pancras.

**Gorchakov, Mikhail** (1795 – 1861) Russian commander in chief of the forces in Moldavia when the Crimean War started, then appointed the commander in Sevastopol when **Menshikov** was recalled.

**Gosse, Philip** (1810 – 1888) Zoologist who did much to popularize natural history through his books and promotion of aquaria. His religious views did not allow him to accept Darwin's theory of evolution, or the geological evidence for the age of the earth. He drew the illustrations to many of his own books himself, often working directly onto the wood block. After his first wife died, Gosse and his son Edmund moved from Islington to Devon.

**Gotch, Frederick William** (1808 – 1890) Baptist minister and tutor at the Baptist College in Bristol.

**Gould, Anne D.** (b̲. c.1820) Artist resident in Camberwell, married, but not living with a husband.

**Gould, John** (1804 – 1881) Ornithologist and publisher who had worked on Darwin's bird collections, when the *Beagle* returned in 1836.

**Graham, Sir James Robert George** (1792 – 1861) Home Secretary under Robert Peel from 1841 until 1846, Graham returned to government as First Lord of the Admiralty in **Aberdeen**'s coalition of 1852. He resigned in February 1855.

**Gray, John Edward** (1800 – 1875) Keeper of the zoology department at the British Museum from 1840; Gray had an honorary doctorate from the University of Munich.

**Gray, Thomas** (1716 – 1771) Poet, whose family had a long connection with Stoke Poges, where he is buried. In 1856 Josiah Whymper had engraved some illustrations by **Birket Foster** to a new edition of Gray's *An elegy written in a country churchyard.*

**Green, Charles Frederick** (1840 – 1898) Watercolour painter and illustrator, who had been apprenticed to the Whympers. He subsequently made a successful career as a black and white artist, providing illustrations for **Dickens**' *The old curiosity shop* and many of the periodicals. He was living next to the Whymper's studio in Canterbury Place during his apprenticeship.

**Green, Samuel Gosnell** (1821 – 1905) Baptist minister who was a lecturer and, from 1863, president of the Baptist college in Yorkshire. From 1876 he was the book editor of the Religious Tract Society.

**Green, Stephen** (c.1796 – 1874) Manager of a pottery works at Prince's Street, near Blackfriar's Bridge. He lived at 3 Union Place in Lambeth, before moving to Clapham. With his first wife Emma (c.1805 – 1851) he was a long–standing member of Maze Pond chapel. He married Mary Clay (c.1815 – ?) in 1856. Stephen Green was a witness at Josiah Whymper's marriage to **Emily Hepburn** in 1866.

**Greenfield, Henry** (c.1813 – 1881) Cabinet-maker at 21 Lambeth Terrace, a neighbour of the Whympers.

**Grimthorpe, Edmund Beckett Denison, Baron** (1816 – 1905) Barrister and amateur horologist, who, along with the Astronomer Royal, George Airy, was joint referee of the competition to build the new clock for the Palace of Westminster. The design and working of the clock owe more to Denison than to anyone else.

**Grisi, Giula** (c.1810 – 1869) Italian opera singer established in London, who performed with her lover, **Mario**.

**Grosvenor, Lord Robert** (1801 – 1893) Third son of the first Marquess of Westminster, Grosvenor was MP for Middlesex until August 1857, when he was elevated to the peerage as Baron Ebury. In 1855 he introduced his Sunday Trading Bill, to prevent shops in London opening on Sundays. Popular hostility, culminating in the riot in Hyde Park on 1 July 1855, caused him to withdraw the bill.

**Gubbins, Martin Richard** (d. 1863) Employee of the East India Company since 1830, his house in Lucknow formed a salient part of the defence of the residency during the events of 1857.

**Guthrie, Thomas** (1803 – 1873) Popular Free Church of Scotland minister, who published his sermons and pamphlets against the evils of drunkenness.

**Haghe, Louis** (1806 – 1885) Watercolour painter, who also worked as a lithographer. His painting, "A public letter writer in the remains of the Theatre of Marcellus, Rome" was shown at the NWCS annual exhibition in 1857.

**Hall, Benjamin** (1802 – 1867) MP for Marylebone until 1859, he brought in the bill to establish the Metropolitan Board of Works in 1855, and became chief commissioner in July that year. His name was given to the bell in the clock tower of the new Houses of Parliament.

**Hall, Samuel Carter** (1800 – 1889) Writer originally from Ireland who settled in London to make a living from journalism and editing. For many years he edited the *Art Journal*, as well as producing such illustrated books as *Ireland, its Scenery, Character, etc.* (1841–3), for which Josiah Whymper engraved some of the pictures. A tireless campaigner for temperance and the improvement of the poor, he may be the model for Pecksniff in *Martin Chuzzlewit*.

**Hallam, Henry** (1777 – 1859) Historian responsible for such works as *The constitutional history of England from the accession of Henry VII to the death of George II* (1827), and *Introduction to the literature of Europe in the fifteenth, sixteenth, and seventeenth centuries* (1837–9). The death of Hallam's son Arthur Henry is commemorated in Tennyson's poem, *In memoriam*.

**Hanbury, Robert Culling** (1823 – 1867) Partner in the brewery firm of Truman, Hanbury, Buxton and Co, he was MP for Middlesex from 1857 to 1867.

**Handel, George Frederick** (1685 – 1759) German composer who settled in London. The hundredth anniversary of his death fell in April 1859.

**Hands, T.** (fl. 1857) Baptist minister in Salisbury.

**Harcourt, James** (c.1799 – aft. 1873) Baptist minister at the chapel in Borough Road, Southwark.

**Harding, George** (c.1822 – 1858/9) Farmer from North Cadbury, Somerset, who married Sarah, the widow of Edward Whymper's uncle Theophilus. He became an innkeeper in Shepton Mallet but was declared bankrupt in May 1856. After his early death his widow worked as a barmaid.

**Hardinge, Henry** (1785 – 1856) Governor–general of India from 1844 to 1848, he succeeded Wellington as general commanding–in–chief on the latter's death in 1852.

**Harvey, William** (1796 – 1866) Wood engraver trained by Thomas Bewick, Harvey moved to London in 1817 on completion of his apprenticeship, settling in Richmond. Gradually abandoning engraving, Harvey became a skilled draughtsman, doing much work for Charles Knight. Many of his beautiful illustrations to Edward Lane's *The thousand and one nights* (Charles Knight, 1839) were engraved by Josiah Whymper.

**Havelock, Sir Henry** (1795 – 1857) Long–serving army officer, who commanded a brigade under **James Outram** during the Indian Mutiny.

[Heath see **Butterworth**]

**Henderson, Frances** (1769 – 1806) Wife of **George Stephenson** and mother of **Robert Stephenson**.

**Hepburn, Emily** (1832 – 1886) Daughter of **Thomas Hepburn** and third wife of Josiah Whymper, whom she married on 4 December 1866 in Battersea. Emily Hepburn exhibited as an artist in her own right, and her drawings illustrated *Beauty in common things* (London: SPCK, 1874).

**Hepburn, Thomas** (1797 – 1880) Wealthy merchant with a tannery business in Bermondsey. Hepburn was a deacon at Maze Pond chapel, became a county magistrate and had a large house on Clapham Common. Besides Emily, he had two other daughters, Maria and Sophia, and two sons, Thomas and Arthur, who all became members of Maze Pond chapel.

**Herbert, Sidney** (1810 – 1861) Follower of Robert Peel, Herbert was Secretary at War in the **Aberdeen** coalition. He resigned with **Gladstone** and **Graham** when **Palmerston** did not give an assurance that there would be no enquiry into the management of the war.

**Hester, Giles** (1829 – 1911) Baptist minister.

**Hewitt, Elizabeth Barnett** (c.1841 – aft. 1891) Born in Liverpool, Elizabeth Hewitt eloped with Edward Whymper's cousin **John Charles Whymper** in 1857.

**Hoddle, John** (1827 – 1869) Boot maker at Fox Court, Holborn.

**Hogarth, John** (1832 – 1895) Photographic printer in the Haymarket, who later moved to Manchester and became a restorer of engravings.

**Hook, Walter Farquhar** (1798 – 1875) High church Anglican, popularly thought to be sympathetic to the Tractarians. Hook was vicar of Leeds from 1837 until 1859, when he became dean of Chichester.

**Howitt, William** (1792 – 1879) Prolific author who, after an ill-advised venture at magazine publishing led to bankruptcy, spent two years in Australia. His *Land, labour and Gold: or, two years in Victoria: with visits to Sydney and Van Diemen's Land* (1855) was published the year after his return. Howitt's wife Mary (1799 – 1888) wrote popular works for the SPCK, for which the Whympers engraved many of the illustrations.

**Huc, Évariste Régis** (1813 – 1860) French missionary who travelled from Canton to Tibet, reaching Lhasa in 1846.

**Hugo, Victor** (1802 – 1885) French novelist best known for *The Hunchback of Notre Dame* (1831) and *Les Misérables* (1862). After **Louis Napoleon**'s *coup d'état* of 1851, Hugo fled to Brussels, then Jersey. From 1855 he lived in Guernsey.

**Hume, Joseph** (1777 – 1855) Radical MP for Montrose.

**Hussey, James McConnell** (c.1819 – 1891) Curate, then vicar, of Christ Church, Brixton.

**Ingram, Herbert** (1811 – 1860) Trained as a printer, Ingram made enough money as a distributor of pills, using some dubious publicity, to allow him to start the *Illustrated London News* in 1842. This made him a rich man, and he was elected MP for Boston in 1855.

**James, Edwin** (1812 – 1882) Queen's Counsel, James acted for the prosecution in the trial of **William Palmer** in 1856. He was later disbarred for fraud and fled to New York owing £100,000. He may be the original for Mr Stryver in *A tale of two cities.*

**Johns, Charles Alexander** (1811 – 1874) Ordained deacon, a school master and writer on natural history. The Whympers engraved the illustrations by **Joseph Wolf** to Johns' *British birds in their haunts* (London: SPCK, 1862).

**Jones, David** (c.1820 – 1887) Baptist minister in Folkestone, who later moved to New Park Road chapel, Brixton.

**Jones, Ernest** (1819 – 1869) Leading chartist, Jones had been one of the main speakers at the great demonstration on Kennington Common, in April 1848.

**Jones, Sir Harry David** (1791 – 1866) Lieutenant-General in the Crimea during 1855, he was wounded in an attack on the Redan.

**Jones, William** (fl. 1856) Baptist minister in Newport, Isle of Wight.

**Joy, William** (1803 – 1867) William Joy and his brother, **John Carihloe Joy** (1806 – 1859) were marine painters from Great Yarmouth. However, it is possible that Whymper's reference is to **Thomas Musgrave Joy** (1812 – 1866), a portrait painter resident in Pimlico.

**Jullien, Louis Antoine** (1812 – 1860) Conductor and impresario, ruined by the bankruptcy of the Surrey Gardens Company in 1857.

**Kane, Elisha Kent** (1820 – 1857) American arctic explorer who led an expedition to the north west of Greenland in 1853, ostensibly to look for **Sir John Franklin**, but in practice to find a way to the North Pole. After two winters in the Arctic, the expedition ended unsuccessfully in some disarray.

**Kearney, William Henry** (1800 – 1858) Founder member and later vice–president of the NWCS; he lived at 114 High Holborn.

**Kelke, William Hastings** (c.1803 – 1865) Rector of Drayton Beauchamp, Buckinghamshire and a writer on law and ecclesiastical history.

**Kingsley, Charles** (1819 – 1875) Author and religious controversialist, best known for his novel, *The water babies* (1863).

**Kirkland, Charles** (1811 – 1886) Baptist minister in Canterbury.

**Knowles, James Sheridan** (1784 – 1862) Playwright and actor, who started a second career as a Baptist preacher in 1844.

**Lablache, Louis** (1795 – 1858) Singer and comic actor from Naples who performed to great popularity in London from 1834 to 1855.

**Lancaster, Richard Bottomley** (c.1813 – 1893) Baptist minister at Regent Street chapel, Lambeth.

**Lance, George** (1802 – 1864) Artist and Baptist.

**Langham, Nat** (1820 – 1871) Bare–knuckle prize fighter.

**Layard, Sir Austen Henry** (1817 – 1894) Archaeologist and liberal politician, Layard had been a strong critic of the government during the Crimean War and lost his seat as MP for Aylesbury in 1857. Josiah Whymper had engraved the illustrations to his books on Nineveh, published by **John Murray**.

**Ledru–Rollin, Alexandre Auguste** (1807 – 1874) French revolutionary politician.

**Leggatt, Henry** (c.1791 – 1858) Senior partner in the firm of Leggatt, Hayward and Leggatt, art dealers in Cornhill. Fosters, the auctioneers, sold his collection of water colour sketches, including works by **Turner**, **Clarkson Stanfield**, **David Roberts** and **David Cox**, at their Pall Mall premises on 26 February 1858.

**Leigh, Jane** (c.1792 – aft. 1861) Sister of **Samuel Leigh**.

**Leigh, Samuel** (c.1794 – 1856) Cashier at the Bank of England, who adopted Edward Whymper's mother, the orphaned Elizabeth Claridge. He lived in Peckham with his sisters **Jane Leigh** and the widowed **Ann Sowerby**.

**Leslie, Charles Robert** (1794 – 1859) Historical genre painter and member of the RA.

**Lewis, John Frederick** (1805 – 1876) Painter who had spent ten years in the Middle East.

**Leyland, John** (c.1815 – 1882) Governor of Bridge House Reformatory, High Street, Wandsworth.

**Livingstone, David** (1813 – 1873) Scottish missionary and explorer, the first European to see the falls on the Zambezi, which he named after Queen Victoria. The Whympers engraved the illustrations drawn by **Joseph Wolf** to Livingstone's *Missionary Travels and Researches in South Africa*, published while he was in London in 1857.

**Locke, John** (1805 – 1880) Barrister and Liberal MP for Southwark from 1857 to 1880.

[Louis Napoleon see **Bonaparte**]

**Lucan, George Charles Bingham, third Earl of** (1800 – 1888) Commander of the cavalry in the Crimea, Lucan was responsible for the immediate order to the Light Brigade, which resulted in their infamous charge on 25 October 1854. This was rancorously disputed between Lucan and **Lord Raglan**, resulting in the former's recall from the Crimea, which he left on 14 February 1855.

**Lyons, Lord Edmund** (1790 – 1858) Naval officer and diplomat, who was second in command to Admiral **Richard Dundas** when the Crimean War started. Lyons captured Balaclava in 1854 and Kinburn the following year. His well–publicised views on the conduct of the war earned him a different reputation from the cautious high command of the navy.

**Macaulay, Thomas Babington Macaulay, Baron** (1800 – 1859) Historian and politician. The first two volumes of his *History of England* were published in 1848 and volumes three and four in December 1855.

**Mackay, Charles** (1812 – 1889) Poet and writer, with an LLD from Glasgow University, who worked as an editor for the *Illustrated London News* from 1848 until 1859.

**McKewan, David Hall** (1816 – 1873) Watercolour painter born in London, probably a pupil of **David Cox**. A member of the NWCS from 1850, McKewan exhibited his pictures of Smyrna at their annual exhibition in 1859.

**Mackness, John Thomas** (c.1831 – aft. 1857) Painter and decorator in Regent Street, Lambeth.

**Maclise, Daniel M.** (1806 – 1870) Historical painter and member of the RA.

**Macmillan, Alexander** (1818 – 1896) Along with his brother Daniel (1813–1857), the founder of the Macmillan publishing house.

**Macpherson, Charles** (c.1789 – aft. 1856) Printer in Edinburgh.

**Mahon, Philip Henry Stanhope, Lord** (1805 – 1875) Politician and historian whose *History of England from the Peace of Utrecht to the Peace of Versailles, 1713-1783* was published in seven volumes, 1836 – 1853. He later succeeded as 5th Earl Stanhope.

**Malcolm, James** (c.1828 – aft. 1861) Baptist minister from Aberdeen, who was pastor at Maze Pond for a few months in 1857.

**Manning, Samuel** (1821 – 1881) Baptist minister at Sheppard's Barton, Frome from 1846 to 1861. From 1863 Manning was book editor of the Religious Tract Society. He started a prolific series of illustrated travel books (*Swiss pictures drawn with pen and pencil, Italian pictures drawn with pen and pencil*, and many others) for which the Whympers did some of their best engravings.

**Mario, Giovanni Matteo de Candia** (1810 – 1883) Italian tenor singer, the lover of **Giula Grisi**.

**Marley, Robert** (c.1817 – 1856) Ticket-of-leave convict who had been transported for housebreaking. He was hung on 15 December 1856 for the murder of Richard Cope, a jeweller's assistant.

**Marmora, Alfonso Ferrero La** (1804 – 1878) Sardinian general, La Marmora, arrived in the Crimea with 15,000 troops in April 1855. He was prime minister of Italy from 1864 to 1866.

**Mazzini, Giuseppe** (1805 – 1872) Italian democratic political activist.

**Menshikov, Aleksander Sergeyevich** (1787 – 1869) Russian commander in chief in the Crimea until being replaced in February 1855.

**Metternich, Klemenz von** (1773 – 1859) Austrian diplomat who played a significant part in the post-Napoleonic settlement at the Congress of Vienna, in 1815.

**Millais, William** (1828 – 1899) Landscape painter, elder brother of **John Everett Millais** (1829 – 1896), pre-Raphaelite artist.

**Millard, James Henry** (1819 – 1883) Baptist minister who moved from Huntingdon to become pastor of Maze Pond chapel in 1858, but resigned in 1863. He was later secretary of the Baptist Union for fifteen years.

**Miller, Hugh** (1802 – 1856) Scottish journalist, writer and geologist, Miller shot himself at his home in Edinburgh in December 1856. His auto-biography, *My schools and schoolmasters*, was published in 1852.

**Miller, William Frederick** (1834 – 1918) Architectural draughtsman and wood engraver.

**Miller, William Henry** (1815 – 1895) Printer, stationer and publisher at 6 Bridge Street, Lambeth.

**Mole, John Henry** (1814 – 1886) Landscape painter, a member of the NWCS.

**Molesworth, Sir William, Bt,** (1810 – 1855) Radical MP for Southwark from 1845 to 1855.

**Montalembert, Charles de** (1810 – 1870) Liberal journalist, whose article entitled, "Un débat sur l'Inde au Parlement anglais," so offended **Louis Napoleon** that he was arrested.

**Moon, Sir Francis Graham, Bt,** (1796 – 1871) Publisher who was Lord Mayor of London during Louis Napoleon's visit of 1855.

**Moore, Thomas** (1779 – 1852) Poet, the author of *Lalla Rookh*. His *Memoirs, journal and correspondence* was published in eight volumes by Longman between 1853 and 1856.

**Morbey, Joseph** (fl. 1857) Carver and guilder with offices at 69 Bishopsgate.

**Morrell, Henry** (fl. 1858) Pen and ink merchant in Fleet Street.

**Morrison, James** (1789 – 1857) Merchant banker, who left property worth four to six million pounds on his death on 30 October 1857.

[Mouriaveff see **Muraviev-Amurskii**]

**Mudie, Charles Edward** (1818 – 1890) Son of a bookseller, Mudie founded a popular circulating library, available to paying subscribers. From his headquarters at 510 New Oxford Street, Mudie also operated as a publisher.

**Muraviev-Amurskii, Nikolai Nikolaevich** (1809 – 1881) Russian general and commander in Armenia.

**Murchison, Roderick Impey** (1792 – 1871) President of the Geological Society, and of the Royal Geographical Society, responsible for important work on geological history in the 1830s.

**Murray, John** (1808 – 1892) Methodical businessman, John Murray took over the management of the family publishing firm in 1843. Josiah Whymper had started his association with the firm by this date, and he and Edward continued to work for Murray's for more than 50 years, engraving the illustrations to accounts of travel, guide books, and numerous scientific and natural history works. Whymper organised the illustrations to all Schliemann's works on his archaeological discoveries, published in English by Murray. John Murray published all Whymper's own books, and at the end of his life Whymper gave the copyrights to the firm. Murray was an early member of the Alpine Club.

**Nakhimov, Pavel Stepanovich** (1802 – 1855) Admiral in charge of the Russian Black Sea fleet and military governor of Sevastopol. He was killed by a sniper's bullet at the Redan.

**Nana Sahib** (1824 – ?) Indian ruler who had quarrelled with the British over his pension, and was involved in the massacre of Europeans during and after the siege of Cawnpore in 1857. After the Mutiny he probably escaped to Nepal, but his subsequent whereabouts and details of his death are not known for certain.

**Napier, Sir Charles** (1786 – 1860) Commander of the naval forces in the Baltic in 1854, Napier was MP for Southwark from 1855 to 1860.

[Napoleon see **Bonaparte**]

**Nasmyth, James** (1808 – 1890) Engineer principally known for inventing a steam hammer.

**Need, Captain Henry** (c.1818 – 1875) Royal Navy captain who made a series of watercolours while on anti-slavery patrols off the coast of West Africa in the 1850s.

**Nightingale, Florence** (1820 – 1910) Nursing organizer known for her work among the allied troops at Scutari during the Crimean War. The subscription opened to support her work there had raised £28,000 by the end of May 1856.

**Nisbet, James** (c.1817 – aft. 1858) Publisher, 21 Berners Street

**Nosotti, Charles** (c.1830 – 1909) Looking glass manufacturer, gilder, cabinet maker and interior decorator, in Oxford Street.

[Nosotty see **Nosotti**]

**Novello, Clara** (1818 – 1908) Popular soprano who retired from public performance in 1860.

**Orsini, Felice** (1819 – 1858) Italian revolutionary, executed along with **Giuseppe Pieri**, for the attempted assassination of **Louis Napoleon** on 14 January 1858.

**Outram, Sir James** (1803 – 1863) Army officer in the East India Company, who with **Havelock** was responsible for the relief of Lucknow in September 1857.

**Palmer, William** (1824 – 1856) Surgeon in Rugeley, Staffordshire, who was convicted at the Old Bailey of poisoning his friend John Parsons Cook. Robert Graves wrote a novelised account of the story, *They hanged my saintly Billy*. Although agreeing that Palmer was 'a scoundrel and spend-thrift,' Graves shared Whymper's opinion that Palmer was probably innocent of the crime for which he was hung.

**Palmerston, Henry John Temple, third Viscount** (1784 – 1865) Foreign minister between 1830 and 1841, and then under **Lord Russell** from 1846 to 1851, Palmerston was Home Secretary when the Crimean War started.

He was made Prime Minister in February 1855 to popular acclaim on the resignation of **Aberdeen's** government. Resigning after the failure of his conspiracy to murder bill in 1858, he returned as prime minister in June of the following year and died in office.

**Panmure, Fox Maule, second Baron** (1801 – 1874) Secretary of State for War in **Palmerston's** government of 1855 to 1858.

**Pasha, Omar** (1806 – 1871) General of Serbian origin who commanded the Ottoman forces in the war against Russia.

**Paul, Sir John Dean, Bt,** (1802 – 1868) Partner in the bank of **Strahan**, Paul and **Bates**. Having been trading while insolvent, bankruptcy was declared in June 1855, with debts of £750,000, but the bank had fraudulently sold securities belonging to its customers. After escaping the police at Reigate station, Paul turned himself in at Bow Street. Strahan and Paul were released from Woking prison in 1859.

**Paxton, Sir Joseph** (1803 – 1865) Landscape gardener at Chatsworth who designed the Crystal Palace for the 1851 Great Exhibition. Paxton was responsible for the extensive gardens in Sydenham, where the building was re-erected in 1854.

**Pease, Edward** (1767 – 1858) Quaker and original promoter of **Stephenson's** railway at Darlington.

**Pélissier, Aimable Jean Jacques** (1794 – 1864) Commander of the French forces in the Crimea during the final year of the war. He was French ambassador to London from 1858 to 1859.

**Pellatt, Apsley** (1791 – 1863) Glass manufacturer and Liberal MP for Southwark from 1852 until 1857, when he lost his seat, having been a director of the Royal British Bank (although he avoided prosecution).

**Penton, Lawrence** (c.1830 – 1889) Painter, sign writer and grainer in Lambeth.

**Peters, Thomas** (c.1826 – aft. 1856) Baptist minister in Rayleigh, Essex.

**Pewtress, Joseph** (1813 – 1887) News vendor and rag merchant who established a large printing and publishing firm, which printed the *Baptist Magazine*. His brother **Edmund Pewtress** (1820 –1915) was a stationer and publisher. A relation and also a Baptist, **Stephen Pewtress** (1828/ 9 – 1910) was a London bookseller. Many of the Pewtress family were members of Maze Pond chapel.

**Phelps, Samuel** (1804 – 1878) Actor and theatre manager who successfully ran Sadler's Wells from 1844 until 1862.

**Pianori, Giovanni** (1827 – 1855) Italian who attempted to shoot **Louis Napoleon** on 28 April 1855. He was guillotined two weeks later.

**Pickersgill, Henry William** (1782 – 1875) Portrait painter and member of the RA. His nephew Frederick Richard Pickersgill (1820 – 1900) was also a painter, but not a member of the RA in 1856, when Whymper mentions his visit.

**Pierce, Earl** (1823 – 1859) American banjo player and comedian who had come to London in 1857 with an offshoot of the original Christy's Minstrels.

**Pieri, Giuseppe** (c.1807 – 1858) Italian revolutionary, executed along with **Felice Orsini**, for the attempted assassination of **Louis Napoleon** on 14 January 1858.

**Pinches, Conrad Hume** (c.1819 – 1881) Whymper's schoolmaster at Clarendon House. Pinches was also a barrister, and practised after finishing as a schoolmaster in the 1870s.

**Price, John** (fl. 1856) Baptist minister in Weymouth.

**Prior, William Henry** (1812 – 1882) Landscape painter and draughtsman, a follower of Bewick's pupil **William Harvey**. Prior worked for Charles Knight and for **Vizetelly** on the *Illustrated Times*. In 1851 he was resident at 72 Oakley Square, St Pancras, then moved to Plumstead.

**Probart, Edward** (c.1798 – 1874) Manufacturing chemist resident in Lambeth.

**Rachel** (1821 – 1858) Stage name of the French actress Elisa Felix.

**Radetsky, Joseph, Count von Radetz,** (1766 – 1858) Austrian field marshal, after whom Strauss's *Radetsky march* was named.

**Raffles, David** (c.1827 – aft. 1859) Gardener resident in Lambeth.

**Raglan, Fitzroy James Henry Somerset, first Baron** (1788 – 1855) Commander of the British force in the Crimea until his death there on 28 June 1855.

**Read, Samuel** (1816 – 1883) Watercolour painter, born at Needham Market, Suffolk. He learnt wood engraving with Josiah Whymper, also studying with **Collingwood Smith**. The *Illustrated London News* sent him to Constantinople in 1853. He provided illustrations for books published by the SPCK, and became an associate of the Old Water Colour Society in 1857, and finally a member in 1880. He lived at 55 Argyll Road, Kensington.

**Reade, Charles** (1814 – 1884) Successful popular author best known for *The cloister and the hearth* (1861).

**Redgrave, Richard** (1804 – 1888) Landscape painter and member of the RA.

**Redpath, Leopold** (c.1816 – aft. 1857) Clerk of the Great Northern Railway Company who was convicted of forging deeds transferring stock, and sentenced to transportation for life.

**Reeves, John Sims** (1818 – 1900) Tenor singer who had studied in Paris and Milan.

**Reid, S.** (fl. 1855) Draughtsman on wood

**Rennie, Sir John** (1794 – 1874) An engineer with extensive factories near Blackfriars Bridge, Rennie was responsible for the new London Bridge built in 1831.

**Richardson, Edward M.** (1810 – 1874) Landscape watercolour painter who became an associate of the NWCS in 1859, is likely to be the Richardson mentioned by Whymper. He had several brothers who were also painters: **Thomas Miles Richardson** (1813 – 1890); **Henry Burdon Richardson** (c.1811 – 1874); **Charles Richardson** (1829 – 1908).

**Rivington, George** (1801 – 1858) Rivington's was a long–established family publishing firm located, after 1853, at Waterloo Place, Pall Mall. During the time of the diary the firm was run by George Rivington, **Francis Rivington** (1805 – 1885), and later by Francis' son, **Francis Hansard Rivington** (1834 – 1913). The family also had a large printing business, based in St. John's Square.

**Roberts, David** (1796 – 1864) Landscape artist who travelled in Egypt and the Holy Land. His paintings and sketches were published as coloured lithographs in five volumes, *Views in the Holy Land, Syria, Idumea, Arabia, Egypt and Nubia* (London: F.G. Moon, 1842 – 9).

**Robins, Thomas** (1814 – 1880) Landscape painter and member of the NWCS.

**Robinson, John** (fl. 1858) Baptist preacher.

**Robson, William James** (c.1820 – aft. 1857) Principal clerk at the Crystal Palace Company from 1853, Robson was convicted of stealing shares and sentenced to twenty years' transportation.

**Roebuck, John Arthur** (1802 – 1879) Independent MP for Sheffield from 1849 to 1868. His motion to set up a select committee to inquire into the state of the army before Sevastopol was carried by 157 votes in 1855.

**Roffey, Thomas William** (1840 – 1928) Schoolfellow of Edward Whymper's, and later his solicitor.

**Rogers, Samuel** (1763 – 1855) Poet, who bequeathed three paintings to the National Gallery, and whose library and art collection raised £50,000 at Christies in May 1856. His poem *Italy* was published with illustrations by **Turner**.

**Rosevear, William T.** (1824 – 1908) Baptist minister in Coventry, born in Cornwall.

[Roseveer, Rosevere see **Rosevear**]

**Rothschild, Lionel Nathan de Rothschild, Baron de** (1808 – 1879) MP for the City of London from 1847 until 1868, then from 1869 until 1874.

**Roupell, William** (1831 – 1909) After a turbulent election Roupell was elected for Lambeth as a Liberal in 1857. Returned as MP in 1859, he resigned in 1862 and absconded to Spain (whereupon **Fred Doulton** was elected). Returning to England Roupell was recognised and convicted of forging a will and a deed. Sentenced to penal servitude for life, he was released in 1876.

**Rowbotham, Thomas Charles Leeson** (1823 – 1875) Watercolour painter of landscapes and a member of NWCS from 1851.

**Rudio, Carlo di** (1832 – 1910) Italian condemned to death for his involvement in the attempt to assassinate Napoleon III on 14 January 1858. His sentence was commuted to live imprisonment on Devil's Island, from which he escaped, reaching London in 1860.

**Russell, Lord John Russell, first Earl** (1792 – 1878) Prime Minister from 1846 to 1852, Russell served in **Palmerston**'s administration after 1855, and was sent to an inconclusive peace conference in Vienna, partly because Palmerston wanted him out of the way. He returned to government with Palmerston in 1859, as Foreign Secretary.

**Russell, William Howard** (1820 – 1907) Russell went to the Crimea as a reporter for *The Times* and stayed there two years, his critical articles having a wide influence on public opinion. Russell's book, *The War: from the landing at Gallipoli to the death of Lord Raglan*, was published in two volumes (1855, 1856).

**Sadleir, John** (1815 – 1856) MP for Sligo, who committed suicide on Hampstead Heath, after being engaged in fraudulent share transactions.

**Salomons, Sir David** (1797 – 1873) Banker who became the first Jewish Lord Mayor of London in 1855.

**Sandall, Henry Blandford** (c.1817 – 1890) Architect resident in St George's Road, Southwark.

**Sandwith, Humphrey** (1822 – 1881) Army physician who served throughout the siege of Kars. When the garrison surrendered in November 1855, the Russian commander **Muraviev** released Sandwith in recognition of his treatment of Russian prisoners, and he returned to London in January 1856. His account of the siege, *A Narrative of the siege of Kars, and of the six months' resistance by the Turkish garrison, under General Williams, to the Russian Army*, was published by **John Murray** in 1856; the Whympers engraved the book's two illustrations.

**Saunders, John** (1811 – 1895) Writer and editor, Saunders was managing his own illustrated monthly, the *National Magazine*, when imposed on Josiah Whymper and **George Clowes** by the SPCK. Edward Whymper was probably mistaken in thinking he was a lawyer.

**Saward, James Townsend** (c.1797 – aft. 1857) Lawyer convicted of forgery in connection with laundering the proceeds of the bullion robbery from the South Eastern Railway in 1855. He was sentenced to transportation for life.

**Sayers, Tom** (1826 – 1865) Undefeated boxing champion.

**Scott, Joseph** (c.1831 – 1888) Wood engraver born in Ireland who trained with the Whympers and afterwards worked for them, particularly on **Cassell's** *Picturesque Europe* (1876–9).

**Scott, Thomas Dewell** (c.1828 – 1911) Engraver and draughtsman on wood, resident in Camberwell.

**Scovell, George** (c.1804 – 1890) Wharf and dock proprietor, born in Lambeth.

**Seymour, Sir Michael** (1802 – 1887) Naval officer, who served in the Baltic during the Crimean War, then took charge of the China station in 1856.

**Shaftesbury, Anthony Ashley-Cooper, seventh Earl of** (1801 – 1885) Politician and an evangelical philanthropist, Shaftesbury was president of the Ragged School Union from 1844.

**Sharp, J. W.** (1817 – 1856) Jack Sharp was a popular comic singer who performed at Vauxhall Gardens.

[Sharpe see **Sharp**]

**Sheepshanks, John** (1787 – 1863) Cloth manufacturer and art collector who donated his collection of British paintings and drawings to the new South Kensington Museum in 1857.

**Shelley, Sir John Villiers** (1808 – 1867) Liberal MP for Westminster from 1852 to 1865 and a supporter of the National Sunday League, established to extend the leisure opportunities available to those who worked for six days of the week, by opening such places as the Crystal Palace and the British Museum on Sundays.

**Sherman, John** (1788 – 1861) Cricketer who played until into his sixties.

**Sibthorp, Charles de Laet Waldo** (1783 – 1855) Tory MP.

**Simpson, Sir James** (1792 – 1868) Army officer who succeeded to the command of British forces in the Crimea on **Lord Raglan's** death. He resigned his command in November 1855, after the taking of Sevastopol.

**Skelton, Percival** (c.1813 – 1887) Illustrator, an unsuccessful candidate for the NWCS. Skelton had a long relationship with the Whympers, for whom he drew designs on the wood block. He is credited as a draughtsman in *Scrambles amongst the Alps* and *Travels amongst the Great Andes of the Equator*. He married **Sir Charles Eastlake**'s sister, Katherine. In 1851 he was resident in Bath, then moved to 7 Ampthill Square, Marylebone.

**Skill, Edward** (1831 – 1873) Wood engraver born in Yarmouth, who worked in London. He moved to Sweden in 1864. His father Frederick Skill (<u>b</u>. c.1801) was a printer born in Norwich, and his younger brother Thomas (<u>b</u>. c.1830) a painter who moved to Lambeth. The draughtsman mentioned by Whymper could also be Frederick Skill (1824 – 1881), an artist and draughtsman on wood, born in Swaffham, who settled in west London.

**Smiles, Samuel** (1812 – 1904) Writer, whose best–known work, *Self help*, was published by **John Murray**, immediately following the biography of **George Stephenson**, for which Edward Whymper draw the illustrations. Before moving to London, Smiles had been the editor of the *Leeds Times*, had got to know George Stephenson, and had a lifelong involvement in the development of the railways. He lived in Lewisham.

**Smirke, Sydney** (1798 – 1877) Younger brother of Robert Smirke, the architect responsible for the British Museum. Sydney Smirke built the reading room between 1854 and 1857, enclosing the rectangular courtyard left by his brother.

**Smith, Albert** (1816 – 1860) Originally a doctor, Smith made his living as a public entertainer. After climbing Mont Blanc in 1851 (the wood–engraver **Henry Vizetelly**, who knew Smith, maintained that he had been carried up the last part of the mountain by his porters), Smith opened his entertainment, *The ascent of Mont Blanc*, illustrated with moving panoramas, at the Egyptian Hall in 1852. By far the most popular show in London, the performance closed two days after Whymper's visit in June 1858.

**Smith, Charles Manby** (1805 – 1880) Author of *The working man's way in the world, being the autobiography of a journeyman printer* (1853).

**Smith, Edward Tyrrel** (1804 – 1877) Impresario who managed the Drury Lane Theatre from 1852 until 1862.

**Smith, Madeleine** (c.1835 – 1928) After a sensational trial lasting nine days, Madeleine Smith was acquitted of murdering her lover, L'Angelier, with the Scottish verdict of 'Not Proven', indicating not that she was innocent but that there was insufficient evidence to convict her. This case formed the basis of Wilkie Collins' novel, *The law and the lady* (1875).

**Smith, William Collingwood** (1815 – 1887) Landscape painter in water colour, who ran a teaching practice at his residence in Brixton. He taught **Josiah Whymper**.

**Smithers, Henry Keene** (c.1813 – 1874) Secretary of the Commercial Dock Company, sentenced to six years' penal servitude in June 1858, for embezzling up to £9,000 from his employer. Resident in Camberwell, he had three sons and three daughters.

**Soper, Thomas James** (c.1817 – 1893) London landscape painter, born in Edmonton, resident in Denmark Hill, then Lambeth.

**Sowerby, Ann** (c.1790 – 1861) Sister of **Samuel Leigh**.

**Sparrow, John** (c.1807 – ?1858) Engraver, resident in Lambeth.

**Spooner, William** (fl. 1859) Printer and publisher in the Strand.

**Spurgeon, Charles Haddon** (1834 – 1892) Popular Baptist preacher, who achieved celebrity for his sermons to enormous crowds in London. He established the Metropolitan Tabernacle at the Elephant and Castle in 1861.

**Stalker, Alexander M.** (c.1815 – 1892) Baptist minister, born in Scotland, who served in Leeds, then Frome.

**Stanfield, Clarkson** (1793 – 1867) Landscape painter who specialised in marine subjects, Stansfield was a member of the RA.

**Stapleton, John** (1815 – 1891) MP for Berwick from 1857 to 1859, Stapleton was one of the directors of the Royal British Bank, along with **Humphrey Brown**, charged with fraudulently publishing false accounts.

**Stephenson, George** (1781 – 1848) An engineer responsible for a new miner's safety lamp in 1815, and then the development of the modern railway locomotive.

**Stephenson, George Robert** (1819 – 1905) Nephew of **George Stephenson**, he worked with his cousin **Robert Stephenson** as a railway engineer from an office in Great George Street.

**Stephenson, Robert** (1803 – 1859) Son of **George Stephenson**, he followed his father as a railway engineer. He was MP for Whitby from 1847.

**Stokes, William** (1803 – 1881) Baptist minister involved in the Peace Society.

**Strafford, John Byng, Earl of** (1772 – 1860) Army officer who fought at Waterloo.

**Strahan, William** (fl. 1831 – 1859) Originally William Snow, a banker convicted of fraud, with **Sir John Paul** and **Robert Bates**.

**Street, George Edmund** (1824 – 1881) Ecclesiastical architect and architectural writer, based in London from 1856.

**Such, John** (1810 – 1878) Printer born in Southwark and resident in Clapham.

**Suffolk, Charles John Howard, seventeenth Earl of** (1804 – 1876) Ten paintings were stolen from the Howard family home at Charlton Park, Wiltshire, in October 1856. John Farbon, a messenger at the War Office, was charged with their theft.

**Sulman, Thomas** (1832 – 1900) A draughtsman on wood, born and resident in Islington.

**Sunter, Edwin** (b̲. c.1835) Edwin Sunter and **Leonard Sunter** (b̲. c.1833) were whitesmiths (metal workers) resident in Lambeth.

**Swinfen, Charles Albon** (c.1830 – 1895) Engraver, born and resident in Lambeth.

**Symons, William Martyn** (c.1817 – 1890) Printer and stationer in Bridge Street, Lambeth.

**Taylor, Robert E.** (1823 – 1897) Printer in Lambeth.

**Tenniel, Sir John** (1820 – 1914) Artist and *Punch* cartoonist best known for his illustrations to *Alice's Adventures in Wonderland* (1865), engraved by the **Dalziels**. **Josiah Whymper** engraved his illustrations to an edition of *Aesop's Fables*. From 1854 Tenniel lived at 10 Portsdown Road, Maida Hill.

**Thackeray, William Makepeace** (1811 – 1863) Author of *Vanity Fair* (1847-8) who wrote prolifically for periodicals.

**Thomson, Arthur Saunders** (1816 – 1860) Army surgeon who worked in New Zealand from 1848 until 1858. He was in London until November 1859, when he left for China. His book, *The story of New Zealand* (J. Murray, 1859), for which the Whympers engraved the illustrations, was the first written history of New Zealand.

**Thornbury, Walter** (1828 – 1876) Author who had travelled widely, and contributed to Dickens' *All the year round*. (His father was a solicitor, from which Whymper may have derived his mistaken opinion of **John Saunders**.)

**Thornton, William** (c.1814 – 1887) Auctioneer, land agent and valuer, resident in Reigate.

**Thynne, Lord John** (1831 – 1896) Later fourth Marquess of Bath, diplomat and politician with Anglo–catholic views.

**Todleben, Eduard Ivanovich** (1818 – 1884) Russian military engineer who organized the defence of Sevastopol during the Crimean War.

**Tomlinson, Charles** (1808 – 1897) Lecturer and schoolmaster, who studied at the London Mechanics' Institute, and wrote on a variety of scientific subjects, his most successful work being *Cyclopedia of Useful Arts* (1852).

**Trench, Richard Chevenix** (1807 – 1886) Dean of Westminster from 1856, where he introduced Sunday evening services.

**Trestrail, Frederick** (1803 – 1890) Baptist minister and secretary of the Baptist Missionary Society from 1849 to 1870.

**Truscott, James Wyatt** (c.1824 – aft. 1858) Printer for SPCK, at Nelson Square, Blackfriars Road.

**Turner, Joseph Mallord William** (1775 – 1851) One of the most important English artists, and a leading figure in the Romantic Movement.

**Underhill, Edward Bean** (1813 – 1901) Secretary of the Baptist Missionary Society, he travelled in India and Ceylon from 1854 to 1857, then lived in Hampstead.

**Ure, Andrew** (1778 – 1857) Scottish chemist who published works on contemporary industrial practices.

**Vacher, Charles** (1818 – 1883) A member of the NWCS who had travelled in Italy.

**Vaughan, Dr John** (c.1793 – c.1859) Vicar of St Matthew's, Brixton, Vaughan was acquitted at the central criminal court of making false entries in the parish register of burials.

**Venables, Richard** (c.1774 – 1858) Archdeacon of Carmarthen.

**Villiers, Henry Montagu** (1813 – 1861) Canon of St Paul's, he began his incumbency as Bishop of Carlisle on 25 February 1856.

**Vince, Charles** (1824 – 1874) Baptist minister of Graham Street chapel, Birmingham.

**Vizetelly, Henry Richard** (1820 – 1894) Trained as a wood engraver in Kennington, Vizetelly ran a printing, engraving and publishing business before moving to Paris in 1865. He worked with **Ingram** on the *Illustrated London News*, then, when newspaper stamp duty was about to be abolished in 1855, started his own *Illustrated Times*, with the publisher **David Bogue** as proprietor.

**Vokins, William** (1815 – 1895) Dealer in works of art in Marylebone.

**Waddington, David** (c.1806 – aft. 1861) Chairman of the Eastern Counties Railway and MP for Harwich from 1852 until 1857.

**Wakley, Thomas** (1795 – 1862) Medical journalist, editor of the *Lancet*, radical MP for Finsbury from 1835 to 1852 and coroner for West Middlesex from 1839.

**Walker, Frederick** (1840 – 1875) Important painter in oil and water colour, who trained as a wood engraver with the Whympers for two years, from the end of 1858.

**Walker, William** (1824 – 1860) American freebooter who intervened in a civil war in Nicaragua in 1855, and, as commander of the army, established a regime there that was recognised by the American government in May 1856.

**Walmsley, Sir Joshua** (1794 – 1871) MP for Leicester and president of the Sunday Society, which campaigned for the opening of museums on the Sabbath, as a result of which he lost his seat in 1857.

**Ward, Edward Matthew** (1816 – 1879) Painter of historical genre subjects.

**Warner, William** (c.1801 – 1886) Wheelwright, married to **Charlotte** (c.1809 – 1877), who lived on Ham Common.

**Warren, Henry** (1794 – 1879) Artist, resident in Chelsea. From 1839 to 1873 he was President of the NWCS. His son, **Edward George Warren** (1834 – 1909), was also a member of the NWCS.

**Warren, Mary** (c.1771 – 1856) Wife of John Warren, a carpenter of 3 Norfolk Row, Lambeth, and neighbour of the Whympers.

**Warren, Samuel** (1807 – 1877) Author of *Passages from the diary of a late physician* (1832).

**Waterlow, Sir Sydney** (1822 – 1906) Printer who became Lord Mayor of London.

**Watkins, John** (c.1823 – 1874) Photographer in Parliament Street.

**Watkins, John** (c.1826 – 1899) Wood engraver, born in London and resident in Highbury, Islington.

**Watson, J.** (fl. 1858) Publisher working for **Nisbet** and Co.

**Watson, Thomas James** (c.1799 – 1857) Superintendent of the Deaf and Dumb Asylum in Old Kent Road.

**Watts, John** (1785 – 1858) Partner in the pottery firm of **Doulton**, Watts in Lambeth High Street. John Watts founded the Baptist chapel in Regent Street, Lambeth.

**Weale, John** (1791 – 1862) Publisher and writer on architecture, with offices in High Holborn.

**Weedon, Edwin** (c.1819 – 1873) London painter of ship scenes. In 1857 his address was 15 Essex St, Strand, then in 1861, 3 Danes Inn, Westminster.

**Weir, Harrison William** (1824 – 1906) Oil painter of natural history and landscape scenes, originally trained by the printer **George Baxter**. Weir worked both as a draughtsman on the wood block and an engraver for the *Illustrated London News*. He lived at Lyndhurst Road, Peckham.

**Wells, Charles Tennant** (c.1808 – 1879) Draughtsman on wood who had worked for Charles Knight, then set up as a manufacturer of engravers' wood blocks, with premises in Bouverie Street.

**Wheeler, Ann** (<u>b</u>. c.1786) Assistant to her son–in–law, James Gwinn, a bookseller and stationer of The Broadway, St Giles, Camberwell.

**White, William B** (fl. 1856) Picture dealer in Holborn.

**Whymper, Alfred** (1843 – 1904) Edward's brother. Alfred trained as a printer, then in 1884 was ordained in the Church of England, working as a vicar in Nottingham and Southwell.

   **Ebenezer** (1811 – 1879) **Nathaniel Whymper's** oldest child and Edward's uncle. Ebenezer Whymper was a Baptist minister but also worked in the wood engraving business with his brother Josiah. He lived at Moore Place, Lambeth, with his wife **Lydia** (c.1817 – 1859); they had three surviving children, Harriet, **John Charles** and Elizabeth. Ebenezer married his second wife Susannah Dearlove in 1860, but she died the following year, whereupon he married again, in 1862. His third wife, Eliza Wade survived him.

   **Elijah** (1822 – 1883) Younger brother of Josiah, and Edward's uncle. Elijah served his apprenticeship as a wood engraver in Josiah's workshop.

   **Elizabeth (**1848 – 1935) Edward's oldest sister. Elizabeth never married but spent her life in social service, becoming a major in the Salvation Army, and a leading temperance campaigner.

   **Frederick** (1838 – 1901) Edward's older brother. Frederick served his apprenticeship as a wood engraver but showed more interest in water colour painting, and had exhibited by the time he was twenty one. In June 1862 he sailed to Vancouver, returning to London at the end of 1867. His book *Travel and adventure in the territory of Alaska* was published by **John Murray** the following year.

   **Henry Josiah** (1845 – 1893) Edward's brother. Henry worked in bookselling and publishing before training as a brewer in Burton on Trent. In 1866 he started work at the recently built brewery at Murree, in the Punjab (modern Pakistan), of which he became the manager. Henry Josiah was a leading freemason.

   **John** (1827 – 1895) Younger brother of Josiah and Edward's uncle. He was a grocer in Watford.

**John Charles** (1838 – bef. 1891) Edward's cousin, the eldest son of Ebenezer Whymper. John Charles Whymper worked as a wood engraver in Lambeth. As recorded on 22 March 1857, he married **Elizabeth Barnett Hewitt** (then aged about sixteen) in Oxford. They settled near the Elephant and Castle and their first child was born in December 1858.

**Joseph** (1850 – 1886) Edward's brother. Joseph trained as a brewer and followed his brother Henry to Murree, later managing the Crown Brewery in Mussoorie. He married there, but died as the result of a cart accident.

**Josiah Wood** (1813 – 1903) Nathaniel Whymper's second son and Edward's father, born in Ipswich. Like his older brother Ebenezer, he married three times. His second wife, **Elizabeth Whitworth Claridge** (1819 – 1859) was the mother of his eleven children.

**Nathaniel** (1787 – 1861) Josiah Whymper's father and Edward's grandfather. He was a brewer and town councillor in Ipswich, of radical political views. He married three times, first to Elizabeth Orris (1791 – 1829) with whom he had eight surviving children; then Elizabeth (1788 – 1838), the widow of Thomas Bradlaugh, whom he married in 1834, and finally **Charlotte Gross** (1818 – 1894), with whom he had one daughter, Charlotte (1851 – 1927), who married Thomas Elkington.

**Samuel Leigh** (1857 – 1941) Edward's youngest brother. Educated at University College School and trained as a chemist, Samuel followed his brothers to India in 1877. He became a manager at Murree before moving to Naini Tal, from where he retired in 1913, then travelled round the world. He was a keen ornithologist and angler.

**Theodosia** (1828 – 1891) Josiah Whymper's youngest sister is almost certainly the aunt mentioned on 30 May 1859. She lived with her father Nathaniel until her marriage to George Barnes in 1860.

**Theophilus** (1840 – 1887) Edward's cousin, the son of Josiah's younger brother Theophilus (1820 – 1843). His father died when he was young and his mother Sarah (c.1818 – aft. 1901), returned to her place of birth, North Cadbury, in Somerset, and married a local farmer **George Harding**. In 1861 Theophilus was a warehouseman in Lambeth, but by 1871 he had become a draper in Yeovil, recently married to his cousin Harriet Whymper (c.1837 – 1875), **Ebenezer**'s oldest child. After Harriet's death, Theophilus married again in 1877.

**William Nathaniel** (1855 – 1917) Edward's brother. William Nathaniel attended University College School and then joined Royal Exchange Assurance when seventeen. He retired as company secretary in 1917.

**Wilkinson, William** (1795 – 1865) MP for Lambeth from 1852 until 1857.

**Willey, W.** (fl. 1856) Baptist minister in Oxford.

**William, Charles Cave** (fl. 1858) A railway carriage maker in Glasshouse Yard, Goswell Street.

**Williams, D.** (fl. 1857) Baptist minister in Accrington, Lancashire.

**Williams, William** (1788 – 1865) Radical MP for Lambeth from 1850 to 1865.

**Williams, Sir William Fenwick** (1800 – 1883) British commissioner with the Turkish army, Williams was in charge of the garrison at Kars that was forced to surrender in November 1855.

**Wire, David** (1800 – 1860) Born in Colchester, Wire was elected Lord Mayor of London in 1858.

**Witherington, William Frederick** (1785 – 1865) Landscape painter and member of the RA.

**Wolf, Joseph** (1820 – 1899) Wildlife painter, born in Germany, invited to London (where he settled in Primrose Hill) in 1848 by the Zoological Society, to illustrate a book on birds. His long association with the Whympers had started by the time of their collaboration on **David Livingstone**'s first book. In 1873, Edward and Josiah Whymper effectively published (under the imprint of **Alexander Macmillan**) *The life and habits of wild animals, illustrated by designs by Joseph Wolf,* a beautifully engraved showcase of Wolf's illustrations. Edward's younger brother Charles was trained by Wolf.

**Woods, William** (c.1832 – aft. 1891) In 1853 he married Josiah's younger sister **Hephzibah Whymper** (1826 – 1895), and is therefore Edward's uncle. Born in Yarmouth, William Woods worked as an accountant before becoming a Baptist minister in Swaffham, later moving to Nottingham.

**Wordsworth, Christopher** (1807–1885) Nephew of the poet William Wordsworth, Christopher Wordsworth was canon at Westminster Abbey from 1844. Twenty two of the illustrations to his *Greece: pictorial, descriptive and historical* (London: William S. Orr, 1839), were engraved by Josiah Whymper.

**Wormull, Henry** (1815 – 1866) Surgical instrument maker in Portland Street, Newington, Lambeth. [Whymper could be referring to the probably related Anthony Wormull, a cutler in Lambeth Walk.]

# Appendix 2  Whymper family tree

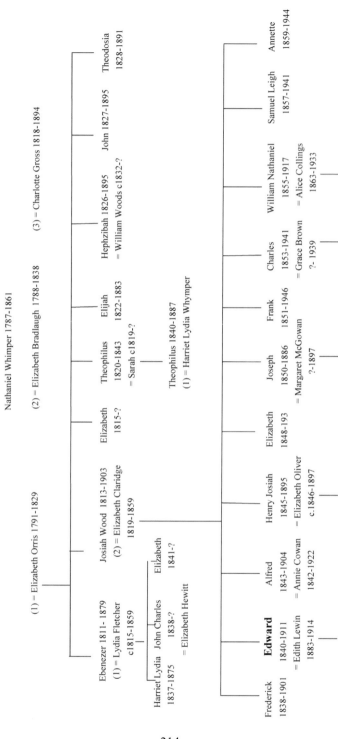

Nathaniel Whimper 1787-1861

(1) = Elizabeth Orris 1791-1829          (2) = Elizabeth Bradlaugh 1788-1838          (3) = Charlotte Gross 1818-1894

Ebenezer 1811- 1879          Josiah Wood  1813-1903          Elizabeth          Theophilus          Elijah          Hephzibah 1826-1895          John 1827-1895          Theodosia
(1) = Lydia Fletcher          (2) = Elizabeth Claridge          1815-?          1820-1843          1822-1883          = William Woods c1832-?                            1828-1891
c1815-1859          1819-1859                                                  = Sarah c1819-?

Harriet Lydia  John Charles      Elizabeth                                        Theophilus 1840-1887
1837-1875      1838-?              1841-?                                          (1) = Harriet Lydia Whymper
                = Elizabeth Hewitt

Frederick          Edward          Alfred          Henry Josiah          Elizabeth          Joseph          Frank          Charles          William Nathaniel          Samuel Leigh          Annette
1838-1901          1840-1911          1843-1904          1845-1895          1848-193          1850-1886          1851-1946          1853-1941          1855-1917          1857-1941          1859-1944
                = Edith Lewin          = Annie Cowan          = Elizabeth Oliver                              = Margaret McGowan                        = Grace Brown          = Alice Collings
                1883-1914          1842-1922          c.1846-1897                              ?-1897                        ?-1939          1863-1933

Ethel Rosa                              4 daughters and 1 son                              2 daughters          1 daughter          2 sons and 1 daughter
1908-1969

214

# Appendix 3 Book illustrations referred to in the diary

*Baptist Magazine* (1858)
The Indian map in the Missionary Herald section, February 1858, is probably that referred to on 15 February 1858.

*Baptist Reporter* (1858).
There are full-page Whymper engravings in the volumes for February, March and May 1858, pages 68, 98, 164.

*The book of Job.* London: J. Nisbet, 1857.
Mentioned by Whymper on 20 December 1856, this contained fifty engravings of which twenty-three are by the Whympers, and sixteen by the Dalziels.

Browne, R.W. *A history of Rome, from A.D. 96 to the fall of the Western Empire.* London: SPCK, 1859.
Edward Whymper drew seven illustrations onto wood blocks, 'Palmyra'(13 – 21 November 1857), 'Diocletian's palace at Spalatro' (21 – 26 December 1857), 'Basilica of St Paul' (3 – 4 May 1858), 'Basilica of Constantine'(30 October – 4 November 1857), 'Baths of Caracalla' (4 – 12 November 1857), 'Castle of St Angelo' (21 – 30 October, 12 – 13 November 1857) and 'Porta Nigra' (8 – 15 December 1857).

Bunyan, John. *The pilgrim's progress.* London: J. Nisbet, 1860.
Described on 25 February, 8 March 1858, this edition contains forty illustrations, drawn by John Gilbert and engraved by the Whympers.

Byron, George. *Childe Harold's pilgrimage: a romaunt.* London: J. Murray, 1859.
Photographs and sketches from a variety of artists were drawn on the wood by Percival Skelton and engraved by the Whympers, Jewitt and J. Cooper. Fifty of the seventy-eight illustrations were engraved by the Whympers. The full page frontispiece to Canto Fourth, page 185, 'Horses of St Marks,' was drawn onto the wood from a photograph by Edward Whymper, 9 – 20 September 1858. Skelton's drawings of the wolf of the capitol and the Pantheon, are those redrawn by Edward Whymper on 22, 28 and 29 October 1858.

Corderoy, Edward. "Progress: life of George Stephenson. A lecture." in *Lectures delivered before the Young Men's Christian Association, in Exeter Hall.* London: J. Nisbet, 1858.
Whymper attended the lecture on 9 February 1858 and completed the two drawings which were published with the text, between 1 and 10 February 1858.

Dufferin, Lord. *Letters from high latitudes; being some account of a voyage in the schooner yacht 'Foam', 85 O.M. to Iceland, Jan Mayen, and Spitzbergen.* London: J. Murray, 1857.
There are nine full page scenes engraved by the Whympers, including one drawing of an arctic fox by Joseph Wolf. The draughtsman Edmund Gibson also drew scenes for this book. Edward Whymper drew the Lapp lady, p.248 (13, 14 May 1857), a diagram of the coast p.227 (14, 20 April 1857), and the basaltic rocks, p.167 (8, 9 April 1857).

Ellis, William. *Three visits to Madagascar during the years 1853-1854-1856.* London: J. Murray, 1858.
Described on 8 March 1858, the book contains twenty-five illustrations, engraved by the Whympers.

*Encyclopaedia Britannica*, 8th ed. Edinburgh: A. and C. Black, 1853-1860.
The volume containing the article on micrometers, mentioned on 28 August 1857, appeared later that year. The optical diagrams described 19 February to 20 March 1858 were for the article 'Optics', in the volume published 1858. This contains 282 diagrams in total.

*Fireside tales.* 2nd series. London: SPCK, 1857.
The volume contains seventeen half-page scenes; the tales originally appeared in the periodical *Home Friend* (26 March 1857).

*Florence.* London: SPCK, 1857.
'Convent of Vallombrosa' (4 – 7 October 1856) appears on page 126, and 'Ponte di Santa Trinita' (8 – 9 October, 1 – 4 December 1856) on page 67.

Gosse, Philip. *A manual of marine zoology for the British Isles.* 2 vols. London: Van Voorst, 1855-6.
The "tunny" referred to on 30 June, 1 July 1856 appears as figure 305.

Gosse, P.H. *The romance of natural history.* London: J. Nisbet, 1860.
Twelve illustrations were drawn by Wolf, and engraved by the Whympers.

*Hannah Lavender, or, Ladyhall.* London: SPCK, 1857.
Whymper appears to have had no more involvement with this anonymously written novel than to read it on 4 July 1857 and decide where the illustrations should go.

*Handbook to the cathedrals of England: Eastern division – Oxford, Peterborough, Norwich, Ely, Lincoln.* London: J. Murray, 1862.
Most of the engravings are by Jewitt, but the illustration of Peterborough west front is signed "EWhymper," and must be that started on 1 December 1858, finished on 15 January 1859, and mentioned 15 March 1859. The illustration of the prior's door at Ely cathedral is that described from 1 to 16 November 1858.

James, Thomas. *Aesop's fables: a new version.* London: J. Murray, 1858.
Joseph Wolf and John Tenniel drew the illustrations; John Murray's ledger records payments of £157 14s to the Whympers, £61 to Wolf and £57 to Tenniel, on 30 September 1858. 'Tenniel's blocks' are referred to on 21 August 1858.

Johns, C.A. *British birds in their haunts.* London: SPCK, 1862.
Mentioned on 19 January 1859, this volume has 190 illustrations drawn by Joseph Wolf, and engraved by the Whympers.

Kingsley, Charles. *The heroes; or, Greek fairy tales for my children.* Cambridge: Macmillan, 1856.
This contains eight illustrations drawn by Kingsley. The last, showing Theseus and the minotaur, which was engraved by the Whympers, is probably the 'ridiculous mythological outline' mentioned on 11 December 1855.

Livingstone, David. *Missionary travels and researches in South Africa.* London: J. Murray, 1857.
There are forty-five illustrations, engraved by the Whympers and drawn on the wood by Joseph Wolf (18 April, 23 May, 22 October, 9 and 11 November 1857).

Moodie, Susanna. *Roughing it in the bush; or, life in Canada.* New ed. London: R. Bentley, 1857.
This book, which Whymper read through on 13 July 1857, contains a frontispeice engraved by the Whympers.

Murchison, Roderick. *Siluria: the history of the oldest fossiliferous rocks and their foundations.* 3rd ed. London: J. Murray, 1859.
The Whympers were paid £25 for work on this book.

Rawlinson, George (ed.). *The history of Herodotus.* 4 vols. London: J. Murray, 1858-1860.
The Whympers were paid £100 by John Murray for work on these volumes. 'Herodotus blocks' are referred to on 7 January 1858.

*Scripture topography: Palestine.* London: SPCK, 1860.
'Valley of Kedron' (28 – 30 September 1859), 'Church at Samaria" (26 September 1859) and 'Northern angle of wall at Jerusalem' (14 – 20 September 1859) were drawn by Edward Whymper.

Smiles, Samuel. *The story of the life of George Stephenson, railway engineer.* London: J. Murray, 1859.
The preface states that 'The illustrations to this volume are from sketches made on the spot by Mr. Edward Whymper.' The commission was first mentioned on 26 April 1858.

Thomson, Arthur S. *The story of New Zealand.* London: J. Murray, 1859.
The Whympers were paid £87 4s for drawing and engraving the illustrations. Edward Whymper met the author on 18 August 1859.

Thomson, W.M. *The land and the book; or Biblical illustrations drawn from the manners and customs, the scenes and scenery of the Holy Land.* London: Nelson, 1860.
Originally issued in 12 monthly parts from mid-1859 at sixpence each with black and white illustrations, for which Bethlehem (23 – 27 November 1858), Baalbec (29 April – 10 June 1858) and Hebron (10 – 11 November 1858) were drawn by Edward Whymper.

Tomlinson, Charles. *Illustrations of trades.* London: SPCK, 1860.

Tomlinson, Charles. *Illustrations of useful arts and manufactures.* London: SPCK, [1859].
Printed by Richard Clay, there are 600 illustrations, mostly printed on double page spreads. 'Tomlinson's diagrams,' first mentioned on 24 February 1859, then 9 June 1859 onwards, probably refer to these two volumes.

Walpole, Horace. *The letters of Horace Walpole, Earl of Orford; edited by Peter Cunningham.* 9 vols. London: R. Bentley, 1857-9.
The title page illustration to volume 6, 'Chimney piece in the library at Strawberry Hill' is probably the drawing mentioned on 2, 3, 9, 14 October 1857). Either the title page illustration to volume 7 or volume 9 is the drawing mentioned on 16, 17, 19, 20 October 1857.

White, Gilbert. *The natural history of Selborne.* New ed, abridged for young persons. London: SPCK, 1860.
First mentioned on 17 January 1859, the frontispiece, 'Residence of Gilbert White, as it existed in his life-time' was begun by Edward Whymper on 2 June and finished 23 June 1859. He drew the map of Selborne and its environs between 27 June and 6 July 1859.

Yarrell, William. *A history of British fishes.* 3rd ed, rev. John Richardson. London: Van Voorst, 1859.
This edition contains 522 wood engravings, begun on 20 January 1859. Edward Whymper was drawing these fish until 22 June 1859 ('on with Rainbow Wrasse and Viviparous Blenny' 1 April 1859).

# Bibliography

## Manuscript material

Scott Polar Research Institute, University of Cambridge
    MS 822/1/1-9; BJ. Whymper, Edward. 'Lecture note books.'
    MS 822/39; BJ. 'Clarendon House School reports, certificates, commendations.'
    MS 822/39; BJ. Whymper, Edward. 'Diary 1855 – 1859.'
    MS 822/4; BJ. Whymper, Edward. 'Diary for the year 1872.'
    MS 822/37/1-2; BJ. Whymper, Edward. 'Proof prints of wood engravings.'
Alpine Club Archives
    1922/B35. Whymper, Edward. 'Greenland correspondence.'
British Library
    Additional MS 63112 (Blakeney Collection). 'Correspondence.'
    Additional MS 46664 (Bentley Papers). 'Bills, receipts.'
    Additional MS 46666. 'Bills, receipts.'
Angus Library, Regent's Park College, Oxford
    Maze Pond Minute Book 1840 – 1860
    Maze Pond Minute Book 1861 – 1871
    Maze Pond Account Book 1844 – 1861
John Murray Archive, National Library of Scotland
    MS 42727. 'Copies ledger C 1828-1849.'
    MS 42729. 'Copies ledger D 1838-1880.'
    MS 42730.'Copies ledger E 1846-1876.'
    MS 42763. 'Commission book 1843-1858.'
    MS 42764. 'Commission book 1851-1873.'

## Published material

Aldis, James A. 'Reminiscences of the Rev. John Aldis of Maze Pond.' *Baptist Quarterly* 5 (1930): 1-10.
Alexander, Herbert. 'John William North, A.R.A., R.W.S., c1842 – 1924.' *The Old Water Colour Society's Club Annual Volume* 5 (1927-8): 35-52.
Altick, Richard D. *The shows of London*. London: Harvard University Press, 1978.
Anderson, Patricia. *The printed image and the transformation of popular culture 1790 – 1860*. Oxford: Clarendon Press, 1991.
Andrews, Malcolm. *Charles Dickens and his performing selves: Dickens and the public readings*. Oxford: Oxford University Press, 2006.

Barnes, James. *Free trade in books: a study of the London book trade since 1800*. Oxford : Oxford University Press, 1964.

Blachon, Remi. *La gravure sur bois au XIX^e siècle: l'âge du bois debout*. Paris: Les Editions de l'Amateur, 2001.

Black, Clementina. *Frederick Walker*. London: Duckworth, 1902.

Bliss, Douglas Percy. *A history of wood-engraving*. London: Spring Books, 1964.

Briggs, J.H.Y. *The English Baptists of the Nineteenth Century*. Didcot: Baptist Historical Society, 1994.

Brown, Philip. *London publishers and printers c1800 – 1870*. London: BL, 1982.

Buchanan-Brown, John. 'British wood-engravers c.1820 – c.1860: a checklist.' *Journal of the Printing Historical Society* 17 (1982-3): 31–61.

Buchanan-Brown, John. *Early Victorian illustrated books: Britain, France and Germany 1820-1860*. London: BL, 2005.

Clark, Ronald. *The day the rope broke: the story of a great Victorian tragedy*. London: Secker and Warburg, 1965.

Clark, Ronald. *Six great mountaineers: Edward Whymper, A.F. Mummery, J. Norman Collie, George Leigh-Malory, Geoffrey Winthrop Young, Sir John Hunt*. London: Hamish Hamilton, 1956.

Clodd, Edward. *Memories*. London: Chapman and Hall, 1916.

Conefrey, Mick and Tim Jordan. *Mountain men*. Cambridge: Da Capo Press, 2002.

Dalziel, George, and Edward Dalziel. *The Brothers Dalziel: a record of fifty years' work in conjunction with many of the most distinguished artists of the period 1840 – 1890*. London: Methuen, 1901.

De Freitas, Leo. 'Commercial engraving on wood in England, 1700 – 1880.' Royal College of Art, Ph.D. diss., 1986.

De Maré, Eric. *The Victorian woodblock illustrators*. London: Gordon Fraser, 1980.

Elliot, Daniel Giraud. *The life and habits of wild animals, illustrated by designs by Joseph Wolf*. London: A. Macmillan, 1874.

Engen, Rodney. *Dictionary of Victorian wood engravers*. Cambridge: Chadwick-Healey, 1985.

Evans, David Morier. *Facts, failures and frauds: revelations, financial, mercantile, criminal*. London: Groombridge, 1859.

Garret, Albert. *A history of British wood engraving*. Tunbridge Wells: Midas Books, 1978.

Gibberd, Graham. *On Lambeth Marsh: the South Bank and Waterloo*. London: Jane Gibberd, 1992.

Goldman, Paul. *Victorian illustrated books 1850-1870: the heyday of wood-engraving – the Robin de Beaumont collection*. London: British Museum Press, 1994.

Goldman, Paul. *Victorian illustration: the Pre-Raphaelites, the Idyllic School and the High Victorians*. Aldershot: Scolar Press, 1996.

Graves, Robert. *They hanged my saintly Billy*. London: Cassell, 1957.

Halliday, Stephen. *The great stink of London: Sir Joseph Bazalgette and the cleansing of the Victorian capital*. Stroud: Sutton Publishing, 1999.

Harris, Judy. *The Roupell's of Lambeth: politics, property and peculation in Victorian London*. London: Streatham Society, 2001.

Hartley, Harold. *Eighty-eight not out: a record of happy memories*. London: Frederick Muller, 1939.

Houfe, Simon. *The dictionary of 19th century British book illustrators and caricaturists*, rev ed. Woodbridge: Antique Collectors Club, 1996.

'Hours of scrambling exercise – Tyndall and Whymper', *Saturday Review* 32 (8 July 1871): 59-60.

Huish, Marcus. 'Birket Foster: his life and work.' *Art Journal* (1890).

Ingram, Glen. 'Joseph Wolf: wildlife artist supreme.' *Wildlife Australia* 26, no. 2 (1989): 16-17.

Kaufman, Paul. 'English book clubs and their role in social history.' *Libri* 4 (1964-5): 1-31.

Kernahan, Coulson. *In good company: some personal recollections of Swinburne, Lord Roberts, Watts-Dunton, Oscar Wilde, Edward Whymper, S.J. Stone, Steven Phillips*, 2nd ed. London: Bodley Head, 1917.

Kerr, Barbara. *The dispossessed: an aspect of Victorian social history*. London: John Baker, 1974.

Lewis, Donald M., ed. *Blackwell dictionary of evangelical biography 1730-1860*. Oxford: Blackwell, 1995.

Lyall, Alan. *The first descent of the Matterhorn: a bibliographic guide to the 1865 accident and its aftermath*. Llandysul: Gomer Press, 1997.

Macdonald, Peter. *Big Ben: the bell, the clock and the tower*. Stroud: Sutton Publishing, 2004.

McLean, Ruari. *Victorian book design and colour printing*. 2nd ed. London: Faber and Faber, 1972.

Mallalieu, H. L. *The dictionary of British watercolour artists up to 1920: volume 1 – the text*. 2nd ed. Woodbridge: Antique Collectors Club, 1986.

Marks, John George. *The life and letters of Frederick Walker ARA*. London: Macmillan, 1896.

Muir, Percy. *Victorian illustrated books*. London: Batsford, 1971.

Ormond, Leonée. 'The Idyllic School: Pinwell, North and Walker.' In *Imagination on a long rein: English literature illustrated*, ed. Joachim Möller, 161-171. Marburg: Jonas Verlag, 1988.

*Oxford Dictionary of National Biography*. Oxford: Oxford University Press, 2004.

Price, Seymour J. 'Maze Pond and the Matterhorn.' *Baptist Quarterly* 10, no. 4 (Oct 1940): 202-208.

Ray, Gordon. *The illustrator and the book in England from 1790 – 1914*. 2nd ed. London: Constable, 1991.

Reid, Forrest. *Illustrators of the sixties*. London: Faber and Gwyer, 1928.

Renier, Hannah. *Lambeth past: Kennington, Vauxhall, Waterloo*. London: Historical Publications, 2006.

Reynolds, Jan. *Birket Foster*. London: Batsford, 1984.

Schulze-Hagen, Karl, and Armin Geus, eds. *Joseph Wolf (1820 – 1899): animal painter*. Marburg an der Lahn: Basilisken-Presse, 2000.

'Scrambles amongst the Alps', *The Hawthorn* 1, no. 1 (April 1872): 46-52.

Selborne, Joanna. *British wood-engraved book illustration, 1904-1940: a break with tradition*. Oxford: Clarendon Press, 1998.

Smith, Ian. 'Edward Whymper – mountaineer and wood engraver.' *Multiples: newsletter of the Society of Wood Engravers* 5, no.8 (March 2004): 228-229.

Smith, Ian. 'Edward Whymper's London.' *AJ* 109 (2004): 234-240.

Smythe, Frank. *Edward Whymper*. London: Hodder and Stoughton, 1940.

Stenton, Michael. *Who's who of British members of parliament. Volume I: 1832 – 1885*. Hassocks: Harvester Press, 1976.

Stephen, Leslie. 'Mr. Whymper's "Scrambles amongst the Alps"', *Macmillan's Magazine* 24 (May-Oct 1871): 304-311.

Taylor, James. 'Commercial fraud and public men in Victorian Britain.' *Historical Research* 78 (May 2005): 230-252.

Taylor, James. 'Company fraud in Victorian Britain: the Royal British Bank scandal of 1856.' *English Historical Review* 122, no. 497 (June 2007): 700-724.

Thwaite, Ann. *Glimpses of the wonderful: the life of Philip Henry Gosse 1810-1888*. London: Faber & Faber, 2002.

Uglow, Jenny. *Nature's engraver: a life of Thomas Bewick*. London: Faber and Faber, 2006.

Underwood, A.C. *A history of the English Baptists*. London: Baptist Union, 1947.

Wakeman, Geoffrey. *Victorian book illustration – the technical revolution*. Newton Abbott: David and Charles, 1973.

Wakeman, Geoffrey. *Victorian colour printing*. Loughborough: Plough Press, 1981.

Wakeman, Geoffrey, and Gavin Bridson. *A guide to nineteenth century colour printers*. Loughborough: Plough Press, 1975.

Webster, Richard and C.W. Alcock, eds. *Surrey cricket: its history and associations*. London: Longman, Green and Co, 1904.

White, Jerry. *London in the nineteenth century*. London: Jonathan Cape, 2007.

White, Joseph William Gleeson. *English illustration – 'the sixties' 1855-70*. London: Constable, 1897.

Whitley, W.T. *The Baptists of London 1612- 1928: their fellowship, their expansion, with notes on their 850 churches*. London: Kingsgate Press, 1928.

Whymper, Edward. 'Greenland.' *AJ* 5 (1870): 1-23.

Whymper, Edward. *Scrambles amongst the Alps in the years 1860-1869*. London: J. Murray, 1871.

Whymper, Edward. 'Some notes on Greenland and the Greenlanders.' *AJ* 6 (1873): 160-168, 208-220.

Whymper, Edward. *The ascent of the Matterhorn*. London: J. Murray, 1880.

[Whymper, Edward]. 'Sir John Gilbert, R.A.' *Leisure Hour* (1880): 183–185.

[Whymper, Edward]. 'The reading-room of the British Museum.' *Leisure Hour* (1880): 685-688.

Whymper, Edward. 'Explorations in Greenland.' *Good Words* 25 (1884): 38-43, 96-103, 183-189.

Whymper, Edward. *Supplementary appendix to travels amongst the great Andes of the equator*. London: J. Murray, 1891.

Whymper, Edward. *Travels amongst the Great Andes of the Equator*. London: J. Murray, 1892.

Whymper, Edward. *Chamonix and the Range of Mont Blanc: a guide*. London: J. Murray, 1896.

Whymper, Edward. *A guide to Zermatt and the Matterhorn*. London: J. Murray, 1897.

Whymper, Edward. 'A new playground in the New World.' *Scribner's Magazine*, June 1903, 642-660.

Whymper, Frederick. *Travel and adventure in the territory of Alaska, formerly Russian America – now ceded to the United States – and in various other parts of the North Pacific*. London: J. Murray, 1868.

Whymper, Robert. 'Edward Whymper: mountaineer, writer, artist, and scientist.' *Quarterly review* 609 (July 1956): 283-296.

Wood, Christopher. *Victorian painters: 1 – the text*. Woodbridge: Antique Collectors Club, 1995.

**Periodicals**

*Baptist Reporter*
*Baptist Magazine*
*A Manual of the Baptist Denomination*
*Ipswich Journal*
*The Times*

# INDEX

Abbreviations used in index

| | | | |
|---|---|---|---|
| EW | Edward Whymper | JWW | Josiah Wood Whymper |
| FW | Frederick Whymper | MP | Maze Pond |

Aberdeen, 84, 90, 196
Aberdeen, fourth Earl of (George Hamilton-
   Gordon), 14, 176, 189, 190, 192, 200
Accrington, 89, 213
Adams Reilly, Anthony, xxii
Admiralty, the, 4, 59, 190
*Aesops' fables*, xvii, 145, 182, 208, 217
Africa, 22, 43, 174, 184, 199. *See also*
   Livingstone, David
*Agamemnon* (British ship), 101
Agar, Edward, 106, 176
Aiguille Verte, xxii
Åland Islands, 6n
Albert, Prince Consort, 9, 10, 106; birthday,
   22; portrait by Gilbert, 49; sees EW's
   drawing, 61; opens Manchester Art
   Treasures exhibition, 91; visits NWCS
   exhibition, 136; EW sees at British
   Museum, 162
Aldis, John, 176; accusation against, xix; EW
   calls on, 113; JWW meets, 80; preaches,
   2–33 *passim*, 62, 160; resignation, xix,
   34–35; visits Whympers, 5, 55–56
Alexander II (emperor of Russia), 6, 29, 36,
   41–42, 51, 53, 66
*Alice's adventures in Wonderland*, xiv, 184,
   208
*All the year round*, 208
Alpine Club, v, xxi, xxii, 182, 198
Alton Grange, 145
Ambergate, 139
*America, U.S.S.*, 101
Anderson, John Henry, 23, 48, 176
Anelay, Henry, 131, 133, 139, 145, 148, 173,
   176
Angus, Joseph, 75, 83, 86, 128, 176
Apothecaries' Hall, 49
Apps, Richard, 162n
*Arabian Nights. See* Lane, Edward
Archbishop's Park (Lambeth Palace), 69, 84,
   91, 92, 95, 96, 98, 99, 106, 138, 139,

141–46 *passim*, 148, 149, 166, 167,
   169–175 *passim*
Armstrong, William King, 176
Arnold, Thomas (1795–1842), 114
*Art Journal*, 191
Art Treasures Exhibition, Manchester, 91,
   96–97
Art Union, 162, 165
Ashman, Mr (butcher, killed in railway
   accident), 111
Ashmead, George, 176
Ashton under Lyne, 176
Ashwell, Samuel, 122–23, 176
Aske, William Henry, 91, 92, 146, 164, 176
*Athenaeum*, 137
Atlas iron works, 12
Attorney General (Bethell, Richard, Baron
   Westbury), 95, 96, 136
Australia, 3, 53, 76, 90, 106, 179, 189, 193;
   Victoria, 38
Austria; and Crimean War, 10, 20, 41; war
   with France and Piedmont, 160, 164,
   165, 167, 170
*Austria* (steam ship), 148
Aylesbury, 195

Baalbek, 165, 166
Bacon, Francis (1561–1626), 76
Badajoz, 23
Baden Baden, 66
Bahadur Shah Zafar (1775–1862), 83
Bailey, Eliza, 47, 176
Bailey, George, 47, 79–80, 176
Baker, George, 24, 177
Balaclava, 196
Baltic; fleet 3, 7, 9, 11, 12, 13, 18, 19, 25, 47,
   49, 179, 186, 204; Hango, 15;
   Cronstadt, 15, 16, 109; Sveaborg, 21;
   Revel, 109; Riga, 26, 29, 30
Bangkok, 117
Bangor; cathedral, 148

230

# LONDON RECORD SOCIETY

President: The Rt. Hon. the Lord Mayor of London

Chairman: Professor Caroline Barron
Hon. Secretary: Dr Helen Bradley
Hon. Treasurer: Dr David Lewis
Hon. General Editors: Dr Robin Eagles, Dr Stephen O'Connor,
Dr Hannes Kleineke

The London Record Society was founded in December 1964 to publish transcripts, abstracts and lists of the primary sources for the history of London, and generally to stimulate interest in archives relating to London. Membership is open to any individual or institution; the annual subscription is £12 (US $22) for individuals and £18 (US $35) for institutions. Prospective members should apply to the Hon. Secretary, Dr Helen Bradley, PO Box 300, Hertford, Herts SG13 9EF (email londonrecord.society@ntlworld.com).

17. *London Politics, 1713–1717: Minutes of a Whig Club, 1714–17*, edited by H.Horwitz; *London Pollbooks, 1713*, edited by W.A. Speck and W.A. Gray (1981)
18. *Parish Fraternity Register: Fraternity of the Holy Trinity and SS.Fabian and Sebastian in the parish of St. Botolph without Aldersgate*, edited by Patricia Basing (1982)
19. *Trinity House of Deptford: Transactions, 1609–35*, edited by G.G.Harris (1983)
20. *Chamber Accounts of the sixteenth century*, edited by Betty R. Masters (1984)
21. *The Letters of John Paige, London Merchant, 1648–58*, edited by George F. Steckley (1984)
22. *A Survey of Documentary Sources for Property Holding in London before the Great Fire*, by Derek Keene and Vanessa Harding (1985)
23. *The Commissions for Building Fifty New Churches*, edited by M.H.Port (1986)
24. *Richard Hutton's Complaints Book*, edited by Timothy V. Hitchcock (1987)
25. *Westminster Abbey Charters, 1066-c. 1214*, edited by Emma Mason (1988)
26. *London Viewers and their Certificates, 1508–1558*, edited by Janet S. Loengard (1989)
27. *The Overseas Trade of London: Exchequer Customs Accounts, 1480–1*, edited by H.S.Cobb (1990)
28. *Justice in Eighteenth-century Hackney: the Justicing Notebook of Henry Norris and the Hackney Petty Sessions Book*, edited by Ruth Paley (1991)
29. *Two Tudor Subsidy Assessment Rolls for the City of London: 1541 and 1582*, edited by R.G.Lang (1993)
30. *London Debating Societies, 1776–1799*, compiled and introduced by Donna T. Andrew (1994)
31. *London Bridge: selected accounts and rentals, 1381–1538*, edited by Vanessa Harding and Laura Wright (1995)
32. *London Consistory Court Depositions, 1586–1611: list and indexes*, by Loreen L.Giese (1997)
33. *Chelsea settlement and bastardy examinations, 1733–66*, edited by Tim Hitchcock and John Black (1999)
34. *The church records of St Andrew Hubbard Eastcheap, c. 1450-c. 1570*, edited by Clive Burgess (1999)
35. *Calendar of Exchequer Equity pleadings, 1685–6 and 1784–5*, edited by Henry Horwitz and Jessica Cooke (2000)
36. *The Letters of William Freeman, London Merchant, 1678–1685*, edited by David Hancock (2002)
37. *Unpublished London diaries. A checklist of unpublished diaries by Londoners and visitors, with a select bibliography of published diaries*, compiled by Heather Creaton (2003)
38. *The English Fur Trade in the later Middle Ages*, by Elspeth M.Veale (2003; reprinted from 1966 edition)
39. *The Bede Roll of the Fraternity of St Nicholas*, edited by N.W. and V.A. James (2 vols., 2004)
40. *The estate and household accounts of William Worsley, Dean of St Paul's Cathedral, 1479–1497*, edited by Hannes Kleineke and Stephanie R. Hovland (2004)
41. *A woman in wartime London: the diary of Kathleen Tipper 1941–1945*, edited by Patricia and Robert Malcolmson (2006)
42. *Prisoners' Letters to the Bank of England 1783–1827*, edited by Deirdre Palk (2007)
43. *The Apprenticeship of a Mountaineer: Edward Whymper's London Diary 1855–1859*, edited by Ian Smith

Most volumes are still in print; apply to the Hon. Secretary, who will forward requests to the distributor. Price to individual members £12 ($22) each, to non-members £20 ($38) each.